THE MAKING OF THE

NEW SPIRITUALITY

The Eclipse of the
Western Religious Tradition

JAMES A. HERRICK

InterVarsity Press
Downers Grove, Illinois

InterVarsity Press
P.O. Box 1400, Downers Grove, IL 60515-1426
World Wide Web: www.ivpress.com
E-mail: mail@ivpress.com

InterVarsity Press® is the book-publishing division of InterVarsity Christian Fellowship/USA®, a student movement active on campus at hundreds of universities, colleges and schools of nursing in the United States of America, and a member movement of the International Fellowship of Evangelical Students. For information about local and regional activities, write Public Relations Dept., InterVarsity Christian Fellowship/USA, 6400 Schroeder Rd., P.O. Box 7895, Madison, WI 53707-7895, or visit the IVCF website at <www.intervarsity.org>.

Scripture quotations, unless otherwise noted, are from the New Revised Standard Version of the Bible, *copyright 1989 by the Division of Christian Education of the National Council of the Churches of Christ in the USA. Used by permission. All rights reserved.*

Cover design: Cindy Kiple

Cover image: Howard Berman/Getty Images

ISBN 0-8308-3279-3

Printed in the United States of America ∞

Library of Congress Cataloging-in-Publication Data

Herrick, James A.
   The making of the new spirituality: the eclipse of the Western
religious tradition/James A. Herrick.
      p. cm.
Includes bibliographical references and indexes.
   ISBN 0-8308-3279-3 (pbk.: alk. paper)
   1. Christianity and other religions. 2. Religion and
science—History. 3. Spirituality—History. I. Title
   BR127.H47 2004
   261.2'993—dc21

2004019204

P	20	19	18	17	16	15	14	13	12	11	10	9	8	7	6	5	4	3	2
Y	20	19	18	17	16	15	14	13	12	11	10	09	08	07	06	05			

for

RUSSEL HIRST

CONTENTS

ACKNOWLEDGMENTS

A large number of people have contributed in important ways to this project. The following individuals deserve special thanks. I want to thank the students in my Senior Seminar class at Hope College over the past fifteen years whose comments in response to early drafts of the manuscript helped me think through a number of issues. There are too many of them to mention by name, but Brian Boersma, John Brandkamp, Timothy Cupery, Daniel Foster, Christopher Poest and Pamela Van Putten have been particularly instrumental in encouraging me along the way. Another student, Jon Adamson, helped a great deal with early research.

Many friends and colleagues have shown constant interest in this project as well. My friend Russel Hirst encouraged me, suggested important themes that shaped several chapters, and responded to early drafts of the book. Marc Baer made helpful suggestions about how to frame the discussion of these issues and directed me to important resources. Richard Poll and Deirdre Johnston also provided a number of useful sources. Peter Payne allowed me to test some of my ideas in talks before his InterVarsity graduate student groups at the University of Michigan. Linda Koetje helped a great deal in preparing the manuscript for the publisher. Gary Deddo and the editorial staff at InterVarsity Press, as well as their outside readers, provided encouragement and made important suggestions about how to present my case. Research grants from Hope College allowed me to devote several summers to writing and research.

I am indebted to a number of writers and scholars as well, again, too many to name individually. However, several deserve special mention. Richard Noll's work on Carl Jung, and Carl Raschke's scholarship on gnosticism were especially helpful in forming my thinking about the origins and direction of contemporary spiritual movements. James Sire's remarkably practical book *The Universe Next Door* has been a helpful guide to my thinking about worldviews in general, while C. S.

Lewis's *The Abolition of Man* was a constant and prophetic reminder of the seriousness of the issues under discussion in the following pages.

One's family always bears the brunt of such a time-consuming enterprise. My children, Daniel, Stephen, Laura and Alicia, have been extraordinarily willing to endure my distraction and even my absence as I worked on the manuscript. Special thanks to Stephen for his help with the index. Finally, my wife, Janet, has provided constant encouragement through the long process of writing and rewriting.

1

INTRODUCTION

A Changing View of the Spiritual World

We are only at the threshold of a new spiritual epoch.

CARL JUNG,
"The Difference Between Eastern and Western Thinking"

These modern movements may be harbingers of a newly dawning and more adequate myth and spirituality.

JOHN P. DOURLEY,
The Illness We Are

We are persuaded that gradually, in religious thought as in the sciences, a core of universal truth will form and slowly grow to be accepted by everyone. Can there be any true spiritual evolution without it?

PIERRE TEILHARD DE CHARDIN,
The Future of Man

We are at the dawn of a new consciousness, a radically fresh approach to our life as the human family in a fragile world. . . . Perhaps the best name for this new segment of historical experience is the Interspiritual Age.

WAYNE TEASDALE,
The Mystic Heart

The idea of changing culture is important to me, and it can only be done in a popular medium.

JOSS WHEDON,
creator of Buffy the Vampire Slayer

Harvard graduate and former Green Beret Gary Zukav, a frequent guest on the *Oprah Winfrey Show*, is just one of dozens of popular writers currently promoting an emerging new spirituality. Zukav confidently anticipates nothing less than the "birth of a new humanity," which even now is apparent in "new perceptions and new values" including the insight that "the Universe is alive, wise, and compassionate." Members of the new humanity are currently participating in "a learning process" that is contributing to "the evolution of our souls." Zukav's books are part of his effort to "serve the needs of the emerging multisensory humanity," for which "current social structures" are inadequate. Thus, these outdated structures "are dissolving" while Zukav and a growing number of like-minded individuals are busily "creating their replacements—seven billion of us, together."[1]

Zukav's *The Dancing Wu Li Masters*, winner of an American Book Club award in 1979, explored the intersection of quantum physics and emerging spiritualities. Like many contemporary writers on spiritual topics, Zukav finds in science a key to human spiritual awareness and development. Science is no longer confined to only physical phenomena, but is the source of a new theology. In his bestselling *The Seat of the Soul* (1989) Zukav writes that the "discoveries of science illuminate both inner and outer experiences," that is, both "physical and nonphysical dynamics."[2] Science has even suggested a new understanding of God, not as the personal Deity of the Judeo-Christian tradition, but as "conscious light" and "Divine Intelligence" that animate, not a single entity, but the universe itself.[3]

The individual spiritual seeker exercising innate rational power is central to the new spiritual views. "The intellect is meant to expand perceptions, to help you grow in perceptual strength and complexity."[4] At the same time, the spiritual seeker may acquire hidden knowledge from "nonphysical Teachers," or spirit entities equipped to assist the process of spiritual evolution to higher levels of awareness. The capacity to "communicate consciously with a nonphysical Teacher, is a treasure that cannot be described, a treasure beyond words and value."[5] Such guidance is crucial, for the "advanced or expanding mind" does not find answers "within the accepted understanding of truth." The old paradigms do not take into account the most important fact about the human race—its continuing evolution.[6] "Our species is evolving," writes Zukav, and this evolutionary process will result in a species that is "more radiant and energetic," more "aware of the Light of its soul," and more capable of communicating with "forms of Life that are invisible to the five-sensory personality."[7] Many members of the human race already exhibit some of these signs of ongoing evolution, and further progress is assured under the guidance of both science and "spirit Teachers."

Gary Zukav is just one example of dozens of writers and media celebrities who have helped both to shape and popularize a medley of religious ideas that I will be referring to throughout this book as the New Religious Synthesis. Such public religious advocates have had enormous influence in the past fifty years, and the audience for their ideas grows steadily. Zukav's books alone, for example, have sold in excess of five million copies worldwide and have been translated into sixteen languages. His appearances on the *Oprah Winfrey Show* have made his ideas available to an estimated twenty-two million viewers.

The new spiritual outlook Zukav and many other talented advocates are promoting stands in sharp contrast to its predecessor, the Judeo-Christian worldview. Proponents of this ancient and venerable worldview have long insisted that it is, not a human discovery, but rather a revelation from a living and personal God. For this reason I will be referring to the tradition emerging from the pages of the Old and New Testaments as the Revealed Word. What I take to be the fundamental, and fundamentally opposed, components of two perspectives currently competing for the Western religious mind—the New Religious Synthesis and the Revealed Word—will be set out in detail below.

So substantial has been the shaping influence of the New Religious Synthesis on contemporary religious thought that it has now displaced the Revealed Word as the religious framework of a large and growing number of Western people. This powerfully persuasive synthesis blends strands of religious thought that began to appear, or reappear in Western religious writing around 1700. Over the past three centuries, and under the guidance of scores of gifted public advocates working in a number of genres and media, the New Religious Synthesis has now successfully colonized Western religious consciousness. The intriguing migration of these provocative ideas from the fringes of religious exotica to Western spirituality's Main Street is the story told in this book.

"One cannot but feel," wrote the famous scholar of religions Joseph Campbell in 1989, that there is a "universally recognized need in our time for a general transformation of consciousness."[8] In a similar fashion, Marilyn Ferguson maintained in her bestselling *The Aquarian Conspiracy* (1980) that scientific and spiritual breakthroughs would soon "thrust us into a new, higher order" of consciousness.[9] As noted in the quotations at the opening of this chapter, the enormously influential psychoanalyst Carl Jung remarked more than seventy years ago that the Western world was "at the threshold of a new spiritual epoch."[10] In apparent agreement, Catholic lay brother Wayne Teasdale has written that "we are at the dawn of a new consciousness, a radically fresh approach to our life as the human family in a fragile world."[11] Though he is deeply concerned about some of its implications, historian of religion Carl Raschke has also noted the recent emergence of a "new religious consciousness."[12] Have we, in fact, now entered a new spiritual era?

For many Westerners, the long-prophesied new spiritual age certainly has arrived. The Revealed Word and its busy, personal God have faded into our collective spiritual memory, and bright new spiritual commitments encourage fresh religious thought. The New Synthesis appears less rigid and systematic than a worldview, less august and enduring than a tradition. And yet, its basic components are considerably more integrated than the simple "toolbox" of religious ideas that French scholar Daniele Hervieu-Leger referred to in 1999 as characterizing the contemporary religious mind.[13] This emerging outlook provides a new theological hypothesis for a dawning age, a user-friendly alternative to the doctrinally insistent Revealed Word. For the spiritual seeker, the New Religious Synthesis has become the Other Spirituality.

In the following pages I want to explore just how this massive transformation in Western spiritual thought has occurred, taking as my focus the work of public religious advocates. At this juncture in the religious history of Western culture, it also seems timely to ask what is gained and what is lost in the dramatic shift now occurring from one spirituality to another. I will begin with the assumption that, in a society accustomed to the free and public exchange of ideas, it takes a great deal of time and enormous effort to replace that society's spiritual base with a wholly new one. After all, two major tasks are involved: dismantling the old view by revealing its inadequacies and fashioning a new and presumably better one in its place. Thus, this act of changing Western culture's religious beliefs has meant going repeatedly before the public in broadly accessible settings and by means of popular religious media—books, speeches, magazines and pamphlets to be sure, but also movies, plays, music, radio interviews, television programs and websites.

In the following chapters I will be drawing attention to a number of authors and artists who have been important to this effort to accomplish the twin tasks of razing the Western world's old spiritual edifice and publicly constructing a new one in its place. What follows, however, is not a comprehensive catalog of the efforts that brought either task to completion. Rather, I have chosen what I take to be representative examples of spiritually influential works from a three-hundred-year-long public persuasive process. Some of the works selected are quite famous and their impact widely recognized. Others were well known in their own day but are now virtually forgotten. In such cases it has seemed to me that the work's influence has nevertheless persisted in the public mind as beliefs, ideas, assumptions, convictions and images. While not including a number of major milestones of religious thought because their influence seems to have been greatest among scholars, I do focus attention on several important intellectual figures who possessed the rare talent for impressing both their academic colleagues and the wider public.

I have been asserting that a massive shift in Western religious attitudes has taken place. Perhaps some basic evidence of such a change is in order before considering the historical sources and impact of the New Religious Synthesis on our religious thought. Even a brief survey of events on the recent Western religious stage suggests that something like a fundamental shift in spiritual assumptions has transpired, almost without our noticing it.

SPIRITUAL CHANGES: A NEW AGE OF BELIEF?

Observers of the religious scene have for some time now noted that an extraordinary redefinition of fundamental religious belief has occurred in the West and that the resultant spiritual transition has been stunning in its rapidity, scope and impact. A decade ago journalist Michael D'Antonio wrote that "sociologists at the University of California, Santa Barbara estimate that as many as 12 million Americans could be considered active participants [in alternative spiritual systems] and another 30 million are actively interested."[14] Perhaps 1,000 to 2,000 new religious movements have arisen in the United States alone in the twentieth century, and few of these are rooted in traditional Judeo-Christian theological assumptions.

The diverse manifestations of the emerging spirituality "obscure its size and its impact on the larger society." Nevertheless, that impact is felt "in public schools, hospitals, corporate offices, and the popular media."[15] And, we might add, in politics. The pervasiveness of alternative spiritualities forcefully confronted Americans with revelations that Ronald and Nancy Reagan sought advice from an (expensive) astrologer and that Hillary Rodham Clinton solicited contact with Eleanor Roosevelt through the offices of psychic researcher Jean Houston. Spirituality, it seems, is no longer confined to the sanctuary and the synagogue, but has now moved into the lecture hall and the classroom, the movie theater and the surgical theater, the corporate office and the Oval Office.

In his book *Spiritual Marketplace: Baby Boomers and the Remaking of American Religion* (1999) Wade Clark Roof suggests that, unlike old established religious denominations, "popular religious culture is more diffused, less contained by formal religious structures." The evidence for a new Western spirituality includes "widespread belief in angels and reincarnation; the appeal of religious and quasi-religious shrines, retreat centers, and theme parks; interest in metaphysical and theosophical teachings; prosperity theology and 'possibility thinking'; and large proportions of Americans reporting mystical experiences." At the level of popular belief, Roof concludes, "we observe an eclectic mix of religious and spiritual ideas, beliefs, and practices."[16]

The success of this "eclectic mix" of ideas is not due to its being "institutionalized," that is, propagated and maintained by formal organizations. Rather, these once exotic but now commonplace notions have pursued a different route into public consciousness. "They persist," writes Roof, "largely as a result of loosely bound networks of practitioners, the publishing industry, and the media." Even the names of many new religions practiced by Westerners are not widely recognized by either government record keepers or scholars in religion. Roof's examples of the new spiritual systems existing just off official radar screens include "the paranormal, Neo-Paganism, astrology, nature religion, [and] holistic thinking," often collected under broader headings such as "New Age, or New Spirituality."[17]

Wayne Teasdale applauds this new Great Awakening noted by D'Antonio, Roof and many others, finding it marked by such positive signs as greater "ecological awareness," a recognition of "the interdependence of all domains of life and reality," as well as "a deep, evolving experience of community between and among the religions." Teasdale writes that more and more of us are becoming aware that "the earth is part of the larger community of the universe."[18] He adds that "each of these shifts represents a dramatic change," and that "taken together, they will define the thought and culture of the third millennium." Teasdale recommends dubbing the new religious era the "Interspiritual Age," and he maintains that new "awarenesses" will profoundly affect all areas of our personal and social lives.[19] "All of these awarenesses are interrelated, and each is indispensable to clearly grasping the greater shift taking place, a shift that will sink roots deep into our lives and culture."

Remarkably, Teasdale believes the new spirituality is "preparing the way for a universal civilization." The basis of this new, universal civilization will be what Teasdale terms "perennial spiritual and moral insights, intuitions and experiences." Moreover, "these aspects of spirituality will shape how we conduct politics and education, how we envision our economies, media, and entertainment; and how we develop our relationship with the natural world."[20]

No assessment of a sea change in religious perspective could be more sweeping than is Teasdale's. Is he overstating the case? Perhaps, but certainly interest in new spiritualities is extraordinarily high if we are to judge by one rough indicator of public interest—book sales. Teresa Watanabe, writing for the *Los Angeles Times*, notes that "sales of religious books skyrocketed 150% from 1991 to 1997, compared to 35% for the rest of the industry." She adds, "Ingram Book Co., the nation's largest book distributor to retail markets, reported a cumulative growth in religion titles of nearly 500% from June 1994 to the third quarter of 1996, an additional 40% increase in 1997, and a 58% rise in the first quarter of 1998."[21] And these figures do not reflect the enormous sales of books on spiritual themes that are ostensibly devoted to business success, medicine and healing, relationships and science.

Clearly, spiritual books sell, as do spiritually oriented seminars, movies and an extraordinary array of personal spiritual products ranging from clothing to candles. However, the beliefs energizing this vast cultural phenomenon are not those of the Revealed Word perspective that held sway in the West for most of two millennia. In fact, our basic spiritual assumptions have changed so dramatically in the past fifty years that sociologist of religion Robert Wuthnow notices nothing less than a "transformation of American spirituality."[22] Wuthnow remarks that "a majority of the public has retained some loyalty to their churches and synagogues, yet," he adds, "their practice of spirituality from Monday to Friday often bears little resemblance to the preachments of religious leaders."[23] Similarly, historian of religion Philip Jenkins has written recently of the New Age phenomenon that "the vast majority of people holding New Age beliefs do not identify themselves as representing a distinct denomination, but describe themselves as Unitarians or Jews, Methodists or Catholics."[24]

It is relevant to note here that self-professed belief in astrology, reincarnation and a non-personal divine energy characterizes upwards of 30 percent of Americans, and these concepts are viable spiritual options for many more. One popular astrology website created for Time Warner Electronic Publishing attracts 1.3 million visitors every month. Another similar site, AstroNet, established with the support of America

Online, attracts an astonishing 300,000 visitors each day.[25] Thus, though church and synagogue attendance remains strong, this fact may not accurately portray the spiritual convictions and practices of millions of Americans and Europeans. Wuthnow writes that whereas "95 percent of the U.S. population claims to believe in God," the nature of that divinity is defined in widely divergent ways.[26]

It seems that the God (or gods) in whom many today believe is not the biblical Yahweh, even for self-identified members of traditional faiths.[27] D'Antonio notes that millions of devotees of new religious systems still "consider themselves Christian, Jewish, Muslim" because they "hold to much of their old religious identity" while at the same time "adopting any number of . . . ideas about health, politics, psychology or spirituality" from new spiritual movements.[28] D'Antonio sees this mixing of spiritualities as "enriching." Whether enriching or simply an expression of spiritual wanderlust, the evidence of spiritual experimentation in the contemporary West is present virtually anywhere one cares to look. Whence this new spiritual orientation?

BESTSELLERS AND BLOCKBUSTERS: SPIRITUALITY GOES PUBLIC

As might be expected when assessing such a massive change in public attitudes, several explanations have been advanced to account for this seismic shift in Western spiritual attitudes. Some observers subsume all of the observed changes under the heading the New Age movement, and find its sources in the experiments of the hippie culture of the 1960s and 1970s. However, the spiritual changes afoot in the West are broader than even the broadest definitions of a so-called New Age movement. By the same token, to emphasize the drug, rock and spiritual experimentation subculture of the 1960s as the principal source of a new Western spiritual paradigm is to risk overlooking the long historical development of the Other Spirituality and to isolate it within a relatively small and easily dismissed subculture.

A longer historical view reveals that major spiritual changes have been afoot in the Western world for some time and that they correspond roughly with scientific advances, corrosive biblical criticism and rising awareness of other faiths on the part of Westerners. Thus, a second explanation of sweeping religious change in Europe and the United States is that it reflects an attempt to "fill the spiritual vacuum" created as Christian assumptions inexorably disintegrated under pressure from cultural pluralism, Enlightenment criticism of the Judeo-Christian tradition and the staggering successes of modern science. This common explanation of recent religious change has merit; the loss of a cherished and ennobling understanding of transcendence leaves one longing for a substitute. But this account's inactive root metaphor of a vacuum being filled distracts attention away from the concerted and highly successful efforts of a host of skilled advocates who have for more than three centuries actively and persistently promoted alternative spiritualities in broadly public settings and through powerful popular media.

Because I have been placing such heavy emphasis on religious advocates as agents of spiritual change, it may be helpful to illustrate their important role by considering several recent examples of their work. Surveying these cases of public spiritual advocacy does reveal that a large number of Western people have indeed been seeking answers in the spiritual realm by moving outside the boundaries of what I have termed the Revealed Word. But this survey also indicates, I believe, something more—that the public spiritual advocate has also functioned importantly to suggest the direction and the destination of our vast cultural quest for spiritual satisfaction.

Spirituality's surprising successes. In the 1980s many commentators noted the stunning popularity of actress Shirley MacLaine's accounts of her spiritual journeying in books such as *Going Within* and *Dancing in the Light*.[29] "God lies within," she taught, "and therefore we are each part of God."[30] It is estimated that fifty million viewers watched her television special based on the book, *Out on a Limb*, the central message of which was the divinity of the individual. "MacLaine's books," writes one observer, "have introduced millions to psychics and channelers, healers and spirit guides."[31] At the same time her captivating narratives made a persuasive case for a new worldview standing in direct opposition to the Revealed Word.

Numerous earlier writers in the genre of the personal spiritual narrative paved the path to MacLaine's astounding popularity. For example, the drug-enhanced mysticism and magic of Carlos Castaneda's phenomenally popular *The Teachings of Don Juan* series, beginning in 1968, fascinated and often convinced college-aged readers that there was more to the spiritual world than the church had suggested.[32] Castaneda's appealing stories related what he claimed were actual experiences under the tutelage of a Mexican shaman named don Juan, a medicine man and sorcerer who taught him how to use hallucinogenic plants to acquire "wisdom, or knowledge of the right way to live."[33] Through arduous training involving intense inner exploration, Castaneda learned the powers and secrets of an alternative spiritual world.

In the nonfiction realm, works like Marilyn Ferguson's *The Aquarian Conspiracy* (1980) set about "challenging our old assumptions" which are "the air we breathe, our familiar furniture."[34] Ferguson argued that the prevailing Western paradigm, founded on the Judeo-Christian worldview, had run its course. A new way of thinking about nature, the divine and human potential had arrived. Ferguson celebrated a growing "conspiracy" of the spiritually informed, a massive collaboration that was changing the way we thought about spiritual matters. *The Aquarian Conspiracy's* dust jacket confidently announced that "a great, shuddering, irrevocable shift is overtaking us. It is not a new political, religious, or economic system. It is a new mind—a turnabout in consciousness in critical numbers of individuals."

Indeed, even a cursory glance at recent artifacts of popular culture suggests that something *was* overtaking us as the twentieth century ended. James Redfield's New Age adventure story, *The Celestine Prophecy,* turned down by publishers but successfully promoted by its determined author, made *The New York Times* bestseller list 165 consecutive weeks starting in 1994. Again, Redfield's path into the public mind was prepared by works like Richard Bach's proto-New Age bestseller *Jonathan Livingston Seagull*—the simple story of a seagull with a profound faith in his capacity to overcome personal limitations. Bach's book sold a surprising three million copies in the mid-1970s. In the cinematic realm, George Lucas's staggeringly successful *Star Wars* movies recently have marketed a decidedly non-Western religious philosophy to their audiences of millions worldwide. Similarly, phenomenally popular television series such as *The X Files* have recently attracted highly receptive, mainly younger audiences as the programs explore alternative understandings of the spiritual realm.

Witches and goddesses. The "great, shuddering, irrevocable shift" in spiritual attitudes has been equally apparent from various cultural vantage points. Many ancient religious traditions, for example, have recently been refurbished and popularized for a new generation of spiritual seekers. Contemporary reworkings of pre-Christian pagan religions, including Wicca, goddess worship, Native American religions, Druidism and the worship of ancient Norse gods are enjoying great popularity. Carol P. Christ writes, "One of the most unexpected developments of the late twentieth century is the rebirth of the religion of the Goddess in western culture."[35] The goddess being worshiped was, in some cases at least, quite close to home. Ms. Christ writes, "I found God in myself, and I loved her fiercely."[36]

One prominent proponent of the goddess revival was the cultural anthropologist Marija Gimbutas, author of *The Language of the Goddess.* Gimbutas hoped for a return to a tradition far older than the Judeo-Christian, a faith she calls "Old European."[37] "We are still living under the sway of the aggressive male invasion [of European] and only beginning to discover our long alienation from our authentic European Heritage," which, Gimbutas contends, was "nonviolent," "earth centered" and "gylanic," that is, making no social or political distinctions between males and females.[38] Similarly, Barbara Walker urges a Western "return" to goddess worship. Her book, *Restoring the Goddess*, calls on women and men to leave the patriarchal religion of the Revealed Word, and to embrace a Nature-centered religion that worships Gaia—the spirit of the earth—as Goddess. Walker finds that goddess worship is more "an evolution than a revolution" in religious thought.[39]

In a similar vein, Akasha Gloria Hull's book *Soul Talk* explores a "new spirituality [that] has arisen among black women."[40] For Hull, spirituality involves "conscious relationship with the realm of the spirit, with the invisibly permeating, ultimately positive, divine, and evolutionary energies that give rise to and sustain all that exists." Though the new spirituality of African American women may draw upon "traditional Christian religions," Hull affirms that it also "freely incorporates elements popularly called 'New Age'—Tarot, chakra work, psychic enhancement, numerology, Eastern philosophies of cosmic connectedness, and others."[41]

Relearning goddess worship has been linked to a striking revival of interest in a related pre-Christian spiritual tradition. Books on witchcraft, both fiction and nonfiction, move briskly from the shelves of the largest bookselling chains. Von Braschler, director of trade sales for the largest occult publishing house, Llewellyn International of St. Paul, Minnesota, states that the "typical reader" of books on witchcraft "is a very young woman in her teens." So intense is the interest in these books that "more than half of the 100 titles that Llewellyn publishes revolve around Wiccan themes."[42] Estimates of actual practitioners of the pre-Christian, nature-based spiritualities known generally as Wicca or witchcraft range up to 1.5 million.[43] Popular teen websites such as Bolt.com direct their mainly female visitors to a wide array of links dealing with witchcraft and the occult.[44]

An example of the many popular books in this genre is Phyllis Curott's *Book of Shadows*.[45] Rejecting what she calls "the Church's crusade to suppress the Old Religion of the Goddess and to establish religious hegemony," Curott writes that she is contributing to "a renaissance of a pre-Hebraic, pre-Christian, and pre-Islamic Goddess worship" through her advocacy of witchcraft.[46] She asks, "How can we rediscover the sacred from which we have been separated for thousands of years?"[47] Old spirituality is suddenly new again.

This is the message of Ashleen O'Gaea's *The Family Wicca Book* as well. Noting that in "pre-patriarchal primal cultures . . . the first human beings were cooperative and gentle with each other," O'Gaea shows families how to return to the Old Religion of our ancient ancestors.[48] Wicca develops around honoring the Great Mother, but acknowledges a large number of gods. It also teaches reincarnation and incorporates rites, spells and holy days from early European tribal groups. With chapters including "Raising Children to the Craft," O'Gaea instructs parents on how to teach basic witchcraft to their children. "Our life as a family of witches is full and satisfying," she writes. "Wicca permeates our lives, enriches our lives, guides our lives."[49] O'Gaea claims that Wicca is gaining wide acceptance, and that growing numbers of covens of practicing witches now meet in many American cities.

Of course, no discussion of the renewed interest in witchcraft and magic can exclude the current international sensation, J. K. Rowling's Harry Potter series. With four books and two movies in release at this writing, the Potter phenomenon is unparalleled. The four books have been translated into two hundred languages, and sales are now in excess of $110 million. The first of the Harry Potter movies, *Harry Potter and the Sorcerer's Stone*, smashed box office records in its first week of release with ticket sales of more than $97 million. After only twenty days in theatres, box office receipts were well in excess of $220 million, putting the Potter movie on a trajectory to match the enormous success of George Lucas's *Star Wars* blockbusters. Though controversy has raged around the witchcraft themes in Rowling's literary and cinematic stories, the public has found little reason to resist the appeal of these captivating supernatural tales created against a backdrop of magic.

Hidden Judaism, emerging Buddhism. This rising tide of interest in "new" religious traditions with ancient roots is not limited to disaffected Christians fleeing Protestantism and Catholicism for refreshingly unfamiliar spiritual territory such as goddess worship and Wicca. Rabbis David A. Cooper and Leibl Wolf, among many others, have successfully revived interest among upwardly mobile American, Australian and European Jews in the ancient mystical Jewish teachings of the kabbalah. Cooper's *God Is a Verb* and Wolf's *Practical Kabbalah* offer popular, simplified treatments of a highly complex and traditionally secret system of textual interpretation.[50] But Yahweh and the increasingly popular deity of kabbalah—an impersonal force known as Ein Sof—appear to be two different entities.

Of course, ancient Eastern traditions have shaped the new spirituality even more dramatically than have ancient Middle Eastern ones. Buddhist influence is evident virtually everywhere on the contemporary cultural scene. Rodger Kamenetz's book *The Jew in the Lotus* affirms the relevance of Buddhist thought and practice for modern Jews.[51] Motivational seminars emphasizing elements of Buddhist thought attract hundreds of thousands of business leaders at great cost by promising power, peace, mystical experience and business success. As early as 1985, John Heider's *The Tao of Leadership: Leadership Strategies for a New Age*, popularized for the business community the teachings of fifth-century B.C. Chinese sage Lao-Tzu.[52] The book taught executives "how to govern or educate others in accordance with natural law." Among the foundational principles of this natural law are "I am one with everything else" and "all creation is a single whole that operates according to a single principle."[53]

Buddhist thought has received a boost from perhaps the most popular person in contemporary America, Oprah Winfrey. Through her television program, website and magazine, Winfrey has introduced her audiences to a variety of new spiritual approaches. The August 2001 edition of *O: The Oprah Magazine* features an upbeat interview with the Dalai Lama. Oprah asks if "there wasn't part of you that had always known you were different?" The Dalai Lama replies, "Sometimes I do feel that, yes, I may feel some effect of previous lives. . . . I have had glimpses of memory from past lives in which I identify with those from, in some cases, one or two centuries ago. I once had the feeling that I may have been in Egypt 600 years ago."[54]

The Dalai Lama himself has had an inestimable impact as a proponent of Buddhist values and practices in the West. One of the nation's most popular business books in 1999 was the Dalai Lama's *Ethics for the New Millennium*, selling more copies than popular books for executives by Bill Gates and Stephen Covey. The Dalai Lama's book resided near the top of *The New York Times* bestseller list for nine weeks, and "was listed as that paper's number two business book for six weeks."[55] In fact, the Dalai Lama has produced a steady stream of popular books for Western readers over the past several years. His recent titles include *Transforming the Mind*, *The Art of Happiness* and *The Path to Tranquility*.[56] Even the Dalai Lama's mother has become an author of note with her recent release of *My Son: A Mother's Story*, which is edited by her grandson, Khedroob Thondup.[57] Of late, the Dalai Lama's spiritual perspective has received a crucial assist from Hollywood as well. A host of recent popular movies including *Seven Years in Tibet* and *Kundun* have presented Buddhist ideas in a sympathetic and persuasive fashion to millions of viewers.

Has all of this emphasis on the wisdom of the Buddha had any particular effect in the traditionally Christian United States? By one estimate, the number of

American adherents to some aspect of Buddhist teaching now exceeds ten million. This number represents an incredible increase from the estimated 200,000 Buddhists residing in the United States in 1960, most of them Asians living in California or Hawaii.[58]

Spiritual science and scientific religion. On the contemporary religious scene, spiritual insights arise nearly as often in the arena of science as in that of religion. Fritjof Capra helped to popularize the idea that science reveals the spiritual nature of the physical universe in books such as *The Tao of Physics* (1975) and his 1982 bestseller, *The Turning Point*.[59] In his recent book *The Web of Life*, Capra contends that science proves that "living nature is mindful and intelligent." Thus, there is no need to maintain the old notion of a specially created universe with "overall design or purpose."[60] Similarly, the notion of "self" or individual identity, a mainstay of Western metaphysics, has yielded to Buddhist-inspired scientific thinking. "The Buddhist doctrine of impermanence includes the notion that there is no self," he writes. "Cognitive science has arrived at exactly the same position . . . our self, our ego, does not have any independent existence."[61]

The New Science often has arrived at conclusions paralleling Eastern religious thought, such as the illusional nature of physical matter. Thus for Fred Alan Wolf the new physics demonstrates that "reality is not made of stuff, but is made of possibilities that can be coherent so that possibility forms into matter" under the direction of consciousness, including even human consciousness.[62] He declares that new scientific findings suggest that "the universe is being created in a dream of a single spiritual entity," and that each individual human consciousness may reflect that entity. "Are we the dreamer?" he asks.[63] Another physicist, Amit Goswami, contends that "science proves the potency of monistic philosophy over dualism—over spirit separated from matter."[64] That is, for these writers science disproves the Judeo-Christian notion of a personal God existing distinctly separate from his creation.

This trend toward spiritualizing science continues in books by a host of contemporary writers working the New Science beat. Examples include Gary Zukav's *The Dancing Wu Li Masters: An Overview of the New Physics* and, more recently, Fred Allen Wolf's *The Spiritual Universe: How Quantum Physics Proves the Existence of the Soul*.[65] Capra and Wolf are physicists who claim that the findings of a spiritualized science will be crucial to the next wave of religion in the West. In several important respects this "new wave" actually reflects a return to ancient spiritual traditions. Similarly, in *The Aquarian Conspiracy*, Ferguson presented her readers nothing less than "a startling worldview that gathers into its framework breakthrough science and insights from the earliest recorded thought."[66]

Turning this idea of a spiritualized science on its head, some anthropologists are now suggesting that we look to the spiritual world for scientific insights. In his essay, "Shamans and Scientists," Canadian anthropologist Jeremy Narby reports a fascinating encounter between three molecular biologists and a shaman residing in the Peruvian Amazon.[67] Each of the biologists voluntarily enters a drug-induced trance under the guidance of the shaman, and each puts several questions to various entities encountered in this state. For instance, one of the scientists specializing in reproductive research asked the spirit guide, "was there a key protein that makes sperm cells fertile?" The answer he received was, "No, there is not a key protein. In this organ there are no key proteins, just many different ones which have to act together for fertility to be achieved."[68]

Narby comments that "in interviews conducted in their respective laboratories four months after the Amazonian experience, the three biologists agreed on a number of key points. All three said that the experience of ayahuasca shamanism changed their way of looking at themselves and at the world."[69] Moreover, all three scientists said they are "planning to return to the Amazon at some point" to pursue further understanding of how shamanism might contribute to scientific knowledge.

Psychology, psychiatry and medicine: insight, healing and alien voices. A sharp tension between science and religion often characterizes public debates about educational policy. Surprisingly, many of today's popular religious works suggest a different picture—the alleged spiritual wasteland of the sciences is, on closer inspection, replete with oases to refresh the spiritual seeker, deep pools furnished by hidden and unstaunchable springs of religious insight.

It is perhaps less surprising that psychology, psychiatry and medicine have recently provided alternatives to traditional Western religious thought for the modern thirster after spiritual truth. For instance, popular psychoanalyst Mark Epstein, in books such as *Buddhism and the Way of Change: A Positive Psychology for the West* and *Going to Pieces Without Falling Apart: A Buddhist Perspective on Wholeness* presents a Buddhist approach to psychology and counseling. Epstein affirms that "within psychotherapy lies the potential for an approach that is compatible with Buddhist understanding, one in which the therapist, like the Zen master, can aid in making a space in the mind."[70] Far from occupying the fringe of psychotherapeutic practice, the *Chicago Tribune* has written that "Epstein is on the cutting edge of change as psychotherapy and spirituality, once antagonistic, move toward a rapprochement."[71]

These particular spiritual springs started flowing early in the twentieth century. Carl Jung, a founder of psychoanalysis, introduced ancient Gnostic and Eastern religious thought to Western psychoanalytic theory and practice. Richard Noll argues in *The Jung Cult: Origins of a Charismatic Movement* that Jung's ideas are steeped in the gnostic teachings that Jung so admired. He is today a more potent influence in counseling circles than is Sigmund Freud, and Jung reading groups meet across the Western world to cultivate spiritual insight.[72]

Navigating rather more alien waters, Harvard professor of psychiatry John Mack attributes shamanic religious insight to the scores of UFO abductee claimants that he has counseled. His original alien abduction book, *Abduction: Human Encounters with Aliens*, was a bestseller.[73] More recent titles include *Secret Life: Firsthand, Documented Accounts of UFO Abductions* and *Passport to the Cosmos: Human Transformation and Alien Encounters*.[74] Mack insists that we must study and heed the spiritual truths being taught us by extraterrestrial visitors through their abductee messengers.

Helen Schucman (1909-1981), a professor of medical psychology at Columbia University's College of Physicians in New York City in the late 1960s and early 1970s, also asks us to listen to the spiritual wisdom of voices from beyond. She and colleague William Thetford, disillusioned with traditional psychological and psychiatric techniques, began to seek "another way." Over a period of three months, Schucman claims to have experienced a virtually uninterrupted flow of "highly symbolic dreams and descriptions" as well as "strange images." For seven years from 1965 through 1972 "a Voice" attributed to Jesus Christ delivered to her a long series of messages which she dictated to Thetford.

The result of this lengthy process of spiritual wisdom transmission was the ponderous bestseller *A Course in Miracles*.[75] The wild popularity of this channeled mix of advice and spiritual insight is indeed surprising to any objective observer who has attempted to wade through its nearly incomprehensible prose. Nevertheless, that humans possess divinity, that sin is an empty concept, that the creation is an illusion, that we save ourselves from spiritual darkness, that "there is not past or future," that "birth into a body has no meaning," that sickness is the result of faulty thinking, and that death is "the central dream from which all illusions stem" are all repeated themes.[76]

This sort of approach to the mind and its latent powers has driven the phenomenon of schools for psychic development. In January 2000 the Associated Press reported "a nationwide surge in facilities known as enlightenment schools and metaphysical institutions." These schools include The Advanced Metaphysical Studies Center in New York, The Berkeley Psychic Institute and the College of Metaphysics in Clearwater, Florida. Students learn to "develop their psychic abilities" and "read the thoughts of others." The Berkeley Psychic Institute has taught classes in "meditation, healing and intuition" to more than 100,000 students over the past twenty-five years.[77]

The body as well as the mind is a subject of interest to practitioners of alternative spiritualities. "Alternative medicine," healing practices often based on a spiritual paradigm rivaling the traditional Western worldview, has now become as popular as more conventional medical treatment with the general public. In 1999, Americans spent as much money out of their own pockets on alternative medical products and services as they did on conventional medical treatments. To satisfy this vast market, numerous authors have advocated healing techniques ranging from "visualizing" health to deep massage. Medical students today are encouraged, and sometimes required, to explore the possibilities in alternative healing techniques such as therapeutic touch, while prominent medical schools have now established centers for the study of the mind-body healing connection. Ruth Walker of *The Christian Science Monitor* reports that "the trend toward inclusion of some form of spiritual practice in healthcare appears to be accelerating." She adds that "this year, 72 medical schools—well over half of those in the United States—have offered some kind of course on spirituality and healing. This represents an increase from only three such courses in 1992."[78]

Works devoted to alternative healing have steadily increased in popularity. Books by authors such as Yale surgeon Bernie S. Siegel, author of *Love, Medicine, and Miracles* and *Peace, Love, and Healing,* have sold millions of copies and occupy dozens of feet of shelf space in book stores. Other prominent figures in the alternative medical field include Indian physician Deepak Chopra, author of *The New York Times* number one bestseller *Ageless Body, Timeless Mind,* and Andrew Weil, author of *Spontaneous Healing* and many other related titles. Journalist Peter Fenton has retrieved the medical secrets of the East for Western readers in his popular book *Tibetan Healing: The Modern Legacy of Medicine Buddha.*

Meditation techniques derived from Eastern religious practices and physical regimens such as yoga have become an integral part of the stress reduction for millions of Westerners. Readers of Stephen Cope's *Yoga and the Quest for the True Self* learn how to employ ancient Hindu religious exercises to alleviate modern Western consumerist stress. And the *Tantric Toning* videotape series brings Hindu insights to physical training for the aerobically inclined.

Finally, we might note that neurologist and Zen practitioner Dr. James H. Austin has suggested that our study of the sources of altruism and other "higher motives" in the human brain might be guided by the insights of ancient Zen masters. "Perhaps we would be advised to begin our searching for their subtler, deeper networks in the limbic system, thalamus, basal ganglia, and brain stem," he writes. "Indeed, there will always be multiple levels of interpretation of Master Chi-chen's statement, 'The way upward is by descending lower.'"[79]

TALKING ABOUT SPIRITUALITY

Though goddess worship, the New Science, Buddhist-inspired motivational seminars, UFO abduction reports, spiritually oriented psychology and alternative medical practices may seem at first glance to have little to do with one another, each phenomenon reflects changes in the Western world's basic spiritual orientation. It is my view, as noted above, that such phenomena also betoken a concerted and successful effort on the part of a large number of spiritual advocates, including writers, speakers and performing artists, to open new religious pathways in the Western mind.

Shaping a society's thinking on an important topic such as religious belief is a complex process involving many sources, pressures and influences. One often-neglected but important force shaping our spiritual views is public religious discourse, that is, the many ways we communicate about and seek to persuade one another regarding spiritual matters. Public religious discourse includes speeches, essays, fiction and nonfiction books, self-help manuals, television programs, movies, plays and other forms of communication about religion. Such communication often is intentionally persuasive, and the success of this persuasive effort is particularly likely when similar messages are encountered repeatedly in various media—print, film, music, television, magazines and so on.

Spiritual advocates engaged in public religious discourse have constituted a powerful force shaping Western religious thought since their first prominent public appearance around 1700, and that shaping influence has continued unabated to the present day. Popular books, widely circulated periodicals and public lectures carried religious ideas in the eighteenth century. To these were added mass circulation magazines and the enormously popular American public lecture circuits in the nineteenth century. Movies, popular music, radio and television and other mass media provided additional avenues for disseminating religious ideas in the twentieth century. Advocates of religious ideas—believing and skeptical, orthodox and heterodox—have exploited each medium as it has appeared. That is to say, advocates engaged in public religious discourse have never simply *reflected* what the public was thinking. They have also persuaded us, changed our minds, shaped our views of what is true or false, right or wrong, assumed or questioned in religion.

In the following chapters I highlight some of these persuasive efforts on behalf of a particular set of religious ideas constituting the New Religious Synthesis. Most of my examples are from the print media, especially books, both fiction and nonfiction. Books have remained a constant source of public discussion of religious ideas since 1700, and books have been the characteristic medium of Western contention over religious ideas. I have also included a number of tracts and pamphlets, some popular movies, several speeches, one or two plays and the occasional television program. The works examined by no means exhaust the important public statements on spiritual themes in the modern period. Rather, they are merely representative examples, occasionally odd ones, of important efforts to persuade the reading and viewing public to new ways of thinking about spiritual matters. This synthesis of concepts now constitutes a widespread framework for understanding ourselves and the spiritual world.

THE REVEALED WORD AND THE NEW RELIGIOUS SYNTHESIS

I referred earlier to two comprehensive spiritual views or systems. One I have termed the Revealed Word, the other the New Religious Synthesis. It may be helpful at this point to outline these perspectives. Some readers will take issue with my characterization of the principal components of either system, but the following overviews will at least serve to express in general terms what I intend by these labels. Subsequent chapters will clarify the contours and expand on the content of each perspective.

Religious thinking is a trait of virtually all human beings. For much of the last two millennia that thinking in the Western world typically has been informed by biblical presuppositions, even when biblical *piety* was notably absent. And yet, the working religious assumptions of many, perhaps most, Western people today are

not the assumptions of what I have called the Revealed Word. Though it would
be difficult to achieve agreement on the point even within the Christian community, the following tenets provide a recognizable sketch of the Revealed Word
perspective. I recognize that not all Christians at all times have accepted this entire set of beliefs. With the exception of the reference to Jesus Christ as God incarnate and the authority of the Christian Scriptures, many orthodox Jews
would affirm these propositions as well, though certainly disparity of belief
marks the Jewish community as it does the Christian. The following, then, are a
reasonable approximation of the commitments making up the spiritual perspective I have called the Revealed Word, the spiritual outlook dominant in the
Western world until relatively recently.

The Revealed Word. I will begin with the very notion of a word from God, which
is, not surprisingly, at the center of the Revealed Word view.

1. *The supernatural authority of the Judeo-Christian Scriptures.* The Bible is taken to
be divinely delivered and thus uniquely authoritative as a source of religious truth.
The Scriptures record messages delivered to humanity by God through various
means—prophetic utterance, the traditions and wisdom of Israel, the life and
teachings of Jesus of Nazareth. The Revealed Word perspective is based on this
written record. Where the record relates events, including miraculous events, these
are usually assumed to be historical and not symbolic or mythological.

2. *A personal, creating and wholly other God.* The traditional attributes of God
present him as all-knowing, present everywhere and all-powerful. That this God is
also personal is assumed in these attributes, meaning that he possesses traits of a
personality—thoughts, motives, emotions and the capacity to form relationships.
This personal, all-powerful God is credited with creating the physical and spiritual
worlds ex nihilo or out of nothing. Moreover, he remains "wholly other," neither
contained in nor equivalent with the created order.

3. *God's creation of the human race.* Assumed in the concept of God's creative activity is his creation of the human race. However, it needs to be noted that the Revealed Word alleges that the human race is a special creation of God, the only part
of the creation said to bear "his image." This commitment to the special creation of
the human race has historically been taken to imply that humans are not a product
of strictly natural processes.

4. *An intervening God.* The Revealed Word affirms that God's activity includes

involvement in the lives of individual human beings. On occasion, this intervening God communicates directly with human beings and at other times miraculously alters the ordinary course of cause and effect. Though this personal and active God invites address and petition through prayer, this does not imply that the divine is a power at the command of human beings.

5. *Humankind's Fall.* The human race experienced a Fall into sin early in its existence, a consequence of the earliest humans' refusal to recognize a divinely mandated limitation on their activities. This Fall carried with it various catastrophic consequences, including spiritual confusion, a state of spiritual separation from God and the inevitability of physical death.

6. *Jesus Christ as God Incarnate.* The historical figure of Jesus Christ uniquely manifested God in human form. Jesus is a revelation of God's nature in a person and the only human being ever to express fully the divine nature. Moreover, the death and resurrection of Jesus Christ are uniquely redemptive of fallen humanity. These events are the sole provision by God for the salvation of the   human race.

7. *Human destiny and divine judgment.* The Revealed Word insists that the destiny of the human race is to be determined by God. Neither the present earth nor the human race exists indefinitely. A final judgment of the human race will occur, and each individual human being will be held accountable for the life lived. It should be noted that the Revealed Word perspective maintains that each human lives only one life.

The New Religious Synthesis. As already noted, the past three centuries have witnessed a stunning shift in Western religious thinking away from the tenets outlined above. For many of us a new set of religious commitments has now replaced the fundamental claims of the Revealed Word. The following are, I will maintain, the basic components of this New Religious Synthesis. This alliance of available, complementary spiritual commitments constitutes the background assumptions currently shaping much of our contemporary religious thought. Moreover, at every critical juncture these new presuppositions pose a dilemma: either the New Synthesis correctly describes reality or the Revealed Word does. But on no crucial point can both systems be true at the same time. Here, briefly stated, are the components of the Other Spirituality.

1. *History is not spiritually important.* History as a record of events in space and time has no particular significance to the spiritual understanding or progress of the

individual human being or of religious communities. In fact, history as traditionally understood may be a hindrance to spirituality by tying people to local beliefs, particular places and individual teachers. Records purporting to be spiritual histories, the prime example being the Bible, are not principally historical. Rather, such sacred texts are largely symbolic, allegorical or mythic.

2. *The dominance of reason.* Reason—also mind, consciousness, intellect, awareness or imagination—is the divine characteristic in humans. It is virtually unlimited in its potential for development through scientific study, mystical experience and evolution. Reason is the principal means for human apprehension of spiritual truth, with the most substantial spiritual insights coming to those with the greatest awareness, the most highly evolved consciousness or the most capacious reason.

3. *The spiritualization of science.* Science, the empirical study of the material universe, is the principal instrument reason employs to acquire spiritual knowledge. Science is both the source and the test of theology—it discovers new spiritual truths and confirms what has long been known to human beings through certain spiritual traditions.

4. *The animation of nature.* Nature is infused with a divine spirit, consciousness or life force. Physical nature is thus alive with divine energy or soul. In short, nature is divine. This fact about physical nature warrants its study by science as a source of spiritual knowledge.

5. *Hidden knowledge and spiritual progress.* Knowledge is the key to spiritual insight and human progress. Such knowledge comes by means of reason employing science, but it may also come through certain individuals specially gifted to understand and directly experience the spiritual realm. Spiritual knowledge, then, is the special preserve of extraordinarily gifted individuals including some scientists, but also a new class of shamans, mediums between the physical and spiritual realms. Because this spiritual knowledge is not immediately accessible to all people, it is, at least initially, hidden or secret.

6. *Spiritual evolution.* Human beings are destined to realize unimaginable spiritual advancement through a process of spiritual evolution. Spiritual evolution is not simply change, but advancement that occurs incrementally over time. The eventual result of this process of spiritual evolution will be actual human divinity. Through science, the means of directing and hastening this process is now within our grasp.

7. *Religious pluralism as rooted in mystical experience.* The only universal religious experience is the mystical experience. Thus, mysticism provides a basis for reli-

gious pluralism, for the uniting of disparate spiritual traditions around common mystical insights. There is a steadily increasing awareness of this fact within each religious tradition.

GOALS OF THE STUDY

This book examines certain representative and highly influential statements that have contributed to a radically new way of thinking about religion in the West. These statements have contributed importantly to the twofold public activity of religious criticism on the one hand and spiritual invention on the other. My goal is to trace the historical trajectory in popular religious discourse of a set of religious ideas that, though once considered exotic or even heretical, now hold sway in the Western religious mind. I hope not only to clarify the sources and interconnections of the ideas making up the New Religious Synthesis, but also to assess the implications of our new spirituality for human happiness. After all, the goal of true spirituality ought to be contributing to our fulfillment, freedom and contentedness as people. Thus, the concluding chapter offers my own assessment as to which system—the New Religious Synthesis or the Revealed Word—is a preferable guide to human spirituality.

The great psychoanalyst Carl Jung, himself an important proponent of a new way in religion, noted in 1933 that a new religious mind was rising in the West as Judeo-Christian thought waned correspondingly. He evaluated the situation as the simple outworking of a powerful psychic law. "I cannot take it as an accident," he wrote. "It seems to me rather to satisfy a psychological law." And what was Jung's law? "For every piece of conscious life that loses its importance and value—so runs the law—there arises a compensation in the unconscious. . . . No psychic value can disappear without being replaced by another of equal intensity."[80]

Jung was right that a fundamental shift in Western religious attitudes was occurring in the twentieth century. However, as indicated above, I do not believe the available evidence supports the notion that this change resulted from the operation of a mindless principle analogous to "the conservation of energy in the physical world." The rise of the Other Spirituality is not so much the outworking of a psychic law as the result of sustained, intentional and successful public efforts to change the Western religious mind. The next chapter surveys some spiritual movements occurring prior to 1700 that helped to prepare the ground for the long program of spiritual persuasion that followed, and of which we are the inheritors.

2

ANTECEDENTS OF THE NEW RELIGIOUS SYNTHESIS

A Brief History of Alternative Spirituality in the West

Secrecy was a trait of all [occult organizations] and was inseparable from the very concept of esotericism, which flourishes among men who enjoy the distinction of possessing rare knowledge.

WAYNE SHUMAKER,
The Occult Sciences in the Renaissance

The human mind "reflected" a divinely ordered universe in such a way that the magus could tap the hidden powers of the universe.

HUGH KEARNEY,
Science and Change, 1500-1700

Before considering the specific persuasive efforts that toppled the Revealed Word outlook and formulated the Other Spirituality, it will be helpful to survey some important early developments that set the stage for a dramatic shift in public religious attitudes. The religious ideas that are our principal focus did not suddenly emerge in 1700, but were in many ways outgrowths of intriguing spiritual movements in medieval and Renaissance Europe. A number of social, intellectual and religious developments between 1300 and 1700 profoundly shaped subsequent Western religious attitudes, thus helping to prepare the ground for a long campaign of public spiritual advocacy.

SPIRITUAL COMMUNITIES IN THE MIDDLE AGES

A number of influential spiritual communities in medieval Europe advocated spiritual practices and doctrines that contradicted the Revealed Word perspective. For example, historian Leonard Levi writes of a fascinating medieval spiritual movement that challenged Christian thought at a time when the church enjoyed perhaps its greatest dominance in Europe. The Free Spirits, young vagabonds who preached free love, mystical union with God, and the rejection of conventional morality, roamed across Europe in the thirteenth and fourteenth centuries. The men in the movement called themselves Beghards, the women Beguines.

Rejecting the trinitarian conception of God, Free Spirits insisted that divinity dwelled in every individual. When a person recognized this truth, she was a step closer to recognizing her own divinity. Free Spirits sought to liberate the soul from its fleshly constraints, and found conventional moral precepts irrelevant and an impediment to spiritual development. As Levi writes, "life itself was incarnation and resurrection. 'The divine essence is my essence and my essence is the divine essence,' said a Free Spirit. Another said he was 'wholly transformed into God,' so that not even the Virgin Mary could tell the difference. 'Rejoice with me, I have become God,' announced a third."[1] The Free Spirits collected their theology from gnosticism, mysticism and other sources.

Of greater concern to the medieval church were the gnostic communities spread through southern and eastern Europe. Gnosticism is the belief that secret knowledge—gnosis—allows certain highly disciplined individuals to transcend the limits of time and the physical body. Gnostic sects such as the Cathars, Bogomiles and Albigensians were common and influential, especially in the Balkans. Some of these groups spread even into Western Europe where the Inquisition eventually wiped them out.

These European sects reflected the typical gnostic division between masters (or *perfecti*) and the uninitiated (or *credenti*, believers). Gnostic sects attributed great power to Satan, including the creation of the world. Some taught that the cosmos reflected a struggle between a good force, associated with light and the God of the New Testament, and an evil spiritual force, associated with darkness and the God of the Old Testament. For this reason, most medieval gnostic groups rejected the teachings of the Old Testament and denigrated the God of creation.

Birth into a body was seen as either a punishment for sins during a soul's prior existence or as an opportunity for the spirit to liberate itself through *gnosis*. Gender itself was an evil consequence of the soul being embodied, and sexual intercourse often was discouraged for the same reason. Among the medieval gnostic sects of Europe, ritual suicide by starvation, called the *endura*, was also practiced. Self-imposed starvation, according to the masters, ensured a soul's advancement if an individual could not master sufficient secret knowledge to become one of the *perfecti*.

Also practiced as a sacrament was baptism into immortality by the laying on of hands by *perfecti,* termed the *consolamentum.* The Church specifically condemned this practice, leading to widespread persecution of gnostic groups. Thus, the *perfecti* dominated the lives of the *credenti,* literally holding in their hands the power of life, death and eternal blessing. Earthly life itself was considered by some groups to be hell, or punishment for sin, a fate from which only *gnosis* could provide release.

MAGIC AND THE HERMETIC TRADITION

Hermeticism is a secret magical tradition based on a set of fourteen books known collectively as the *Corpus Hermeticum* and falsely attributed to a mythical figure known as Hermes Trismegistus. The Hermetic teachings that made their way into Western Europe were based on the systems of various philosophers and teachers in Alexandria, Egypt, between A.D. 150 and 300. Even earlier Greek origins are often claimed for the ideas. Wayne Shumaker writes, "Hermeticism was basically a Greek contemplative mysticism developed on Egyptian soil. Its sources were mainly in popular Greek philosophical thought, . . . but details appear to have been borrowed from Judaism, Persian religion, and, more doubtfully, from Christianity."[2]

Hermetic writings came into Europe when "a monk named Leonardo da Pistoia brought to Florence a Greek manuscript known as the *Corpus Hermeticum.*"[3] A Latin translation and tireless promotion by the enormously influential Humanist Marsilio Ficino (1433-1499) ensured the prominence of Hermetic teachings throughout Europe. Renaissance European scholars ascribed Hermetic secrets to Pythagoras, the ancient Chaldeans, the Egyptians and Zoroaster.[4] Renaissance philosophers were fascinated with the occult Greek and Egyptian teachings contained in Hermetic works. Among the most prominent of these was the handsome, brilliant and charismatic scholar, Pico della Mirandola (1463-1494). Shumaker writes, "the early support of a man who was learned, attractive, and of noble birth contributed to the system's prestige."[5] Another important Renaissance advocate was the famous speculative thinker Giordano Bruno (1548-1600).

Hermeticism emphasized mental or spiritual experience over physical; time and space are irrelevant, and history illusory. Only the interior life of the mind mattered, and God was referred to simply as *Nous* or Mind. This elevation of Mind suggested a corresponding hatred of the body akin to gnostic teaching. Mind "uses the body" to attain ever greater knowledge toward the goal of individual spiritual insight. Thus, Hermeticism often was marked by an ascetic disregard for the body, seen as an impediment to spiritual progress that would eventually be dispensed with. The body had no real significance, and was irrelevant to the spiritual life. As various secret spiritual techniques were mastered, Mind achieved control over time, space and the body. Greek and Egyptian Hermetic teachers suggested that the soul, once liberated from the body, could be ordered from place to place instantly. "Order your soul to transport itself to India; and it is there; send it to the ocean, and it seems not to have to travel to be where you wish it. What power you have, and what speed!"[6]

A pantheistic outlook that found divinity in everything also marked Hermeticism. The *Corpus Hermeticum* repeatedly claims that "the whole world is alive" and "permeated with life." A teacher in the Hermetic book *Asclepius* asks the student, "Have I not said that everything is one and that the one is everything, inasmuch as everything was in the Creator before He created all things."[7] The general view of God is reflected in a famous formulation attributed to various medieval mystics. God is "a circle whose center is everywhere and whose circumference is nowhere." Though this statement is not found in the *Corpus Hermeticum,* followers of Hermetic teachings include it in their own writings.

Divinity in the Hermetic tradition is incapable of description in human language. Thus, the highest spiritual experience is mysticism, or direct contact with the unspeakable divine essence. Such experience is not generally accessible to human beings, but rather is the special domain of the knowing few. This sphere of the divine consciousness is referred to as Poimandres, and great knowledge and self-control are required to enter it.

Hermetic teachers embraced the idea that daemons or spirit beings exercised some control over human destiny. Through the direction of a daemon, the human soul could attain unity with the divine consciousness of Poimandres. In spiritual ascent, the "self is given over to the daemon." The adept or enlightened individual "throws himself upward toward the spheres and is purged of a different vice as he passes through each." He thus moves toward God and "at length can become a Power and enter into God."[8]

The ultimate goal of Hermetic spirituality is the individual's divinity. The Hermetic master "passes into the nature of a god as if he were himself a god; he knows the race of daemons, inasmuch as he is aware that he has the same origin with them." He is "joined with the gods by his shared divinity" and takes on divine traits such as omnipresence. "He is everything at once, and everywhere." This transition to divine status can occur during the earthly life, so that Hermetists believed that "some men are gods."[9] Human beings possessing spiritual secrets actually control daemons (gods) by calling them into their service through occult rituals and incantations. In the *Asclepius* some highly advanced teachers are said to make or create gods.

Such knowledge is, of course, not for everyone. The Hermetic master was a person of extraordinary mental ability, physical discipline and knowledge. This collection of traits proves the presence of mind in the individual, and Hermetic writings contain "constant exhortations to secrecy" and insist "that not all men possess mind."[10] Simply put, some people are spiritually superior to others, and their superiority can be enhanced through training in spiritual secrets.

Implied in Hermeticism—Hermes himself having been a man who became a god—is spiritual evolution from lower to higher states of existence. Human beings are themselves the product of a long spiritual evolutionary process that moves from "creeping things" to fish, mammals, birds and then people. Humans can—through occult knowledge and extraordinary ability—continue this evolutionary process and become daemons, then gods, and finally planets or stars. "This," writes Shumaker, "is the upward path."[11] Thus did the Hermetic tradition seek to absorb Jesus Christ into its cosmic scheme. He is "the Lord God and the Father of every talisman [magic formula] of the whole world." Hermeticism's tradition had broad currency in Renaissance Europe, shaping even popular thinking about the supernatural. As Shumaker writes, "evidently the Hermetic influence was not limited to the scholarly world but filtered down among the populace, and that with surprising rapidity." He concludes, "a predisposition existed in all classes of society" to accept the myths and symbols of Hermeticism, a fact that "suggests vividly an intellectual temper" willing to embrace a "new gospel."[12]

KABBALAH: SECRETS IN THE PENTATEUCH

The kabbalah (also spelled cabala, kabbala and kabala) is a collection of Jewish mystical writings built around the Hebrew alphabet and numerical system, especially as found in Jewish religious writing. Two Hebrew books, the *Sefer Yetzirah* (Book of Formation) and the *Zohar* (Brightness) provide the foundation of the kabbalah, with the latter being the more important source of teachings, though the former is older.[13] Their dating and authorship are contested—some scholars believe they reflect an oral tradition dating back to the Babylonian captivity, while others find them to be the work of medieval rabbis.[14] According to some contemporary teachers of the kabbalah, these mystical teachings were derived from ancient Jewish sages who had traveled to India. As support, they cite Genesis 25:6, which states that "Abraham sent his sons to the east."

By one stream of Jewish lore, the kabbalah was delivered from heaven by angels in order to teach Adam, "after his fall, how to recover his primal nobility and bliss." The more common account is that Moses received these secret teachings on Mount Sinai along with the law, and passed them on to an elite group of seventy elders. Thus, kabbalah is a system intended for the personal spiritual advancement of a spiritual elite through the appropriation of secret insights. "In order to be initiated into this mysterious and sacred science it was necessary to be distinguished not only by intelligence and eminent position, but also by advanced age, as well."[15] Kabbalah has long been viewed by many within Judaism as "a doctrine of superior profundity and purity reserved solely for a small number of the elect."[16]

Kabbalistic teaching shared a low view of the body, history and the physical world with both Hermeticism and Gnosticism, two of its sources. Professor Gershon Scholem, a leading authority on kabbalah, "considers the Kabbalah to be pre-Christian and Zoroastrian in origin."[17] Shlomo Shoham, another important student of the kabbalistic tradition, writes, "both the Kabala and Gnosis regard temporal existence as an incarceration of parts of divinity in profane bodies." Thus, he finds that "the quest for participation in the *Schechina* [mystical presence of God] and in the Sophia [cosmic Wisdom] is a longing for a more benign and boundless reality that contrasts with . . . profane creation."[18] That is, the world of ordinary existence is too limited for the spiritually initiated individual. In keeping with this observation, Adolphe Franck finds the spirit of kabbalah to be mystical.[19]

Creating and controlling God. Kabbalah inverts the Revealed Word relationship of creature to creator, rendering human beings virtually divine and their place of existence a boundless and transcendent reality rather than the profane world. Human beings control and even create God rather than the other way around. In kabbalah, "activation" of God by human beings is the goal, that is, the use of a divine force for human purposes.[20] Moreover, humanity must redeem the entire cosmic order, a task that includes repairing or "mending" (Hebrew: *tikkun*) an imperfect god-force. Shoham writes that the flawed god of kabbalah "can be mended by man and only by man." This limited divinity is "entirely dependent on man for his redemption." In fact, humanity's salvation will "follow with the successful mending of divinity."[21]

Kabbalah suggests that human beings may even "destroy god, or create a new god."[22] This is desirable, for the God of the Old Testament, the God "who created us, made us breathe, eat, reproduce, and write books; who is responsible for our historical existence" is considered to be "blind, arrogant, and merciless."[23] Space and time "were created by a vile God" who needed both to fulfill his selfish plans. It was only "because of God's needs" that "creation and man were created."[24]

Human beings "emanated from God" rather than being created by him. Our role or mission is "to mend the blemished and suffering God," an activity which gives us "meaning and purpose" by making us "a partner to God." Such a partnership "is not possible with a theistic, 'perfect' God" of the type presented by the Revealed Word tradition. Thus, God's limitations or imperfections are actually necessary in order for human beings to assume their rightful role as God's managers and healers. Under the influence of such a theology, the human ego becomes convinced that it is "a unique and exclusive center of the cosmos."[25]

To be created in God's image means only that God and the self "are identical," but with the self firmly in control. The master of kabbalah achieves "transcendence" when he can "grasp" this truth internally. The link with God "through the inner self is direct and immediate—one has only to discover that it exists."[26] Thus, mystical experience of God takes precedence over reading the record of God's activities in revelation, the latter approach to the divine being bound to space and time, and constricted by unnecessary doctrinal concerns.

Shoham concludes, "there could be no greater subordination of transcendence to man than this Kabalist conception of God." The "blemished Kabalist God resigns himself from history," leaving the "management of meaning and values in a godless history to man." God is mankind's puppet who "merely reacts" to human desire. "Man not only influences God's essence and action . . . but actually provides him with the energy for being and doing."[27] By studying and practicing the kabbalah's teachings, human beings complete the creation of an unfinished cosmos.

The kabbalah emerged onto the European intellectual scene at around the same time as the *Corpus Hermeticum*, garnering tremendous interest and exerting unusual influence on Renaissance thought. In fact, Ficino's and Pico's interest in the Hermetic writings was rivaled only by their interest in the kabbalah. Thus, magical thinking dominated much of the European intellectual scene during the Renaissance. Interest in magic greatly affected the development of science as well.

NEO-PLATONISM AND MAGICAL SCIENCE

The philosophical movement known as Neo-Platonism was founded by Plotinus (A.D. 205-270) and developed by disciples such as Porphyry (A.D. 232-303). Neo-Platonism, which claimed to extend the teachings of Plato, was tremendously influential among European Humanists and other intellectuals beginning in the fifteenth century. Historian of science Hugh Kearney writes that by the seventeenth century "its influence extended to the Cambridge Platonists (more properly, the Cambridge Neo-Platonists) and their greatest pupil, Sir Isaac Newton."[28]

A magical worldview characterized Neo-Platonic thought, as it did Hermetic and kabbalistic. The cosmos was secretly coded and would reveal its secrets only to the diligent seeker after truth. Numbers, sometimes revealed by spirits or daemons, were the cosmic encryption method that needed to be broken. Thus, the Neo-Platonic philosopher held to a "mystical reverence for numbers, not a wholesome respect for practical mathematical techniques." Neo-Platonists selected objects of study on the basis of their potential for yielding personal power. This view "encouraged secrecy and an interest in the occult for its own sake by which a work of art was seen as a magical emblem or a coded message for the initiate." Scholarship became a secret enterprise to benefit a privileged elite. Drawing on an ancient Pythagorean principle, the academy's goal was "to preserve its secrets for the favored few," especially those possessing great skill in mathematics.[29]

Like Gnosticism, Neo-Platonism held that the human soul was spirit held captive in matter. This belief set the Neo-Platonists at odds with Christian teaching, which stressed the unity of the human as body and soul, the ultimate redemption of each and the conviction that the material world had been created good. Neo-Platonists looked to ancient sources such as Hermes, Zoroaster and Orpheus, all of whom taught that a divine soul animated the material universe. God was not so much a divine person as a divine energy in all things. The earth and other celestial bodies were alive with a divine spirit.

Magical science. The scientific tradition in Renaissance Europe developed around three basic approaches: the organic, the mechanical and the magical. The organic emphasized living organisms, while the mechanistic searched for mechanical metaphors to explain the universe's operation. But it is the magical tradition that may have provided the Western world with the real impetus for scientific exploration. Hugh Kearney writes that judged by strictly rational criteria "the magical tradition appears to be the least rational of the three; yet judged by its contribution to the Scientific Revolution, we may see it as the most important."[30]

At the same time, this tradition laid the groundwork for many later developments in popular skepticism and in the ascent of a new religious mind.

Neo-Platonism was important to the development of the magical tradition in science. Likewise, magical scientists sought guidance from mystical sources such as the kabbalah and the *Corpus Hermeticum*. An analogy developed between the divine mind in the cosmos and the mind of the human investigator. According to this analogy, "the human mind 'reflected' a divinely ordered universe in such a way that the magus [scholar/magician] could tap the hidden powers of the universe."[31] Thus, the scientist was "a mystic who could hear the magical music of the universe."[32] Astrology took on particular importance.

These early scientists subscribed to the view that light was the giver of all life. The sun was especially important to magical scientists, which many took to be actually divine. Stars also were divine, and the scientists' attention was directed to the night skies in a desperate search for the clues that unlocked vast spiritual secrets conveyed in the movements and harmonies of the heavenly bodies. Astrological studies were rooted in the supposed works of the famous but nonexistent ancient scribe, Hermes Trismegistus, whom we already have met. This Hermetic tradition also found the sun to be "the visible God" who "sits upon a royal throne ruling his children the planets which circle around him."[33] The connection between Renaissance science and astrology could not have been closer.

The universe's music was mathematical in nature, and in numbers lay hidden "the secrets of the cosmos." Thus, phenomena that could be mathematically decoded, including musical harmonies, deserved careful study. The mystical scientist often was an ascetic "studying the occult, within the confines of an esoteric community." Like an ancient Gnostic, he held that the material world was "the last and lowest form of being."[34]

Mystical science became a search for the single element of matter that revealed the secret structure of the whole cosmos. The earth was a microcosm of the macrocosm of all reality. The same was alleged of the human body and of the mind. The universe's structure, once understood, could be manipulated to become a source of virtually miraculous power. Because such power was sought only for personal ends, the scientist's discoveries were always carefully guarded secrets. Obscure language and codes were employed to protect secrets from rivals.

As the Renaissance progressed, interest in cosmic secrets increased. Thus, the sixteenth century witnessed a flourishing of studies such as mathematics, astronomy and alchemy—the search for a means of transforming common metals into gold and discovering an elixir to extend life. Mathematical direction sometimes came through guiding spirits, as in the famous case of Edmund Kelley (1559-1595) who claimed to be "following the directions of the angelic spirits" in his mathematical investigations.[35]

Bruno. Of particular importance to the rise and dissemination of the magical view of science in the Renaissance was the restive Dominican monk Giordano Bruno (1548-1600), a native of Nola near Naples. Fleeing Italy for Geneva, and Geneva for Paris, Bruno lectured widely on Copernicanism and its prospect for unveiling a vast network of cosmic secrets. Bruno believed that a new religious view that would supersede Christianity was at hand, which led to his "repudiation of orthodox Christianity, including the Bible."[36] Eventually Paris became uncomfortable for the unorthodox thinker, and he found refuge in Oxford where he frequently lectured.

European gnostics accepted Bruno's spiritual vision in which the individual "gains access to the divine directly through his own inner illumination." Carl Raschke explains that "while Catholicism required acceptance of revealed truth or 'sacred doctrine' as the first principle from which understanding follows, the new gnosticism, as represented in Bruno's writings, insisted upon *self-consciousness* as the proper window to reality."[37] For Bruno, the path to such spiritual enlightenment was scientific study of the cosmos. Robert Sullivan writes that for Bruno the study of the stars "enabled the adept to internalize the universal order and so preserved him from any fear of death."[38] This kind of liberating scientific knowledge was available only to a small number of highly talented individuals.

Bruno viewed the universe as an infinite system of planets and suns, and held that many planets were inhabited. But his opinion was rooted not so much in the observations of Galileo, from which he drew support, but in his own mystical metaphysics. According to Bruno's speculations, the mind of God or "World Soul" was diffuse throughout the universe; that is, the universe was full of the divine. Moreover, because our own reason participates in the divine reason, there is essentially no limit to human reason.

At the same time, there is no reason to think that God limited his creation of intelligent species to our own small world. The universe is filled with intelligent creatures whose reason, like ours, manifests divine reason. Numbers unlock a store of astronomical secrets, and because these secrets are at the heart of metaphysics, mathematics takes on religious significance. In fact, Bruno subscribed to the gnostic and Neo-Platonic notion that "the earth and the stars were alive," and they speak to us through mathematics.[39] Bruno and other metaphysical scientists gave this originally Greek idea great currency in Renaissance Europe.[40]

Bruno's theology was at its base pantheistic and monistic: divinity is diffuse throughout the universe and all things are ultimately one thing. His defense of this position influenced other European thinkers including Spinoza, and through Spinoza a wide range of religious radicals throughout the Western world.

Brahe. Also important to the rise of the magical view of science was the Danish astronomer Tycho Brahe (1546-1601), the teacher of Johann Kepler (1571-1630) when Brahe was at Prague. Brahe treated his astronomical findings as a private treasure trove, the resources of which he would eventually employ to "build up an unchallenged position of privilege in the world of astrology."[41] Brahe pursued his studies on the model of a "mystic seeking his salvation in the night sky, and jealously guarding the results which he achieved."[42] Brahe's famous Castle of the Heavens on the Island of Hveen, a private observatory funded by King Frederick II of Denmark, became a citadel where he worked tirelessly for twenty years with tremendous success. Brahe labored hard to improve the measurement techniques employed by astronomers, and his findings were crucial to later astronomical discoveries.

But it is the object of that success that is often misunderstood. Brahe was not pushing back the veil of the cosmos for the sake of advancing science. He was, rather, peering into the secrets of the material world in order to advance his own spiritual fortunes. Brahe had a great influence on Kepler, who continued Brahe's search for the keys to the secrets of the cosmos. Kepler's work provided the foundation for the insights of Sir Isaac Newton, perhaps the last of the great magical scientists. Other similar lines of influence from magical to modern science can be traced in chemistry, biology and medicine.

Pluralism. Neo-Platonists and magical scientists advocated a broad and largely undifferentiated view of religious belief. Roland Bainton affirms that "Renaissance mystics . . . sought to discover the same set of truths beneath the symbols of many systems: in the lore of Zoroaster, the mysteries of Hermes Trismegistus, in the alluring number speculations of the Jewish cabala." There were even efforts to found a World Parliament of Religions based on this common core of mystical insight, and the hope was advanced that all nations could be united under a single religious view. Bainton writes, "tolerance became the watchword even at the expense of an emasculated Christianity."[43]

Shumaker concurs: "The Renaissance thirst for synthesis, for syncretism, was unquenchable." Bradford Verter points out that Nicholas of Cusa, a scholar close to the Pope, argued in his *De pace fidei* (1453) for "a fundamental harmony linking all faiths to the worship of a common hidden God." Marsilio Ficino suggested in 1474 that "a member of any faith who displayed the moral virtues of Jesus was properly termed a Christian." Verter adds, "here were seeds of both esoteric mysticism and theological unitarianism."[44] Ficino alleged that Neo-Platonism was compatible with Christianity, while Pico blended Neo-Platonism, Hermeticism, Christianity and the kabbalah.[45] Cornelius Agrippa, another important magical scientist, added to these "astrology, numerology, alchemy, and much else."[46] Christianity, it seemed, was compatible with virtually every philosophy or system conceivable.

The search was on for the irreducible, primitive core of all religions, for "a system of pristine and universally harmonious theology."[47] Thus it was assumed, for example, that "all of Eastern religion must have been reducible to a single pattern, which no doubt would have proved to be a gentile approximation of Christianity."[48] Thus, although Neo-Platonism and magical science, on the one hand, and comparative religious studies, on the other, might seem unrelated, the connections between them were strong and direct.

EUROPEAN MYSTICISM

Various European mystics garnered large followings between 1200 and 1700. Their writings on mystical theology and experience contributed importantly to the development of spiritual alternatives to orthodox, doctrinal Christianity. Two of the more influential mystic writers, both German, were Meister Eckhart and Jacob Böhme.

Meister Eckhart. Johannes Eckhart, often called Meister Eckhart (c. 1260-c. 1327) was the founder of German Dominican mysticism. Joining the Dominicans early in his life, he studied in Paris and returned to Germany to hold a number of positions in the Dominican order. Eckhart's basic theology was pantheistic, and he taught the gnostic idea that the human soul carried within it a divine spark. Clashing with the Church, he was condemned as a heretic by Pope John XXII.

Eckhart's troubles stemmed from his unorthodox mysticism that led to claims such as "God begets his son in the soul," so that, "as some authorities say, the soul is made equal with God."[49] Eckhart's emphasis on a divine spirit in nature, the inherent divinity of the individual and the role of contemplation in spiritual advancement made him a major influence on German intellectuals in the nineteenth and twentieth centuries.

After about the age of fifty, Eckhart's major responsibility in the Dominican order was to preach to contemplative nuns in their convents. During this period of time he wrote both his *Book of Divine Consolation* and *On Detachment*. In these and other works he set out his doctrine of the soul's union with God. As one stage in the process, the soul recognizes this union. Thus the individual and God become spiritually one and the same. Eckhart's teachings tended to reinforce the notion that the individual determined what was true in religion. As R. W. Southern writes, the emphasis on personal spiritual experience and development made "institutions of religion seem less important, and, if not wrong, at least irrelevant." This theme had profound implications for public arguments against Christianity in the Enlightenment period and beyond.[50]

The last stage in Eckhart's mystical path toward union with God was called *breakthrough*. The goal of much of Eckhart's mysticism was direct contact with God or "Godhead" (*Deitas* rather than *Deus*). But this goal can easily be misunderstood. It is not at all clear that Eckhart principally sought ecstatic experience. Rather, his main objective was triumph over the restraints of conventional theology toward the expression of a radical subjectivism in religious life. For instance, Eckhart wished to break through what he saw as the limiting doctrine of the Trinity in order to make contact with the Godhead beyond, the true divine essence.

Jacob Böhme. The mystic cobbler Jacob Böhme (1575-1624) influenced many later religious writers, among them some of the advocates of a New Religious Synthesis. Much of his basic theology is set out in the book *Aurora* (1612). He was not formally educated, but he read widely, particularly the works of mystical writers such as Paracelsus (1493-1541) and Valentin Weigel (1538-1588). Böhme claimed direct divine illumination in 1600, in the midst of which he glimpsed "the Being of Beings" and "the Abyss." He claimed a similar experience again in 1610. Böhme believed the external, physical world was a projection of an inner spiritual power. For him, God was absolute but not personal. The divine is continually expanding in search of self-knowledge, a process in which human beings may participate through contemplation.

The inner spiritual world of the individual is a prototype or analogy of the outward world of the physical universe, an idea similar to Bruno's notion of similitude between the cosmos and the mind. Böhme worked out an elaborate account of the forces at play in the natural world, and then spiritualized these forces by labeling them with names such as "love" and "the Kingdom of God." He believed that mystical insight into the material and spiritual realms could bring about harmony and peace.

For Böhme, progress toward harmony was a matter of spiritual evolution, a process through which God himself has had to pass. A flash of mystical insight (blitz) reveals that one may either remain in the realm of desire or transcend it through self-denial or the death of self. This process, not atonement for human sin, is Böhme's interpretation of the suffering and death of Christ. Such speculation became a major influence on the English Quakers and later Romantic writers.

Mystics like Eckhart and Böhme tended to disregard history as an account of temporal affairs to be transcended and ignored. Christ's advent, for instance, was less important as a historical event than as a stage in divine evolution. Jesus' own life is translated into "an allegory of that which must take place in the inner life." Christ as God incarnate in history is insignificant, but Christ as a metaphor for spiritual progress is highly significant. The mystical view of history also has profound implications for a view of revelation. As Roland Bainton notes, "the Bible is valuable as testimony to an experience which can arise without the book and having arisen can dispense with it."[51] Not regarding the Bible as a historical record of God's redemptive work diminishes its value as history while elevating its value as spiritual allegory.

It is often said that mystics like Eckhart and Böhme emphasized the union of the human and divine. It might be more accurate to say that they sought to move from the material realm where humanity was caught to a spiritual realm where divinity could be apprehended by the individual will. As Bainton has noted, mysticism may be compatible with Christian practice as long as it is clear that the human and the divine are, in fact, different and can never be merged. But, he writes, "if the devotee is believed to be completely merged in the abyss of the Godhead, then the subject-object relationship, the polarity of the I and the Thou, so characteristic of the Hebrew-Christian tradition, is destroyed."[52] Both Eckhart and Böhme taught such complete merging of the divine and human. The old notion was destroyed, but a powerful new notion took its place—that what is human may become divine.

HUMANISM AND THE RISE OF BIBLICAL CRITICISM
During the period running from about 1400 to about 1650, Humanism as a European intellectual movement achieved genuine stature. Many Humanist assumptions provided a foundation for a full-scale popular assault on Christian

thought that began around 1700. A deep interest in the philosophies, languages and religious ideas of the ancient Greek and Roman worlds defined Humanism, first in Italy and later in other parts of Europe. European rediscovery of classical sources had an immediate and profound impact on moral and religious thinking. "At the beginning of the Renaissance," writes historian George T. Buckley, "the classics began to be read once more as literature." As a result "the Humanists soon discovered that in Seneca and Plutarch there was a system of morals worthy to be compared with the Christian."[53]

Humanistic skepticism regarding Christianity was especially powerful at Italian universities in cities such as Florence and Bologna, but gradually spread to northern Europe as well.[54] Questions about the unique truth of Christian theology grew out of the study of writers such as the Roman politician and philosopher Cicero and the Greek physician and philosopher Sextus Empiricus.[55] The recovery of ancient philosophical and religious traditions had a major and lasting impact on the Christian consensus in Europe. In fact, historian C. B. Schmitt writes, "the recovery and the reassimilation of the ancient writings were the primary factors in the evolution of the modern skeptical attitude."[56]

Reason's rise and revelation's decline. Reason—not tradition, revelation or authority—emerged during the Renaissance as the chief criterion of religious truth. Even Jesus Christ, Sebastianus Castellio (1515-1563) pointed out, resolved questions by using his senses and his reason. Sensory evidence and critical reason increasingly were taken as sufficient for resolving religious questions. The Bible was not self-evidently true, for reason determines what is self-evident, and much that the Bible had to say was not apparent to reason. Humanists rejected claims that the biblical texts stood above the critical assessments of reason. The tension between reason and revelation was becoming starkly evident, a tension we will examine more closely in a subsequent chapter.

Increased contact with other cultures and the emerging discipline of textual criticism encouraged Christianity's comparison with other religious systems in the Renaissance.[57] Oxford scholar William Chillingworth (1602-1643) urged in *The Religion of Protestants* (1637) that "schismatics, heretics, even heathen Turks, could find that their good lives led them to salvation."[58] In the seventeenth century, English writers John Toland and Charles Blount compared various religions in search of an irreducible core of common elements. Toland, like Roman Stoics, argued that all religions have many doctrines in common. By reconstructing the "original belief from which the separate religions were supposed to have varied" one could discover the true, rational religion of the human race.[59] Toland and many Deists affirmed a single, primitive source of all religious thought.[60]

Renaissance Humanists sought a new approach to religion built on classical sources, textual criticism, human achievement and reason. A religion of autonomous reason informed by ancient conceptions of virtue began to take shape and was advanced as a rival to the old religion of Christianity based on allegedly irrational concepts such as revelation and miracles. One's apprehension of the divine did not depend upon church authority, Christian tradition or biblical accounts. Religious belief was a personal matter for reason alone to decide.

Early biblical criticism: dismantling the Revealed Word. With the development of literary criticism and a corresponding dramatic rise in knowledge of classical languages and ancient history, the tools were in hand to demonstrate that the biblical texts themselves were open to question. Moreover, as the works of early critics of Christianity were translated into European languages, the arsenal of arguments against the faith was supplied with new weapons. Thus, Humanism provided later writers with much material for developing public arguments against Christian belief.

Of course, the Bible had come under criticism from the first centuries of the Christian church when skeptics such as Porphyry developed arguments against its doctrines and historical claims. As noted above, Italian Humanists of the Renaissance also advanced the project of biblical criticism by comparing biblical teachings to the moral teachings of Greek and Roman philosophies and by encouraging historical study of biblical texts. However, the systematic public criticism of the Bible is a more recent European development, and one that has had greater impact on scholarly *and* popular attitudes toward Christianity than has perhaps any other. The following is not a history of biblical criticism so much as an effort to identify a few important moments in the advent of a critical tradition that became particularly important in shaping religious thought in the modern period.

Benedict de Spinoza. Benedict de Spinoza (1632-1677) laid the groundwork for later biblical criticism in his most famous work, *Tractatus theologico-politicus* (1670).[61] His writings were modified by French and Dutch religious radicals to provide material for the infamous book *Traite des trois imposteurs* (*The Treatise of the Three Impostors*). This scandalous work, which was condemned in both the Netherlands and France, argued that Jesus, Moses and Muhammad were frauds and the religions they established false. The book's subtitle is revealing: *ou l'Esprit d M. Spinoza (or the Spirit of Mr. Spinoza).* In other words, the *Treatise* sought to capture the spirit of Spinoza's corrosive criticism of the Bible. Jonathan Israel, a leading authority on Dutch history, writes that Spinoza's work was "turned by a group of Dutch and Huguenot freethinkers into a potent subterranean force" against Christianity.[62]

Many of Christianity's harshest critics were drawn to Spinoza. He affirmed the supremacy of reason and argued that the only religious truths were ones taught universally. Spinoza wrote, "I determined to examine the Bible afresh in a careful, impartial, and unfettered spirit, making no assumptions concerning it, and attributing to it no doctrines, which I do not find clearly set down therein."[63] Moreover, he suggested that passages he took to be implausible were "foisted onto the sacred writings by irreligious hands," adding that "whatsoever is contrary to nature is also contrary to reason, and whatsoever is contrary to reason is absurd, and *ipso facto*, to be rejected."[64] Spinoza questioned the dating and authorship of many biblical books, particularly in the Old Testament, and advanced philosophical arguments against miracles.[65]

Spinoza sought an acid that would dissolve notions such as traditional authorship and doctrinal inspiration, thus turning biblical criticism in a "negative and destructive" direction. With the publication of the *Tractatus*, "the tools of destruction were at hand."[66] He began with the assumption that "revelation as such does not happen" and had in mind to "discuss biblical interpretation [in order] to discredit the appearance of supernatural authority."[67]

Locke and the early English tradition. The English tradition of biblical criticism extends back at least to Sir Walter Raleigh's *History of the World* (1603-1616) and was more fully developed in Lord Herbert of Cherbury's *De religioni laici* (1645) and Sir Thomas Browne's *Religio medici* (1643), in which Browne challenged such rudimentary biblical doctrines as the Fall and the curse on Adam and Eve.[68]

Late in the seventeenth century the famous philosopher John Locke (1632-1704) also encouraged critical approaches to biblical texts in his *The Reasonableness of Christianity* (1695). Locke's book suggested that the Bible is "a series of documents written at different times, the authenticity of which must often be called into question."[69] Though he sought to appear friendly to Christianity, Locke influenced many radical religious writers in the Enlightenment. Three such writers—John Toland, Anthony Collins and Lord Bolingbroke—all claimed to be his disciples.[70] J. C. D. Clark has written that Locke's "significance for the eighteenth century" was not his political theories, but introducing "heterodox theology into religious speculations."[71]

French critics. Several seventeenth-century French writers assisted the project of biblical criticism by contrasting biblical history to scientific and historical knowledge. In 1655 Isaac de La Peyrere's *Prae-adamitten* was published in which the "new knowledge" of science was contrasted to scriptural accounts. He concluded, for instance, that geographical and chronological evidence suggested that Adam was not the first man.[72] The Benedictine monk Jean Mabillon's *Acta sanctorum* (1668) "worked out the means for determining the date and authenticity of ancient documents, a cornerstone in historical method."[73]

The French priest Richard Simon (1638-1712) is often credited with having been "the direct founder of the historical-critical method."[74] His *Histoire critique du Vieux Testament* (1678) aroused tremendous controversy within the Catholic Church, and Simon was eventually expelled from his order.[75] Undaunted, he proceeded to author a series of books intending to show that the Protestant standard of *sola scriptura* was untenable as a criterion of biblical scholarship and ended only in confusion.[76] His own standards were "the evident and the rational," though he also argued that biblical interpretation must be guided by tradition.[77] As Krentz writes, during the seventeenth century "the scriptures were more and more treated like ordinary historical documents."[78]

The Reformation. The principle of *sola scriptura*, the Reformation's defining commitment, does not seem a fruitful starting point for arguments against the Bible and Christian orthodoxy. Indeed, the Reformation in northern Europe under the leadership of Martin Luther is typically associated with a return to the Bible as the standard of religious truth. However, a number of scholars have pointed out that this powerful Christian movement contributed importantly to skepticism's rise in modern Europe. Perhaps another of the Reformation's guiding principles, the priesthood of all believers, which placed biblical interpretation in the hands of the individual believer, contributed to this effect.

Of critical importance to later developments is the commitment of Reformation leaders to private interpretation of the Scriptures. "The Pandora's box that Luther opened at Leipzig," writes Richard Popkin, "was to have the most far-reaching consequences, not just in theology but throughout man's entire intellectual realm."[79] Similarly, Roscoe Pound argues that "private interpretation of the Bible" had the effect of elevating individual reason.[80] Freedom of interpretation was "a logical deduction from the right of private judgment, which was a basal principle of the Reformation," according to another historian, S. G. Hefelbower.[81]

Luther may have believed that faith was founded on rational certainties that prevented a misreading of Scripture, but thinkers less friendly to Christianity happily used his idea of personal interpretation to justify various attacks in the coming centuries. The English Deists often contended that their assault on the Bible was pursued in the spirit of reformation in Christianity.[82]

CONCLUSION

Several important spiritual and intellectual movements in Europe prior to 1700 helped to shape subsequent thinking about Christianity and alternatives to it. I have noted just a few developments that were of particular importance in preparing the way for more dramatic developments after 1700. Mystical and gnostic communities, fascination with the kabbalist tradition, humanistic studies and magical science, mystical spirituality and experiments in biblical criticism—each had a profound impact on subsequent popular thought about religious questions generally in the modern Western world. These movements often rejected traditional notions of a historically grounded revealed message from a personal God. Also important to several of these trends was a magical view of the cosmos that emphasized coded truths and an impersonal divinity. Finally, the individual's placement at the center of the spiritual cosmos marked a break with the Revealed Word tradition of a sovereign God whose power was unquestioned.

The following chapters consider several crucial components of a potent religious system that has taken shape during the modern period. Though fully formed as a popular religious view only recently, this system represents a synthesis of spiritual tendencies with deep historical roots. It is, thus, a New Religious Synthesis of often quite durable spiritual concepts.

3

THE RISE OF
BIBLICAL CRITICISM

Allegory, Myth, Codes and the End of History

There are concepts in the Bible that are repugnant to the modern consciousness.
BISHOP JOHN SHELBY SPONG,
Rescuing the Bible from Fundamentalism

Carl Jung long ago pointed out, beneath the turmoil of daily activity our unconscious motivations dwell in the mythic world. Inside each of us are primal gods and goddesses.
DEEPAK CHOPRA,
The Path to Love: Renewing the Power of Spirit in Your Life

At the outbreak of the modern era, the [gnostic] system of inverse biblical exegesis was once again activated.

IOAN COULIANO, The Tree of Gnosis

The year 1727 witnessed the beginning of a strange episode in public religious debate. A professor dismissed from the faculty of Cambridge University for his attacks on the Bible—and confined briefly on the charge of mental instability—published a book with the innocuous title *A Discourse on the Miracles of our Saviour*. The book itself was, however, anything but innocuous. In *A Discourse* and the five additional discourses that followed over the next two years, Thomas Woolston systematically subjected Jesus' miracles and even Jesus himself to scathing public ridicule. Claiming that he wrote in an effort to save Christianity from those who read the Bible literally, Woolston argued that Jesus' miracles were never meant as historical accounts. They were simply allegories for spiritual truths, a point he set out to prove by first demonstrating how ridiculous the accounts were when read as history. However, Thomas Woolston's irreverence crossed a line. At the wedding

feast in Cana, for example, Jesus and Mary are "boon Companions" of drunken rev-
elers. Jesus' reaction to Mary—"Woman, what have you to do with me?"—was
"certainly the effect of Drinking." Mary knew that Jesus was "initiated in the Mys-
terys of *Bacchus*" when she asked him to supply more wine.[1]

Bishop Edmund Gibson warned Londoners that Woolston was a madman and a
blasphemer, urged them not to read his books, and threatened to throw him in jail.
But Woolston would not relent. Three more long books kept up the attack on Jesus'
miracles. Thirty thousand copies were sold as quickly as they were published, and
"large quantities were forwarded to the American colonies."[2] Woolston had created
an international scandal, and by 1727 he was the talk of England. Clergy competed to
answer Woolston in print, many reminding King George I that he "did not bear the
sword in vain." Jonathan Swift himself penned verses in honor of the controversy:
"Here's Woolston's Tracts, the twelfth Edition; 'Tis read by ev'ry Politician: The
Country Members, when in Town, To all their Boroughs send them down: You
never met a Thing so smart; The Courtiers have them all by Heart."[3] Late in 1728
Woolston was arrested and charged with blasphemy. The following year he was
tried, convicted and sentenced to three years in jail and a fine of one hundred pounds.

Historians have called Woolston "clinically insane," "eccentric," "psychopathic"
and an "evil genius."[4] And yet, other scholars consider him "the most influential" of
all the eighteenth-century English skeptics, perhaps even the inventor of modern
biblical criticism.[5] Clearly he was a skilled public advocate—clever, provocative,
knowledgeable and daring. Woolston knew that by forcing a divorce between the
spiritual and the historical he was inaugurating a new way of reading the Bible. He
also knew that taking his new method directly to the public was more broadly persuasive than simply fomenting a debate among scholars.

Woolston's influence has been great, although his name is nearly forgotten. His
insistence that the New Testament contains myth or allegory rather than literal
history is now a widely accepted assumption that has been extended to a broad
range of religious texts. If we fast-forward to the year 1991—two hundred and
sixty years after Woolston's trial—a prominent and controversial Episcopal
Bishop has just published the latest in a series of works on the Bible. Bishop John
Shelby Spong's *Rescuing the Bible from Fundamentalism* reads like a seventh install-
ment of Woolston's *Discourses*. Of Jesus' casting a man's demons into pigs who then
destroy themselves by plunging over a cliff, Spong asks, "Are we drawn to a Lord
who would destroy a herd of pigs and presumably a person's livelihood in order to

exorcise a demon (Mark 5:13)?" Similarly, to Jesus' cursing of a fruitless fig tree, Spong replies, "Are we impressed when the one we call Lord curses a fig tree because it did not bear fruit out of season (Matt. 21:18, 19)?" The Woolstonesque tone of Spong's criticism is unmistakable. "If the Bible is read literally, it must be said that Jesus seems to have accepted without question the language of hell employed by his religious contemporaries," which Spong takes as clear evidence of Jesus' lack of spiritual insight.[6] Jesus may be "guilty of what we today would call antisemitism."[7] The "pejorative attitudes found in Christian scriptures and even in the supposed words of Jesus . . . has led to pogroms, ghettos, segregated housing and clubs, defaced synagogues, Krystallnacht, and Dachau."[8]

Spong, like Woolston, suggests that we find the true meaning of the Bible in the "wondrous new meanings to be drawn" from a nonhistorical New Testament. Jesus himself must no longer be understood as a unique historical character, but as one among many mythical figures expressing the human desire for transcendence. Thus, "we must seek the truth that lies beneath the mythology of the distant past so that we might experience that truth."[9] Woolston wrote to save Christianity from the literalists who valued "the letter" more than "the spirit," and Spong professes the same mission. Clinging to a historical Bible means "certain death to all that we have believed."[10] The Bible's truth lies "beneath and behind" its historical façade. Reading Spong leaves one with the distinct impression that Thomas Woolston launched a new era of biblical interpretation.

During the entire modern period the Bible has been the subject of extensive, often corrosive criticism. Critics have concluded that the Christian and Jewish Scriptures are neither historically reliable nor divinely revealed. Rather, these texts are largely symbolic or mythic products of the human religious imagination. This turn away from both history and divine intervention has been justified as an effort to rescue the Bible from narrowly dogmatic literal readings, to liberate Christianity from the confines of history, or as a step toward finding the Bible's deeper, hidden meanings. But this rescue effort has also shifted the very foundations of Western spirituality. Claiming that the Bible is myth rather than history, symbol rather than revelation, now strikes many as a step toward a more personally meaningful faith. The Revealed Word tradition is now viewed as one among many efforts to express the inexpressible experience of the spiritual or "numinous." The objective history and fixed doctrine of the Revealed Word have gradually given way to mythical and metaphorical readings of the Bible as Westerners have sought and discovered a new spirituality. This dramatic change in approach to the Revealed Word tradition has prepared Western people to embrace a wholly new spiritual orientation.

This chapter opens with a closer look at Woolston and his *Six Discourses*, the most important to the eighteenth-century attacks on New Testament history. We will then consider the rise of German biblical criticism, focusing attention on David Strauss and his enormously influential *Life of Jesus*. Two important twentieth-century statements on the Bible as symbol or code conclude the chapter. The first is Bishop Spong's *Rescuing the Bible from Fundamentalism*, one of his efforts to present the Bible as spiritual symbolism rather than historical fact. The last author considered is Michael Drosnin, whose bestselling *The Bible Code* created a sensation by claiming that the Bible's true meaning lay hidden in code.

THOMAS WOOLSTON AND THE ENGLISH DEISTS

The English Deists were a varied group of religious radicals who flourished between 1680 and 1750. Bold and effective strategists, they sought to overturn every major doctrine central to Christian orthodoxy. Among their number were the language scholar John Toland, John Locke's close friend Anthony Collins, a candlemaker named Thomas Chubb, Oxford philosopher Matthew Tindal, Cambridge professor Thomas Woolston, schoolmaster Peter Annet and the aristocrat Lord Shaftesbury.

The Deists specialized in harsh biblical criticism, the goal of which was to help their readers "think themselves out of those notions of God and religion" taught by the church.[11] Hadn't Jesus himself taught his followers to "search the Scriptures" in order to find "their true meaning"?[12] For the Deists, reading the Bible literally was a great barrier to thinking clearly about its meaning. Another approach was needed if progress toward rational religion was to be realized. The Bible could no longer be accepted as the Revealed Word. And the Deists were surprisingly successful in changing public opinions about the Bible. One prominent historian believes that "we cannot overestimate the influence exercised by Deistic thought," adding that their influence extends "right down to the present"[13]

Woolston's "Discourses." Born into a working-class family in 1670, Thomas Woolston's intellectual gifts led him to Cambridge where he specialized in the Christian church's early history. Woolston developed doubts about Christianity and as early as 1705 began questioning whether the New Testament was actually a book of history. Read as history, Jesus' miracles "imply Absurdities, Improbabilities, and Incredibilities," and so "were never wrought." Woolston thus redefined the miracles as allegories with spiritual meanings, claiming he did so "to the Honour of our *Messiah,* and the Defence of Christianity."[14] A strange honor and defense this was, however. Jesus is a "magician" and a "sorcerer," and his miracles "nauseating" works of a charlatan and mere "tricks." Woolston even suggested that Jesus should have been prosecuted, even executed, for fooling the public.[15] Clearly, Woolston's persuasive tactic was to create a public scandal through such provocative language. And the approach worked as a new class of readers—often young men new to urban life—flocked to his books.

A good example of Woolston's controversial approach is found in his treatment of Jesus' healing of a blind man. Woolston rejects the eyewitness accounts because they were from Jesus' followers and thus biased. He notes that to prove the "Cure of a Disease, as of Blindness or Lameness" the testimony of "skillful *Surgeons* and *Physicians*" is required. Perhaps Jesus hid medicines from the crowd, which he then secretly used on the man's eyes.[16] Jesus was just an "impostor" passing himself off as a "miraculous Healer of Disease."[17] If we read this famous "miracle" as literally true, Jesus becomes a mere "*Quack-Doctor.*"[18] Thus, Woolston dismisses the idea that this miracle occurred historically as "absurd, senseless and unaccountable."[19]

Woolston's next step is to suggest what he terms a "mystical and allegorical Interpretation of the story of this Eye-Salve" that will save "*Jesus's* divine Power."[20] As an allegory, the man's blindness is symbolic of spiritual blindness, "Ignorance, Error and Infidelity." Jesus himself is a symbol for "right Reason and Truth," which are "his mystical Names." Finally, the healing mud made of dirt and saliva represents "*perfect Doctrine,* which is Truth" that will "open the Eyes of Mens Understanding."[21] In six separate *Discourses* Woolston offered similar reinterpretations of each of Jesus' miracles.

Woolston's impact. Woolston's *Discourses* were a daring and damaging public attack on the New Testament miracles and on the whole concept of biblical history. His books sold thousands of copies in England and the American colonies, and many readers were convinced that Jesus' miracles were not to be taken seriously as historical events. Simon Browne, a Christian opponent of Woolston, commented that he was "surprised to see so many reasonable people moved to doubts by Woolston and others."[22] Bishop Gibson argued in response to Woolston that if Jesus' miracles were mere allegories, then "when the People were amazed to see the Miracles he did, they were amazed at *nothing.*"[23] However, by forcing a respected figure like Gibson to answer his extreme claims, Woolston succeeded in making the debate appear to be contest between legitimate authorities. Gibson thus inadvertently lent credence to Woolston's claims.

Woolston not only shaped the popular religious mind of the eighteenth century, but also subsequent trends in biblical criticism that have permanently altered how Western people read the Bible. Miracles and other events in the life of Jesus, once viewed as historical, could now be read as symbolic, allegorical or mythological. Thus, the crucial Revealed Word premise of a personal God intervening miraculously in human history was undermined.[24] Similarly, religious pluralism also received a boost from Woolston's work: Christianity founded on unique historical events can stake a claim to being uniquely true, but Christianity based on myths or allegories shares this symbolic footing with many other faiths.

LESSING, STRAUSS AND GERMAN CRITICISM

Woolston sought to substitute allegorical for historical readings of the Bible and in this way rescue Christianity for a modern age. This rescued faith consisted of moral teachings supported by mythic tales. The Revealed Word with its unassailable history was refashioned into symbolic stories under a reader's interpretive control. This prepared the ground for developments in German biblical criticism between 1740 and 1850. The mythic interpretation of the Christian Scriptures would, in the decades following Woolston's highly successful court jester act, achieve a high level of sophistication.

Many German critics were influenced by English Deists like Woolston. For instance, Johann David Michaelis rejected literal readings of the Bible after visiting England in 1741-1742 at the height of the Deist controversy.[25] German biblical criticism accelerated after major works of English Deism were widely circulated in Germany.[26] While Michaelis dismantled Old Testament texts, another German pioneer of biblical criticism, Johann August Ernesti (1707-1781), focused on the New Testament documents.[27] The idea of a uniquely true Revealed Word relating divinely invaded human history would soon be rendered permanently antiquarian to the European mind.

Reimarus, Lessing and the "Fragments." Histories of modern biblical criticism usually start not with the wild-eyed English brawler Woolston, but with the staid German scholar Hermann Samuel Reimarus (1694-1768). Reimarus taught Oriental languages for a time at Wittenberg and then traveled in England where he was influenced by Deists.[28] Respected in German intellectual circles, Reimarus's doubts about the Bible were not widely known. But he and several of his closest associates formed a secret circle of skeptics in otherwise conservative Hamburg. According to Colin Brown, Reimarus held "doubts he had long nursed about revealed religion, the historical worth of the Bible and the origins of Christianity."[29] He gradually accumulated thousands of pages of scholarly criticism of Christianity and the Bible.

A small portion of a massive, four thousand-page manuscript was published anonymously after his death. It took the form, literally, of fragments—a series of disconnected, caustic criticisms of the historicity of various Old and New Testament stories. Clearly the work of a talented and indignant opponent of Christianity, the *Wolfenbüttel Fragments* circulated widely in Germany, creating a great public controversy not unlike that created in England by Woolston's *Discourses*. Reimarus maintained an outward adherence to Christianity throughout his life, in large measure to protect his family from public embarrassment. In the *Fragments*, however, we find a skilled and knowledgeable controversialist angrily attacking the divinity of Christ and the historicity of the resurrection.[30]

Reimarus's friend and admirer, Gotthold Ephraim Lessing (1729-1781) had the *Fragments* published shortly after Reimarus's death. In order to protect Reimarus's family, Lessing falsely attributed the *Fragments* to a well-known skeptic and heretic named Schmidt. Lessing, a gifted playwright best remembered for the provocative play *Nathan the Wise*, rejected Christianity, biblical history, miracles and Jesus' divinity. An apparent pantheist, he proclaimed a "religion of humanity" founded on Reason.[31] Like Woolston, of whom he had some knowledge, Lessing held that "Christian mysteries are symbols and allegories" for spiritual truths.[32] The *Fragments* became an important foundation for later German biblical criticism.

David Friedrich Strauss. Most scholars agree that a new era in biblical criticism dawned with the publication of David Strauss's (1808-1874) *Leben Jesu* or *Life of Jesus* in 1835. This long and technical book placed imposing demands on readers. Nevertheless, *Life of Jesus* was so popular and controversial that the British romantic writer George Eliot made an English translation in 1846.[33] The book's impact was as great abroad as it had been in Germany. It "bewildered and enraged the mass of the clergy in mid-Victorian England."[34] It is no exaggeration to say that *Life of Jesus* permanently changed scholarly attitudes toward the Bible.

Life of Jesus is a massive two-volume work running to more than two thousand pages of "remorseless examination of every fact, every incident in the Gospels."[35]

Strauss sought not history but the mythological core of the Jesus stories. In the process he "etherialized the figure of Christ to the point of making his existence as a man irrelevant."[36] Rejecting all historical claims about the Christian Gospels, Strauss searched for the *mythi* or elemental mythical stories that provided the New Testament's basic materials. For his efforts Strauss was dismissed from his position at Tübingen in 1839. *Life of Jesus* created a public sensation in Germany and England in the 1830s and 1840s. What was Strauss's argument?

Myth displaces history. Strauss was testing "a new mode of considering the life of Jesus," one that would replace historical readings of the Bible. Like Woolston, he justified his work as an effort to rescue the Bible from literalists. Historical readings "had ceased to satisfy an advanced state of culture." Western people needed a "new point of view" on the Bible, which Strauss declared to be "the mythical."[37] History was old and had no future. Myth was modern and satisfied the advanced cultural mind. Strauss argued that previous biblical interpretation was based on two false assumptions. The first was "that the gospels contained a history," and the second that "this history was a supernatural one." Strauss insisted that the idea of historical content in the Gospels "must . . . be relinquished." In fact, biblical studies must begin by actively doubting that "the ground upon which we stand in the gospels is historical."[38]

The time was right for a myth, Strauss maintained, because the West had experienced "internal liberation of the feelings and intellect from certain religious and dogmatical presuppositions" that had blinded philosophers and historians. The Revealed Word was fading into the background of Western consciousness. To critics who found his rejection of history and orthodoxy "unchristian," Strauss replied that accepting such outmoded ideas was "unscientific."[39] Rejecting supernatural explanations out of hand, Strauss strategically affected a concern for the biblical tradition. "The supernatural birth of Christ, his miracles, his resurrection and ascension," he wrote, "remain eternal truths, whatever doubts may be cast on their reality as historical facts."[40] But the enduring significance of the biblical texts is ethical rather than historical. This formula—spiritual truth in the absence of historical truth— was to become an important component in New Religious Synthesis thought.

In a fashion reminiscent of Woolston, Strauss argued that to take some Gospel stories as historical was to believe things unworthy of God. He also maintained that numerous biblical accounts were never intended to be read as history. However, "the most convincing argument" for the "mythical view" is that it instantly eliminates "the innumerable, and never otherwise to be harmonized, discrepancies and chronological contradictions in the gospel histories."[41] Like Woolston's allegorical approach, "the mythical mode of interpretation" relinquishes "the historical reality of the sacred narratives" in an effort to "preserve to them an absolute inherent truth."

Strauss was committed to the idea that the biblical writers used "historical semblance merely as the shell of an *idea*—a religious conception." The "inspiration" for these religious ideas is a "higher intelligence," but not God himself. Strauss contended that "the immediate divine agency" for religious notions like those found in the New Testament was "the spirit of a people or a community." The powerful human spiritual impulse to generate myths is, for Strauss, a "*natural* process."[42]

Much of Strauss's modus operandi is virtually indistinguishable from that of Woolston, though he presents himself as a scholar rather than as a mocking provocateur. Strauss sets before the reader an event in Jesus' life, for example, the transfiguration. He considers various interpretations advanced by scholars ancient and contemporary. Some are dismissed, others are judged plausible, the latter always pointing out impossible obstacles to a literal or historical reading. Strauss the scholar examines Greek terms used to describe an event, considering various translations and nuances. For example, the word *horama*, "vision," used by Matthew to describe the transfiguration suggests a physical event rather than a dream. Reports of the event in three of the four Gospels are compared. Apocryphal Gospels are ransacked for clues about episodes that may have given rise to the transfiguration myth. The alleged occurrence is set in its cultural and historical contexts. Thus, the two men to whom Jesus speaks—allegedly Moses and Isaiah—may be secret followers of his from the Essenes or some similar group. After his critical work is complete, Strauss's final interpretation invariably returns to the myth hypothesis. Thus, just as Woolston's caustic ridicule "cleared the way for allegory," so Strauss's more serious and sustained criticism serves a mythological interpretive scheme.

Strauss recognized, of course, that this sort of mythical criticism demolished the Revealed Word's claim to being historically grounded and uniquely true. But historical literalism was a product of ignorance to begin with, and best dispensed with. The typical Christian "knows no reason why the things recorded in the sacred books should not literally have taken place; no doubt occurs to him, no reflection disturbs him."[43] Christians find "many fictions" in other faiths, while insisting that "the accounts of God's actions, of Christ and other Godlike men contained in the Bible are, on the contrary, true." They assert, "that which distinguished Christianity from the heathen religion is this, they are mythical, it is historical."[44] These conclusions rest solely on the "limitation of the individual to that form of belief in which he has been educated." Such limitation "renders the mind incapable of embracing any but the affirmative view in relation to his own creed, any but the negative in relation to every other."[45] However, rational progress in religion requires Christian openness to the common foundation of all faiths—myth.

Myth and the evolution of religion. "However surprising," writes Strauss, "the Hebrew and Christian religions, like all others, have their mythi," or elemental mythical stories. From this platform Strauss launches an explanation of the origins and development of all human religions. "The inherent nature of religion," that which is "common to all religions," is their origin in myth, the source and essence of religion. Religion is, for Strauss, "the perception of truth" that is subsequently "invested with imagery." Religious communities may underestimate or overestimate the significance of their own sacred narratives.[46] Some see them as mere stories grounded in no particular spiritual insight. Others view their myths as uniquely true and historically valid. Both mistakes place the narrative outside "the proper religious sphere." The only proper understanding of religious narrative is as myth—an imaginative story bearing a transcendent truth.

Strauss developed a theory of the progressive evolution of religions around the globe. Primitives such as the Eskimos, for instance, cannot really be said to have a religion because they do not actually have any myths, only emotions. "They know nothing of gods, of superior spirits and powers," and so their "whole piety" revolves around "sentiment excited by the hurricane, the eclipse, or the magician." However, as religious sense progresses, religious ideas become more "objective." Thus, in more advanced religious systems people worship the sun, the moon, or an animal. Eventually, "a new world of mere imagination" emerges, a realm of "divine existences" whose lives and relationships are "represented only after human analogy, and therefore as temporal and historical."[47] That is, the gods take on lives of their own and are said to inhabit history. Still, all is myth. The most advanced stage of religious evolution is achieved when religious consciousness loses its specific claims to doctrines and historicity, and the reality of myth is embraced for its own sake. Because we share both common experiences and a common imagination, human myths emerge as strikingly similar stories. Thus, "mythical images" arise out of "sentiments common to all mankind." Strauss concludes that "this notion of a certain necessity and unconsciousness in the formation of the ancient mythi" is a point "on which we insist."[48]

David Strauss, then, maintained that humans create myths out of necessity, and these myths are invested with a time dimension, that is, a history. So, the wise student of religion must separate mythical history from the actual human history. However, the Revealed Word consistently fails to make this distinction, fails to recognize the crucial role of myth in religion, and thus treats biblical stories as history rather than as myth. In David Strauss the Revealed Word encounters something new—an explanation of religion that destroys religious history while celebrating the mythmaking capacity of the human mind.

The ultimate mythical insight: a new human religion. In the closing pages of *Life of Jesus*, Strauss muses on the possibility of a new view of Christ that will save Christianity for modern, scientific people. This Christology views the spirit of God and the spirit of humanity as "not essentially distinct." God produced the human mind "merely as a limited manifestation of himself." When human reason rises to a high level of sophistication, when it is "mature enough," it will realize "the truth that God is man, and man of a divine race." At this point there must appear "a human individual who is recognized as the visible God."[49] This is Christ, who lives out in his earthly life the religious evolution of the human race.

But why is this manifestation of the divine limited to one person if we all share a divine nature? Strauss's final position is that "humanity is the union of the two natures—God become man, the infinite manifesting itself in the finite."[50] This fundamental religious insight, writes Strauss, "is the key to the whole Christology." This New Christ—the divine human race—also performs miracles. We should not take more interest in "the cure of some sick people in Galilee" than we do in "the miracles of intellectual and moral life belonging to the history of the world" such as the "almost incredible dominion of man over nature."[51]

Scientific progress, then, reveals the human race to be a race of divine miracle workers demonstrating with ever greater clarity its control over the intellectual and physical realms. This great insight is the ultimate yield of Strauss's biblical criticism. In a final note, Strauss calls for clergy to be "critical theologians" who move beyond the tradition, whereby "the evangelical narratives are received as history," to the recognition that they are "mere mythi."[52] So crucial is this change of orientation that it may require ministers to appear to treat the Scriptures as history while in fact deriving from them their essential mythical sense. When the Christian church recognizes its participation in the universal mythic religious consciousness of the human race, it will finally leave behind its outdated notion of

Jesus as a single divine individual and realize the essential divinity of every human. In this way David Strauss's "scientific" biblical criticism opened the way for a new, mythically based religion of divine humanity. This new faith is now a foundational component of the Other Spirituality.

JOHN SHELBY SPONG RESCUES THE BIBLE

John Shelby Spong was born in Charlotte, North Carolina, in 1931 and grew up under the influence of Southern fundamentalism. Spong was educated at the University of North Carolina, Chapel Hill, and at Duke University. A prolific author, Spong has published more than a dozen books. In 1978, he became the Episcopal Bishop of Newark, New Jersey. During his career, Spong has been known for his strong stands against traditional doctrines of the church and for his staunch advocacy for civil rights.

As noted in the introduction, Bishop John Shelby Spong sometimes writes like a modern incarnation of the radical Deist Thomas Woolston. In literal and historical readings of the Bible Spong found a God he could not worship. "The picture of God that began to emerge from the Bible for me was neither a pleasant one nor one to which I was drawn in worship. It did not get better."[53] He provides his readers dozens of examples of God's acts by which he is "repelled" and comments that "the list of objectionable passages could be expanded almost endlessly."[54] It is not surprising, then, that in a number of popular books Spong seems determined to disabuse the public of whatever confidence it had in the historicity of the Christian Scriptures.

In *Rescuing the Bible from Fundamentalism* and *Liberating the Gospels*, Spong introduces many readers to the techniques of earlier biblical critics such as Woolston and Strauss. For example, Spong engages in ironic character assessment similar to that with which Deists provoked the British public in the eighteenth century. "Moses was a murderer," he writes, "but this was not a character flaw because his victim was an Egyptian (Exod. 2:11ff.)." Again, "Joseph was an arrogant and spoiled favorite son upon whom his father heaped lavish gifts and special favor (Genesis 37)." Finally, "adultery was said to be evil, but both Abraham and Isaac tried to pass their wives off as their sisters, even though this meant having them sexually used by Abimelech, King of Gerar (Gen. 20:1-18; 26:6-11)."[55] Such stories offend "the modern consciousness" and his own conscience.

Blaming the Jesus of history. Bishop Spong rejects biblical literalism as untenable in the modern world. "A literal Bible," he writes, "presents me with far more problems than assets." One problem is that such a Bible "offers me a God I cannot respect, much less worship; a deity whose needs and prejudices are at least as large as my own."[56] And Spong finds the historical character of Jesus of Nazareth no more appealing as presented in the Bible. One problem is that the Jesus of the Bible is often ignorant. "Jesus is presented in the Bible as believing that epilepsy is caused by demon possession (Mark 9:14-29). That is hardly a viewpoint that any of us would accept today." Moreover, Jesus reveals certain off-putting character traits. "There are passages in the Gospels that portray Jesus of Nazareth as narrow-minded, vindictive, and even hypocritical.... He called gentiles 'dogs' (Matt. 15:26).... He disowned his own family (Matt. 12:46-50)."[57]

Spong rejects the notion of biblical history when he writes, "the biblical writers had no sense at all of the sweep of historic times." But he goes a step further, calling in question the very notion of objective history. When we get down to cases, "we need to remind ourselves that even in this modern world with its technological genius, there is still no such thing as 'objective' history.'"[58] Moreover, if modern people have no objective view of history, then certainly the tribal Hebrews could not have held such a view. They inhabited the "ancient world with its narrow focus, its limited embrace of reality, its pre-scientific mind-set of miracle and magic, and its nationalistic tribal understanding of deity itself."[59] Spong rehearses a variety of scientific evidences, setting these beside the naïve and corrupted history of Scripture to convince his readers that the Bible is not a historical book. He leads his readers through a variety of critical discoveries such as the numerous sources of the Old Testament texts, problems of dating and manuscript transmission, and internal contradictions in Bible accounts.

Spong also engages in damaging psychological assessment of biblical writers. For example, "Paul's writings reveal the combination of intense levels of self-negativity covered by intensely cultivated images of superiority," he notes. "At first these forces fed Paul's devotion to Judaism at the same time that they created his defensiveness." Paul's marginal self-concept "became operative in his later devotion to and understanding of the gospel." This deeply conflicted apostle was also benighted by his cultural limitations. "Paul was not a universal man. He was indeed a man of his times. He reflected the common assumptions of his day, assumptions that time has eroded badly."[60] Paul was "uncritically part of the patriarchal system that so informed the Hebrew Scriptures." But "modern standards" reveal many of Paul's attitudes to be "not only inadequate but wrong."[61]

Spong's purposes, like his methods, seem akin to those of Woolston and Strauss. He strips Christianity of its historicity through moral critique, historical analysis, character assessment and comparison with the modern mindset. Then he revives the lifeless body of traditional Christianity through the "wondrous new meanings to be drawn" from a nonhistorical New Testament. In the process, a reinvented Christianity emerges, complete with a new understanding of Jesus. No longer a unique historical character incarnating God, Jesus is now one among many mythical figures expressing in narrative form the human desire for transcendence.

The end justifies the means for Spong, though, and courage is called for. "For those who are willing to take the journey, the stakes are high. But not to take the journey means, in my opinion, certain death to all that we have believed. So the task moves on."[62] Whether one follows Spong on his journey, or chooses to demur, the death of *historical* Christianity ensues. This, however, is a necessary step toward redefining Christianity for the modern mind.

Refitting Christianity for modernity. Spong commends to his readers a new Christianity refitted for a modern world, the Holy Grail of Woolston and Strauss as well. Rather than accepting surface historical meanings in the Bible, "we must seek the truth that lies beneath the mythology of the distant past so that we might experience that truth."[63] That truth is that God is not personal and wholly other, as the Revealed Word suggests. Rather, "God is the *Ground of Being*," the essence of existence, an idea central to New Religious Synthesis. Spong asks, "How did Jesus reflect this ground of being?" As "the Christpower we meet in Jesus," an idea quite distinct from Jesus *being* the historical Christ.[64]

Spong urges his readers to express "being" in a fashion similar to Jesus by embracing their own existence. John Spong sets history aside in order that the real spiritual truth "beneath and behind" it may emerge. This truth supports a new spirituality built on the affirmation of the self. The loss of an objective ground for religious experience renders subjective experience ultimate. "The call of Christ is an eternal call to the affirmation of that which is," and that which is, is us. "To have the courage to be oneself, to claim the ability to define oneself, to live one's life in freedom and with power is the essence of the human experience." This is what it means to express being as Jesus did. Real faith for a modern world means elevating humanity. Or, as Spong puts it, "true Christianity ultimately issues in a deeper humanism." This "deeper humanism" in turn issues in "new dimensions of consciousness and transcendence," a conclusion strikingly similar to that advanced by Strauss at the end of *Life of Jesus*. Such is the spiritual fruit of John Spong's biblical criticism.[65]

MICHAEL DROSNIN'S *THE BIBLE CODE*

The last section of this chapter is an excursion into an unusual treatment of the Bible that may not seem to be extending the tradition of Woolston, Strauss and Spong. However, this unexpected bestseller from the late 1990s treats the Bible as bearing a message "beneath and behind" its historical surfaces, something, moreover, more important than those surfaces.

In the emerging Western spiritual view—the *Other* Spirituality—religious truth is not found in readily accessible historical texts. Rather, the truths of sacred narratives are apprehended by those prepared to ferret out their underlying allegories and myths. Of course, it takes special skill to read past the historical surfaces to deeper mythical meanings. One highly successful author has recently recommended another interpretive skill important to discovering hidden spiritual meanings in the biblical record—deciphering the complex numerical code embedded within it.

Michael Drosnin is a journalist who has worked for *The Washington Post* and *The Wall Street Journal*. On a visit to Israel in 1992 to meet with members of the intelligence community he encountered a mathematician by the name of Eliyahu Rips. Rips introduced Drosnin to the ancient idea that the Hebrew letters of the Old Testament contain a code that predicts a number of future events and describes events in the distant past. Drosnin was convinced of the hypothesis and went on to write his incredibly popular book, *The Bible Code*, a bestseller not only in the United States, but also in Germany, France, Australia, Taiwan, Korea, South Africa, Portugal, Japan and England. Drosnin, who professes no particular religious affiliation, claims in the book to lay bare the hidden messages of the Old Testament.[66] "The Bible code," he writes, "was discovered in the original Hebrew version of the Old Testament, the Bible as it was first written. That book, now translated into every language, is the foundation of all Western religion."[67] In *The Bible Code*, however, the historical sense of the biblical message is inconsequential compared to the remarkable warnings and predictions that lie hidden in various combinations of the Hebrew letters.

Reviving the spirit of kabbalah. Though Drosnin does not mention the kabbalah anywhere in *The Bible Code*, he replicates some of the approaches of the ancient rabbis who found hidden in the Torah a set of secret messages and spiritual truths. The secret of reading the Bible code, according to Drosnin, first came to light a mere fifty years ago. "Rips told me that the first hint of the encoding had been found more than 50 years ago by a rabbi in Prague, Czechoslovakia. The rabbi, H. M. D. Weissmandel, noticed that if he skipped fifty letters, and then another fifty, and then another, the word 'Torah' was spelled out at the beginning of the book of Genesis." Not only this, but "the same skip sequence again spelled out the word 'Torah' in the book of Exodus. And in the book of Numbers. And in the book of Deuteronomy."[68] Perhaps the rabbi from Prague was familiar with kabbalah, and was seeking just such a hidden message.

Rips pointed out to Drosnin early in their association that seeking a hidden code in the Bible has been a preoccupation of some impressive thinkers of the past. "At first I tried just counting letters like Weissmandel," says Rips. "You know, Isaac Newton also tried to find the code in the Bible, and he considered it more important in some ways than his Theory of the Universe." Drosnin adds, "The first modern scientist, the man who figured out the mechanics of our solar system and discovered the force of gravity, Sir Isaac Newton, was certain that there was a hidden code in the Bible that would reveal the future."[69] As noted in chapter two, Newton is sometimes identified as the last of the magical scientists, thinkers whose understanding of science was rooted in a worldview that elevated esoteric knowledge.

Apocalypse now. According to Drosnin, "details of today's world are encoded in a text that has been set in stone for hundreds of years, and that has existed for thousands of years."[70] Drosnin argues that what he calls the "plain text"—the ordinary, historically grounded meaning of the Bible—actually points to the deeper meaning hidden in code. For example, Drosnin writes that "crossing the words 'Bible code'" that is, literally forming a cross with this encoded phrase in the Hebrew text, "is a hidden text that states it was 'sealed before God.'" Drosnin takes this to mean that "the Bible code is the 'sealed book,' the secret revelation found in the plain text of the Bible."[71]

Drosnin's writing is drenched in contemporary apocalyptic warnings, a fact that renders his "decoding" work suspect while at the same time dramatically enhancing interest in his book. For instance, he writes near the end of the book that the Bible code predicts an imminent nuclear holocaust in the Middle East. "I felt compelled to warn both Peres and Netanyahu that the code seemed to predict an atomic attack," he breathlessly announces, "as I had warned Rabin that the code predicted his assassination." Continuing in this vein, Drosnin writes, "I never imagined that

I would ultimately find myself searching for the details of the real Apocalypse. I never imagined that the 'End of Days' would be encoded in the Bible with the current year. I never imagined that the long-known biblical prophecies of Armageddon might in some level be real."[72]

Asteroids and dinosaurs: biblical history versus coded history. Certain logical and factual problems attend Drosnin's argument about the Bible code. "The Bible code is ecumenical," he writes, "the information is for everyone." Then why were the Hebrews singled out for receiving and transmitting the code? Drosnin's reasoning on this point begs rather than answers questions. "The code only exists in Hebrew, because that is the original language of the Bible."[73] Moreover, many "predictions" Drosnin attributes to the Bible code appear to be inaccurate. The assassination of Yitzhak Rabin was, allegedly, foretold by the code. But so was a nuclear holocaust to follow—an event that did not occur.

But logic and factual accuracy are not the point of *The Bible Code*. The issue here, as in Woolston, Strauss and Spong, is the control of history. That is, Drosnin's argument that the *real* history of the Bible is a hidden history allows him to determine which historical events will occupy the foreground, and which the background. Consider, for example, a particularly odd message contained in the code—the destruction of earth's dinosaur population by a comet. Drosnin writes that "'asteroid' and 'dinosaur' are encoded together in the Bible." He explains this unexpected and surprisingly contemporary juxtaposition of terms as follows: "The name of the dragon the Bible says God fought—'Rahab'—appears in the Bible code exactly where 'asteroid' hits the 'dinosaur.'" Drosnin concludes that this "suggests that the extinction of the dinosaurs was the real slaying of the dragon, the cosmic event recalled by Isaiah: 'Was it not you who cut Rahab in pieces, and pierced through the dragon?'" Thus, God slew the dinosaurs—the dragon Rahab—for a reason.

A direct conflict between the literal biblical history and Drosnin's coded history now ensues. The opening chapters of Genesis suggest that human beings were the special creation of a personal God. However, Drosnin's coded message about an asteroid destroying earth's dinosaurs suggests a different account of human origins. "Scientists now agree that mankind would never have evolved unless the dinosaurs had been wiped out by the asteroid."[74] Thus, Drosnin's coded history teaches the evolution of the human race, albeit with cosmic assistance, while biblical history teaches special creation. Coded history is placed in the attended-to foreground, literal history the ignored background. Similarly, Woolston placed allegorical meaning in the foreground and literal history in the background, while Strauss and Spong worked the same inversion with mythical and literal readings. In all four cases, the originator of the interpretive approach subjectively determines the meaning of the text, that is, decides what it "actually" says. Likewise, in all four cases the biblical text is discovered not to contain what is ordinarily understood as history.

In *The Bible Code* Michael Drosnin acts the part of a latter-day seer reading the biblical text with the aid of computer enhanced magical spectacles. And, like antihistorical critics before him, Drosnin does not find the actual history of the nation of Israel to be the principal message of those sacred pages. Rather, he finds a time-sensitive code filled with strange glimpses of the past and stunning warnings about the future. In fact, *The Bible Code* reads like a media-influenced encapsulation of stories of recent public interest, *National Geographic*-meets-*Newsweek*, with Drosnin as editor-in-chief. Regardless of how we understand his discovery, it is clear that traditional biblical history takes a back seat to the coded messages of the Hebrew text. Thus, *The Bible Code* represents a late twentieth-century demotion of biblical history, albeit a particularly novel one.

CONCLUSION

Throughout the modern period, the Bible as a book of history has been under a sustained, public and largely successful assault. From the early eighteenth-century Deists down to the most recent biblical critics and popular speculators, the idea that the Bible reports historical events has been questioned and even ridiculed. Nevertheless, the Revealed Word's commitment to history remains central to its conception of religion. For example, biblical scholar John Stott writes that traditional Christianity "does not rest only on a historical person, Jesus of Nazareth, but on certain historical events which involved him, especially his birth, death, and resurrection."[75]

Opponents have long recognized both Christianity's need of history and its reliance on the Bible to substantiate its claim to being historical. Thus, to attack the Bible's historicity was to attack Christianity generally. Some modern biblical criticism grows out of this specific persuasive goal. The particular school of biblical criticism emphasizing allegorical or mythological interpretations of the Bible has been our focus because this school's principal claim—that spirituality does not need history—has become an important component in the New Religious Synthesis. Connections between antihistorical readings of the Bible and the rise of a new way in religion will be developed throughout this book.

Rescuing Christianity from historical literalists has been an important justification of much modern biblical criticism. Woolston argued that he was saving Christianity from irrationality and superstition by demolishing historical readings of Jesus' miracles and rendering the accounts allegorical. On a similar line of argument, Strauss set about to prove that the New Testament incorporated myths common to many faiths, a fact obscured, he alleged, by parochial claims that the Gospel accounts were historical. The source of true religion was not a personal God's activities in history, but rather our own collective human experience. Bishop John Spong finds biblical history repulsive in many of its particulars and argues that Christianity is better off without history. Dispensing with obsolete historical claims also removes the obstacle of a personal and locally active God and opens the way to universal religious insights and experiences. Michael Drosnin finds literal history a mere carrier of coded messages, a surface that must be stripped away to reveal something more valuable beneath. That more valuable truth is an odd combination of metaphysical speculation, political prediction and recent news.

What the antihistorical critics have in common is their rejection of the Revealed Word's determined divine interventionism—the view that a personal God has been continuously and actively involved in human history. Instead, the Revealed Word's central narratives have been gradually transformed into allegories for the religion of reason, a mythic system akin to others found throughout the world, metaphors for a "new humanism," and conduits for coded messages from beyond. Correspondingly, its central figure, Jesus, is now changed from Son of God into a religious philosopher, a mythic hero, a mystic, a character in a morality play or a symbol for something more meaningful.

De-historicizing of the Bible has been strategically important to creating the New Religious Synthesis for a variety of reasons that will become more evident in subsequent chapters. Among these reasons is establishing the link between myth and secret spiritual knowledge or *gnosis*. At this point it may be sufficient to point out that severing history from spirituality renders biblical interpretation almost infinitely plastic. Subjective readings reign as history fades into the background. Moreover, the Revealed Word notion of history as the scene of God's sovereign acts is neutralized, and history itself becomes a suspect category. Events critical to the Revealed Word tradition such as Jesus' crucifixion and resurrection must also be reinterpreted, not as moments in redemptive history, but as symbolic of stages in the spiritual life of humanity or the individual.

The rise of antihistorical criticism of the Bible is just one indication that we are now, and have been for some time, in the presence of a dominant new religious view that sees no particular need for history, that in fact sees history as a problem. In the chapters that follow I will examine how this turn away from the historical path in religion is a vital component in a new spiritual view that is everywhere present in Western religious thought.

4

THE ASCENT OF REASON

Birth of a Deity

The system of modern nihilism starts with a powerful substitute for transcendence, which is belief in Reason.

IOAN COULIANO, The Tree of Gnosis

Reason . . . is God incarnate.

PETER ANNET, Lectures

The fall of one god is often the precondition for the rise of another. Historian Franklin Baumer reported the strange events that took place in the famous Cathedral of Notre Dame in Paris on the morning of November 10, 1793. The cathedral was that day the site of the first, and the last, Festival of Liberty and Reason. As citizens and dignitaries of Paris entered the great church "they saw, some doubtless with astonishment, the insignias of Christianity covered up and their place taken by the symbols of a strange new religion." Baumer continues:

> Rising up in the nave was an improvised mountain, at the top of which perched a small Greek temple dedicated "To Philosophy" and adorned on both sides by the busts of philosophers, probably Voltaire, Rousseau, Franklin, and Montesquieu. Halfway down the side of the mountain a torch of Truth burned before an altar to Reason. Then ensued a bizarre ceremony.[1]

The "bizarre ceremony" involved an actress emerging onto the stage dressed in red, white and blue robes. The assembled crowd was directed to pay homage to this personification of Liberty. A little later Notre Dame was designated "the Temple of Reason."

The dramatic, almost unbelievable events at Notre Dame beg for explanation. Historian Baumer's effort focuses on a writer considered in this chapter, one of the most famous and successful opponents of the Revealed Word tradition. The strange worship service held at the Temple of Reason in 1793 "was a symbol, first of all, of Voltairean skepticism which scored Christianity as an 'infamous thing' to be crushed . . . and replaced by a religion imbued with 'reason,' 'virtue,' and 'liberty.'"[2] Indeed, Voltaire's goal in a lifetime of activist writing was to eliminate Christian belief in Western Europe. In its place he offered the new god Reason. Reflecting on the events in Notre Dame, Carl Jung wrote, "The enthronement of the Goddess of Reason in Notre Dame seems to have been a symbolic gesture of great significance to the Western world—rather like the hewing down of Wotan's oak by the Christian missionaries. For then, as at the Revolution, no avenging bolt from heaven struck the blasphemer down."[3]

The following year, 1794, a brilliant French mathematician, the Marquis de Condorcet (1743-1794) published his *Sketch of the Progress of the Human Mind*. Condorcet argued that humanity would achieve perfection through gradual, inevitable progress guided by reason. Condorcet's "new doctrine" involved a profound belief in "the indefinite perfectibility of the human race."[4] Reason and its instrument, science, would eliminate the need for religion. Though he authored his optimistic *Sketch* while a warrant for his arrest was current and he was under sentence of death from the French Revolution, Condorcet nevertheless maintained that his own century was the great turning point in human history. According to Baumer, Condorcet believed that "in the foreseeable future, thanks to the power of reason and the discovery of new knowledge, mankind would rise to unprecedented heights, to perfectibility, in fact." Condorcet wrote, "No bounds have been fixed to the improvement of the human race." In addition, he contended that "the perfectibility of man is absolutely indefinite," and that "we are approaching one of the grand revolutions of the human race."[5]

Condorcet dubbed his new age of human perfection "the tenth epoch," mankind having already passed through nine identifiable stages of progress. The tenth epoch would be a time of world peace and scientific utopia. Food supplies would increase, wars would cease, injustice would end, disease would be vanquished, and leisure would replace labor. Condorcet referred to this perfected state of the human race as "heaven which . . . reason has created."[6] He maintained a profound aversion to the Revealed Word, the enemy of Reason—human rationality elevated to the status of a divinity. Condorcet was eventually captured by agents of the French Revolution and died in prison. Nevertheless, his hope of a human race improved by Reason never died.

This chapter explores several popular arguments for Reason as a limitless power, a virtually divine capacity, in humans. The substitution of human rationality, self-awareness, imagination or consciousness for the Revealed Word's "wholly other" deity is a critical component of the New Religious Synthesis. Reason, thus broadly defined, has been transformed into a full-fledged deity for a new spiritual age. The writers considered include the English Deist Peter Annet, for whom Reason was "God incarnate." The famous French advocate and playwright Voltaire is also considered. Voltaire advanced Reason as the antidote to the rational poison of Revealed Word theology. Though nineteenth-century Romantic writers are alleged to have rejected Enlightenment infatuation with reason, their exaltation of imagination and intellect is often difficult to distinguish in principle. We will be exploring the early Romantic writer Thomas De Quincey's arguments for what he termed Majestic Intellect.

Tracing the ascent of Reason into the twentieth century brings us to the exotic claims of the New Thought movement that held such powerful sway over the popular religious mind at the turn of the century. Mind or Consciousness—new names for the interior divinity earlier called Reason—offered healing and escape from all of our present limitations. The final section of this chapter examines novelist Ayn Rand's powerful argument that Reason prepares an elite to escape the ancient fetters of faith and to assume their rightful place as the rulers of the human race. Rand provides a fitting terminus for our pilgrimage toward the god of a new spirituality.

PETER ANNET

Englishman Peter Annet (1693-1769) trained for the ministry, but encounters with religious bigotry turned him against Christianity. Between 1738 and 1747 Annet, who made his living as a schoolteacher, created controversy in England by attacking Christianity in several popular speeches, pamphlets and books. His most controversial and successful pamphlet, *The Resurrection of Jesus Considered by a Moral Philosopher* (1744), relentlessly questioned the evidence for the central Christian miracle. In 1761 Annet began publishing a periodical called *The Free Enquirer*, a weekly collection of essays on topics of general interest with special attention to religious subjects. Annet's main purpose in this early experiment in popular journalism was to raise doubts in the public mind about the Bible.

According to Annet and other Deists, the universe follows "the rule of Reason," an omnipresent law that even a divine being cannot violate. Having thus tied his hands and ushered him out of the cosmos, Reason took the place of the Revealed Word's God. "Reason," proclaimed Annet, is "the divinity operating within us" and our "inward illumination."[7] Adding a daring flourish to his radical claim, Annet taunted Christians by calling Reason "the only begotten son of God, the God incarnate, or God humanized."[8] Reason, not God, is "that authority . . . above all other authorities." In a new apocalypse "the dead shall rise" when they hear "the trumpet of reason." A spiritually reborn humanity will embrace Reason as "the basis of true religion."[9] But this new god—like Yahweh of old—is a jealous deity. In the new era, any "religion rebellious against Reason shall be compelled to . . . yield to the divine authority of Reason."[10] Legal sanctions and perhaps force will ensure the universal worship of Reason. In Annet's vision of the religious future, Reason replaces each member of the Trinity. Like the Father, it is "that authority . . . above all other authorities." Like the Son, "Reason is God incarnate." And like the Holy Spirit, Reason is "the divinity operating within us."

The upward fall. For Deists like Annet, the original religion of the human race was the pure and worshipful recognition of Reason's sovereignty in the universe. The first three chapters of Genesis present a rather different account of humanity's early spirituality. These passages recount the special creation of human beings by a personal God, and their subsequent tragic Fall. Relational intimacy with God was lost, and humanity was cast into spiritual darkness and rational confusion. Reason, like other capacities, fell along with the human race.

Annet, however, strategically reinterpreted the Genesis account in *The Free Inquirer* to support his spiritualized understanding of Reason. If human beings are the fallen creatures the Revealed Word makes them out to be, he asks, how is it that they find themselves in possession of the powerful faculty we call Reason? Annet advances a fascinating answer to this question in *The Free Inquirer* of November 3, 1761, a response that turns the traditional reading of Genesis on its head. The alleged Fall of Adam and Eve was not a ruinous disaster but rather a great leap forward for humanity. By asserting their independence from Yahweh, Adam and Eve gained Reason and thus became Godlike. Far from injuring human rational capacities, the Fall actually inaugurated Reason—the divine capacity for self-determination. The much-maligned serpent of Genesis was right all along—by ignoring the commands of the restrictive divinity Yahweh, Adam and Eve gained a divine quality of their own. Moses, the supposed author of Genesis, was wrong to suggest in Genesis that God would punish people for thinking on their own.[11]

The heroes of Annet's Genesis, then, are the serpent, who created a truly human race by giving us Reason, and Adam and Eve, the first rationally autonomous human beings who gained their freedom by a bold act of courage. Yahweh—if he exists at all—is a weak and malevolent deity, and Moses a purveyor of bad theology. Annet, the rationally liberated biblical interpreter, reads the story's true meaning beneath the historical surface of the text. He thus inverts the Revealed Word creation account in his effort to advance a new spiritual view that captivated audiences by the sheer exotic intrigue of its audacious inventiveness. Reason, not God, saves us and guarantees our "eternal salvation."[12] A sound moral principle will always "approve itself, to the true, genuine reason of man."[13] Thus, the worshiper of Reason follows a law higher than the constricting, arbitrary moral code of the Revealed Word. Like Adam and Eve who decided to eat the fruit of the tree of the knowledge of good and evil, only Reason's worshipers are free moral agents.

Peter Annet sought to convince his readers that Reason was a gift acquired when humans first asserted their rational independence from the Revealed Word's God. This new quality rendered human beings themselves virtually divine. Writers like Annet popularized the cult of Reason in the eighteenth century by taking the case for Reason directly to the public. These religious advocates celebrated autonomous individualism as a spiritual value, and their message was highly persuasive. In the following section we will observe how Europe's greatest skeptical writer fleshed out the practical moral implications of a religion of Reason in opposition to the irrational dictates of the Revealed Word.

VOLTAIRE AND LIBERATED REASON

Thomas Babington Macaulay has said of Voltaire (1694-1778), the most influential and prolific of all Enlightenment writers, that "he could not build, he could only tear down."[14] But there can be no question that Voltaire's irreverent wit contributed substantially to shaping the popular religious mind in the modern West. Voltaire's utter rejection of authority, his doubtfulness about all objects of reverence, his dismissal of anything claiming to stand above Reason are all marks of the serious as well as the casual intellectual of today. Among the several mottoes that sum up his life and work, one is cited perhaps more often than any other by Voltaire's biographers: *"Ecraser l'infame,"* that is, crush the infamous thing. The "infamous thing" was the superstition and hierarchy of the Catholic Church, but also, by extension, the beliefs and structures of Christianity. For all of the justice implicit in his opposition to ecclesiastical tyranny, it cannot be doubted as well that Voltaire was an ardent foe of not just church authority but Christianity itself. He commented at one time that he was tired of hearing that it took only twelve men to establish Christianity. "I'd like to prove that only one man is called for to undermine its foundations."[15] Among the passions motivating Voltaire to write, then, was his abhorrence of the Revealed Word tradition, and particularly of its tendency to limit Reason.

An enormously prolific writer, Voltaire published more than ten million words and left over twenty thousand letters. His greatest talent was as a playwright, and his works dominated French theater for more than half a century. His epic poem *Henriade,* which he considered his greatest achievement, celebrated the life of France's last liberal king, Henry IV. But Voltaire was also an able historian as evidenced by his *Age of Louis XIV.* His most lasting fame, however, derives from one short novel, *Candide.*

Voltaire's life. François-Marie Arouet, who adopted the pen name de Voltaire, was born in Paris to a prosperous family on November 21, 1694. The son of a successful legal secretary, Voltaire was sent at the age of ten to the college of Louis-le-Grand where he received an excellent classical education under the Jesuits. Initially committed to the study of law, he eventually abandoned that ambition to become a writer. As a young man he was influenced by French Deism of the type revealed in Montesquieu's *Persian Letters,* and in his twenties by the English Deism of Collins, Woolston and others. Very early in his writing career Voltaire revealed a genius for satire, often offending prominent citizens of Paris. He became a hero to many for his stand against religious fanaticism, and he vowed to "seek revenge" for acts of religious persecution and intolerance.[16]

So sharp and well aimed were his shafts that he was banished from Paris on more than one occasion. During these banishments he lived for a time in Holland, and for most of a year in the Bastille. Though often considered a perpetually smiling wit who staved off the pain of his penetrating perceptions by mocking the injustices of life, Voltaire suffered throughout his life from depression, anxiety and hypochondria. Often ill, he nevertheless lived to the age of eighty-four.

Called the most characteristic writer of the Enlightenment, Voltaire was also a great popularizer of Enlightenment ideas such as the rejection of the Bible, contempt for authority and the elevation of Reason. Voltaire's confidence in Reason was encouraged by the epoch-making work of Isaac Newton, a thinker for whom Voltaire maintained unbounded admiration. Voltaire sought not only to understand Newton's *Principia* but to provide the public an accessible interpretation of it. He found in this new science a wonder and explanatory power sufficient to ground a substitute for traditional religion.

Voltaire was exiled to England in the 1720s. During this time he read the English Deists and engaged England's leading thinkers. Exposure to Deism profoundly shaped Voltaire's religious ideas. His approach to biblical criticism—dismissing miracles as fabrications, searching for contradictions, questioning the character of biblical figures—are reminiscent of Deists like Woolston. In spite of the Christian faith of his father and brother, as well as of the teachers he so admired at Louis-le-Grand, Voltaire rejected all of Christian theology.

Voltaire's influence on popular religious thought in the Western world has been great. One scholar writes, "We have . . . completely absorbed the ideas of his polemical books and pamphlets."[17] His *Lettres philosophiques* are considered the greatest single force shaping European liberal religious thought. Much of Voltaire's religious philosophy is an angry response to the great Christian mathematician Pascal (1623-1662), who died a generation before Voltaire's birth. Pascal believed passionately in both the Fall and innate human sin, two concepts Voltaire repudiated with equal passion. Such Christian doctrines enslave the mind, and come not from Reason but revelation. Ancient priests likely invented these ideas and their modern counterparts perpetuate them.

Voltaire is best remembered for his strange novelette *Candide*, a haunting and humorous story that presents the absurdity and cruelty of human life. It was originally written as an answer to Leibniz's philosophical optimism. A man highly sensitive to human suffering, Voltaire was moved by events such as the disastrous earthquake that struck Lisbon, Portugal, on October 31, 1755. The city was virtually wiped out by the quake, and many thousands of citizens died in fires while attending church services celebrating All Saints Day. How could a loving God allow such evil, particularly when so many of the victims were the devout? Voltaire posed a dilemma: Either God is not all-powerful, or he is not all good. If he is all good and allows evil to persist, he must not be all-powerful. If he is all-powerful and allows evil to persist, he must not be all good. *Candide's* summary sentiment is Voltaire's famous maxim, "tend your own garden," but no man ever was less inclined to tend his own garden than Voltaire. Throughout his long and successful literary life he was perpetually involved in criticizing actions he thought unjust and ideas he deemed ludicrous.

"Zadig": liberating reason. Nothing occupied Voltaire's thinking more than the goal of emancipating human reason from the restrictions of the Revealed Word. His short novel *Zadig* presents a view of religion that today sounds almost contemporary. Voltaire assumes the moderate position that a reasonable person can only affirm a tentative belief in God's existence. What we can know and trust is Reason. Moreover, all established religions contain much pure superstition while at the same time each insists that it is uniquely true. Such foolish insistence on doctrinal correctness produces religious intolerance and violence. Reason leads freethinking modern people to avoid dogma and to embrace pluralism. This is the message of *Zadig,* the spirit of which has been incorporated into the New Religious Synthesis.

At the age of fifty-three, with his literary powers in full force and his freedom as a writer fully realized, Voltaire wrote this fascinating Oriental romance to convey his ideas about the place of Reason in a new religious outlook. From its first appearance in 1747 the book has been considered "among his masterpieces of light narrative."[18] More subtle and whimsical than *Candide, Zadig* is thus also more appealing and convincing. Theodore Besterman writes that *Zadig* was "intended to persuade with a smile."[19] A wily advocate, Voltaire chose the genre of humorous narrative to create a winsome and convincing case for Reason as the basis for religion. Besterman notes, "Voltaire's tales are carefully wrought works of art: that is, their forms fit perfectly their content and purpose."[20]

A highly sympathetic character, Zadig is the wisest of men. His adventures and misadventures tend to prove that there is no point in relying on divine providence to see one through life. Rather, one should trust Reason and hope for the best. In his elegant and captivating prose Voltaire spins a virtually irresistible tale of Zadig's life, and in the process of reading we are drawn into Voltaire's account of religion. So pleasant and accessible is *Zadig* that even today it is more likely to be required reading for French school children than is the disturbing satire *Candide.*

Zadig's full title is *Zadig, or Destiny: An Oriental Tale.* The story of Zadig is set in Babylon in the middle of the fifteenth century A.D. Zadig is introduced as a man "whose innate goodness had been strengthened by his upbringing." Voltaire adds that "despite his wealth and his youth he held his passions in check, was utterly sincere, did not always expect to be right, and made allowances for human frailty."[21] Thus, in Zadig we encounter a person of impeccable manners and character, and one who enjoys social status as well. Moreover, Zadig is just and fair-minded. "Above all," Voltaire writes, "Zadig did not pride himself on despising women and keeping them in subjection." In addition to his other qualities, Zadig is handsome, frank, wise and noble.

Early in this elaborate tale readers learn of Zadig's suspicion of religious authorities and pompous scholars. Like a good Deist, Zadig looks to Nature and Reason, not revelation or authority, for his religious guidance. "'There is no one more fortunate,' he thought, 'than a philosopher who reads in the great book that God has spread before our eyes,'" that is, the book of Nature. "The truths he discovers are his own," that is, they come through his own reason. "He nourishes and elevates his soul. He lives in peace. No one can harm him.'"[22] Reason examining Nature discovers spiritual truth, and thus discovers the transcendent. Zadig's autonomous Reason liberates itself from the constraints of Revealed Word religion, escapes the bonds of revelation and declares unequivocally its independence.

Reason resolves religious controversy. During his days as a member of the Babylonian court, Zadig developed a reputation for Solomonic wisdom and saintly generosity. "He showed day by day the subtlety of his intellect and the goodness of his character. He was admired but he was also loved."[23] At the height of his popularity Zadig is called upon to resolve a religious dispute that "split the empire into two rigid sects" for more than fifteen hundred years. And what was the question at issue in this dispute? Just this: One of the two sects "claimed that the only way to enter the temple of Mithra was left foot first, while the other sect held this custom in abhorrence and always went in right foot first."[24]

Zadig resolves this nettlesome controversy by jumping over the threshold of the temple with both feet at the same time. He then makes a speech affirming that "the God of heaven and earth is no respecter of persons," following which an envious listener complains that Zadig has not relied sufficiently on eloquence. But, "Zadig was quite satisfied with a rational style."[25] In this episode Voltaire argues that the disputes of official religion often are ridiculous and predicated on distinctions of no consequence. Any rational observer recognizes this immediately. He also affirms that Reason is superior to the religions of the priests, the disputations of the debaters and the eloquence of the orators. Reason reigns supreme.

Reason defeats religious abuse. Through many travels, adventures and perils Zadig's reason also triumphs over brutality, bigotry and religious intolerance. Zadig challenges the Arabian practice of burning widows on their husband's funeral pyres. A widow has requested this form of death, and a defender of the practice argues: "Women have been allowed to burn themselves to death for more than a thousand years. Which of us dares to alter a law consecrated by time? What can be more respectable than an ancient abuse?"[26] These questions sum up Voltaire's argument against religious abuses; they are brutal and persistent *because* they are unexamined by Reason.

Zadig's response reflects the belief that humanity's original religion was both natural and rational: "Reason is still more ancient." Reason is older than all religious practices, and the one source of true religious ideas at all times. Zadig convinces both the widow in question and her tribal leaders to forsake their plans. In fact, so persuasive is his argument that it eventually leads to the cessation of the practice.

Reason reveals religious unity. In one of the narrative's culminating scenes, Zadig sits down to a banquet in Egypt with representatives of several different faiths. His companions include "an Egyptian, an Indian from the Ganges, an inhabitant of Cathay, a Greek, a Celt, and several other foreigners." As the evening progresses a dispute breaks out over religious practices. An Egyptian complains that he has not been loaned money against the excellent collateral of his aunt's mummified body, while an Indian instructs Zadig not to eat a piece of chicken because "the soul of the deceased may have passed into the body of that hen." The Egyptian fails to see the problem for, he asserts, "we worship a bull but we eat it all the same." The Indian is appalled, but the Egyptian says he and his countrymen have been doing the same for over one hundred thousand years. And in this vein the argument continues with each person present defending his religion as the true one. Ridiculous claims such as that a great fish taught the human race to read or that mistletoe is sacred characterize the discussion.

Zadig listens politely to this religious babble, and is finally moved to suggest a resolution to the swirling, groundless controversy. "Gentlemen . . . you are all in agreement." Zadig's argument unfolds as follows. "'It is a fact, isn't it,' he said to the Celt, 'that you don't worship this mistletoe, but the creator of mistletoe and oak?' 'Of course,' replied the Celt. 'And you, the Egyptian gentleman, revere in the form of a certain bull the maker of all bulls?' 'I do,' said the Egyptian. 'Oannes the fish,' he went on, 'must bow before the creator of the sea and all fishes.' 'Granted,' said the Chaldean."[27] In this passage Zadig sounds one of the leading themes of Deism as well as of the New Religious Synthesis: differences among religions are superficial; what they hold in common is essential. Only the common elements in various religions can claim Reason as their source. Voltaire's "creator" of all things, however, is never quite defined.

Voltaire's intolerance and the limits of Reason. Zadig is a winsome and rational Everyman, avoiding the excesses of revealed religion while maintaining a sense of the transcendent. Voltaire has created the perfect paradigm for the religious individual for a new era, a confident and reasonable resident of the new world. Gone are the meaningless disputes over doctrine that have divided believers in various faiths, that have set nation against nation and church against synagogue. Zadig tends his own garden, but helps when he can his less rational fellow travelers still trapped in creeds outworn.

Indeed, Voltaire is said by his admirers to have "succeeded in pulling the poisoned fangs of religious intolerance."[28] However, this lifelong opponent of intolerance was, as one biographer notes, "always intolerant of Christianity."[29] Voltaire was also a notorious anti-Semite. Perhaps these contradictions in Voltaire's character are due to the fact that he was much more confident about what he sought to oppose than about what he sought to establish. Zadig, after all, has no creed. Voltaire worshiped only the god of Reason whose altar in Notre Dame his followers helped to design, a god who sharpened his famous wit but who, apparently, could not soften his heart. Writers belonging to a new century would rename Voltaire's interior god.

THOMAS DE QUINCEY

Romantic writers, like Enlightenment critics before them, substituted for the outmoded wholly other God of the Revealed Word a new interior divinity. William Covino refers to this internal power as the "magical imagination." Romantic devotion to imagination is evident in the works of Blake, Wordsworth, Coleridge, Shelley and others.[30] So thoroughgoing was the Romantics' devotion to imagination that it led some to disregard the body as its hindrance. Wordsworth attributed "Coleridge's physical decay" to his intensely interior focus and the resultant "withdrawal from the sensible world into a miraculous and improbable one."[31]

Belief that a spark of divinity animated the human soul drove Romantics' intense interest in Imagination. Moreover, the knowing devotee might nurture this inner divinity through virtual self-worship. Thus Coleridge made a "godlike representation of himself" in one of his major works, *Biographia.*[32] This section draws attention to the early Romantic writer Thomas De Quincey and to a strange and very popular book that sacralized Imagination. De Quincey, like Peter Annet, made a god of the human mind.

Opium eating. Though essayist and critic Thomas De Quincey (1785-1859) was born in Manchester, England, he ran away from home at the age of seventeen, lived in London for a time, and later attended Oxford University. By 1813 he had become addicted to opium, his use of the drug beginning with an effort to relieve severe pain in his face and head. Though his collected works run to fourteen volumes, he is remembered principally for one book based on two articles for the *London Magazine*. This book, *Confessions of an English Opium Eater*, was widely read and highly influential in the early Romantic period. De Quincey's argument helps us to understand how the cult of Reason developed in the nineteenth century.

Confessions of an English Opium Eater created a sensation when it first appeared in 1820. De Quincey's remarkable ability as a prose stylist, combined with his capacity for ushering readers winsomely into the world of London's street denizens—prostitutes, orphans, thieves—attracted readers from across a wide spectrum of the British and American public. Much of the early part of the work is taken up with De Quincey's description of unusual events from his childhood and with his ill-fated relocation to London as a student in the opening years of the nineteenth century. Through various illnesses and chance encounters, De Quincey discovered opium, a drug that would become central to his life and work. The middle chapters of *Confessions* offer an elaborate defense of opium's capacity to stimulate the mind, while the closing chapters present an equivocal lament over De Quincey's struggle to overcome the effects of his long addiction to the drug.

However, *Confessions of an English Opium Eater,* for all of its other intriguing qualities, offers the reader more than a glimpse into the drug-induced state of imaginative excitement. It also makes a religious statement, an *apologia* for the superior mind liberated from the limits of conventional social life. In this way, De Quincey's book can be read as an exaltation of Reason, the inner divinity, albeit under the influence of a powerful chemical. Opium reveals to the disciplined user a transcendent inner world of unlimited rational potential and phantasmagoric imaginative experience. In this way De Quincey prefigures later hallucinogenic writers such as Aldous Huxley.

Dreaming. In another work, *Signs from the Depths*, De Quincey wrote approvingly of what he termed "dreaming," a drug-enhanced activity in which Imagination grows unrestrained by ordinary social limitations. "Among the powers in man which suffer by this too intense life of the social instincts, none suffers more than the power of dreaming." Dreaming was crucial to this nineteenth-century worshiper of Reason. After all, "the machinery for dreaming planted in the human brain was not planted for nothing." Then what is its purpose? Interestingly, De Quincey makes dreaming a means of connection to the supernatural realm. Dreaming, when guided by something he called the "mystery of darkness"—apparently esoteric knowledge that allows one to direct the dreaming mind—becomes for De Quincey a "great tube" through which one can "communicate with the shadowy," an apparent reference to the spiritual world. Of course, opium assisted this communication.[33]

In elevating dreaming, De Quincey rejected not only social convention but also, like the biblical critics, history. He proposed a new understanding of religion as free from history and rooted in what he termed "profound philosophy." Profound philosophy was an act of rational rebellion against ordinary life, conventional morality, and traditional history, a rebellion achieved only by the few truly superior minds. In this way, profound philosophy was something like the Deists' practice of freethinking, an act of extraordinary rational strength by which autonomous Reason liberates itself. William Covino comments that De Quincey wrote his *Signs from the Depths* as "a manifesto for superhumanity, an oration on the dignity of the human potential for reaching beyond [the] mundane" by employing "magical imagination" against history and society. For De Quincey, this profound philosophy constituted an "act of cultural insolence." His loathing of ordinary humanity was well known.[34]

Carrying God within: restoring the mind to its natural state. Just as the Enlightenment god of Reason was eternal and omnipresent, the Romantic's interior deity of Imagination was everlasting and infinite. V. A. De Luca writes that the devotee of Imagination "houses the infinite in his own finite corporeality," that is, carries divinity within.[35] Annet found his own thinking to mirror the movements of eternal Reason. Thus, for De Quincey as for Annet, Reason became "God incarnate." Similarly, the Romantic recognized in Imagination a divine expansion of the self. When in his dream state, "which is for De Quincey the product of an isolated, drugged, defiant, and haunted sensibility," writes Covino, "one composes the giant self."[36]

Oddly, constructing this "giant self" was enhanced by opium use. De Quincey contrasted opium's effects with those of alcohol. "The main distinction lies in this," he wrote, "that whereas wine disorders the mental faculties, opium, on the contrary, (if taken in a proper manner,) introduces amongst them the most exquisite order, legislation, and harmony."[37] Thus, opium enhanced Reason by bringing order and harmony to an otherwise inconstant, unpredictable human capacity. Opium returns

Reason to a natural, unspoiled state. As he puts the point, opium brings about "a healthy restoration to that state which the mind would normally recover upon the removal of any deep-seated irritation of pain that had disturbed and quarreled with the impulses of a heart originally just and good."[38] Annet found the elixir of freethinking to place Reason in sync with Nature. De Quincey takes the quicker and truer path to the same end; the powerful narcotic opium was a restorative medicine healing the mind of wounds inflicted by life in human society. "Opium," he writes, "always seems to compose what had been agitated, and to concentrate what had been distracted."[39]

Putting a somewhat finer edge on his description of the mind's restoration, De Quincey maintains that "the opium-eater . . . feels that the diviner part of his nature is paramount; that is, the moral affections are in a state of cloudless serenity; and over all is the great light of the majestic intellect." Opium puts one in touch with the god within, one's own rational faculties—"majestic intellect"—whose true powers have been obscured by mundane routines, obligations and fatigues. Opium achieves its effects by "greatly increasing the activity of the mind."[40] A new spiritual age dawns when profound philosophy and opium set the mind free, that is, awaken the sleeping interior god. Alluding to Christ's description of himself in the book of Revelation, De Quincey assumes the role of prophet of a new spiritual order. "This is the doctrine of the true church on the subject of opium: of which church I acknowledge myself to be the only member—the alpha and the omega."[41] De Quincey's language becomes more religious as his devotion to opium and dreaming grows. In his dream state he finds "hopes which blossom in the paths of life" and "motions of the intellect as unwearied as the heavens."[42] Reason under the influence of opium offers hope, rest, peace and even freedom from the fear of death.

De Quincey awakens an interior god possessing power to create extraordinary beauty and elevate the spirit to divine heights. He praises the virtual omnipotence of divine Reason under opium's influence. De Quincey must, then, be considered an early writer in the Western hallucinogenic tradition, the cult of employing chemical substances to enhance the power and perceptual experience of the mind. In 1922 Aleister Crowley, the infamous Victorian occultist, would follow suit with his popular and controversial work *Diary of a Drug Fiend*, and in the 1960s Aldous Huxley introduced a new generation of spiritual seekers to the possibilities of mind-enhancing drugs in *Doors of Perception*.

An elite of the mind and a new religion. De Quincey's views on the powers of the human mind incorporated a kind of spiritual elitism. "Whatever may be the num-

ber of those in whom this faculty of dreaming splendidly can be supposed to lurk,"
he writes, "there are not perhaps very many in whom it is developed."[43] The preoc-
cupations of ordinary work prevent the laborer from achieving such heights of intellectual self-realization. Moreover, a certain inborn capacity is required in the
greatest of minds. In order for the intellect to "dream magnificently," an individual
must possess "a constitutional determination" to elevated thought.[44]

It is also true that the gift of dreaming great dreams is hindered by modern technological culture. But liberation comes by way of a new religion that replaces the
Revealed Word. Amidst the din of urban culture "the brain is haunted" as if by
"ghostly beings moving amongst us." This "colossal pace of advance" is not likely to
be reversed, and so another remedy is needed. That remedy is "counter forces of
corresponding magnitude," which meant for De Quincey the force of a new religion.[45] Guided by this new faith the great dreamer rises above the mundane tragedy
of "the merely human" through extraordinary rational ability, all-conquering will
power, and opium.

The great mind has a destiny to fulfill: to deliver the self from the ordinary
world of people through contact with another world. The mind of the dreamer
is a "magnificent apparatus" that discovers "eternities below all life."[46] For De
Quincey, a new religion of the exalted Self allows access to a supernatural realm,
but only to a specially gifted vanguard of the human race. They enter this realm
of superawareness through secret knowledge—"the mystery of darkness"—
combined with their extraordinary will power, which "forces the infinite into the
chambers of the human brain." Eternity itself is within their grasp. Superior intellect, freedom from the drudgeries of daily labor, secret knowledge and extraordinary will power liberate the great minds among us from the mundane world.
Reason triumphs over all of the limiting forces of life, and the human mind assumes its place as master of eternity.

The goal of De Quincey's works on opium and dreaming was to probe the great
capacity of some human beings, through the exercise of "magnificent intellect," to
rise above their companions. The idea of an elite of the mind has had many advocates in the modern period, Annet, Voltaire and De Quincey among them. One of
the most influential recent advocates of such a view of Reason, though certainly not
the subtlest or most talented, is the subject of this chapter's final section. But before
turning to the works of Ayn Rand, it will be instructive to consider a peculiarly
American expression of the notion of divine Reason.

AMERICAN NEW THOUGHT: MIND AS DIVINE HEALING FORCE

In nineteenth-century America, Reason's elevation was manifested in widespread interest in New Thought—the use of mental power to achieve psychological and physical healing. Ultimately, New Thought may have its origins in the animal magnetism theories of the Austrian physician Franz Friedrich Anton Mesmer (1733-1815). Mesmer taught that certain cosmic powers akin to magnetism could be harnessed for healing by the knowing practitioner.[47] He is often credited with having developed the technique of hypnosis.

The American line of descent in the New Thought movement runs from Phineas Parkhurst Quimby to his patient Mary Baker Eddy, and from Eddy to Ralph Waldo Trine, the great popularizer of New Thought philosophy in the late nineteenth century. Characteristic of these thinkers, and a host of others in the New Thought and Harmonialism tradition, is a belief in the powers of the human mind or human reason. As Stephen Gottschalk writes, these thinkers stress "the adequacy of the human mind as a source of power and meaning rather than the necessity for the radical salvation of mankind through an agency outside of the self."[48]

Quimby and Eddy. Quimby (1802-1866), a clock-maker from Belfast, Maine, practiced both mesmerism and hypnotism for a time. His observations of patients and their responses to medicines and other treatments convinced him that "there was no causal connection between prescriptions and resultant cures."[49] He concluded that healing was a consequence of patients *believing* that a medicine or other treatment was effective. As Dennis Voskuil writes, "Quimby concluded, therefore, that disease was a mental problem and that health depended upon a mental cure."[50] Quimby's metaphysical speculations upon this point led him to a striking conclusion: "He viewed man as a spiritual being who possesses an unconscious soul, which is directly related to and partakes in the divine mind."[51] Healing was a matter of understanding properly our essential divinity. This discovery Quimby dubbed the "science of healing."

Mary Baker Eddy (1821-1910) visited Quimby in search of healing in the early 1860s, and became for a time a devoted disciple. She adapted—some would say plagiarized—Quimby's basic ideas and formulated her own science of healing around an idealism that taught that illness was an error in thinking. Eddy always insisted that she had made a sharp break with Quimby and his views.[52] Quimby's ideas were also advanced by Warren Felt Evans, another former patient. In a series of books including *The Mental Cure* and *The Primitive Mind Cure*, Evans "reiterated the basic positions of New Thought."[53]

New Thought advocates organized themselves in 1914 into the New Thought Alliance, a group that officially proclaimed "the Divinity of Man and his infinite possibilities through the creative power of constructive thinking." The group also urged attention to the "voice of the Indwelling Presence which is our source of Inspiration, Power, Health and Prosperity."[54] Mind was the indwelling divinity in human beings. As such, Mind, not the Revealed Word's God, was the source of all good things.

The Fillmores and Unity Christian School. The religion of Mind or Reason continued to develop its own distinctive theology under the guidance of Charles and Myrtle Fillmore, founders in 1889 of the Unity Christian School. The mind possessed boundless powers that were released through a practice Charles Fillmore called simply "prayer." Through prayer the skilled practitioner concentrated mental energy on a problem in such a way as to unleash the "electronic, life imparting forces" and "vibrant energies" of the "spiritual ethers" which are present also in the "cells of our body."[55] Mind was again, as with Quimby, Eddy and Evans, the sole agent of divine power.

It did not take long for religious mentalism to become the key to worldly success and even power. Prentice Mulford stands as an important example of this trend. "To think success brings success," he wrote in the 1880s. But a greedy edge bordering on megalomania begins to appear in the Mulford's religious mentalism: "Set the magnetic power of your mind persistently in the desire and *demand* the best of everything, and the best will, by an inevitable and unerring law, eventually come to you."[56]

Ralph Waldo Trine. The real popularizer of religious mentalism, however, was Ralph Waldo Trine (1866-1958). In 1897 his book *In Tune with the Infinite: Fullness of Peace, Power and Plenty* first appeared. Voskuil reports that "this book sold an astonishing one and a half million copies."[57] Trine turned "mentalism" in a direction best termed rational magic. He emphasized a technique of visualization that actually turned ideas into material realities. Through the exercise of Trine's rational techniques, the practitioner of mentalism "set into operation subtle, silent, and irresistible forces that ... actualize in material form what is today merely an idea." Trine adds, with suggestive phrasing, that "ideas have occult power, and ideas when rightly tended are the seeds that actualize material conditions."[58] Thus, the skilled human manipulator of ideas creates reality, and the master of Reason is rendered a divine agent. Voskuil maintains that Trine's book created "a new form of religious literature . . . that would become as common as aspirin by 1960."[59] Later proponents of Trine's mentalism included Emmet Fox and Glen Clark, who taught that "'things are thoughts' and that external reality is 'an outpicturing of our minds.'"[60]

Reason elevated to a divine status is inherent to religious and secular metaphysics ranging from the positive thinking teachings of Norman Vincent Peale to the works of New Age writers who urge their readers to create their own realities through mental projection or *maya*. The power of Reason to discover spiritual truth, to transcend earthly constraints, even to shape present reality, are now basic tenets of the New Religious Synthesis. So widely assimilated are these ideas that they have also been advocated by writers who claim no particular religious view whatever. Novelist Ayn Rand provides an important and highly influential example of just such a writer. Her morality of unrestrained egoism constitutes a luminous instance of the terminus of Reason's elevation.

AYN RAND'S ARGUMENT FOR REASON

Russian émigré Ayn Rand (1905-1982) arrived in the United States in 1926. She was highly successful as a Hollywood screenwriter, an occupation she pursued until 1943. Beginning with *We the Living* in the 1930s, Rand developed a philosophy of "enlightened self-interest" and the "virtue of selfishness." This perspective is skillfully advocated in phenomenally popular and controversial novels, including *The Fountainhead* (1943) and *Atlas Shrugged* (1957), books that continue to sell more than 250,000 copies annually. Rand achieved a degree of cultural influence enjoyed by few writers. She stated repeatedly in her fiction, as well as in nonfiction works such as *The Virtue of Selfishness* (1964), that her philosophy—a version of Nietzsche's philosophy of will—is based on regard for reason alone. The extended narrative was by far her most successful vehicle for advancing the philosophy of radical self-interest. Rand represents the twentieth-century fruition of the cult of Reason.

John Galt speaks . . . and speaks. Ultimate regard for something called Reason is powerfully portrayed in Rand's ruthless prose. John Galt, the principal character in her largest and most important novel, *Atlas Shrugged*, presents Rand's philosophy of Reason in a long speech near the end of that book. Galt's speech is perhaps the most powerful example of Rand the didactic storyteller, Rand the public advocate, Rand the popular philosopher. This famous interlude in *Atlas Shrugged* also provides a fascinating example of how Rand defines the role of autonomous Reason in reaction against the traditional moral perspective of the Revealed Word.

Some background is important to understanding the origin and purpose of John Galt's speech. In *Atlas Shrugged*, the wealthy industrialist Galt arranges for all of America's powerful and influential elite to join him in a secret enclave in the Rocky Mountains. He intends to demonstrate once and for all that the followers of Reason, a small human vanguard, are the "great ones" who make civilization possible. The speech's secondary purpose is, apparently, to convince the ordinary working drones of the world that they are parasites who make victims of their betters. At the novel's climactic moment a rapidly deteriorating nation, bereft of its most talented leaders, hears from the mighty Galt a prolonged argument for his basic philosophy of life and a harsh account of social justice.

Sacrificing Reason to faith. Despite Rand's remarkable popularity, Galt's speech reads like a rant from a self-absorbed amateur philosopher who has read Nietzsche without much power of penetration. Galt declares, "I am the man who loves his life. I am the man who does not sacrifice his love or values," by which he means that he has lived according to the rule of Reason, which for Rand is the law of complete selfishness. By taking the strong, like himself, out of the world, Galt has deprived the weak of their "victims" and thus "destroyed [their] world." The weak and poor are in their present state because they "dread knowledge."

And why have the majority of America's citizens forsaken knowledge for something lower? Rand's answer is that they have allowed the apostles of religious faith to delude them. "You have sacrificed reason to faith," Galt alleges. Consequently the masses have acted according to conventional and irrational morality. "You have sacrificed wealth to need," which constitutes a sin against Reason. John Galt makes clear, repeatedly, that for him there is no higher source of power than Reason, no greater entity than Mind. People who choose to live by Reason are "the men of the mind," an elite destined to rule.[61] Such people are not moved by human need; they find selfishness, not mercy, the highest virtue. With the great ones out of the picture, the remainder of humanity faces "a world without mind" according to Galt.[62] Speaking on behalf of the best of us, John Galt tells the rest of us, "*We do not need you*" (emphasis in original). Is this the ultimate destination of Voltaire's liberating deity, Reason? In Rand, Reason dissolves into vindictive self-importance posturing as moral philosophy.

Galt alleges that trading Reason for religious morality caused humanity's Fall.

The "scourges and disasters" of history are "brought about by your code of moral-ity." The feeble Revealed Word moral code demands love, service, charity and sac-rifice. The meek do not inherit the earth; rather they are the "incompetents on earth" who have failed to follow Reason. "Reason does not work automatically," Galt alleges. "Thinking is not a mechanical process; the connections of logic are not made by instinct." To think requires "effort," an effort the poor have not made.[63]

The Revealed Word tradition takes a severe beating in Rand's case for a new mo-rality. The despicable masses admire the old religious virtues of altruism and service, and for this they are punished. "Yes," declares Galt, "you *are* bearing punishment for your evil."[64] Their sin was to fail to follow Reason to the place it had led Galt himself. But this is an odd judgment, for Rand makes clear that following Reason is *not* within the reach of most people. The "men of the mind" are a very small elite, and Reason is the omnipotent tool of the few possessing the will to master it.

Saving knowledge. For Rand, mastering Reason is self-salvation, the gods of the religions being merely "ghosts in heaven."[65] Death is always a lurking threat, and holding on to life requires "the knowledge needed to keep it."[66] Thus, the follower of Reason seeks the special knowledge necessary to maintain and extend the life of Reason. Galt argues that one "must obtain his knowledge and choose his actions by a process of thinking, which nature will not force him to perform."[67] "Man's life" is thus "life by means of achievement." Good and evil are defined with reference to Reason. "All that which is proper to the life of a rational being is the good, all that which destroys it is the evil."[68]

Galt places this ferocious, triumphant morality of Reason in opposition to the pathetic, self-destructive morality of religion. Conventional religion preaching ser-vice and self-sacrifice "gives you *death* as your standard."[69] The founders and leaders of conventional religions are "hatred-eaten mystics who pose as friends of human-ity and preach that the highest virtue man can practice is to hold his own life as of no value."[70] Thus, Rand vehemently rejects such dictums as Jesus' proclamation that "those who want to save their life will lose it, and those who lose their life for my sake will find it" (Mt 16:25; Lk 9:24). Saving oneself in Rand's cosmos is a mat-ter of devoting oneself fully to the interior god Reason.

CONCLUSION

This chapter has explored writers who find in Reason, Mind, Imagination or Con-sciousness unlimited potential for human advancement. Elevation of Reason was a hallmark of the Enlightenment, and Reason's central role in human spiritual life has been a theme of Western metaphysical writing ever since.

I have selected for special attention several writers who addressed a popular audience and treated some aspect of the human rational life as a substitute for either the Revealed Word or its personal God. Annet made Reason a divinity within us, the standard of human morality and the source of our spiritual life. Voltaire emphasized reason's critical qualities, its capacity to cut through the dense fog of confusion cast up by various revelations. De Quincey called attention to the intellect's imaginative dimension, making it the center of human experience and calling for its expansion through opium use. The advocates of New Thought explored the mind's capacity to heal and to otherwise alter reality. Rand made Reason the basis of ego's triumph over life's obstacles, the source of both personal success and political order, and the basis of a self-serving moral view. What each author has in common with the others is the determination to place human rational capacities, or some particular rational capacity, at the center of spiritual or moral life. Each venerates Reason, placing it figuratively, as Voltaire's followers did literally in Notre Dame, at the center of the temple of human spirituality.

The New Religious Synthesis recognizes a force, a virtual divinity, within the human cerebrum. This power of human rationality, will and creativity displaces the sovereign and wholly other God of the Revealed Word. Annet's God Incarnate, Voltaire's Reason, De Quincey's Majestic Intellect, Trine's Mind, Rand's Reason—each is an expression of rational autonomous individuality transformed into a god. The following chapter considers the public case for Reason's own creation—science—as a new source of theology. In the Other Spirituality, science reveals to Reason new spiritual truths.

5

SCIENCE AND SHIFTING
PARADIGMS

Salvation in a New Cosmos

O what a world of profit and delight,
of power, of honor, of omnipotence
Is promis'd to the studious artisan!

CHRISTOPHER MARLOWE, Dr. Faustus

Do not be surprised if physics curricula of the twenty-first century include classes in meditation.

GARY ZUKAV, The Dancing Wu Li Masters

I thought of all the books I had read—and tried to understand—on quantum physics . . . the
new physics, they called it. It sounded so much like ancient Eastern mysticism.

SHIRLEY MACLAINE, Dancing in the Light

Christianity is to be found an enemy to civilization, and the struggle which modern thought and
science are compelled to conduct with it is . . . a "cultur-kampf [culture war]."

ERNST HAECKEL, The Riddle of the Universe

Auguste Comte (1798-1857), founder of the school of thought known as logical
positivism, maintained "that humanity progresses through stages of thought."
Each of these stages represents a rational advance over the previous one. The first
stage he identified as the theological, which, as the name implies, presents God as
the cause of all that exists. The second stage Comte dubbed the metaphysical, a period in our rational progress which dispenses with theological explanation in favor
of more refined philosophical accounts of objects and events.

However, both the theological and the metaphysical stages in human thinking
are mere stepping stones along the way to the final stage of rational progress, which

Comte called the "positivist." This is the highest achievement in human thinking, a period in which only scientific explanations are accepted as legitimate and rational. Science was for Comte the ultimate achievement of human Reason. It explained the cosmos and offered a method of controlling it. Moreover, science performed both tasks without reference to a deity.[1] Science, then, was a substitute for religion.

Comte discarded theology and enthroned Science as the sole source of knowledge, transcendence and higher experience. Comte "literally made a cult of science," and by the 1870s his many readers "invested science with power, promise, . . . even with sacredness."[2] He developed an elaborate calendar of inspirational readings from the world's great thinkers and included what can only be called holy days. "The year," wrote one observer, "is divided into thirteen lunar months, each named after some great man. Every day is dedicated to some minor celebrity—one day to the dead in general, and one day to the memory of holy women. The calendar is studded with *fete* days just like a calendar of the saints." Churches of "the Religion of Humanity" sprang up in London and other cities, and Comte himself occasionally "preached and performed marriage and burial services."[3] Comte himself, however, eventually moved from his scientific worship of humanity to the worship of his deceased paramour, Madame Clotilde de Vaux, to whom he prayed on a regular basis.[4]

If science is empirical method employed to resolve questions of physical causation, Science is that method sacralized as the sole source of saving knowledge for the human race. This chapter considers some efforts to convert science into Science, to transform a method of investigation into a source of theological insight. Science as a window on a sacred cosmos is a cornerstone of the New Religious Synthesis, the instrument of Reason in search of ever greater spiritual insight.

Joseph Ernest Renan (1823-1892), philologist, historian, director of the College de France and author of the enormously controversial *Life of Jesus* (1863), shared and helped to shape the late nineteenth-century hope in Science as a substitute for religion. "He was sure," writes historian Jacques Barzun, "that science would make all other works of the mind obsolete: philosophy, theology, literature would disappear."[5] Speaking of the Christian faith of medieval people, Carl Jung wrote in 1933 that "natural science has long ago torn this lovely veil to shreds." In the old religious view "men were all children of God under the loving care of the Most High, who prepared them for eternal blessedness."[6]

Is not Science a strictly rational endeavor intentionally denuded of such gaudy baubles that have always attended "mere faith"? Surely the picture must be more

complex. When Mary Baker Eddy invented a new religion in the nineteenth century, she called it Christian *Science*. Similarly, Philip Jenkins has noted that occult
writers of the nineteenth and twentieth centuries often alleged that they were simply applying scientific discoveries to the solution of spiritual problems.[7] And physicist Amit Goswami has recently written in his book *The Self-Aware Universe* that
"modern science is venturing into realms that for more than four millennia have
been the fiefdoms of religion and philosophy." Consequently, "we are privileged to
be a part of this evolutionary and transcendent process by which science is changing not only itself but also our perception of reality."[8] The dean of twentieth-
century spiritual scientists, Fritjof Capra, arrived at the same conclusion in 1975
when he wrote that "the influence of modern physics . . . extends to the realm of
thought and culture where it has led to a deep revision in our conception of the universe and our relationship to it."[9]

The following pages focus attention on several popular arguments over the
past three centuries that advance Science as the pathway to a new spirituality, one
prepared to replace the outdated and unscientific Revealed Word perspective.
We will survey a famous eighteenth-century work that treats Science as a new
source of transcendence, a nineteenth-century argument that Science opens the
way for a new humanistic religion, and several twentieth-century arguments for
Science as the new religion. Recently the argument about the spirituality of Science has turned decidedly in the direction of mysticism. The elevation of Science
as a means of discovering a new and verifiably true spirituality is a crucial component in the Other Spirituality.

THOMAS PAINE ON THE HOPE OF SCIENCE

Thomas Paine was born January 29, 1737, at Thetford in Norfolk, England. His father was Quaker, his mother Anglican. As a young man Paine served for a time as a
sailor, and later as a tax collector for the English government. Self-educated, he used
the small amount of money he could save to purchase books and rudimentary scientific equipment. Paine also attended lectures in London and was particularly drawn
to discussions of Newtonian physics. During a visit to London, Benjamin Franklin
encouraged Paine to sail for America, which he did in October of 1774. Talk of revolution was heard everywhere in the Colonies in the 1770s, and Paine began to write
pamphlets that eventually made him one of the independence movement's principal
proponents. His wildly popular pamphlet *Common Sense* played a decisive role in

convincing many colonists that separation from England was inevitable.

"The Age of Reason." Paine had long believed that Christianity prevented people from thinking about the injustices of government, and was convinced that a free and just government could not exist simultaneously with Christianity. For Paine, the Deists' veneration of Reason was the only true religion, and it could not exist side by side with Christianity. "Tyranny in religion" is the worst of all tyrannies. Always a popularizer, Paine provided Americans in the 1790s what Deists of the 1730s provided England—a clear and accessible argument for rejecting the Revealed Word in favor of a "religion of Reason."

Voltaire vowed to show the world that, if it took only twelve men to establish Christianity, it would take only one to destroy it. Similarly, Paine boasted that he would "march through the Christian forest with an axe." *The Age of Reason* was to be that axe. So extreme were the views expressed in this book that Samuel Adams and Benjamin Rush refused to associate with Paine after its publication. The publisher of the book's first edition was actually tried for blasphemy and imprisoned. Paine's deep hatred of Christianity rang clear in the book's pages. "Whenever we read the obscene stories, the voluptuous debaucheries, the cruel and torturous executions, the unrelenting vindictiveness, with which more than half of the Bible is filled," he wrote, "it would be more consistent to say that it was the word of a demon than the word of God. It is a history of wickedness that has served to corrupt and brutalize mankind; and, for my part, I sincerely detest it as I detest everything that is cruel."[10]

While *The Age of Reason* is infamous for such antireligious sentiments, Paine's argument for a religious hope in science is seldom recognized. Nevertheless, he incorporated into this caustic and provocative work a groundbreaking view of science as spiritual solace, as the source of a new religion suited to the modern world. *The Age of Reason* is his manifesto on a new era in human consciousness, his plea for taking leave of all of the errors of the past and embarking on a new scientific path in religion. Paine spent many pages in *The Age of Reason* rehearsing the Bible's errors and other offenses to reason, making the case that Reason, not the Bible, leads us to God. "It is only by the exercise of reason that man can discover God," he wrote.[11]

Paine was above all a highly capable rhetorical tactician, and two strategic goals regarding religion are evident in *The Age of Reason*. The first is to undermine the Revealed Word perspective through corrosive biblical criticism of the type pioneered by the Deists and with which Paine was intimately familiar. The second is to advance an alternative religious perspective based on Science, one that prefigures components of the New Religious Synthesis. Paine sets about accomplishing these goals by writing as an angry opponent of all superstition and rational tyranny. Tyranny in the spiritual realm was even more objectionable than tyranny in the political realm, and Paine knew better than anyone how to rouse public ire over tyranny.

But Paine's tone changes in the second book of *The Age of Reason*. Here he writes as the reader's friend and guide into the mysteries of an incomparably complex and wonderful universe. Book Two presents Paine as the diligent student of nature and nature's God, a thinker and observer ready to share discoveries that might actually form the basis of a new perspective on religion.

A glimpse of this new religious perspective is afforded in Paine's discussion of the Bible's two worthy passages. The book of Job and the nineteenth psalm garner Paine's approval because they "take the book of creation as the Word of God, they refer to no other books, and all the inferences they make are drawn from that volume [of creation]."[12] The physical world—Paine's "book of creation"—is elevated in these two portions of Scripture in a commendable, scientific way. More to the point, Paine is particularly interested in what careful study of the sky reveals about the original human theology.

Paine argued that Psalm 19 and the book of Job "are theological orations comformable to the original system of theology."[13] That is, all theology can be, and originally was, derived from observing nature, especially "the structure of the universe."[14] Like the magical scientists of the Renaissance, Paine sought to understand the underlying principles of the cosmos—for this is all he can mean by "theology"—through a study of the stars. As Hugh Kearney writes, these early scientists sought "to recognize the fundamental structure of reality."[15] It was thought that such a science placed its practitioner in virtual control of the cosmos.

Science, understood as grasping the mathematical structure of the universe through study of the planets and stars, has always been, according to Paine, Christianity's mortal enemy. Indeed, he alleges that early Christian leaders tried to prevent science's development. They "could not but foresee that the continually progressive knowledge that man would gain, by the aid of science, of the power and wisdom of God, manifested in the structure of the universe and in all the works of creation, would . . . call into question the truth of their system of faith." Thus, these first Christian leaders actively opposed the development of science. They "cut learning down to a size less dangerous" to faith, and so "restrict[ed] the idea of learning to the dead study of dead languages."[16]

Christian myth versus scientific pantheism. If Christianity cannot be supported by science, how should we understand the faith? For Paine the Deist, faith is simply "another species of mythology" and a corruption of "an ancient system of theism."[17] To reclaim this pre-Christian system of rational belief, one must turn to science, especially astronomy. In fact, Paine traces the rise of theism itself to the worship of the planet Saturn. "The supposed reign of Saturn was prior to that which is called the heathen mythology, and was so far a system of theism that it admitted the belief of only one god." He adds, "All the corruptions that have taken place in theology and in religion have been produced by admitting of what man calls *revealed religion*," that is, the Revealed Word tradition and all of its offshoots.[18] Rational religion, on the other hand, derives from the scientific examination of nature, especially the careful study of celestial bodies.

In a section entitled "Comparing Christianism with Pantheism," Paine recommends a scientific alternative to Christianity. He labels this faith Deism, but it is a brand of pantheism that locates God in creation. "How different is [Christianity] to the pure and simple profession of Deism! The true Deist has but one Deity," he announces, "and his religion consists in contemplating the power, wisdom and benignity of the Deity in His works," that is, in nature.[19] For Paine, the Judeo-Christian tradition is a corruption of an ancient pantheism that can be reclaimed through science—the study of God "in His works." Nature does not so much point to a God outside of itself as it suggests that there is something divine in nature.

Astronomy, extraterrestrial life and scientific religion. Paine compared Science as the study of "the structure of the heavens," with the various "systems of religion."[20] Science, "the progression of knowledge," was the one true source of religion. Early Christians had recognized this fact, and thus tried to stop Science. Had Christianity not stifled Science, human knowledge of the cosmos would have developed indefinitely. This limitless scientific knowledge would have become the foundation of a scientific religion based on the mathematical structures of the universe and resulting in the limitless "progress of the human mind."[21] Christians had, then, prevented the advent of heaven on earth by their vision of a heaven beyond life.

Paine began developing his theology of Science at an early age. Even as a youth he "doubted the truth of the Christian system or thought it to be a strange affair."[22] From early childhood the "natural bent" of his mind "was to science." Thus, as soon as he was able he "purchased a pair of globes and attended the philosophical lectures of Martin and Ferguson" and became acquainted with other eminent astronomers.[23] He made himself master of the use of globes and of the orrery," a term referring to a "machinery of clock-work representing the universe [solar system] in miniature." Paine eventually became convinced of "the infinity of space, and the eternal divisibility of matter."[24]

In a section entitled "Advantages of Life in a Plurality of Worlds," Paine explains that this idea of an infinite space filled with divine life led him, as it had earlier led Giordano Bruno, to speculate that there are other intelligent species in the universe. "Since, then, no part of our earth is left unoccupied, why is it to be supposed that the immensity of space is naked void, lying in eternal waste?"[25] Rather, as we contemplate its vastness, "the immensity of space will appear to us filled with systems of worlds."[26] Recognizing that the universe contains "a *plurality* of worlds" should elicit "the gratitude of man as well as his admiration." Paine is confident that these other worlds are inhabited, and that "the inhabitants of each of the worlds of which our system is composed enjoy the same opportunities of knowledge as we do."[27] Though he claims to be following Science alone, Paine ends in speculation about inhabited planets in other parts of the universe as a source of religious awe and spiritual comfort.[28]

"The cheerful idea of a society of worlds" ought to function as an antidote to Revealed Word's puny vision of a single inhabited planet. "In the midst of those reflections, what are we to think of the Christian system of faith that forms itself upon the idea of only one world, and that of no greater extent, as is before shown, than twenty-five thousand miles? . . . Alas, what is this to the mighty ocean of space, and the almighty power of the Creator?" Christianity is wrong, for when one reflects on the skies "every evidence the heavens afford to man either directly contradicts it or renders it absurd."[29] Nature clearly teaches a religion, but that religion is not the Revealed Word.

Morality and transcendence. The perennial religious contest, then, pits the Revealed Word and its God against Science and Nature. Rather than trusting "that which is called *the Word of God,* as shown to us in a printed book that any man might make," Paine commends "the real word of God existing in the universe."[30] However, Paine faced two problems in advocating a scientific religion that venerated the natural order.

The first problem was finding moral content for a new religion inspired by merely contemplating the vastness of space and the numerous inhabited planets swimming in that vastness. Paine discovered a solution to this problem that has been employed many times since—morality in the new scientific faith derives from "contributing to the happiness of the living creation that God has made." This is the chief moral duty of scientific religion.[31] "Living creation" is an important phrase for Paine. Despite his references to a creator God, his strong implication in the second book of *The Age of Reason* is that the creation is, in fact, a living thing generating other living things.[32] Thus, actions that increase the happiness of the living natural order are moral, while those that work against its happiness are not.

Second, Paine needed a source of transcendence to replace the worship of the Revealed Word's personal God. Again, he invents a source of reverent awe often repeated since his day. Transcendence is discovered in contemplating the intricate order of the cosmos, an act of worship for Paine. Religious feelings "become enlarged in proportion as we contemplate the extent and structure of the universe."[33] Thus, Science can provide a sense of wonder that expands our spiritual consciousness and deepens our religious feeling.[34]

For Thomas Paine, Science was the basis for a new spiritual hope. Pantheism coupled with a close study of the structures of the universe—"the real word of God"—generates a rational, unifying religion as an alternative to the old, irrational tradition of the Revealed Word. Paine's argument hearkens back to the magical scientists of the sixteenth and seventeenth centuries who "looked forward to a Golden Age of universal wisdom (pansophia)" that would follow our deciphering of the secrets of the cosmos.[35] As the Enlightenment closed, Thomas Paine became an ardent advocate of this universal and scientific religion. His vision was pursued in the next century by a great American orator whose admiration for Paine was well known.

ROBERT GREEN INGERSOLL: SCIENCE AND DELIVERANCE

The public lecture was a popular form of entertainment in nineteenth-century America, and an important means of disseminating ideas. In the absence of radio, television and national newspapers, the public lecture performed some of the functions of modern mass media. Well-known political, religious and academic figures held large audiences in thrall with their eloquence and erudition. Even in small towns large crowds gathered on Main Street to hear Abraham Lincoln and Stephen Douglas debate, or congregated in a lecture hall to contemplate the philosophy of Ralph Waldo Emerson or the political ideas of Susan B. Anthony. Particularly famous speakers made regular appearances on the Chautauqua, Lyceum or other prominent lecture circuits. The Lyceum Movement, established in 1834, at one time had more than three thousand local branches.

Among the most famous and successful of these traveling speakers was a former army officer and Attorney General of the state of Illinois, Robert Green Ingersoll (1833-1899), known to his Christian opponents as Mr. Injure-soul. Born in Dresden, New York, the son of a Congregational minister, Ingersoll had little opportunity for formal education as a child but diligently educated himself. After studying law, Ingersoll was admitted to the Illinois bar in 1854, eventually developing a legal practice that brought him considerable income. He served as a Union cavalry colonel during the Civil War, and following the war became involved in politics as a persuasive Republican spokesman during presidential campaigns.

Ingersoll's interest in arguments against Christianity, coupled with his legal training and oratorical skill, led him to write volumes in opposition to traditional faith. He eventually became a highly sought-after speaker with a national reputation for eloquence and wit. At the peak of his fame in the 1870s and 1880s Ingersoll commanded the astonishing sum of $3,500 for a single evening of speaking. A prolific writer and lecturer, he published numerous books, articles and lectures on a variety of subjects, but was most famous for his brash attacks on Christianity and the Bible. The personal cost of his passionate assault on the Revealed Word was substantial, as Republican leaders refused to appoint Ingersoll to prestigious cabinet and diplomatic posts.

Ingersoll more than any other figure in late nineteenth-century America popularized a virtually religious faith in scientific progress. His lectures were intelligent, provocative, bombastic and superficially scientific. Ingersoll presented himself as a freethinking citizen asking tough questions and looking for honest answers. He was an ordinary person of common sense too clever to be duped by biblical myths and legends. Ingersoll invited his audiences to join the ranks of forward-looking, scientifically minded thinkers liberating themselves from outdated and unexamined religious notions. His most famous and influential speech, "The Mistakes of Moses," dismantles key narratives in the Pentateuch using scathing satire and biting wit. The speech places science in the dual role of critic of the old superstitions and source of a new spirituality. Ingersoll thus reflected a view of science now characteristic of the New Religious Synthesis.

According to Ingersoll, "all religious systems enslave the mind."[36] No existing religion is founded on "the facts of nature" as revealed by science. The goal of Science is "to go into partnership with these forces of nature" in order to benefit humankind.[37] No longer would modern thinking people need the Revealed Word's superstitions to explain either their existence or their destiny. Religious ideas bear no relationship to scientific knowledge. "What does religion have to do with facts? Nothing. Is there any such thing as Methodist mathematics, Presbyterian botany, Catholic astronomy, or Baptist biology?"[38] Liberating the popular mind from the dictates of the Revealed Word became Ingersoll's great public work. To light the way out of the dungeon of unscientific religious belief he held aloft "the torch of reason." And Science was reason's purest flame.[39]

The scientific attack in "The Mistakes of Moses." Ingersoll's goal in "The Mistakes of Moses" was to challenge on scientific grounds certain claims in Genesis and Exodus. He lived his entire life during the nineteenth century, a century of astonishing advances in the various sciences. Scientific discoveries in biology and geology seemed to render miracles incredible and the earth incalculably ancient. Ingersoll cast his critical gaze on famous biblical passages such as the creation of Eve from Adam's rib, the miraculous crossing of the Red Sea and the Israelite's subsisting on manna in the desert, subjecting them to scornful examination. Ingersoll attacked the Genesis notion that the sky is a "firmament" over the earth. "The man who wrote that believed the firmament to be solid. He knew nothing of the laws of evaporation."[40] He ridiculed the Noahic flood in Genesis. "How deep were these waters? About five and a half miles. How long did it rain? Forty days. How much did it have to rain a day? About 800 feet. How is that for dampness?"[41] Concerning the rainbow that appeared after the flood, Ingersoll asked his audiences the scientific question, "Now, can anybody believe that that is the origin of the rainbow? Are you not all familiar with the natural causes which bring about those beautiful arches before our eyes?"[42] In these and many similar examples Ingersoll hoped to demonstrate that Science employed by common sense overturns a literal reading of the Bible. And Science would also provide the Revealed Word's replacement.

The creed of Science: a new salvation. Ingersoll repudiated the Christian notion of salvation by faith. "Are we to get to Heaven by creed or by deed?" he asked. "Shall we reason, or shall we simply believe?" Christ's substitutionary atonement was an "infamy" that taught "that one man can be good for another, or that one man can sin for another." According to Ingersoll, "you have to be good for yourself; you have to sin for yourself." Thus, "the trouble about the atonement is, that it saves the wrong man." His alternative to such unscientific religion is summarized in three words: "Liberty, love, and law." With minds unencumbered by worries of an after-life, our goal becomes to make ourselves and others happy. "One world at a time is my doctrine," Ingersoll told his audiences. "Let us make some one happy here. Let every man try to make his wife happy, his children happy . . . and God cannot afford to damn such a man."

Ingersoll's gospel was that "humanity is the only real religion." Guided by Science, a new humanity will reject destructive ideas such as hell, sin, guilt and judgment and will "grasp each other's hands in genuine friendship."[43] A new spirituality elevates the title "human" above labels such as Baptist or Methodist. "Forget that [you] are Baptists or Methodists, and remember that [you] are men and women. These are the biggest titles humanity can bear—man and woman; and every title you add belittles them. Man is the highest; woman is the highest."[44] Recognizing our common humanity is spiritual fulfillment enough for the dawning age. "Instead of loving God, we love each other." In this way "real religion" is to "live for each other." A scientific society will emerge when we "build the fabric of civilization on the foundation of demonstrated truth."

To hasten the advent of this new spiritual order, scientifically minded people must "destroy the guide-boards that point in the wrong direction," a reference to the old spirituality of the Revealed Word. Like the futurist prophet that he understood himself to be, Ingersoll called his audiences to "dispel the darkness of ignorance" by turning toward "the sun of science."[45] And what is the creed suggested by the rising sun of Science?

In an important speech entitled "The Foundations of Faith," Ingersoll set out his moral code for the new religious age. He entitled it "The Creed of Science," though it makes no direct reference to science. Like the Deists' Reason, Ingersoll's Science teaches an ethic evident in the natural order of things. In fact, Ingersoll referred to this natural and universal morality as "the religion of reason." I will present the creed in its entirety, as it is the clearest and most complete statement of the scientific moral perspective Ingersoll hoped would replace the Revealed Word:

> To love justice, to long for the right, to love mercy, to pity the suffering, to assist the weak, to forget wrongs and to remember benefits—to love the truth, to be sincere, to utter honest words, to love liberty, to wage relentless war against slavery in all its forms, to love wife and child and friend, to make a happy home, to love the beautiful; in art, in nature, to cultivate the mind, to be familiar with the mighty thoughts that

genius has expressed, the noble deeds of all the world, to cultivate courage and cheerfulness, to make others happy, to fill life with the splendor of generous acts, the warmth of loving words, to discard error, to destroy prejudice, to receive new truths with gladness, to cultivate hope, to see the calm beyond the storm, the dawn beyond the night, to do the best that can be done and then to be resigned—this is the religion of reason, the creed of science. This satisfies the brain and heart.[46]

For Robert Green Ingersoll, then, Science had a clear spiritual dimension. It sought not simply facts about the physical universe, but a universal moral order. Only "the sun of science" could provide religious insight. Despite his experiences in the Civil War—a vicious conflict ignited by a loathsome practice—Ingersoll remained confident that natural human goodness, informed by Science, would provide the foundation of a new spiritual awareness destined to replace the Revealed Word. Science was the engine of religious progress, the source of a new religion that would carry us to a bright future.

CARL SAGAN: FROM *THE DEMON-HAUNTED WORLD* TO ALIEN *CONTACT*

No writer of the late twentieth century did more to popularize science than Carl Sagan. Prior to his death from cancer in 1996, Sagan was the David Duncan Professor of Astronomy and Space Sciences and Director of the Laboratory for Planetary Studies at Cornell University. He had also held such prestigious positions as the Distinguished Visiting Scientist at the Jet Propulsion Laboratory, California Institute of Technology. Sagan was cofounder and President of the Planetary Society, the world's largest space interest group. A prolific writer and television commentator on scientific issues, Sagan was a Pulitzer Prize recipient as well as the recipient of the Public Welfare Medal, the highest award offered by the National Academy of Sciences. Sagan was also involved in the American space program for many years. He received twenty-two honorary doctorates and the Oersted Medal from the American Association of Physics Teachers.

Sagan's public fame resulted from books such as *Cosmos* (which became an Emmy and Peabody Award-winning television documentary), *Billions and Billions* and the science fiction novel *Contact*, which was made into a popular movie starring Jodie Foster. *Cosmos* was the most widely read science book ever written. Carl Sagan wrote these extraordinarily popular scientific and fictional works as a bona fide scientific scholar, an expert with few peers. To unquestioned expertise he added charm, wit and transparency. Sagan brought science out of the laboratory and into the living room. Science was now for everyone's enjoyment, and it had wonderful and unexpected things to teach us. For his vast and attentive audience, Carl Sagan spoke as an unquestioned authority.

However, despite his impeccable credentials, numerous awards and unprecedented fame, Sagan was a controversial figure in the scientific community. This controversy had one source—Sagan's life-long interest in discovering intelligent beings on other planets. An enthusiastic backer of SETI, the Search for Extraterrestrial Intelligence, his passion for this project led to his rejection by many scientists who considered his quest to be pseudo-science.[47] Undaunted, the charismatic Sagan placed all of his considerable influence and personal charisma behind the project. He lived to see Harvard University establish the 8 million channel META/Sentinel survey, and an even more powerful NASA program begun as part of the ongoing search for intelligent life in the cosmos.

"The Demon-Haunted World." *The Demon-Haunted World: Science as a Candle in the Dark* was Carl Sagan's last book. The metaphor in the subtitle is revealing: in the twentieth-century's gathering darkness of rampant superstition and religious fundamentalism, science is a saving presence, a lone light in a dark place. In short, science offers humanity's only real *spiritual* solace. The book is a historical exploration of how scientists and other critically minded individuals have fought to expose spiritual charlatans, overturn groundless superstitions, and still the voices of religious enthusiasts. *The Demon-Haunted World* also elevates science as a source of wonder and transcendence, and argues that science and democratic values will provide the foundation for a progressively improving and increasingly peaceful human future.

According to its title, Sagan's lengthy statement on "science as social hope" is written against a religious idea—that demonic or other hidden spiritual forces exist and that they influence the daily lives of human beings. This benighted notion of a "demon-haunted world" becomes Sagan's metaphor for all that science seeks to dispel—occult causes, esoteric knowledge, dark superstitions, religious fundamentalism, barbaric persecutions and inhumane inquisitions. Though one would expect that the late twentieth century would no longer be witness to such irrational excesses, they are, in fact, on the increase. Moreover, this new dark night of the mind threatens to engulf the most scientifically advanced culture ever produced on planet earth. The world is again on the verge of submitting to the demons of our darker imagination, and in the process losing all that science has achieved. The light of science can alone rescue us from the new Dark Age. The fight is on.

Throughout his book Sagan contrasts fruitless religious practices with productive scientific ones. For example, he draws attention to science's enormous progress in overcoming human diseases. What hope does religion provide in such cases? Sagan poses the dilemma between science and faith: "We can pray over the cholera victim, or we can give her 500 milligrams of tetracycline every 12 hours."[48] And yet, Sagan can employ essentially religious phrasing to describe science. Of medicine's progress he writes, "This is a precious offering from science to humanity—nothing less than the gift of life."[49] Science is a magnificent edifice of demonstrable facts, while faith is an illusory house of imaginary cards. Thus he writes, "For me, it is far better to grasp the Universe as it really is than to persist in delusion, however satisfying and reassuring."[50]

Like Ingersoll and Paine, Sagan confidently affirmed that science would displace all spiritual explanations, and thus all false hopes. We have already embarked on the path of trading one worldview for another. "Plainly there is no way back. Like it or not, we are stuck with science. We had better make the best of it."[51] Nevertheless, some of us stubbornly try to make the return trip. Because of our discomfort with the power and sobriety of science we reach out to "pseudo-science," such things as creationism and alternative medical practices. These function as "a kind of halfway house between old religion and new science, mistrusted by both."[52] *The Demon-Haunted World* is as much an assault on pseudo-science as it is a rejection of religious explanations. And though Sagan is willing to concede that "science is far from a perfect instrument of knowledge," it nevertheless remains for him "the best we have."[53]

Responding spiritually to the cosmos. Sagan was a staunch opponent of what he took to be the excesses of religion. However, he was no enemy of "spirituality," by which he meant the human quest for the transcendent. Like many scientists writing for the trade book market today, he argues in *The Demon-Haunted World* that "science is not only compatible with spirituality; it is a profound source of spirituality." But, what does this surprising statement mean? By way of example, Sagan writes that "when we recognize our place in an immensity of light-years and in the passage of ages, when we grasp the intricacy, beauty, and subtlety of life, then that soaring feeling, that sense of elation and humility combined, is surely spiritual."[54] Scientific spirituality, then, means having an appropriate emotional response to the vastness and complexity of the cosmos science reveals. Sagan was not bothered that he lacked a scientific basis for calling such feelings spiritual. He simply chose to label them as such, apparently assuming his readers would find the label apt.

Sagan willingly blurred the line between what science can provide—explanations of physical events—and what it cannot—transcendence, moral guidance and a sense of the spiritual. *The Demon-Haunted World* is salted with such unscientific terms and phrases as "our place," "beauty," "subtlety," "soaring feeling," "elation" and "humility." Such ideas as these, however, have no empirical verification; no study provides their proof. On the other hand, terms such as "immensity," "light years," "ages" and "intricacy" may be scientific because they imply units of measure, or comparisons of physical phenomena. But Sagan freely mixed such terms and notions in his effort to find a transcendent science to satisfy the human soul, itself an entity incapable of scientific verification. Sagan the *scientist* held that only those objects and events that are physically present and empirically verifiable are "real" in any meaningful sense. As he said, "it is far better to grasp the Universe as it really is than to persist in delusion, however satisfying and reassuring."[55]

New objects of worship for a New Religion. For Sagan, science makes determinations about existence, and thus about worth. That is, science reveals what actually exists, and what actually exists is all that is worthy of our attention. In this discovery of true worth through science—the term *worship* literally meaning "to attribute worth"—Sagan replaced Revealed Word theology with what might be called Scientific Cosmology. By spiritualizing the cosmos, physical objects of worship replace spiritual ones in Sagan's new scheme. Similarly, Paine's worship of "God in his works" or Ingersoll's worship of "humanity" replaced Revealed Word worship of the God who created both the cosmos and humanity. Nevertheless, Sagan denied that his goal was to make science a matter of faith and worship. "Is this worshipping at the altar of science? Is this replacing one faith with another, equally arbitrary? In my view, not at all."[56]

However, Carl Sagan repeatedly opposed the Revealed Word to science, thus suggesting a contest between two *religious* views. Each claims a source of transcendence—God on the one hand, the cosmos on the other—and each recommends appropriate human emotional response to that transcendence. After all, Sagan urged that the appropriate response to the immensity of the cosmos is "a soaring feeling" and a "sense of elation and humility combined." A feeling of absolute, suicidal despair at the emptiness of space apparently is not an appropriate emotional response. Truth about the physical universe provides, for Sagan, the doctrine of a new scientific religion. Accordingly, scientists like Sagan function as a new order of priests assisting us to respond with the correct emotions to these truths.

In fact, Sagan argued that science is a better religion than the Revealed Word because science tests its doctrines empirically. Sagan asks, "What sermons even-handedly examine the God hypothesis?"[57] Forcing a face-off between the Revealed Word and science for the role of the one true religion, Sagan taunts: "Despite all the talk of humility, show me something comparable [to testing hypotheses] in religion." Divine inspiration and miracles are two ideas central to the Word, and neither idea can be tested empirically. Thus, each is rationally suspect. "Scripture is said to be divinely inspired—a phrase with many meanings. But what if it's simply made up by fallible humans? Miracles are attested, but what if they're instead some mix of charlatanry, unfamiliar states of consciousness, misapprehensions of natural phenomena, and mental illness?" Traditional religion is simply less reasonable than science when scientific standards are applied to it. "The fact that so little of the findings of modern science is prefigured in Scripture to my mind casts further doubt on its divine inspiration."[58]

Science thus becomes the only legitimate source of transcendence for Sagan. Even modern religions, those established after the rise of science, fail to "take sufficient account of the grandeur, magnificence, subtlety and intricacy of the Universe revealed by science."[59] Sagan's commitment to exploring the intersection of science and transcendence is even more pronounced in his science fiction work *Contact*.

"Contact." In Sagan's 1985 novel *Contact*, the brilliant maverick astronomer Ellie Arroway fights against great odds to convince a hidebound scientific establishment that a search for extraterrestrial life is a good use of scientific research funds. She succeeds, but only to have her funding yanked by self-interested scientific bureaucrats who are too narrow minded and ambitious to see the brilliant possibilities in her search.

Ellie Arroway is, then, a thinly veiled representation of Carl Sagan himself. On a shoestring budget she manages to set up a listening station with radio telescopes pointed heavenward. The climactic day finally arrives when a clear signal from outside our solar system reaches Ellie's listening station—beams of prime numbers, repeatedly transmitted. The heavenly signals, called suggestively "the Message," come from the Vega star system, and are followed by an enormous amount of numerical data which, it turns out, is a long series of instructions for building some sort of space craft. In Sagan's prophetic vision the stars have finally yielded up their numerical secrets.

Eventually Ellie Arroway secures funding from an eccentric and secretive billionaire who makes it possible to actually build the craft. Ellie and four others are allowed to enter the craft—referred to in the novel as "the Machine"—and are whisked away through a series of black holes and wormholes until they reach Vega thirty-three light years away from earth. The trip takes little more than an hour.

On Vega, Ellie carries on a long conversation with a Vegan who has assumed the exact appearance of her deceased father in order to alleviate her fears of the first contact. Sagan writes in a strikingly religious way of this strange encounter: "It was as if her father had these many years ago died and gone to Heaven, and finally—by this unorthodox route—she had managed to rejoin him. She sobbed and embraced him again." Ellie concludes, "this was their way of calming her fears. If so, they were very . . . thoughtful."[60] As it turns out, the aliens had entered her dream life the one night she slept on the new planet and taken memories of her father as the plans for this model. Apparently alien thoughtfulness does not extend to respect for the privacy of one's memories.

The Vegan who has assumed her father's form reassures Ellie that her science fiction notions of the work of intergalactic empires are passé. The Vegans are not space warriors, but cosmic bureaucrats.

VEGAN: "Don't think of us as some interstellar sheriff gunning down outlaw civilizations. Think of us more as the Office of Galactic Census. We collect information. I know you think nobody could learn anything from you because you're technologically so backward. But there are other merits to a civilization."

ELLIE: "What merits?"

VEGAN: "Oh, music. Lovingkindness. (I like that word)."[61]

Presumably, the Vegans are died-in-the-wool scientists like Sagan himself. And yet they, like Sagan himself, exhibit peculiarly unscientific moral preferences. The alien tells Ellie, "last night we looked inside you. All five of you. There's a lot in there: feelings, memories, instincts, learned behavior, madness, dreams, loves. Love is very important."[62] Love may be very important to Sagan, but is this a concept that can find validation through science, Sagan's candle in the dark?

Alien creators. As the dialogue between Ellie and the Vegan alien progresses, more facts come to light. It turns out that the Vegans are producing galaxies by redirecting energy that is being sucked into two black holes at the very center of the Milky Way. The galaxy currently under construction, Cygnus A, is one with which Ellie is familiar. Not surprisingly, she is surprised. "You're *making* Cygnus A?" The alien answers nonchalantly, "Oh, it's not just us. This is a . . . cooperative effort of many galaxies. That's what we mainly do—engineering." Civilizations abound in Sagan's universe as they did in Paine's. "You mustn't think of the Universe as a wilderness. It hasn't been that for billions of years," he said. "Think of it more as . . . cultivated."[63]

The reason for alien interest in galaxy creation is simple—the universe is slowly winding down. The Vegan explains:

> The basic problem is easily stated. . . . The universe is expanding, and there's not enough matter to stop the expansion. After a while, no new galaxies, no new stars, no new planets, no newly arisen lifeforms—just the same old crowd. Everything's getting run-down. It'll be boring. So in Cygnus A we're testing out the technology to make something new. . . . It's good honest work.[64]

The Vegans and their allies are working to create new matter in a universe that will eventually disappear without their efforts. That is to say, these superevolved, godlike beings are controlling the destiny of the universe itself. In fact, the Vegans already were involved in "galactogenesis"—the creation of galaxies—before life on earth had even gotten a good evolutionary start.

Scientific religion: pi in the sky. Ellie says at one point in her conversation with the alien: "I want to know about your myths, your religions." She then asks, "What fills you with awe? Or are those who make the numinous unable to feel it?" Here is the big question: What do virtual gods think about God? What is their understanding of ultimate reality, of "the numinous"? Sagan created the ultimate authority to answer our ultimate questions, presumably from a scientific point of view. The alien's answer is both intriguing and instructive. "I'll give you a flavor of our numinous. It concerns pi, the ratio of the circumference of a circle to its diameter." He continues, "After calculating pi out to ten billion places, the randomly varying digits disappear, and for an unbelievably long time there's nothing but ones and zeros." Ellie replies, "And the number of zeros and ones? Is it a product of prime numbers?" "Yes," he says, "eleven of them." "You're telling me there's a message in eleven dimensions hiding deep inside the number pi? Someone in the universe communicates by . . . mathematics?"[65]

This sequence of numbers, the virtually infinite calculation of pi, is referred to in *Contact* as "the Message," and the entire visible universe is created to reveal this hidden message to those knowledgeable enough to read and understand it. Ancient mathematicians such as Pythagoras, Renaissance astronomers like Brahe, even the great eighteenth-century physicist Sir Isaac Newton: all sought such a numerical key to the cosmos. Sagan reveals what he thought this key might be, thus aligning himself with an earlier scientific tradition. Is this the mystery of the universe unveiled, the final answer to humankind's religious longings?

Sagan the scientist, a determined materialist, suggested a source of transcendence in superevolved extraterrestrials, a means of conquering death through complete re-creation of individuals, the possible origins of some galaxies by the engineering feats of intelligent beings, and the notion that the universe is constructed around a numerically coded message. Carl Sagan wished that the world might find in science what he found there—hope, a sense of transcendence, and an antidote to religious superstition. Carl Sagan propagated the hope in science of the New Religious Synthesis as a source of numinous awe. As we shall see in the next section, the distinction between new and old religions is breaking down under pressure from a new breed of scientists who, like Paine, Ingersoll and Sagan, find in science a spiritual hope to rival the Revealed Word.

THE NEW PHYSICS: SCIENCE AND ANCIENT WISDOM

In his book *From Atom to Kosmos: Journey Without End*, Gordon Plummer demonstrates how the insights of astronomy reestablish "ancient wisdom."[66] Plummer is not alone in his assertion that what has been called the New Science confirms an old spirituality. Gary Zukav provided an early indication of the trajectory of much New Science writing in his bestselling book *The Dancing Wu Li Masters: An Overview of the New Physics,* published in 1979. After examining some of the findings of quantum physics, Zukav determined that the greatest insights of modern science were actually ancient theological insights capable of transforming Western spirituality. "The development of physics in the twentieth century," he writes, "already has transformed the consciousness of those involved with it."[67]

The specific religious insights of the New Science often contradict those of the Revealed Word, while simultaneously confirming Eastern religious thought. Zukav writes, "the study of complementarity, the uncertainty principle, quantum field theory, and the Copenhagen Interpretation of Quantum Mechanics produces insights into the nature of reality very similar to those produced by the study of eastern philosophy." He adds, "We need not make a pilgrimage to India or Tibet. There is much to learn there, but here at home, in the most inconceivable of places, amidst the particle accelerators and computers, our own Path without Form is emerging."[68] Ancient wisdom and the New Science are so similar, teach so many of the same truths, that the terms *experiment* and *pilgrimage* become synonymous.

Science in the New Religious Synthesis is a means of discovering spiritual knowledge. But for many of its advocates, science also confirms ancient wisdom. Thus, Marilyn Ferguson writes in *The Aquarian Conspiracy*, "Science is only confirming paradoxes and intuitions humankind has come across many times but stubbornly disregarded."[69] This ancient wisdom—of consciousness in stars and planets, of spiritual energy in objects, of magical properties in numbers, of mystical forces in nature, of fundamental spiritual unity in the human race, of a spiritual world just beyond our sensory experience—anticipates many discoveries of the New Science. "The new science," writes Ferguson, "goes beyond cool, clinical observations to a realm of shimmering paradox where our very reason seems endangered."[70]

Advocates of the New Science present these paradoxes as scientific discoveries. For example, physicist Amit Goswami suggests that science now shows that "consciousness is fundamental" to all that exists. Moreover, "science proves the potency of monistic philosophy over dualism—over spirit separated from matter."[71] That is to say, science proves that God and the physical universe cannot be two different things, as the Revealed Word suggests they are. This scientific discovery is, Goswami admits, essentially a religious tenet. "This philosophy accommodates many of the interpretations of human spiritual experience that have sparked the various world religions."[72] Still, Goswami and other New Scientists treat it as a scientific discovery.

Another physicist writing about the New Science, Fred Alan Wolf, also finds ancient wisdom to be proven by modern scientific investigations. Hindu philosophy posits that present experience is *maya*, a self-generated illusion. Wolf maintains that science proves that "the universe is being created in a dream of a single spiritual entity" and that our own consciousness and our own dreams are but reflections of that one great cosmic soul. "Reality," writes Wolf, "is not made of stuff, but is made of possibilities that can be coherent so that possibility forms into matter."[73] Again modern science confirms the ancient Eastern religious idea that we create our own personal realities.

Fritjof Capra is quite explicit that such spiritual insights came to humankind originally through religious channels, not through science. In his groundbreaking 1974 publication *The Tao of Physics*, Capra announced that even though the "changes brought about by modern physics have been widely discussed by physicists and philosophers over the past decades, very seldom has it been realized that they all seem to lead in the same direction, toward a view of the world which is very similar to the views held in Eastern Mysticism."[74] He writes, "In modern physics, the universe is always experienced as a dynamic, inseparable whole which always includes the observer in an essential way." Capra adds that this experience "is very similar to that of the Eastern Mystics. The similarity becomes apparent in quantum and relativity theory, and becomes even stronger in the 'quantum-relativistic' model of subatomic physics where both theories combine to produce the most striking parallels to Eastern Mysticism."[75]

More recently, Capra has again asked readers to reject "the concepts of an outdated worldview"—apparently the Revealed Word—and called on them to embrace a new spirituality supported by the insights of a new physics. Science now provides us with "spiritual or religious awareness." He adds, "It is . . . not surprising that the emerging new vision of reality is consistent with the so-called perennial philosophy of spiritual traditions, whether we talk about the spirituality of Christian mystics, that of Buddhists, or the philosophy and cosmology of the Native American traditions."[76] Thus, not only is science the source of fundamental spiritual insights, but it is also the source of a new pluralism that unites various religious traditions.

The Revealed Word tradition, however, insists upon the reality and persistence of individual identity. That is, individuals possess an identity or "self" that continues to exist even after the end of physical life. But, Capra argues, science proves that such a view is unfounded. "The Buddhist doctrine of impermanence includes the notion that there is no self—no persistent subject of our varying experiences. It holds that the idea of a separate individual self is an illusion, just another form of *maya*, an intellectual concept that has no reality." Science, then, proves Buddhism correct in its assumption that our experience of a fixed reality and a separate identity are more apparent than real. Buddhism teaches that "to cling to this idea of a separate self leads to the same pain and suffering *(dukha)* as the adherence to any other fixed category of thought." Interestingly, "science has arrived at exactly the same position."[77] The Revealed Word repudiates such a view, and must now do so in the face of scientific objection.

The old distinction between religion and science, then, has all but disappeared. Goswami writes that "today, modern science is venturing into realms that for more than four millennia have been the fiefdoms of religion and philosophy." Under the guidance of science, we are evolving to a higher level of spiritual understanding that confirms the ancient wisdom. "We are privileged to be a part of this evolutionary and transcendent process by which science is changing not only itself but also our perspective on reality."[78]

CONCLUSION

Canadian anthropologist Jeremy Narby has written recently that while "shamanism, as classically defined is reaching its end, . . . bringing scientists and shamans together seems more like a beginning."[79] Narby's suggestion would have been unthinkable to any self-respecting member of the scientific community forty years ago, but something dramatic occurred in the sciences during the second half of the twentieth century. The wall between the scientific and the spiritual was breached, and spiritual insight became a matter of scientific interest as it was for the medieval alchemists and Renaissance magical scientists. Zukav has written that we should "not be surprised if physics curricula of the twenty-first century include classes in meditation."[80] What are these popularizers of science as spirituality telling us about the impending spiritual future?

They may be telling us that the Revealed Word's role in that future will be limited, for its assumptions impede the progress of scientific spirituality. First, Revealed Word theology is dualistic, separating God and the physical universe, but science now proves that all things are a single thing or essence. Second, a writer like Carl Sagan would likely say that the very idea of a Creator impedes scientific advancement by filling the world with unobservable "demons." Third, the Revealed Word renders nature a mere artifact of such a Creator, thus obscuring its inherent divinity.

Writers in the New Science are also telling us that science's role as a source of spiritual insight and guidance will only increase, and for good reason. More than a century ago, Ingersoll argued that science promotes harmonious human relationships and conquers humanity's perennial ills such as war, hunger and disease. Two centuries ago Paine was already contending that science provided a sense of transcendence as we contemplate the vast inhabited spaces of the cosmos. Today, a host of writers urge that science confirms the perennial philosophy, that ancient wisdom of primitive human spirituality lost under the disastrous dominion of the Revealed Word. In fact, among the New Science's two principal goals today is to establish on empirical grounds this ancient wisdom, the early and foundational spiritual outlook of the human race before we were encumbered by Revealed Word theology. Its other great goal is explored in the next chapter—infusing modern religious thought with the hope of humanity's inevitable and complete spiritual transformation through evolutionary change.

6

EVOLUTION AND
ADVANCEMENT

The Darwins' Spiritual Legacy

As I lay in the tub thinking, I wondered how long it would be before scientists would find ways to verify the evolution of the soul in the same way that they had verified the evolution of the body.

SHIRLEY MACLAINE, Dancing in the Light

The soul has come to the body, and the body to life, for the purpose of evolution. You are evolving, you are becoming.

NEALE DONALD WALSCH, Conversations with God

Evolution is a continuous breaking and forming to make new, richer wholes. Even our genetic material is in flux. If we try to live as closed systems, we are doomed to regress. If we enlarge our awareness, admit new information, and take advantage of the brain's infinite capacity to integrate and reconcile, we can leap forward.

MARILYN FERGUSON, The Aquarian Conspiracy

Where do advanced human souls go? There are many forms of Life that exist as advancements of this one. There are literally millions of options. There is life in numerous galaxies.

GARY ZUKAV, The Seat of the Soul

The young prophet spoke confidently, his words an unquestioned revelation to his rapt listeners. The death of a friend that year, 1844, had prompted a discourse on the human soul, the nature of God and the relationship between the two: "There are very few beings in the world who understand rightly the character of God," he announced, and some clarity on this question was needed. "I will go back to the beginning, before the world was, to show what kind of being God is." The prophet promised to reveal "the designs of God in relation to the human race, and why he interferes with the affairs of men."[1]

His next statement, which the prophet termed "the great secret," clearly demarcated his theology from the Revealed Word and its preexistent divinity: "God himself was once as we are now, and is an exalted man, and sits enthroned in yonder heavens. That is the great secret." Were a human being able to see God, "you would see him like a man in form—like yourselves, in all the person, image, and very forms as a man." The traditional idea that "God was God from all eternity" was erroneous, for "God himself the Father of us all, dwelt on earth." Of perhaps even greater import to the listeners gathered that April day in the frontier town of Nauvoo, Illinois, was the admonition, "you have to learn how to be Gods yourselves . . . by going from one degree to another, and from a small capacity to a great one."[2]

Employing an apt analogy for gradual spiritual ascent, the Prophet continued his exposition on the advancing soul. "When you climb a ladder, you must begin at the bottom, and ascend step by step until you arrive at the top; and so it is with the principles of the Gospel: you must begin with the first, and go on until you learn all the principles of exaltation." Their own minds and spirits could develop endlessly, with divinity itself within their grasp. "All the minds and spirits that God ever sent into the world are susceptible of enlargement."[3] This truth of the enlarging mind, the expanding soul, the ever-evolving, divinity-destined human spirit was central to the new gospel of Jesus Christ, as it had been delivered to the prophet Joseph Smith.

Bestselling research psychologist Robert Ornstein has written extensively on the topic of the evolution of human consciousness, and is today perhaps the leading expert on the subject. His books include *New World, New Mind: Moving Toward Conscious Evolution* and *The Evolution of Consciousness: The Origins of the Way We Think*. Ornstein thinks the time has come for human beings to seize control of the evolution of the mind. The human mind possesses "an endless supply of possible capabilities, waiting to be called on in response to the new necessities of the new world we've created." Thus, we must undertake "conscious evolution," a process that "may be easier, closer at hand, and more liberating than we might normally think."[4] "Conscious selection," as opposed to natural selection, is the means by which we "take our evolution in our own hands by developing the ability to select parts of the mind."[5] In *New World, New Mind* Ornstein and coauthor Paul Ehrlich call for a "solution" to our inability to adapt to a rapidly changing world. They write, "the 'solution' is not simple—to generate the social and political will to move a program of conscious evolution to the top of the human agenda."[6]

Ornstein's vision of evolving consciousness is neither new nor unique. It also occurred to many readers of Darwin's *On the Origin of the Species* in 1859 and is today a foundational component of the New Religious Synthesis. Even prior to Darwin, progressivist thinking had suggested continual evolution of the body and the spirit. Joseph Smith's progressive theology was fully developed by 1844, while Herbert Spencer had postulated in 1855 that "mind had evolved out of life as a form of adaptation."[7]

This chapter considers several early proponents of continuing human evolution, including Charles Darwin's brilliant grandfather Erasmus Darwin. But not until Charles Darwin provided evolution with a credible scientific foundation was it possible for writers such as T. H. Huxley in England and Ernst Haeckel in Germany to make a convincing public case for continuing evolution as human destiny, one resting on more than speculation or prophetic utterance. After Darwin's *Origin of the Species*, proponents made continuing human evolution seem inevitable, indeed morally essential. The scientific vision of a spiritually evolving human race set the stage for writers of fiction to furnish us with vivid images of an exalted future for the human race.

ERASMUS DARWIN

Charles Darwin's brilliant and eccentric grandfather Erasmus (1731-1803) was England's most famous physician and perhaps its most knowledgeable scientist at the end of the eighteenth century. His advanced studies began at St. John's College, Cambridge, and his medical degree was completed in 1756 at Edinburgh University. The elder Darwin was also a tireless inventor, a talented poet and an ardent opponent of Christianity. He helped to start the Industrial Revolution in England along with other members of the famous Lunar Society of industrialists and inventors, including Josiah Wedgwood and Richard Edgeworth. Erasmus Darwin was also a theorist of education, basing many of his ideas on the work of Rousseau, with whom he corresponded.[8]

Despite his reputation as an original thinker and talented writer, admirers of his famous grandson at one time suppressed Erasmus Darwin's works. This tactical historical censorship was an effort to save Charles Darwin from the charge that his grandfather's strange theories—Erasmus believed that plants possessed a soul— had any influence on his own. Moreover, Erasmus Darwin, for all his brilliance, was an eccentric who delighted in writing erotic poetry and whose romantic escapades were legendary. Any link between Erasmus and Charles Darwin might compromise the latter's status as an original and respectable scientific thinker.

Fluid materialism. Erasmus Darwin's greatest influence came through his own theory of evolution. His famous book, *Zoonomia, or the Laws of Organic Life* (1794-1796), is a massive medical treatise arguing a straightforward evolutionary hypothesis.[9] In *The Temple of Nature*, a popular poem setting out his evolutionary views for the public, he "traced the progress of life from microscopic specks in primeval seas to its present culmination in man."[10] These works advance a concept dubbed "fluid materialism." As Edward Reed explains, "For [Erasmus] Darwin all of animate nature was possessed of sensibility and feeling, even plants." Thus, Darwin "sought the material basis for this sensibility in a subtle fluid or ether in the body and nerves, basing his ideas on the influential fluid theory of electricity developed by his friend Benjamin Franklin."[11] Darwin subjected many of his medical patients to electrical shocks in hopes of understanding the universal life force he was so certain existed. His theories and experiments gave Mary Shelley the idea for her book *Frankenstein*.

Erasmus Darwin believed that life evolves toward higher levels of complexity and happiness, a commitment that became for him a virtual religion. As one biographer notes, Darwin "weaves his evolutionary ideas into the wider philosophy of organic happiness."[12] Thus, "evolution was no casual speculation" for Erasmus Darwin, "but a belief he lived with for thirty years and one which moulded his whole philosophy of life."[13] As we shall see, Erasmus's grandson Charles shared much of his grandfather's faith.

Finding a cure for religion. According to Erasmus Darwin, the human mind or soul has a physical basis. In both *Zoonomia* and *The Temple of Nature*, Darwin speculated that "objects of thought" were merely "the movements of the relevant neural fibers" and that these movements were vibrations, an idea found earlier in the work of David Hartley.[14] The upshot of Darwin's speculation was to put human mental or spiritual life on a biological and evolutionary plane, making all aspects of our conscious existence products of natural processes. Thus, human religious feelings and beliefs—including those expressed in the Revealed Word—also were material in nature, simple movements of "relevant neural fibers."

In fact, the staunchly anti-Christian Darwin found conventional religious beliefs pathological and prescribed appropriate psychological cures in *Zoonomia*. To cure the mental illness of belief in hell, for instance, Darwin prescribed the remedy of ridicule. "Those who suffer under this insanity are generally the most innocent and harmless people," he conceded. And though "the voice of reason is ineffectual . . . that of ridicule may save many."[15] Religious beliefs result from environmental factors such as early training, which cause "intellectual cowardice" to be "instilled into the minds of the people from their infancy." This cowardice "prevents inquiry" into religious beliefs. The medical cure in such cases "is to increase knowledge of the laws of nature." In this way we are able to "emancipate ourselves from the false impressions we have imbibed in our infancy, and to set the faculty of reason above that of imagination."[16] That is, science is the proper cure for religious belief. Similarly, so-called sins were simply the result of nerve vibrations, and could also be cured by proper therapy. Wrong action was merely a matter of doing what one's nerves told one to do; right action could be engendered by sound nerve therapy. Moral guidelines would be derived from what Darwin termed "universal love."[17]

Darwin, Frankenstein and the Romantics. Though his name and ideas are not widely known today, Erasmus Darwin's influence on writers and thinkers of his own day was enormous. Considered by some contemporaries to be the greatest intellectual figure of the day, his idea of fluid materialism was particularly influential in the early development of Romantic thought. Around the time of Darwin's greatest popularity, the poet William Blake in his *Marriage of Heaven and Hell* has the devil repeat a distinctly Darwinian idea: "Energy is the only life and . . . Reason is the bound or outward circumference of Energy."[18] Edward Reed writes that his "relative obscurity nowadays should not lead us to ignore the impact of Darwin's fluid materialism, which was, at the very least, one of the major physiological and psychological theories propounded between 1798 and 1815."[19] Among those falling under the Darwinian spell was the great English surgeon William Lawrence and, through Lawrence, his patient Percy Shelley. Shelley's wife, Mary, was the author of the famous novel *Frankenstein*, a work she acknowledged to have written while pondering Erasmus Darwin's ideas. She and her husband "talked of the experiments of Dr. Darwin," concluding that "perhaps a corpse would be re-animated" through electrical shock treatment if "the component parts of a creature" could be "brought together, and endued with vital warmth."[20] Darwin had suggested to the great writer that life—physical, mental and moral—might arise out of matter alone without divine intervention.

Erasmus Darwin's influence on a generation of English thinkers and artists was extraordinary. Coleridge, Wordsworth, Percy Shelley and Keats all took Darwin's ideas seriously. Desmond King-Hele writes that "Darwin was the most important single influence on the English Romantic poets."[21] For Wordsworth and Coleridge, Darwin's *Botanic Garden* "had a longer and stronger effect" on their thinking than did the French Revolution.[22] Wordsworth "came to adopt a religious creed very similar to Darwin's, including the idea of a vague Power lying behind the processes of Nature, and as much concerned with Nature as with Man." In addition, Shelley's great poem *Prometheus Unbound* advocates "regeneration of the world through Universal Love" on the model of Darwin's *The Temple of Nature.* Blake, Byron and Crabbe are among the other English Romantics who looked to Darwin for inspiration.[23]

Erasmus Darwin was a skilled public advocate, one remarkably successful in propagating his ideas about evolution, nature and the progress of life. He wrote with the intellectual confidence of a noted medical expert, but also with the grace and force of a poet. His ideas were both popular and controversial from the moment they appeared in *Zoonomia* and *The Temple of Nature.* Many contemporaries considered the elder Darwin the greatest and most original thinker of the age. Others understood that this eccentric scientist's ideas were revolutionary and intentionally anti-Christian. Within two years of its first publication, Thomas Brown answered *Zoonomia* in his 560-page *Observations on the Zoonomia of Erasmus Darwin.*

LAMARCK AND SPENCER

Herbert Spencer (1820-1903) is an important transitional figure in the development of ideas about human evolutionary progress. Before Charles Darwin had published *On the Origin of the Species,* Spencer had already formulated and advocated a theory of human social progress based on the early evolutionary theories of French naturalist Jean Baptiste Lamarck (1744-1829). Lamarck's theory emphasized progress and improvement, and "Spencer must have delighted in the notion, easily extractable from Lamarck," that both nature and society were on "an exciting, buoyant, optimistic course, bouncing onwards and upwards."[24] Spencer, armed with his Lamarckian view of an ever-progressing cosmos, exerted tremendous influence over nineteenth-century thought. John Passmore writes that Spencer's "agnostic-evolutionary philosophy" literally "swept the world."[25]

Lamarck rejected the traditional notion that animal species were unchanging. His *Philosophie zoologique* (1809) argues the descent of current species from earlier ones, but his ideas about *how* evolution occurred were not convincing. Lamarck imagined organisms adapting to actual physical constraints more or less on the spot, and then passing these changes on to their offspring. In his most famous example, early and greedy giraffes slowly stretched their necks to reach leaves at the tops of trees. As these giraffes were more successful at getting food, they also had a greater chance of reproducing. Though eventually overturned, Lamarck's theories were nevertheless employed to justify various theories of human progress. Spencer never abandoned Lamarck's theory.[26] However, when Darwin's more plausible theories were made public, Spencer recognized their greater persuasive potential for supporting his theory of human social and moral progress.

An evolving society, an evolving race. Spencer argued in *Social Statics* (1850) that human progress was inevitable, the increasing complexity of organisms over time being his chief evidence. Spencer, not Darwin, coined the phrase "survival of the fittest," and he argued for a ruthless social system of free enterprise that paid no heed to the needs of the "unfit" poor. Some human beings are more advanced than are others, and they demonstrate this fact by their capacity to acquire knowledge, wealth and power.

Racism seemed always to emerge from evolutionary thinking at this time. According to Spencer, the European race was the most highly evolved. In *First Principles,* Spencer wrote of the residents of Papua New Guinea, "Though often possessing well-developed body and arms, the Papuan has very small legs; thus reminding us of the man-apes, in which there is no great contrast in size between the hind and fore limbs." However, "in the European, the greater length and massiveness of the leg has become marked." Similarly, facial features proved the higher evolutionary status of Europeans. Spencer argued that "the higher forms" of human race are "distinguished by the relatively larger size of the bones which cover the brain, and the relatively smaller size of those which cover the jaws." Moreover, "this trait, which is stronger in Man than in any other creature, is stronger in the European than in the savage."[27] And, we might add, even more pronounced in the celluloid alien than in the European, a notion to which we will return toward the end of this chapter.

Spencer's melding of the metaphysics of progress and the biology of evolution would have many imitators, and he remained a major figure in the development of the doctrine of progressive evolution. A. N. Wilson has written that Spencer "bolstered up two . . . key superstitions: the idea of life as perpetual progress— the life of the universe as well as the life of societies and individuals; and, secondly, the idea that Science would provide the key instrument of progress."[28] These "key superstitions" of the Victorian age have now been incorporated into the New Religious Synthesis.

CHARLES DARWIN: NATURALIST PROPHET

The period from 1840 to 1900 was one of profound and extensive intellectual change in the Western world. In the wake of the Enlightenment's caustic criticism of the Revealed Word, powerful new explanations of the human condition emerged to challenge the traditional account of creation, fall and redemption. The most influential intellectual figure of this period was Charles Darwin (1809-1882), whose *Origin of the Species* (1859) changed forever how life's origins and development on earth were understood.

It goes without saying that Darwin's evolutionary hypothesis has affected assumptions about biological life's development. Most educated people today accept that biological advancement takes place by degrees over a long period in response to external pressures. This basic biological hypothesis has also greatly influenced thinking in a range of disciplines including religion. Darwin's life is important to understanding his most famous idea and its considerable influence on contemporary religious thought.

Charles Robert Darwin was born into a prominent and prosperous British family in 1809. His mother was the daughter of the wealthy potter and industrialist Josiah Wedgwood—friend of Erasmus Darwin—and his father was the successful doctor Robert Waring Darwin. Darwin's early life was one of unusual social privilege and stimulating intellectual contact. Robert Darwin, son of Erasmus, adopted his father's beliefs about both evolution (he accepted it) and Christianity (he rejected it). Thus, though Charles Darwin was born six years after his brilliant grandfather's death, Robert Darwin became a conduit to his son of much of Erasmus Darwin's thought.

Charles Darwin received a good early education, and in 1825, at his father's direction, he went on to study medicine in the family tradition at Edinburgh University. A sensitive boy, Darwin was repulsed by macabre scenes in the dissection theatres. Consequently he turned most of his attention to naturalism. In Edinburgh Darwin came under the influence of the famous marine biologist Charles Gray, an evolutionary theorist in his own right. But Charles was not seriously committed to his studies and spent much of his time hunting and collecting natural specimens.

In 1828 his father directed him to enter Cambridge University to study for the ministry. Darwin had no real interest in the ministry, but a clerical position would allow him leisure to pursue his real passions—hunting and naturalism. Darwin spent much of his time in Cambridge collecting and categorizing species of beetles.

In December 1831, at the recommendation of his beloved botany professor, Reverend John Stevens Henslow, Darwin was made naturalist on the H.M.S. Beagle, which was sailing to the South American coast. This famous voyage lasted nearly five years, Darwin returning to England October 1836. During the Beagle's long Pacific adventure, Darwin became an expert on the plants and animals of several regions.

Between 1836 and 1846, Charles Darwin's reputation as a naturalist grew due to his many publications on topics ranging from volcanic islands to the anatomy of tropical birds. He had become one of England's leading naturalists. In 1844—fourteen years prior to publication of the Origin—Darwin developed a theory of the means by which one species gradually changes into a distinct and separate species. That year he wrote to his friend, the botanist James Hooker, "I think I have found out . . . the simple way by which species become exquisitely adapted to various ends."[29] He termed the mechanism of evolutionary change "natural selection."

Though he arrived at his fully developed theory of evolution by natural selection in the early 1840s, Darwin waited to announce his speculations in a scientific paper read in 1858. His theory of transmutation from one species to another resulted from long and serious study of natural phenomena, including painstaking collection and dissection of many species of animals, barnacles being his special interest. Darwin finally published his theory of evolution in book form in 1859, largely due to concern that another naturalist would get credit for it. This other naturalist, Alfred Russel Wallace (1823-1913), had not only developed a theory of evolution strikingly similar to Darwin's, but had also arrived at the mechanism Darwin called natural selection. Wallace sent a manuscript describing his own evolutionary theory to Darwin for review in 1858, an act that finally persuaded Darwin to publish On the Origin of the Species.

Darwin's famous book first appeared November 1859 and went rapidly through six editions. Though the initial print runs were small, On the Origin of the Species was soon selling as many volumes in England and America as were the novels of Dickens.[30] The Origin created enormous controversy and is one of the few works whose publication can be said to have changed all subsequent intellectual life.

Darwin's diminishing religion. Darwin's famous theory has created as much controversy in the realm of religion as it has in the life sciences, and for understandable reasons. His hypothesis challenges the Revealed Word view of special creation by providing a scientific justification for believing that life on earth progressed from single-celled organisms to human beings without divine intervention in the process. Darwin's religious views apparently influenced his interest in evolution and may have shaped both his basic theory and the arguments he employed publicly to defend that theory. But what were Darwin's religious views, and what relationship do they bear to his ideas about evolution? The answer to this question has been the subject of much speculation and controversy.[31] The following facts seem matters of general agreement.

Raised in a family of Unitarian women and skeptical men, Darwin was not much exposed to traditional Christian thought in his home. As his views on evolution developed, his faith in God diminished further. The apparent cruelty and randomness of nature eroded his trust in Paley's argument from design. Darwin found nature a ruthless, barbaric battleground in which the random variations of survivors accounted for the physiological features of all species. Paley's argument from design had once drawn Darwin toward theism, but his own theory of evolution by natural selection tended to "banish design from the universe."[32] Darwin eventually saw no need for God or design "to explain the beautifully effective hinge of a bivalve shell or even more perfect adaptations."[33] The power behind nature was not a personal and creative God but impersonal natural forces producing design through evolution. For Darwin, brute biological facts argued against a benevolent God and for the heartless "deity" of natural selection.

The Unitarianism with which he grew up also affected Darwin's thinking about spiritual matters. Theology is insignificant in Unitarianism because God is an inexpressible enigma. The universe operates according to natural laws that preclude miracles, and these laws render God's activity in nature unnecessary. Darwin came to embrace a completely materialist view—nothing exists but physical matter. As his biographers Adrian Desmond and James Moore write, Darwin concluded that "wild animals are not the product of God's whim any more than planets are held up by his will."[34] Frank Brown adds, "Considerably after Darwin's rejection of Christianity, theism itself began to seem to him difficult to establish."[35]

Once Darwin's case against Revealed Word assumptions was fully developed in his own thinking, the great naturalist became an ardent foe of the faith. "Disbelief crept over me at a very slow rate, but was at last complete," he wrote. "The rate was so slow that I felt no distress and have never since doubted even for a single second that my conclusion was correct."[36] The strident nature of Darwin's opposition to Christianity is not well known in part because relatives excised from his papers angrier comments about the faith so as to save the family embarrassment and to protect Darwin's public image. These hostile comments have now been restored to the text of his autobiography.

"The mystery of the beginning of all things is insoluble by us," he wrote, "and I for one must be content to remain an Agnostic."[37] But this bland statement hardly captures the real tenor of Darwin's thought on the issue. His position regarding Christianity resembles the adamant Deism of his grandfather Erasmus. "I can hardly see how anyone ought to wish Christianity to be true, for if so the plain language of the text seems to show that the men who do not believe, and this would include my Father, Brother and almost all my best friends, will be everlastingly punished. And this is a damnable doctrine!"[38]

Darwin had other reasons for rejecting traditional Christian teachings. An intensely sensitive man prone to various illnesses, Darwin found it difficult even to be present in public settings. Throughout his long life he was deeply bothered by the suffering that he knew to be an inherent part of natural existence. The suffering of animals was for Darwin a powerful argument against God's care for living things. Like Voltaire, Darwin reasoned that God, if he exists, must be omnipotent. And yet, if God is omnipotent he has chosen not to prevent the suffering of animals. Darwin concluded that the idea of a benevolent and omnipotent God "revolts the understanding, for what advantage can there be in the suffering of millions of the lower animals throughout almost endless time?"[39] The loss of a beloved daughter to a painful disease at the age of ten cemented Darwin's conviction that the Christian idea of a loving God was a charade.

Charles Darwin, then, made public his argument for evolution for a variety of personal and professional reasons. He sought to advance science by presenting a plausible mechanism for the development of different species. Darwin also wanted recognition for an important scientific discovery, fearing credit might go to Wallace if he did not publish his views. But Darwin was also interested in arguing from biological science against the Christian doctrine of an omnipotent and benevolent deity.

Darwin the rhetorical strategist. Darwin did not disseminate his ideas in public lectures nor in the classroom; his patrician social status ensured that he never actually had to teach or lecture to earn a living. Rather, his advocacy of evolution was done through his many publications. As Edward S. Reed writes, "The most famous scientist of the [nineteenth] century never once gave a public presentation of his revolutionary theory, not even in the form of a classroom lecture!"[40] But the success of Darwin's ideas was not hindered by the absence of their author from the public lecture stage, for Charles Darwin was a skilled rhetorical strategist and an accomplished writer of persuasive prose.

Though readers assume that Darwin wrote as a scientist for other scientists, he is clearly also seeking to persuade the general reading public in *On the Origin of the Species*. He certainly sought fame beyond the halls of the academy, and his great work was intended for the common reader as much as it was for the scientist. One measure of his rhetorical success is the fact that the *Origin's* impact has always been felt as dramatically in popular thinking about science, society and religion as it has been in the realm of professional biology. Darwin's rhetorical maneuvering deserves closer examination.

Darwin scholar John Campbell has focused attention on Darwin's efforts to make his ideas persuasive to a dubious public.[41] Both the scientific world and the public were disinclined to accept that species of plants and animals emerged gradually through evolutionary change, and were thus not the products of special divine creation. Even Darwin's term "natural selection" was selected more for its persuasive potential than for its actual descriptive accuracy.

In positing natural selection, Darwin was applying to biology the theories of controversial English economist Thomas Robert Malthus (1766-1834). Malthus observed that "food supply increases arithmetically while population increases geometrically." The result is that "not as many organisms live as are born." Darwin added this "thoroughly negative" economic doctrine to the biological notions of variation and inheritance. Campbell notes that "when one combines variation, inheritance, and the struggle for existence" the result is "differential reproduction"—the idea that some members of a species have a reproductive advantage over others. "Allow differential reproduction to continue over virtually unlimited time in an unlimited variety of changing environments and the result is organic change or evolution."[42]

This, in a nutshell, is Darwin's theory of evolution, and it owes much to Malthus's ruthless reasoning. As Franklin Baumer states the point, Darwin pictured nature as "a great battleground, not unlike the world of contemporary economics." In the economic world of mid-nineteenth-century England, "individuals competed for an insufficient food supply, and . . . victory went to luck rather than to cunning."[43] Many readers then and now import the notion of progress to Darwin's basic theory, the idea that evolution involves not merely change, but improvement. However, progressivism is not actually present in Darwinism as advanced in *On the Origin of the Species*. Evolution under the Darwin theory is random, unintentional and undirected. His carefully chosen metaphor of "selection," with its implied analogy to domestic animal breeding, suggests something the theory does not deliver. Biological life in a Darwinian world is not headed anywhere in particular—it just happens.

Darwin on progress: nature imperfectly solving problems. Darwin was himself largely responsible for the interpretation that evolution is progressive, for his carefully chosen language was intended to implant the idea in his readers' minds. Darwin writes in the *Origin*, "natural selection tends only to make each organic being as perfect as, or slightly more perfect than, the other inhabitants of the same country with which it has to struggle for existence. And we see that this is the degree of perfection attained under nature."[44] Within the limits of his theory, however, Darwin's term "perfection" can only mean "reproductively advantageous change." In the same section in which he mentions "perfection," Darwin also draws attention to the limits of that perfection. The stinger of a honeybee, for instance, functions in such a way that the bee dies after stinging an intruder. This, clearly, is not a perfect design, though the bee's actions benefit the colony.[45]

Darwin's strategic reason for placing the notion of "perfection" next to examples of "imperfection" is to argue a specific point: natural selection, not a divine hand, solves practical problems in the natural order. Improvements do occur in the evolutionary process, but they are not the perfect solutions one would expect of God. A divine designer would not create the stinger that kills the bee. This contrivance came about because at one time the stinger was a tool for boring—thus, barbed or serrated—that later was "adapted" to use as a weapon of defense. God would never have set out to design the bee's stinger in this clearly imperfect way, creating in the very process of design a fatal disadvantage to the individual creature. However, the bee's adaptation is still perfect in a limited sense, that is, reflecting the "degree of perfection attained under nature." Darwin's argument from an "imperfect perfection" is tactical, allowing him to argue *for* adaptation by natural selection while at the same time arguing *against* divine design.[46]

Darwin also sought to make *ultimate* progress by means of natural selection appear benevolent compared to certain temporary natural states which, if the result of divine design, rendered God cruel. Darwin thus strategically presented these biologically momentary states as mere steps along the way to something more advanced, that is, as stages in a progressive succession toward "higher" or more complex forms of life. As Campbell points out, "Darwin takes several of nature's ingenious adaptations and underscores the embarrassment they cause to the customary belief in divine goodness." Campbell quotes a relevant passage from Darwin's works:

> Finally, it may not be a logical deduction, but to my imagination it is far more satisfactory to look at such instincts as the young cuckoo ejecting its foster-brothers—ants making slaves—the larvae of the ichneumonidae feeding within the live bodies of caterpillars—not as especially endowed or created instincts, but as small consequences of one general law, leading to the advancement of all organic beings.[47]

Darwin's argument is couched in such a way as to make evolution *compatible with* theism, a view Darwin had himself already relinquished. It appears that he wished to maintain the public appearance of faith in God, while arguing the opposite thesis throughout the *Origin*. Darwin argued that if evolution moves toward improved species or "higher animals," then God is saved from the charge of cruelty. But, as we shall see, saving the dignity of God clearly was not Darwin's motive in advancing this argument and thus his theory.

Natural and artificial selection. The master strategy behind Darwin's eventual persuasive success was his metaphor of "natural selection" itself, an implied comparison of the undirected and wholly physical processes of evolution to the highly intentional, goal-directed work of the animal breeder. In deploying this metaphor, Darwin walked a very fine line between rhetorical stratagem and outright deception. Darwin compares nature to a breeder, both of whom "eliminate certain individuals from their breeding stocks." But, Campbell adds, "nature is not like the breeder in that nature does not consciously choose certain animals or plants to achieve a foreseen end."[48] Campbell notes that Darwin's particular use of the term "selection" in the *Origin* "is unusual and technically false," "misleading" and "inaccurate." And, we should add, enormously successful, for Darwin was able to not only win a hearing for his views, but to convince many readers who, frankly, did not understand his argument while being convinced that they did.

Charles Darwin eliminated the need for divine involvement in the biological world. In fact, he seemed to have eliminated the need for purpose in nature altogether. There was no Designer behind the design of nature, and even the apparent design, if one looked closely, was flawed in just such a way as to suggest that all living things were the survivors—albeit improved survivors—of a great battle rather than the products of a divine craftsman. A playwright behind nature's scenery was unnecessary to explain the drama of life; it was all about a fight over food among the players on stage. "If Darwin's hypothesis was correct, then mind was indeed 'pitchforked' out of the universe, as Samuel Butler put it."[49]

Darwin the progressivist: a new divinity. Nevertheless, another component must be added to the story of Charles Darwin and his theory before considering its later applications. Apparently Darwin *did* believe in evolutionary progress, and himself held out the hope of a physically and morally perfected human race. In spite of the fact that his famous theory clearly is not progressive, Darwin both believed in ultimate human progress and thought his theory supported such a belief.

The leading expert on the question of Darwin's views on progress is Robert Richards of the University of Chicago. In his book *The Meaning of Evolution* Richards points out that "Darwin expressed his belief in a progressive, natural selection dynamic" in his notebooks as early as 1839, twenty years before the publication of the *Origin*.[50] In fact, Richards argues that Darwin's "notion of an innate tendency to change gradually faded in his theory" and was replaced by "the supposition of environmental forces producing the kind of variation that could be transmuted into progressive forms during the development of species."[51]

What is Richards saying? Just this—that Charles Darwin increasingly attributed to the completely undirected process of natural selection a virtually willful concern for progress. As Richards writes, "In the *Origin*, Darwin augmented the power of this progressive dynamic by attributing to natural selection the beneficent concern for the good of creatures, a concern that had been formerly expressed by the recently departed Deity." For Darwin, "natural selection altruistically looked to the welfare of the creatures selected."[52] Thus, the theory of evolution, with its central mechanism of natural selection, was specifically intended by Darwin to take the place of God in a scheme of natural relationships that tended inherently toward progress. Richards adds that progressivism had been incorporated into every theory of evolution that had influenced Darwin's thinking, including those of his teacher Grant, his grandfather Erasmus Darwin, the great French scientist Lamarck and several others.[53]

Darwin's theory "banished God from the universe" and introduced in his place the possibility of scientifically justified "progress." Of course, the Darwin theory does not posit a mechanism for continuing improvement or progress through evolutionary change. Rather, Darwinian change within members of a species is random and does not tend toward any particular culmination point or eventual destiny. It may be said to suggest improvement only when that term is defined as "improved capacity to reproduce," or perhaps as "greater biological complexity." Thus, though Darwinism is popularly taken to imply gradual progression toward "higher forms of life" and perhaps eventually toward biological perfection, his theory of evolution does not support such an interpretation. When Darwin spoke of progress, he was not speaking as a biologist.

Some Darwin defenders have argued that progressivism was a misinterpretation of evolution by those wishing to use the theory to support political and social concepts. However, according to Richards, progressivism was close to Darwin's heart, and Darwin himself was largely responsible for this erroneous interpretation of his theory. Hopeful of a meaningful natural world tending in some discernable direction, Darwin sometimes spoke as a believer in progressivism. For instance, he wrote in his autobiography: "Believing as I do that man in the future will be a far more perfect creature than he now is, it is an intolerable thought that he and all other sentient beings are doomed to complete annihilation after such long-continued slow progress."[54] Thus, the Revealed Word notion that the human race would one day be annihilated with an ensuing judgment was an intolerable doctrine to Darwin. His rival hope, now a mainstay of the New Religious Synthesis, was for ultimate human perfection by means of evolution.

Edward Reed writes, "The mid-nineteenth century was a time when most serious thinkers in Europe were eager to hear progressivist accounts of both natural and civil history."[55] In the nineteenth and early twentieth centuries, however, progressivism could not be separated from racism, and for most European believers in progressivism, the future of the human race was a white future. "Humans were the most highly developed creatures on earth, were they not? And certain humans (European, male, well heeled) were the best of the best—who could doubt it?"[56] It is not clear whether Charles Darwin himself accepted the racist implications of evolutionary progressivism, but he also did not attempt to overturn the use of his theory to prop up such speculations by others. After all, belief in racial progress helped to promote his theory, something Darwin never obstructed.

Many Victorian intellectuals found Darwin's dismissal of God from the universe spiritually liberating, in large measure because it seemed to open the way for unlimited human progress. God's dismissal put humanity squarely in the cosmic spotlight and placed human destiny in human hands. George Bernard Shaw, always on the lookout for an exotic theory to prop up his humanistic egoism, wrote that Darwin's friends "actually regarded the banishment of mind as 'a glorious enlightenment and emancipation' from a moribund theology and Biblicism. 'We were intellectually intoxicated with the idea that the world could make itself without design, purpose, skill or intelligence: in short, without life.'"[57]

Frederick Pollock recalled the reaction of Cambridge students after steeping themselves in the basics of Darwinian antitheology: "We seemed to ride triumphant on an ocean of new life and boundless possibilities. Natural Selection was to be the master-key of the universe; we expected it to solve all riddles and reconcile contradictions. Among other things, it was to give us a new system of ethics." W. K. Clifford, a friend of Pollock's at Cambridge, developed a system of ethics based on natural selection.[58] As we shall see, the tendency to appropriate the progressive aspects of Darwin's theory have persisted, and they have been propagated in various arenas including popular religious thought.

THE SPIRITUAL VISION OF DARWIN'S EARLY DEFENDERS

The notion of perfecting the human race was a potent idea well before Darwin published his *Origin* in 1859. For example, the lapsed American Congregational minister John Humphrey Noyes (1811-1886) advocated controlled breeding to achieve human progress in the 1840s. Procreation was strictly forbidden in his Oneida Community (est. 1848) without Noyes's approval. He called his approach to eugenics "stirpiculture," and considered it a logical outgrowth of progressive thinking. Noyes determined which men and women would be allowed to reproduce in order to propagate certain physical, mental and spiritual characteristics.

Noyes wrote before such thinking about human progress had any real scientific grounding, however. Following the publication of *The Origin of the Species*, a host of English and Continental intellectuals speculated about the moral and spiritual possibilities inherent in Darwin's solidly scientific theory. These thinkers often authored works for the general public that provided a highly credible, scientifically grounded case for a new view of human advancement.

Prominent British scientist, physician, lecturer and close Darwin family friend T. H. Huxley (1825-1895) was known as "Darwin's bulldog" for his tenacious defense of Darwin's theory of evolution. Huxley, perhaps the leading naturalist of his day, did what the reticent Darwin could not—mount an energetic, even flamboyant public defense of evolution through natural selection. A charismatic speaker and gifted debater, Huxley relished the opportunity to address large crowds of working class men—the "cloth hats"—about the new scientific discoveries that were challenging the settled convictions of the church. Huxley sought nothing less than to foment a revolution in religious thought predicated on his friend Darwin's discovery.

T. H. Huxley recognized the many implications of Darwin's evolutionary ideas for an emerging Western culture that would be governed by a scientific rather than a Christian worldview. What principle would provide the moral foundation of a world without traditional "revealed" religion? Perhaps evolution itself suggested the contours of a new morality. Huxley often speculated about the possibilities of human moral evolution, a progression from survival of the fittest to survival of the morally soundest. In his book *Evolution and Ethics* (1893), for instance, he wrote that "social progress" for human beings meant "checking the evolutionary process at every step" and substituting for biological evolution the process of moral evolution, "which may be called the ethical process." The result of this process is the survival of the morally fittest. Though Huxley detested the spiritualism and occultism that had captivated the Victorian mind, he did view life's emergence through biological evolution as a springboard into an even more astounding possibility—the process of human evolution from one level of moral attainment to another. That is, Huxley recognized that Darwin had discovered the spiritual future of the human race, a future free of the constraints of religion.

Another British scientist directly influenced by Charles Darwin on the point of human advancement was Darwin's own cousin, Francis Galton (1822-1911). Galton, with Darwin's approval, advanced the first fully developed theory of eugenics in books such as his *Hereditary Genius* (1869). His ideas took Darwin's strategic analogy of evolution to animal husbandry and applied it to the breeding of humans. J. W. Burrow writes, "One decided whom one wanted to breed and rear offspring and then tried to arrange the environment accordingly. It was akin to what Darwin in *The Origin* had called 'artificial selection.'" Such selective breeding of humans was to be overseen by "a rational elite."[59]

Many of Darwin's ideas were also adopted and developed by the phenomenally popular German evolutionary theorist, Ernst Haeckel (1834-1919). The first important advocate of Darwinism in Germany, Haeckel popularized the idea of human evolutionary progress in Europe through his many books and lectures. His ideas provided a foundation for eugenic theories and experiments in the late nineteenth and early twentieth centuries. Just one of Haeckel's books, *The Riddle of the Universe*, sold 100,000 copies in one month soon after its publication in 1899. The tone of his writing was ferociously anti-Christian, and he argued strenuously for a new religion founded on evolutionary theory. The details and surprising success of Haeckel's effort to found an evolutionary religion will be discussed in the next chapter.

As noted above, the hope of scientifically improving the human race intoxicated a wide range of European intellectuals in the late nineteenth and early twentieth centuries. Eugenics was often viewed as a vehicle to achieve a physically and morally perfected human race. The examples of intellectual figures who promoted the practice are too numerous to list, Haeckel being one of the more prominent and credible. Another important figure in the eugenics movement was the French psychiatrist August Forel (1848-1931). Forel wrote, "We hope that the eugenics of the future, if well applied, will even be able to improve by small degrees the quality of our higher races," by which he meant Europeans.[60]

Forel, like Haeckel, was enamored of the evolutionary possibilities for human advancement and envisioned a future in which science supplanted religion. He advocated a "scientific religion of man's well-being" that would be "the religion of the future." Sounding much like Robert Green Ingersoll, Forel wrote that this religion "must be free from doctrine and metaphysics, uniting all that is truly good and purely human in the ancient religions."[61] The doctrine-bound Revealed Word tradition would have to be set aside in favor of a modern, scientific religion capable of encouraging evolutionary advances.

The works of Huxley, Haeckel, Galton, Forel and many other leading European intellectuals at the end of the nineteenth century show some tenets of the New Religious Synthesis already solidly in place. Clearly, any notion of a sovereign God directing human destiny had been rejected, and reason was given the task of shaping humanity's destiny following the principles of evolution. Science replaced the Revealed Word as a source of religious hope by providing the techniques necessary to bring about humanity's perfection. The spiritual future of the human race would derive from humanly directed, evolutionary moral advancement.

JULIAN HUXLEY: TRANSHUMANISM AND THE MORAL ELITE

T. H. Huxley's grandson Sir Julian Sorell Huxley (1887-1975), brother of the famous essayist and novelist Aldous Huxley, has been called the greatest Humanist of the twentieth century. An accomplished scientist and graduate of Balliol College, Oxford, Huxley was appointed the first director of the United Nations Educational, Scientific and Cultural Organization (UNESCO) in 1947. In the mid-twentieth century Huxley was a famous news broadcaster and a frequent lecturer in America and England. His many books include *Religion Without Revelation* (1927), *Evolution: The Modern Synthesis* (1942) and *New Bottles for New Wine* (1958). Huxley was a leading figure in evolutionary biology and a highly successful popularizer of both scientific findings and his own metaphysical speculations based on those findings.

Julian Huxley presented his message of freethinking, human evolutionary destiny and moral advancement to hundreds of thousands in the Western world. His "transhumanism" was a doctrine of evolutionary progress toward a morally or spiritually perfected human race. The religion of the new human race would consist in the reverent contemplation of its own evolutionary destiny. A fundamental change in the universe occurred when evolution finally produced human consciousness. "As a result of a thousand million years of evolution, the universe is becoming conscious of itself, able to understand something of its past history and possible future."[62]

The conscious life of a human being is the ultimate goal that biological life has been seeking from the very beginning. The next stage in human evolution is cosmic self-awareness—a conscious awareness of the direction and purpose of human evolution. This stage of development is "being realized in . . . a few of us human beings." Though it offends liberal notions of democracy, the idea that only an elite will take the next evolutionary step seems in keeping with the basic mechanics of evolution. So only a few human beings are destined to take remarkable evolutionary bounds. "Do not let us forget that the human species is as radically different from any of the microscopic single-celled animals that lived a thousand million years ago as they were from a fragment of stone or metal."[63]

Evolution, metaphysics and human destiny. In his hugely successful and frequently reprinted work *Evolution: The Modern Synthesis,* Julian Huxley described the current state of evolutionary science for English and American readers between 1942 and 1974.[64] For Huxley, as for his brother Aldous, evolution was undeniably progressive, a fact the public readily accepted. "The confusion appears to be greater among professional biologists than among laymen," Huxley writes.[65] Evolutionary progress was crucial to Huxley's metaphysical system, and he drives the point hard against those who reject the idea as unscientific.

For Huxley, "dominant types" branch out and take over territory inhabited by other species. Such biological conquest demonstrates, not just change, but progress. It is clear that these dominant types reveal "efficiency in such matters as speed and the application of force to overcome physical limitations."[66] The "final results" of progress appear in "the historical fact of a succession of dominant groups" occupying ever more territory.[67] Thus, "evolutionary progress" means "increased control over and independence of the environment," and by this criterion humans are the current evolutionary leaders.[68]

Though he was a scientist, Huxley's interest in evolution was ultimately metaphysical, focusing on a human race whose evolutionary destiny had to be recognized in order to be realized. In the climactic section of *Evolution,* entitled "Progress in the Evolutionary Future," Huxley argued that "conscious and conceptual thought is the latest step in life's progress." There will not be a proliferation of new species from the human stock, but rather one new species resulting from the "crossing and recombination" of human genetic material. Human beings will "set limits" on this process based on the environment available for the new species to inhabit.[69]

In keeping with New Synthesis thinking, science will direct the creation of this new human species. Scientists must insist on "greater disinterestedness and fuller control of the emotional impulse," an idea Sir Julian attributed to his brother, Aldous. Old-fashioned moral restraint of the type suggested by the Revealed Word, as well as irrational limits on scientific research rooted in concerns over "playing God," must be dispensed with. The "brain's level of performance could be genetically raised" in various ways. "Castes" could be created with special capacities needed by the society.[70] The very best among us—"the best endowed ten-thousandth"—would be the model and goal of such experimentation with human genetic engineering. "Nor is there any reason to suppose that such quantitative increase could not be pushed beyond its present upper limits."[71]

Progress, mysticism and the religious impediment. Capacities such as "telepathy and other extra-sensory activities of the mind" would be goals of genetically guided evolution in humans. Of course, inherited traits that hinder advancement may have to be eliminated from a more evolved humanity, just as our earlier ancestors got rid of scales and grew hair. Human "values" themselves must be examined and determinations made about which ones to keep and which ones to jettison. "Control and independence," the twin criteria of progress, would guide such decisions.[72]

Huxley muses that "true human progress consists in increases in aesthetic, intellectual, and spiritual experience and satisfaction." His foundational concern appears to be spiritual, with a particular spiritual tendency viewed as the most desirable—the mystical experience. "Control" rests with the human being when he achieves "independence of inessential stimuli and ideas." The result is "the satisfaction of mystic detachment and inner ecstasy."[73] His brother's well-known experiments with hallucinogens may have suggested such a view.

Rejecting as "wholly false" the idea that human destiny is directed by "some external power"—the view of Darwin's rival, Alfred Russel Wallace—Huxley argues for *human* directedness in future evolution. "It is we who have read purpose into evolution," he writes. "If we wish to work towards a purpose for the future of man, we must formulate that purpose ourselves. Purposes in life are made, not found."[74] And finding such purpose is our destiny. "The future of progressive evolution is the future of man," he writes. "The future of man, if it is to be progress and not merely a standstill or a degeneration, must be guided by a deliberate purpose."[75] That "deliberate purpose" ought to be the ultimate driving force of science.

A great conflict of fundamental human values will occur between those who can envision the human evolutionary future and those who cannot, those who have moved beyond the traditional religious values of the Revealed Word, and those who remain rooted in the past. Repeating Darwin's own complaint against Christianity, Huxley writes, "another struggle still in progress is between the idea of a purpose directed to a future life in a supernatural world," that is, in heaven, "and one directed to progress in this world." However, "until such major conflicts are resolved, humanity can have no single major purpose, and progress can be but fitful and slow."[76] The Revealed Word's dominance in the Western world, where science is the most advanced, has been the principal impediment to human evolutionary advancement. "Man must work and plan if he is to achieve further progress for himself and so for life."[77] This "work" might reasonably involve propagating a new spiritual view more amenable to such progress.

PIERRE TEILHARD DE CHARDIN: REACHING THE OMEGA POINT

French Jesuit priest, geologist and paleontologist Pierre Teilhard de Chardin (1881-1955) was perhaps the twentieth century's greatest advocate of spiritual evolution. "During his formative years, Teilhard was greatly influenced by both of his parents: his father was an avid naturalist while his mother was a devout mystic." As a result, from an early age "Teilhard became interested in both science and religion."[78] One commentator writes that Teilhard offered "a new framework for those believers who take science seriously and concern themselves about the future of humankind."[79] The Catholic Church withheld publication of many of his works until after his death, fearing that his ideas were unorthodox. His books are now foundational works of progressive spiritual thought.

Henri Bergson's book *Creative Evolution* (1907) "convinced Teilhard of the truth of evolution." He thus "devoted the rest of his life to a personal attempt at reconciling science and theology within an evolutionary interpretation of this dynamic universe."[80] Evolution was the fundamental principle of the cosmos, and Teilhard afforded humans a central place in the "evolving universe." The evolution of the cosmos was "both progressive and directional."[81] Teilhard dubbed the terminus of human evolution the Omega Point, a state of "mystical unity" and "spiritual love."[82]

Writing in *The Future of Man* (1959), Teilhard praised the efforts of Aldous Huxley "to formulate and crystallize . . . the basis of a common philosophy on which all men of goodwill can agree in order that the world may continue to progress." Teilhard believed such an effort would hasten the day when, "in religious thought as in the sciences, a core of universal truth will form and slowly grow to be accepted by everyone." He asked, "Can there be any true spiritual evolution without it?" In Teilhard's vision, "mankind is to achieve a breakthrough straight ahead by forcing its way over the threshold of some higher level of consciousness."[83]

One commentator writes, "Teilhard always maintained that the whole universe is evolving spirit (since matter is energy and, for him, all energy is ultimately spirit)."[84] Humanity as part of this evolving universe is destined to evolve with it. Teilhard referred to the elite group destined to achieve a spiritual evolutionary breakthrough as the "Sacred Union" and "the active minority" of the human race. These spiritually gifted individuals constitute the "solid core around which the unanimity of tomorrow must harden."[85]

The final step in spiritual evolution results in "all the separate consciousnesses of the world converging" into one great consciousness centered on love. When this breakthrough occurs, humanity will have created out of itself a new divinity. This is the Omega Point, the messianic moment when an evolving, converging human consciousness issues in "the rise of God."[86]

Teilhard de Chardin joined the scientific and the religious ideas of a new age, making the evolutionary notion of constant, incremental improvement the foundation of a new spirituality. Recently a number of popular writers have developed this idea to the point that it has become the centerpiece of the New Religious Synthesis. One of those authors is the focus of the next section.

JAMES H. AUSTIN: EVOLVING BRAIN, EVOLVING SPIRIT

James H. Austin is emeritus professor of neurology at the University of Colorado. His recently published *Zen and the Brain: Toward an Understanding of Meditation and Consciousness* is an encyclopedic 840-page synthesis of brain research and Zen philosophy. His book serves as a bridge between the biological progressivism of Darwin and the more spiritually oriented evolutionary thinking explored in the next chapter.

Austin, writing as a recognized expert in brain science, argues that Zen Buddhism's emphasis on meditative techniques holds the key to understanding the brain's continuing evolution. He contends that Westerners, accustomed to understanding God as the Creator, are not immediately open to Eastern explanations of human consciousness. However, "as we learn more about Zen's subtler mechanisms, we shall discover . . . [that] its messages are not really that alien to the West after all." In fact, Austin suggests that "human brains everywhere gravitate toward the same kinds of natural messages."[87] And these natural messages are more closely aligned with Eastern than with Western spiritual systems.

Following his exhaustive overview of the literature on the brain's development, Austin offers his readers a musing on the future of the brain and, indeed, of the human soul. He accepts the notion of continuing human evolution, one of the most persistent consequences of the Darwinian worldview and a mainstay of the New Religious Synthesis. Austin asks his readers to consider whether "still other forces" in addition to biological ones might have been at work in our continuing evolution. "The Jesuit Teilhard de Chardin thought so," he notes. "He perceived that humankind was also progressing through sequences of *spiritual* development" as a "natural consequence of the fact that the human species was still evolving biologically."[88]

Evolution and human destiny. Where will this continuing process of human spiritual evolution end? Teilhard apparently believed that at some distant moment that he termed the Omega Point all human beings would achieve the equivalent of the Buddha's enlightenment. Austin is less sanguine. When looking at the history of the human race, the idea of "universal enlightenment" sounds to Austin "like too grandiose a Utopia."[89] Nevertheless, Austin finds various kinds of evidence pointing to the spiritual progress of at least a portion of the human race.

For instance, he argues that early Buddhist philosophers "were especially far-sighted" about our evolutionary destiny. "In the old city of Nara, there exists today a sublime statue which depicts their long-range faith" in our spiritual evolutionary progress. This seventh-century statue is of "*Miroku* (Maitrea), the Buddha of the future" and this statue bears "remarkably 'modern' facial features." Moreover, "a closer look discloses another curious feature about this Buddha of the future." The statue, as it turns out, "has *two* protrusions, one on either side of the top of the head *next* to the midline" when other Buddha heads "are limited to only one *ushnisha* in the midline." Austin asks, "Was the remote sculptor sending us some kind of message? Will evolved brains of the future be twice as enlightened?"[90]

Austin explores the crucial assumption of the New Religious Synthesis that human spiritual evolution follows directly from the notion of biological evolution, though he lacks Teilhard's confidence that such evolution is in store for everyone. "So, how realistic is an expectation that fallible human beings will evolve" to a point where they are "*all* Buddha-like in their degree of enlightenment?"[91] Still, some of us are already spiritually well on our way. Those capable of experiencing "advanced alternate states of consciousness" demonstrate that at least some human brains possess great capacity for change. Thus it seems likely that "some of our adaptable descendants," in particular "those whose education has gentled them and made them more flexible," are certain to "build on their experiences" and thus "become increasingly free to adapt creatively to survive future crises."[92] Some future humans with the right genetic equipment and access to the right kind of education will evolve to the next plane of spiritual achievement.

New Age stirpiculture? For Austin, the key Darwinian mechanism of natural selection may carry us onward to our spiritual destiny. "Let a few more persons multiply who had survived because they had greater capacities for such adaptability, and the resulting series of events might go on slowly to change the ethical and religious climate of the far distant future."[93] But why wait for the spiritual future to arrive by the slow conveyance of natural selection when we can speed up the process of change? "One can at least imagine," Austin writes, "a new era when some religious group within a culture might decide that it needed to raise and train a new leader." In the distant future "the ancient custom of searching all over for the right baby" would have disappeared. Moreover, "'reincarnation' would finally be appreciated as something determined solely by the laws which govern the human genome."

Lining up these possibilities, Austin concludes that "in this far-distant future it might be realized that the desired child could best be conceived in a test tube and nurtured in a surrogate mother." Sounding a bit like John Humphrey Noyes, Austin writes, "entering into the ever-braver union would be the ovum donated perhaps by a virginal nun, plus the sperm from an exemplary monk, both of whom had been screened and selected on the basis of their outstanding lineage and capacity." And what ought our response be to such hopeful spiritual eugenics? Austin replies, "Our task is to take a deep breath and to accept that such a blessed event is now *technically* possible. And not to scoff too quickly."[94]

For Austin, the progression from biological to spiritual evolution is a natural one that suggests the trajectory of ultimate human destiny. "Infinitesimal steps" akin to those of biological evolution slowly reveal "the human potential to evolve toward illumination at more advanced levels. For ours is still a species on an endless journey into an unimaginable future."[95] In addition, Austin seems confident that this future may be hastened by scientific research into the mechanisms of the brain, under the direction of the insights of Zen and other meditative traditions. Such research might suggest how to direct the process of evolution toward enlightenment. "As one of the byproducts of such research, it would be of interest to develop ways of identifying at a young age, *prospectively*, those persons who do have the potential to mature into our classic ideal of the saintly sage: a next Dalai Lama, a future Mother Theresa, or a Krishnamurti in the making, so to speak."[96] Austin's speculations bring us to the brink of an intentional union between spirituality and reproductive science in the search for our spiritual future.

JAMES REDFIELD: THE CELESTINE PROPHET

Spiritual evolution is now a potent spiritual idea reflected in a wide range of both popular nonfiction and fiction. James Redfield's bestselling adventure story *The Celestine Prophecy* (1993) reflects the concept's centrality to a new genre of spiritual fiction. For Redfield, spiritual advancement is a direct outgrowth of biological evolution, and his story presents the idea in a winsome and persuasive fashion as a matter of modern common sense. *The Celestine Prophecy*'s protagonist searches a Latin American country for a mysterious manuscript bearing spiritual secrets. In an instant of cosmic insight after reading the manuscript, he realizes that he is on an evolutionary journey that began with the first helium atoms beginning to "vibrate." Vibration is the fundamental principle of life itself in *The Celestine Prophecy* and has been a common theme in evolutionary writing since the days of Erasmus Darwin and "vitalism."

According to Redfield, evolutionary progress is tied directly to an individual's insights into the evolutionary process itself, a view not far removed from Julian Huxley's thinking on the matter. "I perceived everything to be somehow a part of me," Redfield's unnamed narrator tells us, this insight triggering a personal recollection of the evolutionary hypothesis in an almost mystical vision. "The science of evolution had always bored me, but now, as my mind continued to race backward in time, all the things I had read on the subject began to come back to me . . . [and] the recollection allowed me to look at evolution in a new way."[97]

Matter, he realizes, is not solid, but rather is vibrating energy operating under a "ruling principle" that causes it to continuously organize itself into more and more complex forms. Basic matter—hydrogen—organized itself into helium, helium into stars, and hydrogen and helium into lithium. "The stage was now set," he understands in an instant of illumination, "for the next step of evolution."[98] To make a long evolutionary story short, matter continues to organize itself into progressively more complex systems until "great lightning storms" on earth cause matter in "shallow pools and basins" finally to "leap past the vibratory level of carbon" to become amino acids. Inevitably life appears, and then more complex life. At the end of it all, "the progression ended. There at the pinnacle stood humankind."[99]

As Redfield tells the grand story, evolutionary progress came about through increasingly higher pitched "vibration." The progressive evolution of matter, guided by a "ruling principle," produces "humankind" as its final outcome. But, as with Julian Huxley and Teilhard de Chardin, humanity is not a finished work.

The spiritually sensitive Father Sanchez patiently explains the mechanics of spiritual evolution in *The Celestine Prophecy*. "We fill up, grow, fill up and grow again. That is how we as humans continue the evolution of the universe to a higher and higher vibration." In this way, "evolution has been going on unconsciously throughout human history." This fact "explains why civilization has progressed and why humans have grown larger, lived longer, and so forth. Now however," Sanchez adds, "we are making the whole process conscious. That is what the Manuscript is telling us. That is what this movement toward a world-wide spiritual consciousness is all about."[100] The emerging "world-wide spiritual consciousness" will involve the elimination of all distinctions among the world's various religions as realization dawns that each in its own way is assisting human spiritual evolution. The new consciousness also means the elimination of unhelpful concepts such as a fall from grace, sin and evil as inherent components of human nature.

SCIENCE FICTION AND HUMAN EVOLUTIONARY DESTINY

Inevitable human progress through evolutionary processes is a theme in some of the most imaginative and persuasive science fiction. It is particularly important to the works of three pillars of British science fiction: H. G. Wells (1866-1946), Olaf Stapledon (1886-1950) and Arthur C. Clarke (b. 1917). That Wells would have devoted attention to human evolutionary advancement is not surprising considering that he was a student at Huxley's London School of Science.

Bulwer-Lytton's "The Coming Race." The idea of human evolutionary progress appears in some of the very earliest works in the science fiction genre. Sir George Edward Bulwer-Lytton (1798-1871) was a popular English fiction writer of the nineteenth century who produced an extraordinary number of novels and short stories between about 1835 and his death in 1871. Among his last works was the strange novella about a journey beneath the surface of the earth entitled *Vrilya: The Power of the Coming Race*, better known simply as *The Coming Race*. The book "created a sensation" when it first appeared in 1871.[101] A skilled storyteller, Bulwer-Lytton combined current scientific theories, racialist dogma, speculation about the ancient Egyptians and a love story to create a captivating but troubling early work of science fiction.

The Coming Race bears a haunting message about the possible racial and cultural implications of evolutionary theory. Bulwer-Lytton, a Rosicrucian and occultist with an interest in languages, presents the Vrilya people as descendants of the original Aryan race that once inhabited the earth's surface. Following a great deluge early in human history the Vrilya were forced to develop their civilization below ground and largely in isolation from other races. Adolf Hitler is known to have been influenced by Bulwer-Lytton's works, and may even have absorbed this Victorian writer's theories about a master race descended from the Aryans.[102] Madame Blavatsky, herself a racial theorist and proponent of Aryan superiority, was also known to have been a fan of *The Coming Race*.

In *The Coming Race* a young American explorer falls through a chasm in the lower reaches of an abandoned mine shaft. The protagonist finds himself in a new world inhabited by advanced human beings—the Vrilya—who are physically perfect, extraordinarily intelligent, godlike creatures capable of flight with artificial wings. Seeing a member of this superrace "reminded me of symbolical images of Genius or Demon that are seen on Etruscan vases or limned on the walls of Eastern sepulchres—images that borrow the outlines of man, and are yet of another race."[103] This creature had "the face of man, but yet of a type of man distinct from our known extant races." As if encountering a god, the narrator's initial "terror" gives way to "a sense of contentment, of joy, of confidence in myself and in the being before me."[104] Appearing like "sculptured gods," these new people constitute "a race akin to man's, but infinitely stronger of form and grander of aspect, and inspiring [an] unutterable feeling of dread."[105]

The Vrilya have mastered a mysterious force known as Vril. By means of Vril—a kind of psychic or spiritual energy providing enormous power—the subterranean humans illuminate their dark world. Vril also powers their air ships and land vehicles. The Vrilya are vegetarians, and practice a benign form of fascism, having dispensed with democracy as a "crude experiment." In every way, including spiritually, the Vrilya have evolved beyond their surface-dwelling cousins. And like Julian Huxley's "dominant types," the Vril intend one day to return to the earth's surface and annihilate the inferior human species living there.

The inexplicable force known as Vril is used to perform virtual miracles. It provides a limitless source of light and can be employed to control the thoughts and actions of others. Vril is the Life Force itself, the key to godlike control over all that exists and the key to extending life indefinitely. "These people," says the protagonist, "consider that in Vril they have arrived at the unity in natural energic agencies, which has been conjectured by many philosophers above ground."[106]

The Vrilya discovered Vril because they perceived by scientific means that "the various forms under which the forces of matter are made manifest have one common origin."[107] That is, science led the Vrilya to monism, and monism led them to Vril, the power that propels life forward toward ever more perfect states. The highest point so far attained in the evolutionary progress of life is the Vrilya themselves. The protagonist is calmly informed by a leader of the master race that they will one day return to the surface of the earth and subjugate or destroy the other races. This is their destiny and the destiny of life itself as it moves toward ultimate perfection. That which is inferior must be set aside to make room for that which is progressing toward perfection—this is the rule of life.

George Edward Bulwer-Lytton used The Coming Race as a forum in which to advance his theory of a spiritually evolved master race destined to rule or destroy all other races.[108] And his theories proved quite popular with his Victorian reading audience. Vril societies formed in England and on the European Continent, lasting well into the twentieth century. The Vril Society of Munich attracted several members who would later become prominent figures in Hitler's National Socialist Party.

"Close Encounters." In closing this chapter, I would like to look briefly at two other examples of science fiction as a messenger of continuing human evolution. Steven Spielberg's classic 1977 UFO movie, *Close Encounters of the Third Kind*—the title a reference to direct human contact with aliens—was among the first of many highly successful big-budget science fiction blockbusters. In the film a small number of humans are subconsciously instructed to await a visit by aliens at a mountain location in Wyoming. There, the process of instructing human beings in their further progress will begin. As one character says in the opening moments of the actual visit, "This is the first day of school."

In the climactic scene of Spielberg's *Close Encounters*, alien beings emerge bathed in light from an enormous spacecraft to make contact with humans. Suggestively, these aliens look vaguely like some members of the gathered humans waiting breathlessly for this moment of contact with a more advanced species. The camera focuses on the now familiar face of a celluloid alien—narrow chin, large eyes, high forehead, pale skin. Then, the camera pans the human audience, focusing at last on a similar human face—narrow chin, large eyes, high forehead, pale skin. Through the juxtaposition of cinematic images, Spielberg seems to be making a point—the aliens reflect what the human race is destined to look like somewhere in the distant evolutionary future. In addition, some of us have already taken important genetic steps in this direction.[109]

One is reminded of Herbert Spencer's speculation that among the various human races "the higher forms [are] distinguished by the relatively larger size of the bones which cover the brain, and the relatively smaller size of those which cover the jaws, etc. Now this trait, which is stronger in Man than in any other creature, is stronger in the European than in the savage."[110] And, apparently, stronger yet in the extraterrestrial than in the European. Spielberg and Spencer seem to be reading from the same script. As *Close Encounters* closes, a minister reads the biblical passage "He will give his angels charge over you," as actor Richard Dreyfuss is awarded the unimaginable privilege of entering the alien craft and departing on a grand cultural adventure. Alien culture, it is suggested, will become for us a source of innumerable insights, certainly scientific, perhaps also spiritual.

"Star Trek." Another example of science fiction exploring the evolutionary hypothesis is important if for no other reason than its massive cultural impact. *Star*

Trek is perhaps the most popular and long lasting and influential media phenomenon of all time. So vast has been its cultural influence that a number of terms and phrases have entered the English language through the show.

In a groundbreaking study of the hidden messages of *Star Trek* from the first appearance of the television program through the latest movie manifestation of the saga, Daniel Bernardi has examined, among other issues, how the writers and producers of *Star Trek* treat the topic of evolution. Under the doctrine of "parallel evolution"—the notion that humanoid beings would have evolved at a rate approximately that of humans on earth—*Star Trek*'s creator Gene Rodenberry and subsequent writers have often speculated about where humanity is headed, both physically and spiritually.[111] According to Bernardi, "the pinnacle of evolution in Trek is a creature who looks white and becomes god-like." A virtually divine race of beings known as the Organians choose "to take humanoid form, thus representing our divine destiny." Mr. Spock comments regarding these minor divinities: "I should say the Organians are as far above us on the evolutionary scale as we are above the amoeba."

According to the Trek myth, human evolution began when aliens seeded the earth's oceans with their DNA. In a *Next Generation* episode entitled "The Chase," a holographic image of an early galactic humanoid states, "the seed codes directed your evolution toward a physical form resembling ours."[112] Thus, the human race is created—not in the Revealed Word's image of God—but in the image of a dying race of aliens anxious to perpetuate itself throughout the galaxy.

If this is where we started, the nearly divine character Q may be where we finally will arrive on our evolutionary march. The first episode of the television series *Star Trek: The Next Generation* featured Q, an "omniscient being who can manipulate the space-time continuum with the snap of a finger."[113] Played by actor John de Lancie, Q is an arrogant and sarcastic demi-god who represents the evolutionary terminus of a species that apparently started its cosmic climb in a fashion similar to human beings. In several episodes featuring immortal, omnipotent and omniscient Q, the point is made that human beings also are embarked on an evolutionary journey and will one day resemble Q and the members of a guild of gods known as The Continuum. In this way, *Star Trek*, like much science fiction, incorporates evolutionary spirituality and its vision of a divine future for the human race.

CONCLUSION

Aldous Huxley, Sir Julian's brother, wrote in 1947, "Human progress in happiness, virtue, and creativeness is valuable in the last analysis, as a condition of spiritual advance toward man's Final End." For Aldous Huxley, "If happiness, morals and creativeness are treated as ends in themselves instead of means to a further End, they can become obstacles to spiritual advance no less serious, in their way, than wretchedness, vice, and conventionality."[114] That is, all of the aspiration, attainment and virtue of our present lives are simply preparing the way for something grander and more consequential—the ultimate spiritual End of human evolution. The idea that human beings are embarked on an inevitably successful and increasingly self-directed journey toward spiritual perfection via the mechanisms of evolution is now a crucial and taken-for-granted component in much religious thought. This idea exerts a powerful grip on contemporary religious thinking.

Under the New Religious Synthesis, evolution is the principle animating the cosmos. Human beings, evolution's conscious products, can now achieve ever-higher levels of consciousness by directing their own evolution. The goal is spiritual fulfillment, absolute consciousness, blissful experience. Most advocates of spiritual evolution agree that humans can and should hasten the process. Marilyn Ferguson wrote in *The Aquarian Conspiracy* of a "new paradigm" that now "attributes evolution to periodic leaps by small groups." The efficient operation of this new paradigm will require "a mechanism for biological change more powerful than chance mutation," which will open "the possibility of rapid evolution in our time."[115] For some theorists of the "next step," assistance is available to us from entities further along the evolutionary path. Gary Zukav, for example, refers to such helpers as Angels. "An Angel," he writes, "might be thought of as a force of consciousness that has evolved into an appropriate teaching modality for the planetary village called earth."[116]

Charles Darwin saw evolutionary perfection as a rival to the Revealed Word's hope of heaven, and he certainly was not alone in looking forward to an era of a fully evolved human race. Similarly, Darwin's grandfather Erasmus found in evolution a mechanism for moral as well as biological progress, provided we cured the plague of conventional religious thinking. Herbert Spencer did much to popularize the notion of human evolutionary progress. Spencer also recognized that evolution could assist the invention of a powerful moral philosophy, indeed, a new religious view, provided traditional religion could be jettisoned. This idea is still powerfully with us. A. N. Wilson asks, "Do we not share with Spencer a generalized belief that the scientific outlook, however that may be defined, compels the religious outlook to be modified, if not actually abandoned?" Wilson adds that "the existence on this planet of two generations of Europeans who believed Herbert Spencer to be the greatest thinker of their time might have something to do with our own outlook."[117]

Franklin Baumer writes that evolution "persuaded people to think of everything in nature as the fruit of a gradual growth rather than an original creation." Such gradualist thinking means that it is "now difficult if not impossible for an educated man to conceive of a primitive revelation such as traditional Christianity taught, or even of an original natural religion from which men had declined." This difficulty arises because "in an evolving world, perfection obviously lay, not in the past, but in the future."[118] Evolutionary, progressivist thinking has reversed the direction of Western spirituality—we did not fall from perfection, we are gradually heading toward it. Moreover, the idea of "conscious evolution" has shifted the locus of spiritual agency: we do not need to turn to God for salvation; we shall do that work ourselves as we learn to control evolution.

Darwin's idea is now taken as final proof that the universe is governed, not by a divine will that created humans out of dust, but by a virtually divine force Darwin called natural selection. Having produced human consciousness, evolution may now, according to its prophets, be brought directly under the control of its own product. Humanity, the accomplishment of natural selection, is on the threshold of mastering Darwin's divinity. The hope of the New Religious Synthesis is that the mechanisms of evolution can be taken by force and consciously employed to guide human progress toward the next level of existence, Aldous Huxley's "Final End."

7

PANTHEISM IN THE MODERN WORLD

Nature or God

"What is that mysterious force?" I asked.
"It's a force that is present throughout everything that is," he said.

CARLOS CASTANEDA, The Fire from Within

Science proves the potency of monistic philosophy over dualism—over spirit separated from matter.

AMIT GOSWAMI, The Self-Aware Universe

Pantheists usually believe that God, so to speak, animates the universe as you animate your body: that the universe almost is God, so that if it did not exist He would not exist either, and anything you find in the universe is part of God. The Christian idea is quite different.

C. S. LEWIS, Mere Christianity

Teilhard de Chardin saw in the rising religious awareness of humankind "the progressive Spiritualization of Matter." The destiny of the cosmos is for spirit and matter to be revealed as "the same cosmic stuff."[1] The universe is "falling . . . in the direction of spirit," which is its "stable form."[2] The matter of which the universe is made up is not inanimate, but carries within itself "an extraordinary capacity" for "complexification."[3] That is, matter continually organizes itself into more and more complex forms, with consciousness being the end of the process. Human consciousness is finally awakening to the reality and inevitability of the universe's evolutionary process, while at the same time recognizing that it—human consciousness, that is—represents the very pinnacle of the universe's spiritual evolution.

Teilhard claims that even as a child he recognized in himself the operation of "Cosmic" and "Christic" forces, which led him into a virtually worshipful relationship first with a piece of iron and later with quartz. He writes that these substances "opened my groping mind into the vast structures of the Planet and Nature."[4] And what did he see when viewing these "vast structures"? He saw that the earth is enveloped, not just in an atmosphere, but also in a "noosphere," a thinking layer of spirit that is, in fact, the sum of all human minds. The noosphere is, in his words, "totalized Mankind," all human minds as one great Mind.[5] Moreover, this noosphere drives forward the evolution of the universal spirit. The noosphere is not static, but is currently experiencing an "accelerated drift toward ultra-human states, under the influence of psycho-physical convergence (or Planetization)."[6] We are, that is, becoming something other than, something higher than human. We are gradually but inexorably becoming one with the divine consciousness that is in everything that exists.

The idea that nature or the cosmos is divine is an ancient and persistent one that stands in direct contradiction to the Revealed Word's personal and transcendent God. The notion appears throughout history in a variety of guises. Ancient writers such as Plotinus imagined a universe in which "soul" animated all physical objects. "It is the soul that lends all things movement," he wrote.[7] In the seventeenth century, the Dutch philosopher Benedict de Spinoza advocated pantheism. Shortly afterward the idea was popularized in the controversial writings of the Irish religious radical John Toland. A form of pantheism was at the root of the vast nature-worshiping movements in Europe during the nineteenth century. Richard Noll has written that "the 1890s in Central Europe were marked by the rise of volkish utopianism" based on the rejection of Christianity "and emphasis on the worship of nature." Noll takes this movement to have been rooted in the pantheistic monism of the enormously influential German naturalist Ernst Haeckel.[8] Haeckel wrote that it was "quite certain that the Christian system must give way to the monistic," that is, to an understanding of all things as one divine entity.[9]

Writers in the New Science genre now routinely describe a universe charged with divine energy or consciousness. For example, physicist Fred Alan Wolf writes of "our present modern vision of an abstract God and mysterious eternal soul" present in all material things.[10] Wolf believes that pantheism returns us to an earlier, more fundamental human spiritual view. The "early modern vision of raw and to-be-conquered nature" he finds to be "vastly different from that of the pre-Greeks." Moreover, "this pre-Greek vision of the soul, life and death" that incorporated the notion that "everything in nature, including rocks, mountains, the sky, animals, and plants, was alive, bristling with sacred energy" is a worldview Wolf sees "returning to our time."[11]

This basic idea is found in many contemporary spiritual works as well. For instance, in Helen Schucman's *A Course in Miracles*, students are instructed to repeat the "lesson" that "God is in everything I see." Schucman instructs, "Begin with repeating the idea to yourself, and then apply it to randomly chosen objects about you, naming each one specifically, . . . 'God is in this coat hanger. God is in this magazine. God is in this finger. God is in this lamp.'"[12] Pantheism has become an essential component in the New Religious Synthesis. God is no longer outside of creation, no longer either "wholly other" or personal. Rather, the new god is in all things as a divine energy, animating force or cosmic consciousness.

This chapter considers the reemergence of pantheism as a popular religious idea and building block of the Other Spirituality. John Toland coined the term *pantheism* in the early eighteenth century, and Toland's influence on religious ideas in England and later in France, Germany and America was great. Indeed, this early pantheist was the first truly successful and popular religious radical in the modern period. This chapter also explores pantheism's development as a popular religious idea in America under the influence of Ralph Waldo Emerson. Emerson exerted extensive influence over religious thought in the rapidly expanding American republic of the 1800s.[13]

From Emerson we will shift our focus to the pantheistic monism of Ernst Haeckel, a late-nineteenth-century scientist, evolutionist and popular writer who for years held Europe in thrall on a wide range of scientific and metaphysical topics. So successful was Haeckel's case for seeing all that exists as one entity that monistic churches began to spring up on the Continent. Moving from the sciences to the arts, we will consider the pantheism inherent in an important play by the English playwright George Bernard Shaw. The chapter concludes with a consideration of the fundamental pantheism inherent in much of the New Science.

SPINOZA AND TOLAND

Baruch or Benedict de Spinoza (1632-1677) was a member of the Jewish Diaspora in the Netherlands. For his unorthodox writings he was expelled from the Synagogue of Amsterdam in 1656. The reclusive Spinoza made his living grinding lenses for telescopes and other optical instruments, and once refused a prestigious chair in philosophy in order that he might continue to live a tranquil life as a lens grinder. Spinoza is famous for his attacks on the Bible in *Tractatus theologico-politicus*. The *Ethics* sets out his pantheistic view that the natural realm is God, and God is all of nature. Spinoza's view is captured in a famous Latin phrase, *Deus sive natura* (God or nature). The two terms are, for Spinoza, interchangeable. This god/nature is infinite, one substance extended indefinitely in such a way as to preclude the possibility of any other entity in the cosmos. That is, Spinoza literally leaves no room in the cosmos for God. There is no mind behind the physical matter of Spinoza's universe, and thus no divine purpose in the cosmic order of things. Matter in motion is the only principle at work in the universe. The material/divine universe is all of one essence. Human beings and all other physical objects share this common essence. This makes human beings a part—albeit a uniquely rational part—of the vast cosmic order.

In his own day, Spinoza's rendering God equivalent to the physical world was taken as simple atheism. But Spinoza insisted he had a theology and that it was in keeping with an ancient Jewish tradition. That tradition, however, was the kabbalistic mysticism of writers such as Rabbi Moses Cordovero, the author of the famous mystical work *A Garden of Pomegranates*. Cordovero argued that "God the knower" and the objects that God knows are one and the same thing, partaking of the same essence. Thus, Spinoza may have seen himself as providing philosophical grounding for a theological view that had been alive in Judaism for centuries. To identify God with nature is to make science and theology the same discipline. As Daniel C. Dennett writes, "Benedict Spinoza, in the seventeenth century, *identified* God and Nature, arguing that scientific research was the true path of theology."[14]

Spinoza influenced a number of late seventeenth and early eighteenth-century religious radicals. One famous skeptical work that circulated in this period, *The Treatise of the Three Impostors*, provided curious readers a sensational and popularized version of many of Spinoza's skeptical arguments. The Irishman John Toland (1670-1722) was among the most colorful and controversial of the public religious advocates directly influenced by the great Dutch philosopher. He is, in fact, credited with having coined the term *pantheism* in a 1705 publication, the word coming into general use among English speakers by the time of Toland's death in 1722. His most important work was *Christianity Not Mysterious* (1696), in which he attacked the Bible on the argument that the true religion of humanity was established well before Christianity.

In works such as *Pantheisticon* (1720) Toland advocated a pantheistic theology that popularized the ideas of both Spinoza and the earlier Dominican writer Bruno, who had championed the infinity and "divinity of the universe" as well as the plurality of habitable worlds.[15] If Bruno was correct that the universe was infinite, Toland reasoned, this left no room for a God who exists externally to it. Thus, if there is a God he must be indistinguishable from the physical universe. Moreover, in an infinite universe shot through with a life force, intelligent life might be expected to arise and flourish in many places.

Such views were dangerous to express in the early eighteenth century, and so Toland adopted a strategy of advocating pantheism without appearing to be committed to the idea. Thus, historian Robert Sullivan notes that "insinuation" of pantheism into the minds of the British reading public became Toland's "ultimate literary purpose."[16] Avoiding direct statement of his religious views was in keeping with Toland's approach to religion generally. A believer in esoteric theology, he found secrecy a necessary means of guarding spiritual truths against the corrupting influence of the public.

John Toland was committed to the pantheistic principle that "everything was full of God, who was in everything."[17] In *Pantheisticon* he wrote of "the Force and Energy of the Whole, the Creator and Ruler of All, and always tending to the best End is GOD, whom you may call the Mind, if you please, and the Soul of the Universe."[18] Sullivan writes that "Toland's aim was to eliminate both the separation of God from the universe and the distinction between a supreme intellect (or soul) and the natural activity of matter." That is, Toland sought to usher out of the Western mind the Revealed Word's conception of God. However, Toland's new deity was incapable of providing either "divine guidance of individuals" or "loving care, and intervention."[19]

Toland studied the texts of a wide range of ancient and modern religions, often in the original languages. He was particularly fascinated with the ancient British Druids, reading their works in Celtic. His interest in the Druids was driven largely by his desire to discover the most primitive human religious beliefs and practices. Druid nature worship, Toland argued, suggested that the primitive religion of humanity was pantheism, not theism. Early humans did not worship a transcendent and personal God, but nature itself as god. In *Pantheisticon*, Toland developed his fullest argument to the effect that pantheism was the natural religion of the human race. It was also, he claimed, the spiritual view expressed by "all wise men" at all times.[20] Among the groups that he believed to have been pantheistic in their theology were the Pythagoreans of Greece and the Brahmans of India.

Many others also held to this view of a unity between God and the physical universe. These included "most ancient Egyptians, Persians, and Romans, [and] the first Patriarchs of the Hebrews," all of whom understood "the simplicity of the Divine Nature."[21] In *Letters to Serena*, Toland remarks that "a great many eminent Persons in Europe and Asia, both understood themselves the Origins of the Religions commonly received . . . and thus asserted the Unity of the Deity."[22] Thus, Toland viewed his project as "laboring to restore forgotten truths" by reintroducing pantheism to human religious thinking.[23] After all, pantheism was the natural religion of the human race. Sullivan remarks that Toland's account of human spirituality's devolution from pantheism into belief in various personal gods "dominated European writing on the subject for almost two generations after his death."[24] This view— that all religious faiths share a common ancestry in primitive pantheistic and mystical spirituality—is now an important component of the New Religious Synthesis.

RALPH WALDO EMERSON

Ralph Waldo Emerson (1803-1882) was the son of a Unitarian minister, William Emerson, who died in 1811 when Ralph Waldo was eight. Born in Boston at the opening of the nineteenth century, Emerson grew up in the context of a religiously saturated and spiritually jaded New England. Emerson's father was fond of both Paine and Priestley, and so a strong deistic influence is evident in the elder Emerson's thinking. One of Ralph Waldo Emerson's biographers calls the religion of the great essayist's father "calm deism." In this way, the religious atmosphere in which Emerson grew up was remarkably similar to that in which Charles Darwin, born only six years after Emerson and dying the same year, was reared. Emerson's mother is described as "deeply religious," but was drawn to works of "spiritual self-help" rather than to theology.[25]

However, the greatest early spiritual influence on Ralph Waldo Emerson was his aunt Mary Moody Emerson, a self-styled mystic, visionary and prophet compared by one writer to the German mystical writer Jakob Böhme.[26] This strange woman wrote and traveled a great deal, wore a burial shroud when she traveled, and slept in a bed fashioned in the shape of a coffin. Mary Emerson's "effect on [Ralph Waldo Emerson] was permanent."[27] She was drawn to authors with pantheistic, mystical and deistic leanings—Plotinus, Spinoza, Goethe, Law, Coleridge—and Emerson himself owed a great debt to these same authors.

It is no mere coincidence that Mary Baker Eddy, Joseph Smith, Henry David

Thoreau and Emerson all were born around the same time and in the same region of the United States. Each threw off the dominant Protestantism of New England and suggested an exotic spiritual alternative that drew adherents into a variety of closely related teachings. The New England of the first half of the nineteenth century has been called the "burned over region" because of the extensive evangelizing that had taken place there and the resultant spiritual weariness of the residents.

Emerson entered Harvard at the age of fourteen, where he studied John Locke's empiricism, Dugald Stewart's commonsense philosophy and William Paley's ethics. Graduating in 1821, he was drawn increasingly toward the ministry and became a Unitarian minister in 1829. Emerson married Ellen Tucker in 1829, a woman for whom he had a deep and passionate love. She died only eighteen months later, dealing a severe blow to Emerson's beliefs about the immortality of the individual soul. At this time, around 1831, he began to formulate his distinctive religious ideas.

Swedenborg, Schleiermacher and Reed. To understand Emerson it is important to recognize the writers he read, admired and emulated. Emerson owed a considerable debt to Emanuel Swedenborg (1688-1772), the enormously influential Swedish mystic who claimed numerous conversations with spirits over a period of several years. Swedenborg repudiated Christianity's historical orientation, stressing instead the inner search for divine consciousness. Biographers have difficulty reconciling Emerson's apparent genius with his profound interest in Swedenborg's strange theology.

Another writer who profoundly influenced Emerson was Friedrich Schleiermacher (1768-1834), the prominent German theologian who also stressed the importance of interiority, emotion or feeling *(Gefühl)*, and individual reflection in the religious life. Critics labeled Schleiermacher a pantheist, perhaps because he advocated a central mystical core common to all religious faiths. Jesus was unique only in the degree of his God-consciousness, that is, his awareness of the divinity at work in the world. Sin, for Schleiermacher, was a matter of wrong belief, rather than evil, and could be overcome by increasing one's God-consciousness. In both Swedenborg and Schleiermacher, Emerson found a religion of interior experience and god as a diffuse spiritual essence in nature.

Emerson was also drawn to the mental evolutionist Sampson Reed, for whom humanity was in the midst of a "revolutionary change."[28] In Reed's major work, *Observations on the Growth of the Mind,* he wrote, "all the changes which are taking place in the world originate in the mind."[29] Another of Emerson's mentors was the mystical and gnostic writer Guillaume Oegger, especially through his work *The True Messiah*.[30] The seventeenth-century mystic and gnostic Jakob Böhme (1575-1624) was another strong influence on Emerson. Böhme, who claimed direct divine illumination in 1600 and again in 1610, believed the external, physical world was a projection of an inner spiritual power. His theology is set out in the book *Aurora*.

Finally, Emerson was influenced by eastern religious works, and he himself eventually popularized in America a fundamentally Hindu religious view for the first time. Philip Jenkins writes that "Emerson was influenced by the Upanishads, and in 1883 his widow hosted a lecture by a visiting Hindu teacher."[31] Emerson apparently also read magical works and advanced a theory of correspondence like the one undergirding occult thinking. The view is summarized in the adage, "As above, so below." That is, there is a correspondence between the physical world of events and objects in the spiritual world; thus, the former is an analogy or map for the latter.

Emerson's career. Emerson was one of those rare intellectual figures who both ably translate their ideas into the language of ordinary citizens and relish the opportunity to write for that audience. Moreover, Emerson was unusually successful in this enterprise of popular persuasion. As far as the public was concerned, he was the most compelling thinker of his age—and his age lasted a very long time indeed. Because Emerson had such extensive influence on religious ideas as both a lecturer and author of popular essays, it will be helpful to understand the course of his public career.

Ralph Waldo Emerson assumed the pulpit of the Second Unitarian Church of Boston in 1831. As his theological views drifted ever further from even liberal Christian thought, he resigned from the church and traveled to Europe where he met both Wordsworth and Coleridge. But it was his visit with Thomas Carlyle that moved him most. The two carried on a famous correspondence for the next thirty-eight years. In 1834 Emerson received an inheritance from Ellen Tucker's estate, the money being sufficient to ensure that he did not have to hold a steady job ever again. Eager to disseminate his developing theological views, Emerson became involved in the growing Lyceum movement of public lectures. Part education, part entertainment, the Lyceum circuit gave Emerson the opportunity both to promote and to hone his ideas.

As his fame increased, newspapers often reprinted his lectures. Emerson's many public addresses over several decades popularized an unorthodox spiritual view that has come to be known as Transcendentalism. His short book *Nature* (1836) and his lecture "Address Before the Divinity Class" (1838) are perhaps his best-known explications of his now well-developed theology. The basic argument in these addresses is that individual consciousness is the one crucial component in religion, not doctrine, creed or ceremony. This subjective religious consciousness is triumphant over all historical and cultural constraints, including the teachings of all religions.

Emerson held that "the religious spirit does not reside in external forms, words, ceremonies, or institutions," affirming that "the one thing of value in the universe is the active soul." Thus, "subjective consciousness" is the essence of religion.[32] But Emerson also insisted on the general similarity of religious consciousness in all people. Holding to the idea of "one mind and common humanity," he argued that individualism was wrong because it tended to isolate us from those of other religious persuasions.[33] This unifying view of human religious experience was joined in Emerson's thought to a pantheistic understanding of divinity itself. When the term *god* carried any meaning at all for Emerson, it described a spirit present in all things. His radically subjective spirituality created controversy when he first expounded it. But by the end of the 1830s Emerson was beginning to be accepted as America's heterodox prophet of pantheism, the divine self and reverence for Nature.

By 1840 Emerson was directing most of his writing and speaking to the general public, and his influence was considerable. This "confident American prophet" traveled and lectured extensively in the Northeast and along the Atlantic seaboard.[34] He felt, as one biographer records, "that the nation needed him."[35] His fame continued to grow throughout the 1840s and 1850s, and his lecturing now took him to the Midwest. Emerson was a "magnificent rhetorician," according to one biographer, a speaker with "the power to communicate feelings even better than ideas."[36]

Emerson was the forefather of today's motivational speakers, and in this role served as spiritual counselor to thousands of Americans. Audiences found him inspiring even when they did not adopt or perhaps even fully understand his philosophy. Still, some ideas stuck, becoming part of the American religious consciousness: place your trust only in self, it is a cosmic law that good deeds are rewarded and bad deeds punished, God is present in all nature.

Emerson's religious thinking. It has been said that Emerson set about to invent a religion, doing so at a time when inventing religions was an American growth industry. Most of Emerson's writing is theological, whether implicitly or explicitly, and he has been accused of attempting to force all of his thinking into each essay, book and speech. Moreover, he aggressively sought converts to his point of view and was quite successful in this effort. From 1835 through 1870 he was the most respected and influential American religious teacher. What religion, then, did Emerson teach?

It is clear that Emerson's personal and public theology was a reaction *against* Christian theology. Though never an orthodox Christian, Emerson moved further and further from Christianity throughout his life. Influenced by Romantics, mystics and naturalists, his "skepticism toward Christianity" was also bolstered by German biblical criticism.[37] Emerson developed his spiritual system as a tool for overturning Christianity and replacing it with something he thought better—an American version of monistic pantheism. God was not a divine judge or father, but rather a spirit present in all physical objects. He appears, Emerson wrote, "with all his parts in every moss and cobweb."[38]

On this "divinity in nature" view, Emerson erected an anthrotheology common to other nineteenth-century theological speculators: Humanity is the embodiment of the divine spirit moving through the universe, and thus each individual person is, in this sense, god. It followed that trust could be placed only in the self. In his essay "Self-Reliance," he writes about the individual as akin to a deity. For instance, spiritual peace must be discovered in the resources of the individual and not in an external deity. "Nothing can bring you peace but yourself," he writes.[39] Moreover, the individual explores the unmapped inner regions of consciousness in the search for religious truth. Only the self can explore the "undiscovered regions of thought."[40] The individual is embarked on an internal spiritual quest to discover the divinity residing within the human soul.

"I am part or particle of God." The similarity between the human mind and nature was so thoroughgoing for Emerson that he could write, "The whole of nature is a metaphor for the human mind."[41] And if nature is a *metaphor* for the human mind, nature was *identical* with the divine mind. In *Nature* Emerson affirms two essences in the universe, "Nature and the Soul," with Soul being his name for the divine spirit in all things and in each individual.[42] Because the human mind is analogous to the divine mind infusing nature, Emerson's theology led him to the view all pantheists eventually arrive at—the individual is divine. In Emerson's radically subjective theology, the observing, experiencing, intuiting self displaces a transcendent creator God. Moreover, the divine self takes on qualities traditionally attributed to God, such as omniscience and omnipresence. In *Nature* Emerson writes: "I see all. The currents of the Universal Being circulate through me; I am part or particle of God."[43]

For Emerson, truth comes not from a Revealed Word but rather from within the divine self. Malcolm Cowley notes that for Emerson, "each of us can find the laws of the universe by searching his own heart."[44] Similarly, the search for God also takes one on an inward path. Thus, in his "Divinity School Address" Emerson affirms that "if a man is at heart just, then in so far is he God; the safety of God, the immortality of God, the majesty of God do enter into that man with justice."[45] His "sublime creed" was that "the world is not the product of manifold power" as taught by the Revealed Word. Rather, the world is the product of what Emerson terms "one will" and "one mind." That "one mind," he writes, "is everywhere, in each ray of the star, in each wavelet of the pool."[46] All things emerge "out of the same spirit, and all things conspire with it."[47] For reasons not clearly articulated, this spirit in all things is a moral spirit, which encourages right action and discourages wrong.

For Emerson, a cosmic "law of laws" awakened "the religious sentiment" which is the source of "our highest happiness." All of the world's religions are expressions of this sentiment because it called each of them into existence. This "sentiment lies at the foundation of society, and successively creates all forms of worship," Emerson assured the Divinity School students.[48] The same elemental religious spirit also teaches human beings that they are divine, suggesting that the concept of human divinity resides at the heart of all religious systems. "This thought dwelled always deepest in the minds of men in the devout and contemplative East; not alone in Palestine, where it reached its purest expression, but in Egypt, in Persia, in India, in China."[49]

Life is a great mystery that the individual unravels, resulting in spiritual self-reliance. Mind, not the Revealed Word's God, rules in Emerson's cosmos. Emerson grew ever more suspicious of the physical nature of human beings, and thus ever more inclined to spiritualize human existence. This spiritualizing tendency eventually led him to reject the central emblem of human physicality—the act of procreation itself. In *The Conduct of Life* (1860), his last important book, he urged his readers to invest themselves "in spiritual creation and not in begetting animals."[50]

In his own day, Emerson's more astute critics understood his views to be derived from Swedenborgian mysticism, Romanticism and ancient pantheism. As Hershel Parker writes, "all the reviewers understood *Nature* was not a Christian book but one influenced by a range of idealistic philosophies, ancient and very modern, Transcendentalism being merely the latest name for an old way of thinking."[51] Emerson's influence on American thinking in his own day was considerable; his was the most important hand shaping the nation's religious views in the mid-nineteenth century. Emerson's influence was always felt more keenly by searching individuals than by the society as a whole. Richardson writes, "Transcendentalism did not transform American life, but it did change—and continues to change—individual American lives."[52]

ERNST HAECKEL AND *THE RIDDLE OF THE UNIVERSE*

Ernst Haeckel (1834-1919), professor of zoology at the University of Jena, was one of the leading scientific voices on the European continent at the end of the nineteenth century. An ardent proponent of Darwinism in Europe, the first in Germany, this daring explorer and gifted writer and artist exercised extraordinary influence on popular thought. Haeckel sought a religious view rooted in scientific study of the natural realm, a religion he dubbed "monism." On Haeckel's view, the old religious system was "dualistic" in that it posited both nature and a God outside of nature, with worship properly directed to the latter. Monism, on the other hand, affirmed a single essence in all things. In this way the cosmos itself became the only possible god.

Haeckel envisioned nothing less than a new model of culture built on the foundation of a new scientific religion. Richard Noll writes that Haeckel "designed secular paths of cultural renewal or regeneration that were greatly influenced by evolutionary biological training."[53] Haeckel's new way in religion, his monistic religion, was explicitly "anti-Christian."[54] The utopian Volkish movement that swept central Europe in the 1890s rejected Christianity and emphasized "the worship of nature (particularly the sun)." Haeckel's bestselling *The Riddle of the Universe* (1899)—an early version of the popularized science genre—openly promoted pantheism as the basis of a new order of civilization. Noll adds, "Haeckel himself exhibited a messianic zeal in promoting his logical, new pantheistic 'nature religion'" to a public ready to be persuaded that science provides solid answers to ancient metaphysical puzzles.[55]

Under Haeckel's monistic-pantheistic religious revolution, nature alone demands our adoration. Modern people should not repeat the ancient mistake of placing a Revealed Word above reason, thus derailing religious thought. Haeckel's *The Riddle of the Universe* presents "our godlike reason" and its clear superiority to revelation. "We must at once dispose of this dangerous error" of thinking that revelation ought to rule reason.[56] Reason employing "triumphant" science would lead humankind out of the darkness of revealed dualism and into a bright new monistic day.

Science as the foundation of monistic religion. For Haeckel, science was a metaphysical as well as a physical enterprise. "The greatest triumphs of modern science—the cellular theory, the dynamic theory of heat, the theory of evolution, and the law of substance—are *philosophic achievements*," he writes in *The Riddle*.[57] Moreover, the philosophy revealed by science is pantheistic monism, the same view advocated by the great German Romantic writer Goethe, who stood for Haeckel as a modern prophet. "At the end of the nineteenth century we have returned to that monistic attitude which our greatest realistic poet, Goethe, had recognized from its very commencement to be alone correct and fruitful."[58]

And what distinguishes this monistic religion that both science and the Romantics have taught us? "Monism," writes Haeckel, "recognizes one sole substance in the universe, which is at once 'God and nature'; body and spirit (or matter and energy) it holds to be inseparable." Monism thus stands opposed to "the extra-mundane God of dualism," belief in whom "leads necessarily to theism." However, "the intra-mundane God of the monist leads to pantheism," the one true religion for a scientific age.[59] Haeckel explains that "matter cannot exist and be operative without spirit, nor spirit without matter." He referred to "spirit" and "energy" as simply "sensitive and thinking substance." Spirit and energy are then the "attributes or principal properties of the all-embracing divine essence of the world, the universal substance."[60] Thus Haeckel the scientist rejects Revealed Word dualism in favor of a universe comprised of a divine energy defined as "sensitive or thinking substance."

The soul's evolution. One of Haeckel's principal interests in *The Riddle of the Universe* was to develop a case for the evolution of the human soul based on two principles: pantheism and the evolutionary theory of Charles Darwin. "It becomes one of the main tasks of modern monistic psychology," he writes, "to trace the stages of the historical development of the soul of man from the soul of the brute."[61] Haeckel grounds his argument in a theory of a "soul substance" capable of creating consciousness. Within us resides a "protoplasm which seems to be the indispensable substratum of psychic life." Haeckel dubbed this substance *psychoplasm*, which he defined as "the 'soul-substance,' in the monistic sense."[62]

The cells exhibiting the greatest capacity for a soul life are the "sexual cells," all cells in any way connected with the human sexual response. "Each of these sexual cells," he writes, "has its own 'cell-soul'—that is, each is distinguished by a peculiar form of sensation and movement." In such cells are found "potential energies" that are "inseparable from the matter of the protoplasm."[63] That is, there is no need to posit a soul *in addition to* the biological functions of cells within the human body. The soul—a name for our capacity to think, feel and move—evolved in a cellular fashion as did all other human functions.

In this way Haeckel's spiritual version of materialism renders dualism unnecessary. Of course, a key strategic purpose of *The Riddle* is to refute a major component in the Revealed Word worldview—that the human soul is a special creation of God. Haeckel believed that his argument about the souls of cells sufficed "for the destruction of the still prevalent superstition that man owes his personal existence to the favor of God." On the contrary, the soul's origin "is rather to be attributed solely to the 'eros,'" or sexual life of some human cells.[64] Thus, in the evolution of sexuality and the erotic impulse is found "the evolution of the soul."[65]

The highly specialized sex cells "not only conduct the commerce between the muscles and the organs of sense, but they also affect the highest performances of the animal soul, the formation of ideas and thoughts, and especially consciousness."[66] The "soul" function of these cells leads eventually "to that marvellous structure of the human brain which seems to entitle the highest primate form to quite an exceptional position in nature."[67] Thus, Haeckel believed that his sexual/cellular evolutionary theory of the soul demonstrated that "consciousness is simply a natural phenomenon like any other psychic quality, and that it is subject to the law of substance like all other natural phenomena."[68] Where does all this leave us with regard to rational religion? In a rather unexpected place, as it turns out.

Sun-worship as scientific religion. Haeckel recognized that directing his readers to reverent contemplation of nature might fail to arouse the sense of transcendence found in traditional religion. He thus sought a brilliant divinity worthy of the new pantheistic/monistic faith he had invented. Haeckel found his new god in the sky. The nature-worshiping Volkish movement sweeping central and Eastern Europe as the nineteenth century waned revered the sun as nature's true god. For Haeckel as well, the sun became the perfect emblem of the constant cycle of evolutionary advancement that characterizes the cosmos. "This universal movement of substance in space takes the form of an eternal cycle or of a periodical process of evolution," he wrote, and the sun perfectly represents this cyclical, universal and eternal process.[69]

Evolution was the very basis of the cosmos, its foundation and organizing principle. And, in keeping with this conviction, Haeckel understood human beings as but a point along an evolutionary trajectory toward something grander. "Humanity is but a transitory phase of the evolution of an eternal substance, a particular phenomenal form of matter and energy," he affirmed.[70] The sun best manifested this eternal progression of cosmic energy, leading Haeckel the scientist to a remarkably unscientific conclusion: "Sun-worship (solarism, or heliotheism) seems to the modern scientist to be the best of all forms of theism."[71]

Interestingly, Haeckel found sun-worship a more scientific faith than worship of a triune God. In a striking passage he wrote, "in the light of pure reason, sun-worship, as a form of naturalistic monotheism, seems to have a much better foundation than the anthropistic worship of Christians."[72] For support, Haeckel turned to the leading lights of science and philosophy. "Many distinguished scientists and philosophers of the day, who share our monistic views, consider that religion is generally played out," he claimed. In short, the Revealed Word tradition was dead; monism had taken its place as the faith of thinking people, and was thus the basis of a new religion. "Clear insight into the evolution of the world which the scientific progress of the nineteenth century has afforded us will satisfy, not only the causal feelings of our reason, but even our highest emotional cravings."[73]

Science reveals evolution as the foundational principle of the cosmos, and evolution in turn instructs us that our new religion is pantheistic monism—everything is one thing, and that one thing is divine. Haeckel is now "convinced" that "truth unadulterated is only to be found in the temple of the study of nature," a conclusion Thomas Paine had arrived at a century earlier in his *The Age of Reason.*[74] And thus, with prophetic confidence Haeckel affirms that "the modern man who 'has science and art'—and, therefore, 'religion'—needs no special church, no narrow, enclosed portion of space."[75]

Monistic morals, self-love and a world religion. Of course, any religion worthy of the name must instruct us about how we ought to live. And, according to Haeckel, any adequate ethic "must be rationally connected with the unified conception of the cosmos which we have formed by our advanced knowledge of the laws of nature."[76] What, then, is the unified moral system taught by Haeckel's new monistic religion? Clearly it must not simply replicate the moral view of the Revealed Word, the perspective Haeckel set out to destroy.

Sounding like his contemporary and fellow countryman, the anti-Christian philosopher Friedrich Nietzsche—and Nietzsche's twentieth-century disciple Ayn Rand—Haeckel takes Christianity to task for overemphasizing love of others. He writes, "The supreme mistake of Christian ethics . . . is its exaggeration of love of one's neighbor at the expense of self-love." Haeckel is offended that "Christianity attacks and despises egoism on principle." And yet, the natural selfishness we call egoism "is absolutely indispensable in view of self-preservation," while love of others—"a very ideal precept"—is "as useless in practice as it is unnatural."[77] Darwinian science and its spiritual offspring, pantheism, direct us down another moral pathway—self-preservation through self-love.

Haeckel realized, of course, that the Revealed Word tradition and his scientific monism were diametrically opposed spiritual forces. Christianity denounced "all that invaluable progress of science, especially the study of nature, of which the nineteenth century is justly proud." Christians find "worthless" the scientific advances that enjoy "so high a value in the eye of the monist," or so Haeckel argued.[78] For Haeckel, science and Christianity are sworn enemies locked in a "culture war" to determine control of the Western mind. "Christianity is to be found an enemy to civilization, and the struggle which modern thought and science are compelled to conduct with it is . . . a 'cultur-kampf.'"[79] Haeckel was nevertheless confident that "the older view" was "breaking up with all its mystic and anthropistic dogmas." A new religion—scientific monism— was already rising out of the ashes of Christianity. In a heroic flourish Haeckel asserted that "upon the vast field of ruins rises, majestic and brilliant, the new sun of our realistic monism, which reveals to us the wonderful temple of nature in all its beauty. In the sincere cult of 'the true, the good, and the beautiful,' which is the heart of our new monistic religion, we find ample compensation for the anthropistic ideals of 'God, freedom and immortality' which we have lost."[80]

Haeckel proposed that a single unified religious view—monism—be adopted throughout the world in the coming twentieth century. "We may, therefore, express a hope that the approaching twentieth century will complete the . . . construction of pure monism" and thus "spread far and wide the desired unity of world-conception."[81] The spread of Haeckelian monism was, in fact, surprising. "By 1904, groups all over Central Europe had formed and were known as *Monistenbund* (the Monistic Alliance), with some trying out rituals based on this new scientific religion."[82] Haeckel actually organized the various cells of the *Monistenbund* under "a single administrative umbrella." Moreover, the new religion of "the Monistenbund attracted prominent cultural, occultist, and scientific celebrities as members."[83] The movement spawned various other organizations devoted to the worship of a "'life-principle' in all matter."[84]

BERGSON AND SHAW

Belief in a pantheistic "Life Principle" or "Vital Impulse" was widespread among intellectuals in the early twentieth century, and its foremost advocate was the French philosopher Henri Bergson (1859-1941). As Bergson influenced many twentieth-century advocates of a divine principle at work in the evolving cosmos, it will be helpful to survey his thought on this point. Bergson, like many writers of his day, affirmed that the Vital Impulse worked through the mechanism of evolution, and that its principal activity was evident in the evolutionary ascent of the human race. Physical matter was being organized by the Impulse into organisms of greater and greater complexity, and thus higher and higher levels of consciousness. The Vital Impulse was "an inward impulse that passes from germ to germ through individuals, that carries life in a given direction, toward ever higher complexity."[85]

In human beings this impulse expresses itself in various forms of higher order intelligence, each form a step along the way to divinity. "The creative effect progressed successfully only along that line of evolution which ended in man. In its passage through matter, consciousness assumed in that case, as it were from a mould, the shape of tool-making intelligence."[86] Such high-order intelligence was also the source of what Bergson called "the myth-making function that contrives the patterns of religion."[87] In other words, religion—including the Revealed Word variety—is an expression of the myth-making quality found only in highly evolved human intelligence. Thus, our myth-making ability binds us together as producers of religions, the ability to create religion being itself simply a stage in our evolutionary development.

However, human evolutionary progress does not manifest itself in all places equally for Bergson. Some races clearly lead the pack in the race toward human spiritual destiny. Bergson spoke freely of "the inferior races" who did not show the signs of advancement, brackish evolutionary backwaters cut off from "a great current of creative energy" that is the main stream of the Vital Impulse's flow toward the larger evolutionary sea. He also spoke of "static religions" that kept people from recognizing their destiny, spiritual systems that insisted on a fixed dogma, an unchanging orthodoxy unresponsive to developments in human evolution.

Shaw's Supermen. George Bernard Shaw (1856-1950) was one of the twentieth century's most prolific and influential writers and is considered by many the most important English playwright since Shakespeare. Shaw was also a strident political polemicist and a speculative religious advocate. A member of the socialist Fabian

Society, Shaw tirelessly promoted radical social change as well as revolutionary ideas in religion. Not the least of these ideas was the spiritual evolution of the human race under the direction of a pantheistic presence Shaw referred to as the Life Force, a variation on Bergson's Vital Impulse.

Shaw's Life Force continually organizes itself into higher and higher forms of life. Such is the basis of life in the cosmos most clearly present in Shaw's play *Man and Superman* (1903). A principal character in the play speaks of "the working within me of Life's incessant aspiration to higher organization, wider, deeper intenser self-consciousness, and clearer self-understanding."[88] This continually advancing Force directs the cosmos toward a specific goal. In Shaw's vision, Revealed Word religion was "a mere excuse for laziness, since it had set up a God who looked at the world and saw that it was good." The alternative was better: "The instinct in me that looked through my eyes at the world and saw that it could be improved."[89]

Shaw advocated "evolving a mind's eye that shall see, not the physical world, but the purpose of Life."[90] Developing such a perspective will "thereby enable the individual to work for that purpose." Shaw thus praises the person who seeks "to discover the inner will of the world," and who, on the basis of that discovery, takes "action to do that will." In other words, the person of great intellect and great will works in consort with the moving spirit in nature to shape the evolutionary future of the human race. Thus, the wise or strong individual "chooses the line of greatest advantage," becoming nothing less than "Nature's pilot."[91]

The Life Force's goal is to ensure that intelligence in the universe evolves to the point of divinity. In *Man and Superman* Shaw states the point this way: "Life is a force which has made innumerable experiments to organize itself . . . [and] to build up that raw force into higher and higher individuals, the ideal individual being omnipotent, omniscient, infallible, and withal completely self-conscious: in short, a god."[92] The fully evolved divine human race will rule the cosmos. Our guide to this glorious future is not the Revealed Word's suffering servant, but rather Shaw's "Man of Philosophy," a determined and talented student of the Life Force who masters its power.

"The Revolutionist's Handbook." Though Shaw was a proponent of human advancement, he utterly rejected the Victorian notion of inevitable social progress. In an essay attached to *Man and Superman,* entitled "The Revolutionist's Handbook and Pocket Companion," Shaw argues that unless we take evolution into our own hands and provide the Life Force some assistance in perfecting us—an idea borrowed from T. H. Huxley—we humans will never see significant progress. As

Shaw urges, without evolution "we must frankly give up the notion that Man as he exists is capable of net progress."[93] All apparent evidence of progress is "an illusion." Thus, he concludes, nothing will become of the human race "unless we are replaced by a more highly evolved animal—in short, by the Superman." Without these highly evolved Supermen, "the world must remain a den of dangerous animals among whom our few accidental supermen, our Shakespeares, Goethes, Shelleys, and the like, must live as precariously as lion tamers do."[94]

In order to hasten the advent of this new breed, Shaw advocated "the selective breeding of Man," thus providing assistance to "human evolution." Progress by means of "political, scientific, educational, religious or artistic" developments—so far as we remain in our present evolutionary state—is simply meaningless. "Our only hope, then, is in evolution. We must replace the man by the superman."[95] And as we seek superman, "we must eliminate the Yahoo" as well, lest he ruin the eugenic project.[96] Government could assist the Life Force by establishing a "State Department of Evolution." Such a bureau might develop a "private society or a chartered company for the improvement of human live stock."[97]

It goes without saying that Shaw's proposal for directing human evolution toward the goal of a new race of supermen assumed the rejection of Revealed Word theology and ethics. The "men and women" who would give themselves to Shaw's exalted plan of directed human advancement are individuals who "no longer believe that they can live forever." Having rejected the Revealed Word's notion of spiritual transformation through repentance and salvation, citizens of a new world "seek for some immortal work into which they can build the best of themselves before their refuse is thrown into that arch dust collector, the cremation furnace."[98] Shaw's new hope—a highly evolved race of superhuman beings transforming life on earth—replaces the antiquated Revealed Word hope of eternal spiritual existence with God. His Darwinian vision was joined to a pantheistic faith in a universal Life Force that drove the cosmic evolutionary project ever forward. With human assistance, the terminus of this project would be superman.

At the end of the twentieth century and beginning of the twenty-first, a pantheism akin to that of Toland, Emerson, Haeckel, Bergson and Shaw found support among members of the scientific community. The following section overviews recent efforts in popular scientific writing to provide empirical grounding for a self-organizing Life Force driving the life of the universe. New Physics writers claim to have irrefutable scientific proof for the foundational pantheism of the Other Spirituality.

A NEW PANTHEISTIC PHYSICS

German physicist Max Planck revolutionized the study of physical phenomena in 1900 when he announced a theory that light acted like it was comprised of particles. As Catherine Albanese writes, "Planck described energy 'packets' in which, he said, light was emitted and absorbed. He called these packets '*quanta*,' and in his work quantum mechanics, the 'new physics' of the twentieth century, had its early beginnings." Quantum theory opened not only a new era in physics, but a new era in metaphysical speculation as well. The cosmos, once apparently made of solid matter and bound by inflexible laws, now seemed composed of energy operating according to indecipherable rules. "At the subatomic level, many scientists were saying, matter was not the solid entity that appeared to commonplace observation [and so] the line between matter and energy was fluid, the boundary not so fixed as it seemed."[99] Furthermore, if this boundary was flexible, perhaps so was the boundary between the material and the spiritual. In fact, perhaps the physical *was* the spiritual. In this way the new physics gave birth to a new pantheism.

In *The Quantum Society*, science writers Danah Zohar and Ian Marshall advocate a new pantheistic psychology and sociology grounded in quantum theory. Sounding much like Emerson positing his famous analogy between the human mind and nature, they assert that "there is an uncanny analogy between the structures and processes underlying quantum reality, and the structures and processes underlying the conscious mind."[100] This section explores the new pantheism as presented in Zohar and Marshall's fascinating and engaging *The Quantum Society*.

Emerson once referred to himself as an invisible eye observing nature, but at the same time participating in the formation of what he observed. More recently, Zohar and Marshall have affirmed what they term "the mutually creative relationship between the observer and the observed in the quantum domain." They explain that "the quantum observer does not stand outside his observations. He does not see nature as an object. Rather he *participates* in nature's unfolding" because "the observer is *part* of what he observes." No longer is the human agent distinct from the natural order, with a creator God standing above both. Rather, humans reside within that order, while at the same time participating in its creation through their observations of it.

Zohar and Marshall discover a breathtaking range of practical implications in the "fundamental physics that underlies all else that is in the universe." A common physics of existence suggests a new view of the self, of society and of personal and social ethics. But such is only to be expected, for "the nature of the mind, the nature of society, and the nature of nature are all one and the same thing," for all three are "linked by a common physics."[101] But the ultimate discovery of the New Physics is a final scientific proof of the basic correctness of Benedict Spinoza's pantheistic theology—nature *is* god. The components of that proof are worth setting out in some detail, and they focus on a particle called the *boson*.

Bosons: particles of relationship. Zohar and Marshall describe bosons as "one of only two *basic* sorts of 'particles' that make up the whole universe. The other sort are called *fermions*." Fermions, they explain, "are particles that make up things." Thus, fermions include "protons, neutrons and electrons, the basic constituents of the atom." In other words, "all of the matter of the universe is made of fermions."[102] Thus, there are two kinds of things in the universe, and all of one kind of thing is what we call matter or the physical universe. What does this leave? The inescapable answer appears to be that bosons must be *spiritual* or *mental* particles, though our authors prefer "particles of relationship." They explain that "all the fundamental forces that bind the universe together—the electromagnetic, the gravitational, the strong and weak nuclear—are made of bosons." Bosons actually exhibit "social" qualities. For instance, they appear to "like clustering together" in various experiments. In fact, Zohar and Marshall posit that "consciousness itself" may be a "boson phenomenon."[103]

Sounding at times more like philosophers than physicists, Zohar and Marshall contend that "there is a whole new 'metaphysic' of the human in this history of boson evolution." They contend that the boson is implicated in basic evolutionary process, thus taking on metaphysical implications. "If the same tendency of two bosons to bunch together at the most basic level of early physical processes can be traced in unbroken sequence to the principles underlying the physical basis for conscious mind," they write, then "we have traced the origins of the human mind back to primordial physical reality." That is to say, in the social tendencies of bosons we have discovered the evolutionary origins of the human soul itself. The boson provides a critical link between the previously immaterial human soul and the entire evolutionary process of both biological life on earth and of the universe itself. "The self carries within itself the whole history of the physical universe," they write.[104]

Of course, if this is the case then the Revealed Word idea that the human soul makes us distinct from the rest of creation is erroneous. "There is no basis, then, in the quantum worldview for any ontological distinction between the human and the natural." Zohar and Marshall recognize that this conclusion represents "a radical shift away from the whole earlier Western worldview." They also find, however, a new source of ethical insight to be derived from this new metaphysical view. When we move to a "deeper level" we discover a "quantum source of empowerment to act as personal and moral agents" rooted in "the nature and function of what physicists call the 'quantum vacuum.'" Emerging understanding of this vacuum "and our relationship to it" is causing a "revolution in our understanding of human reality."[105] What, then, is the nature of the quantum vacuum that may prove the foundation of a new reality and a new religion?

Confronting the void: Buddhist Sunyata and modern science. When physicists and astronomers probe the deep recesses of the universe, they find an indefinite and apparently infinite field of energy. As Zohar and Marshall put it, "We are confronted by a 'void,' a background without features and that therefore *seems* empty." Of course, the particles and waves of physicists must be made of something, but what? The answer to this question tells us where all physical objects originate. "All the waves and particles that we can see and measure, literally, as in the Greek, *ex*-ist or 'stand out from' an underlying sea of potential that physicists have named the vacuum . . . just as waves undulate on the sea."[106] This "sea" of proto-physicality is "an all-pervasive, underlying field of potential—the vacuum." On this view, all physical objects are surfaces on the underlying cosmic vacuum. "It is as though all surface existing things are in constant interaction with a tenuous background of evanescent reality."[107]

This view is strikingly similar to some Hindu and Buddhist accounts of the origins of physical objects as emanations from the One. In fact, Zohar and Marshall do not dispute this similarity. "The vacuum spoken of by quantum physicists, like the Buddhist concept of *Sunyata*, or the Void, to which it is so similar, is replete with all potentiality." The ineffable vacuum or void is, moreover, the ground of all true religious experience. The Buddhists say that "it is the basis of all . . . the absolute, the truth, that cannot be preached in words." The void, then, is that ultimate and divine ground of being experienced by mystics. As the beginning and ending of all reality, the vacuum is "the vast sea of all else that is." Moreover, "*We* are excited states of the vacuum."[108] The vacuum is, then, ultimate reality. "In more religious language, the vacuum is *the* All of everything."[109]

Perhaps Zohar and Marshall's most striking conclusion is that "the vacuum has the same physical structure as human consciousness." If this is the case, then the soul of the universe and the human soul are one and the same *substance*. "There is, then, quite possibly a common physics linking human consciousness to the ground state of 'everything that ever existed or can exist' in the universe," write Zohar and Marshall. They add, "This is a very exciting idea, filled with wide implications."[110] Thus, one of religion's perennial questions receives a scientific answer—we now know with certainty who we are. "We are *part* of it. Each one of us as an individual *is* an excitation of the vacuum, an individual being on the sea of Being." That we are part of the vacuum, that the structure of consciousness is the structure of the universe "is a straightforward conclusion of orthodox physics. It is, if you like, proven."[111]

Mysticism and modern physics. For Zohar and Marshall, recent physical discoveries provide us "a whole new sense of finding human beings at the center of things." But perhaps these findings are new only to science, for this essentially religious insight has been understood in other arenas for ages. That the universe is consciousness and that we are part of that consciousness "is a vision more common to the great wisdom traditions of native peoples or to the ancient Greeks, but here it is derived from the latest insights of science." Science has discovered the divinity of the great mythic and mystical traditions, the god of the New Religious Synthesis. "If we are looking for God in physics, the vacuum would be the most appropriate place to look," they write. "As the underlying ground state of all that is, the vacuum has all the characteristics of the immanent [all-pervading] God, or of the Godhead, spoken of by mystics, the God within, the God who creates and discovers Himself through the unfolding existence of His creation."[112]

The vacuum is posited as a new and scientifically proven god, though certainly not the personal and wholly other God of the Revealed Word. The New Physics has birthed a new myth with the power to inform and unify an array of religious traditions. "In this new 'myth' of the vacuum, all things that are, are expressions of the immanent God's being. All are precious and awe-inspiring, all 'filled with spark of the divine.'" Science proves that our consciousness participates in cosmic consciousness. Thus, "there is no real sense in which we are 'created in God's image.'"[113] It would be more accurate to say that we are becoming godlike.

Zohar and Marshall embrace a version of spiritual evolutionism built upon a new *gnosis*—the knowledge of quantum physics. "Because we may be possessed of *the most complex version of physics in the universe*, we may, in a strict physical sense, actually be at the vanguard of evolution." This new *gnosis* of physics, then, provides the key to our spiritual ascent. That is, because we are aware of our own thoughts, there is "a real, physical importance to the constructs of human reason." Could it be that our minds are evolving toward godhood? "This is the true, the awesome, significance of 'being created in God's image.'" That is, we are directing our own evolution, and thus the very evolution of god.[114] This notion is common to various ancient and modern gnostic and mystical systems, a fact that Zohar and Marshall acknowledge. "Indeed," they write, "there is a similarly uncanny link between many older, mystical visions and recent scientific insight."[115]

CONCLUSION

Pantheism has a long history in Western religious thought and has now, as we have seen, taken up residence in Western science. The English Deist John Toland reintroduced the ancient notion into popular religious discourse in the early eighteenth century, and since that time it has found many advocates. In America, a species of pantheism found a powerful advocate in Ralph Waldo Emerson, while in Europe the philosopher Henri Bergson provided the concept with intellectual credibility. Pantheism continued to appear in a number of popular authors in Europe and America in the early twentieth century, George Bernard Shaw being an important example. Other literary figures exploring pantheism included the German novelist and 1946 Nobel laureate Herman Hesse, who achieved extraordinary popularity in Europe in the 1920s and 1930s, and in America of the 1950s and 1960s, and who affirmed the fundamental unity and divinity of the cosmos. In his Buddhist novel *Siddhartha,* the principal character affirms, "This stone is a stone. It is also animal, God and Buddha." This fundamental insight gained through arduous effort and self-discipline leads Siddhartha to a worship of the god in nature. "This is what pleases me," he states, "and seems wonderful and worthy of worship."[116]

More recently, as we have seen, scientists and popularizers of science have found in quantum physics a new foundation for pantheistic thinking. Under the banner of pantheism, science and theology become virtually indistinguishable in some writers. Consequently, mystical spirituality is increasingly advocated by writers in the genre of the New Science, often presented as a rediscovery of an ancient spiritual truth. Clearly the appeal of pantheism and its "older, mystical visions" extends to scientists other than Danah Zohar and Ian Marshall. Daniel C. Dennett, Director of the Center for Cognitive Studies at Tufts University, also finds in pantheism a religion for a new era. This expert on the evolution of consciousness writes in his book *Darwin's Dangerous Idea* that "Darwin has shown us how, in fact, *everything* of importance is just such a product" of what Dennett terms "mindless, purposeless forces." He adds, somewhat incongruously, "Spinoza called his highest being God or Nature (*Deus sive Natura*), expressing a sort of pantheism."

So why does Dennett's book on Darwinian evolution end with a discussion of Spinozan pantheism? Apparently because Dennett finds in Darwin "a convincing *explanation* of just how God is distributed in the whole of nature." Darwin's convincing account of what can only be called pantheism draws support from "the distribution of Design throughout nature." This fact alone suggests "an utterly unique and irreplaceable creation, an actual pattern in the immeasurable reaches of Design Space that could never be exactly duplicated in its many details."[117] In other words, the design of nature is itself a kind of divinity for Dennett that does not require positing the Revealed Word's personal and wholly other deity in the cosmos. The cosmos *is* deity because the cosmos is design. Dennett asks, "What miracle caused it? None. It just happened to happen in the fullness of time." But this amazing product of happenstance does not lead Dennett to reject the idea of a spiritual reality behind the physical universe. Rather, it issues in a pantheistic faith in a divinity that *is* the universe. "The Tree of Life," Dennett's shorthand for the exquisitely designed cosmos, "created itself . . . slowly over billions of years." Does this make the cosmos "a God one could worship? Pray to? Fear? Probably not." Nevertheless, the universe "is surely a being that is greater than anything any of us will ever conceive of in any detail worthy of its detail." So what should be our response to this sort of "being"? Dennett's response recognizes it as sacred. "Is something sacred? Yes, say I with Nietzsche. I could not pray to it, but I can stand in affirmation of its magnificence. The world is sacred."[118]

Similarly, physicist Fred Alan Wolf hearkens back to an earlier time in our religious history when human spiritual vision was clearer, revealing a universe more in keeping with the findings of modern science. "According to many historians," he writes, "our ancient forebears saw God everywhere, in all nature and in all the universe. . . . Gods were seen as nature itself and observed everywhere."[119] These early spiritual explorers—Wolf dates the insight at three to four thousand years B.C.—found God to be indistinguishable from the physical objects making up their world. "Our ancient forbears envisioned a universe forming from a great void sometimes imagined to be primordial waters." Our ancestors "discovered the Creator of the universe . . . was in all nature and in all of the universe, constantly becoming."[120]

This "creator" was "contained by the creation He created" according to Wolf. This "creator," however, so common in New Synthesis writing, is certainly not of the kind envisioned in the Revealed Word, a God who willfully creates a universe that exists as something other, something distinct from its creator. Rather, Wolf's creator is the "world soul" of the pantheists, a divine essence within all things. And our own souls are simply a part of this world soul. Perhaps, he writes, "the soul inside you and the soul inside me are simply reflections of one soul living . . . in the universe at large." If this is the case, "then my soul is your soul is the only soul that ever was or ever will be."[121]

Certain implications follow from this insight. For instance, Wolf argues that suffering results from believing that I am an independent entity with lasting personal identity, a concept at the heart of the Revealed Word tradition. However, "when we realize that at another level, perhaps at a mythic one, we are God—the Universe—our children—our mothers—the apes in the trees—the rocks on the ground—when we see that we are all that there *is*, all suffering appears to melt away just as the boundaries separating our visions of ourselves vanish."[122] Can this be right? Does pantheism eliminate the problem of suffering? We will be pursuing this and other spiritual implications of New Synthesis pantheism in subsequent chapters, as pantheism has ushered in a number of ancient spiritual practices now dressed in modern garb.

8

THE REBIRTH OF GNOSTICISM

The Secret Path to Self-Salvation

His study fits a mercenary drudge,
Who aims at nothing but external trash
Too servile and illiberal for me
When all is done, divinity is best.

CHRISTOPHER MARLOWE, Dr. Faustus

The fallen angels are in prison, that is, embodied, so that Man is an apostate Angel and a Body.

JACOB ILIVE, The Oration Spoke at Joyner's Hall

You have got to learn how to become gods yourselves; to become Kings and Priests to God, the
same as all gods have done, by going from a small degree to another.

JOSEPH SMITH, King Follett Discourse

Now open your eyes and look at all the gods in hiding.

JEAN HOUSTON, A Passion for the Possible

The scene in the mansion at 18241 Colina Norte Drive in Rancho Santa Fe shocked the world. Thirty-nine bodies of men and women of various ages, identically clad in black, lay within the estate, the victims of mass suicide ordered by Marshall Applewhite, leader of the Heaven's Gate UFO cult. Among them were a thirty-nine-year-old mother of five from Cincinnati, a seventy-two-year-old grandmother from Iowa, and the fifty-nine-year-old brother of an actress from the original *Star Trek* television series. The Hale-Bopp comet, according to Applewhite, announced the arrival of a vehicle from another dimension that would usher "a select group" of followers to their destiny in the stars.[1] All they had to do was "shed their containers," the bodies containing their preexistent spirits, and move to the "Next Level."

Applewhite had been preaching his message of celibacy, secret knowledge and cosmic ascent for more than twenty years. Recruits were told that they were "highly evolved" and thus were among the "chosen ones." According to a report in *U.S. News & World Report*, "Applewhite believed that he and his followers were aliens who had been planted [on earth] years ago."[2] Descending from "a level above human in distant space," they sought to return to "their world," or the place of their cosmic origin, by following secret teachings and, eventually, destroying the material containers—their bodies—that were not part of their true nature.

THE FUNDAMENTALS OF GNOSTICISM

Marshall Applewhite's message was derived from gnosticism, a spiritual view reasserting itself today and an important component in the New Religious Synthesis. The term *gnosticism* may conjure up images of second- and third-century Christian heretics practicing secret rites, disseminating occult knowledge and challenging the stability of Christian theology.[3] For some scholars, the term *gnosticism* has itself become a contested category.[4] While *gnosticism* itself may be difficult to define with precision, a spiritual inclination I will term the gnostic impulse has been both powerful and persistent in Western religious thought.[5] This impulse manifests itself in the veneration of secret spiritual knowledge, the elevation of spiritual elites in possession of such knowledge, a denigration of time and history, a tendency to view the physical realm as evil and a corresponding tendency to view human embodiment with suspicion. The elements of the gnostic impulse are increasingly important to contemporary spiritual thought, often being joined to the notion of spiritual evolution. As will be shown in the following chapter, shamanism—the idea that secret spiritual knowledge comes by way of spirit guides—also plays a part in the gnostic impulse. Some voices for a new gnosticism will occupy our attention in the present chapter. But first it will be helpful to gain a fuller historical view of gnosticism itself.

Gnosticism is often traced back to Simon Magus (fl. A.D. 40-55), whom Peter opposed in Acts 8, and his student Menander (fl. A.D. 90-100). Valentinus, a second century teacher condemned as a heretic, was also a major figure in the establishment of Gnosticism in Europe, as was Marcion of Pontus (fl. A.D. 135-145), who actually established a series of Gnostic churches in the Roman Empire. Other early sources of Western Gnosticism include Mani (216-275), whom Augustine followed before his conversation to Christianity, and the various Neo-Platonic philosophers such as Plotinus (205-270) and Proclus (d. 466). Much of the available information about the teachings of such early Gnostics, however, comes from Christian sources who opposed them. Mystical speculation of the type that later Gnostics drew upon in developing their views can also be found in Greek philosophers, including Plato and Pythagoras, and even earlier in the works of Zoroastrian writers.

As already noted, gnosticism was a persistent and highly influential force in the development of the Western religious tradition, one constantly in tension with the Revealed Word. I will be arguing in this chapter that gnostic thought has powerfully reasserted itself over the past three centuries. However, because gnosticism is itself a contested term, it will be important to clarify what I take to be the defining marks of the gnostic impulse in contemporary spiritual systems. So, what makes a religious view gnostic?

Rising above it all: transcending time and the physical. In its most elemental form, gnosticism is the systematic spiritual effort to escape the confines of history and physical embodiment through secret knowledge (*gnosis*) and technique (magic). Gnostics seek to rise above the crowd of ordinary mortals who lack the will to break the chains of time and earthly existence. Thus, Henri-Charles Puech has called gnosticism "a 'revolt' against all myths and belief systems which purport to give time some indwelling meaning."[6] Time, history and the earthly realm are the gnostic's enemies. Conventional religious "myths" that give history legitimacy and that make the physical world a significant place—Christianity with its emphasis on both history and incarnation being the singular example—must be demolished. Yuri Stoyanov, an expert on medieval gnosticism, notes that gnostics advanced "allegorical interpretations of the gospels and parts of the Old Testament" because of their aversion to history and historically based faith.[7] One is reminded here of both Woolston and Strauss.

Gnostic spirituality, then, exhibits a deep suspicion of history and any attendant notions such as God's redemptive work in history. The gnostic dispenses with the historical Christ of Christianity, choosing instead to pursue self-salvation through secrets that come from beyond the earthly and historical scheme of things. Sin—a historical category associated with the Fall as well as with particular actions in time—is not humanity's captor, as the Revealed Word would have it. Rather, ignorance is—particularly ignorance of liberating spiritual secrets or *gnosis*. Thus, *gnosis*, not the Revealed Word's divinely initiated redemption, is the solution to our collective predicament. Gnosticism also typically involves demeaning the creator God of the Old Testament, the God of history and of the entire physical realm that he created in time and out of matter. True divinity—known to gnostics as the *pleroma* or fullness—is inaccessible and unknowable in our present limited state.

Secrecy and the spiritual elite. The central component in gnosticism is *gnosis* itself, esoteric knowledge unavailable to and, importantly, unattainable by the general run of humanity. Such secret knowledge usually developed around a myth about a titanic struggle between the highest divine being along with his cohort, and a lower creator God over the creation of the human race itself. In short, humanity resulted from a misdirected effort to combine pristine spiritual consciousness with fallen physical matter. To apprehend this myth, this *gnosis*, was to take the first step toward spiritual self-liberation. Other steps followed as additional secrets were learned. Thus, gnostics "purported to offer knowledge of the otherwise hidden truth of total reality as the indispensable key to man's salvation," writes Hans Jonas.[8] Gnosticism taught "salvation by enlightenment," and enlightenment always came in the same way—by mastering hidden knowledge. *Gnosis* allowed the soul's ascent into the higher reaches of spiritual experience, divinity itself being the ultimate tantalizing possibility.

In all gnostic systems, ancient or modern, spiritual awareness comes to and through a small minority of the spiritually capable. The members of this spiritual elite go by many names: seers, ascended masters, prophets, pneumatics, *perfecti*, shamans, illuminati, mystics, magi and adepts. Typically these individuals alone determine which other mortals will enter the inner sanctum of *gnosis*. As Carl Raschke writes, gnosticism always depends on "esoteric wisdom accessible only to the privileged or initiated few."[9]

Spiritual elitism, then, is an essential aspect of the gnostic impulse. Moreover, the enlightened ones loath the unenlightened as spiritually inferior beings incapable of spiritual ascent. The initiated or *pneumatikoi* are the "truly 'spiritual' people, despising the uninitiated as *psuchikoi*, doomed to an animal life on earth."[10] As a result of their exalted spiritual perspective, spiritual masters often reject conventional morality as belonging to a lower order of things, and thus consider themselves to be living lives above morality. The gnostic master, writes Hans Jonas, is "free from the yoke of the moral law, and all things are permitted to him."[11]

The power promised to initiates by gnostic masters of the ancient world was truly mind-boggling. Divinity itself loomed as a seductive possibility. Disciples were taught to envision themselves as one with the universe. Jack Lindsay, a leading expert on the spiritual beliefs of the classical world, quotes an ancient source of gnostic lore known as the *Asclepius*. A man possessing the appropriate secret knowledge is promised dominion over a world, or "as the Greeks say more correctly, an order [cosmos]."[12] The initiate literally takes on the qualities of a God. "Grasp . . . in your mind that nothing is impossible for you," he is taught. "Consider yourself immortal and capable of understanding everything. . . . Gather into yourself the sensations of creation, fire and of water, of dryness and of humidity, imaging that you are at one and the same moment everywhere, on earth, in the sea, in the heaven, that you have not yet been born, that you are beyond death."[13]

JACOB ILIVE: ENLIGHTENMENT GNOSTIC

Carl Raschke has written that a "wistful recollection of a marvelous prehistory" animates the gnostic mind, a yearning for a time before historical forces corrupted human religious belief.[14] The spiritual view of the earliest human beings has often been seen as a key to discovering an authentic spirituality that would provide the basis for a new religion to replace the Revealed Word. In pristine prehistory, it is assumed, human beings enjoyed uninhibited access to spiritual truth. For instance, Enlightenment Deists affirmed a primitive and universal religion of Reason, a faith uncorrupted by a devious priestly caste and literal notions of history. According to the Deist Jacob Ilive, Adam and Eve practiced a pure religion of Reason. But modern religions have departed "so far from their origin" that they have "lost their primitive intention."[15] Ilive and many others set about to reclaim that early religion or to invent a new religion that would capture its content. His work in this regard is intriguing and has proven surprisingly influential.

Jacob Ilive (1705-1763) was a prominent member of the London printers' guild. As early as the 1730s he began delivering lectures in London guildhalls. He affirmed that the human soul was not created, but preexistent and eternal.[16] Ilive identified this eternal human soul with the key Deist term *reason*. More startling was his additional claim that each human soul was a fallen angel imprisoned in a human body.[17] Over a period of twenty years Ilive reinvented and popularized a brand of gnosticism in which his unusual theory of human origins and spiritual progress played a prominent role.

Fallen angels on their own planet. Like most other ancient people, early gnostics found the stars crucial to shaping human destiny. The force of such "astral fatalism" in the ancient world is difficult for modern people to apprehend, but even educated and powerful people feared to make a major decision or begin a journey without consulting the stars. Moreover, the stars were thought to reflect the actual presence of spiritual beings—sometimes referred to as elemental spirits—who held the keys to human spiritual advancement. Some of these star-dwelling beings had at one time been humans who employed spiritual secrets to achieve their divine ascent. Ilive brought such ancient notions to life again between 1730 and 1750.

In a 1733 lecture presented at the London Joyner's Hall, Ilive envisioned a massive and ancient struggle for control of heaven. A lower divinity named Jesus defeated Lucifer, who was subsequently expelled from the celestial realm.[18] Lucifer and his host of fallen angels were imprisoned on earth where human bodies were fashioned as "certain little Places of Confinement for the reception of [these] apostate Angels."[19] However, the highest God was intent on "bringing back again the rebellious and apostate angels" by putting them through a series of purgatorial exercises on the prison-planet earth.[20] Thus, in keeping with the dominant gnostic myth, the human race was created as the consequence of a spiritual struggle, and represents the imperfect combination of deposed angelic spirits and physical bodies.

Ilive also imagined numerous other inhabited planets, founding his speculations on Jesus' statement, "In my Father's house are many mansions." These other planets are "Celestial Mansions" that humans may eventually inhabit and govern provided sufficient progress toward their spiritual redemption is achieved. Greater advancement will be rewarded with assignment to more prominent planets. But for now the purgatorial period must be endured. Earth, "that Globe we now inhabit," is hell, which is not so much a place of torment as it is a correctional facility created specifically "for the reception of the Rebellious Angels." Thus, "no new Order of Beings was created on Purpose to people [the earth]" as the Revealed Word tradition affirms.[21] Far from being the special creations of God, humans are "fallen Angels . . . in Prison," each of us being "an apostate Angel and a Body."[22] Repeatedly Ilive affirmed the myth at the center of his new *gnosis*: "the very fallen Angels [are] cloathed in Flesh, and . . . the Place we now inhabit, is Hell, and no other place."[23] This account closely parallels second- and third-century Gnostic accounts of a "world dominated by the evil angels."[24] But Gnostics held out the hope that these fallen spirits might "return to the heights of knowledge" provided they gained access to the appropriate mythic secrets, or *gnosis*.[25]

Other Enlightenment writers were familiar with gnostic thinking, and some hinted at its merits. Charles Gildon commended the view of "the *Pythagoreans* and *Chaldeans*," who believed human souls "were created in Heaven, and thence transmitted to the Bodies for punishment." As a result, "we are Devils."[26] Charles Blount in *Anima mundi* (1678) elevated the gnostic myth that "the fall of those evil Angels" who assisted Lucifer in his rebellion "occasioned our Corporeal Creation." Human bodies are places for "those wicked Spirits" to be imprisoned, the spirits being now human "souls." These fallen angels were placed in human bodies "for expiating their guilt," and thus "our Sublunary Orb," or earth, became "the only Hell."[27]

"Astro-Theology." Ilive found support for his gnostic theology in an earlier eighteenth-century work, William Derham's *Astro-Theology* (1715).[28] Derham had argued, based on astronomical observations, that the universe contained innumerable planets. These other planets "consist in all probability of Land and Water, Hills and valleys, having atmosphere about them, and being enlightened, warmed and influenced by the Sun, whose yearly visits they receive as Seasons, and frequent Returns for days and nights."[29] Some of Derham's planets, comets and stars are, like Ilive's earth, hells.[30] There is much more going on in the universe than we can know from our puny planet, which, Derham points out, is insignificant on a cosmic scale.[31]

Derham claimed that the Dutch astronomer Huygens had observed planets orbiting other stars. "The usual Question is," Derham writes, "what is the use of so many Planets as we see about the Sun, and so many as are imagined to be about the Fix'd Stars? To which the answer is, that they are *Worlds*, or places of *Habitation*, which is concluded from their being *habitable*, and well provided for habitation."[32] Some astronomers, according to Derham, had actually seen human-like beings moving about on these planets. Thus, extraterrestrials make an Enlightenment appearance, and in direct connection with a new theological view—Ilive's gnosticism. As we saw at the beginning of this chapter in the description of the Heaven's Gate UFO cult, the connection between extraterrestrials and new gnostic theologies is an active one on the contemporary spiritual scene.

Moses the magician. Scholars have often wondered about the "fierce anti-Jewish polemics of ancient Gnosticism."[33] Gnostics rejected anything to do with the Jews or the Old Testament, treating Yahweh the Creator-God as a bungler or worse. Anti-Semitism, hating this inferior God's chosen people, followed logically. A similar anti-Semitic thrust is clear in Ilive's writings. Moses in particular comes in for harsh treatment. The great and deadly plagues that struck Egypt were "wrought by Moses's Knowledge in the Magick Art."[34] Moses and his general Caleb plotted and personally helped to carry out the murder of all of the first-born children of the Egyptians. He and his henchmen were guilty of "killing the harmless babies while they sleep."[35] Moses also masterminded the theft of Egyptian property. Thus, Ilive concludes that "by Murder and Theft [Moses] procured their Freedom" from Egypt. Far from being the chosen people of God, the Jews are portrayed as a murderous band of renegades under the leadership of the vicious general Caleb and the cunning sorcerer Moses. For Ilive the biblical history of the Jews is a lie, and "the *Jewish* Religion . . . a grievous Yoke."[36]

The Book of Jasher. In 1751 Ilive published a transparent forgery entitled *The Book of Jasher*, a lost book mentioned twice in the Old Testament, once in Joshua 10:13, and again in 2 Samuel 1:18. This unusual and controversial work—which is still published by the Rosicrucians—is moral fiction intended to register a series of theological points or, more accurately, corrections. That is, *The Book of Jasher* is a myth based on stories from Genesis and advances several speculative theological ideas that support Ilive's gnostic views. The book's wide readership for two centuries and its lasting influence suggest it is worthy of our attention.

As noted above, Deists speculated that early human beings practiced a pure religion of reason, an idea central to Ilive's theology. Early gnostics often taught a similar concept—that early and universal knowledge of *gnosis* had been lost to humanity over long eons of time. Gnostic interpretations of the Garden of Eden narrative cast the serpent in a hero's role as the bringer of liberating knowledge, an idea also reflected in the Deist Peter Annet's theology. The Fall was thus a "fall up," as humans gained knowledge that set them on a path toward divinity. In similar fashion, Ilive's recounting of the Eden incident in *Jasher* involves no human fall into sin. Ilive affirms in *Jasher* that Adam practiced a pure religion, later corrupted by the first priest, Enos, who invented something Ilive terms "the worship of the body."[37] Enos and his ilk wrongly directed humanity's religious thinking away from the unsullied realm of reason and spirit, and toward the physical and the temporal.

Moreover, the concept of sin—a time-bound notion rejected by gnostics—developed out of early religious stories corrupted during centuries of transmission. Ilive is at pains to remove the stain of human sin from the Genesis stories through strategic retellings in *Jasher*. For example, Cain never actually murdered his brother Abel; he merely slew Abel's beast, and the story was related with the crucial error that one brother had killed the other. "From this act of Cain slaying the beast of Abel, it seemeth, arose that story recorded in the book of Moses, that Cain slew

Abel." Nor did God employ a flood to punish human sin. Rather, Noah simply invented "a floating cave, a vehicle, a house to remain upon the surface of the waters."[38] Other biblical stories were similarly corrupted over time. For instance, Abraham was not instructed to sacrifice Isaac, but misunderstood the angel's instructions.[39]

In *The Book of Jasher* Ilive also sought to provide natural explanations for miraculous events. Miracles were offensive to the Deist mind as violations of the rule of reason by which the cosmos operated, and which even God was bound to follow. Gnostics rejected the notion of miracle as well, for the transcendent God—always distinguished from the lower Creator God—does not meddle in the evil material world. Thus, the miracle of Isaac's birth to Sarah and Abraham after Sarah had grown too old to conceive is creatively refashioned. In Ilive's telling, Isaac is born to the aging patriarch and his wife after Sarah instructs her husband to circumcise himself, thus allowing a stronger flow of semen. In one stroke, so to speak, what appeared to be a miraculous pregnancy is explained away.[40]

In sum, by his strategic rewriting of Genesis accounts, Ilive suggested to his readers—many of whom would have believed they were reading a translation of a lost Hebrew text—that the Bible they usually read was not a Revealed Word but a priestly deception. Moreover, his approach to history in *Jasher* as an invented narrative to be shaped and adapted according to theological need reflects the gnostic's disdain for history. Another author drawn to imaginative historical reconstruction began shaping the American religious mind early in the nineteenth century. As with Ilive, gnosticism likewise informs the religious invention of Joseph Smith.

JOSEPH SMITH'S YANKEE GNOSTICISM

Americans are so familiar with the Mormon Church, a common name for the Church of Jesus Christ of the Latter Day Saints, that they have difficulty imagining that its theology is only vaguely Christian. And yet the teachings of Mormonism's founder, Joseph Smith, are much closer to those of ancient gnostics than they are to New Testament Christianity. Smith (1805-1844) helped to popularize a gnostic cosmology in mid-nineteenth-century America.[41] Harold Bloom correctly observed in 1992 that "the Gnostic components in Mormonism are overt, but called by different terms," and it is to these components that I wish to drawn attention in this section.[42] As one of the fastest growing religious groups in the world, and one of the most aggressively evangelistic, Mormonism wields tremendous influence and demands attention.

Spirit guides and secret revelations. Joseph Smith insisted that the revelations on which he based Mormonism were private, coded and delivered to him by spirit guides, each element in this set suggesting his gnostic orientation. Spirit or angel visitation was a feature of Smith's young adulthood. He claimed to have been visited in 1820, at the age of fourteen, by two spiritual beings now referred to as angels by the Mormon Church. In 1823, another spiritual entity identifying himself by the name Moroni appeared to Smith. The Moroni visitations continued yearly between 1823 and 1827. D. Michael Quinn notes in his well-researched book *Early Mormonism and the Magic World View* that these visitations always occurred on the autumnal equinox, September 22, in keeping with Smith's deeply rooted astrological convictions regarding auspicious days for such contact.[43]

Moroni directed Joseph Smith to a number of golden plates buried in a hill near Palmyra, New York. The plates contained the narrative history of North America's ancient inhabitants, one among them being Moroni himself during his physical life on earth. Smith had to visit the specified site near Palmyra regularly over a period of three years before he was allowed to actually take possession of the plates.[44]

Smith alleged that the golden plates were inscribed with characters from a hitherto unknown version of Egyptian hieroglyphic. Moroni, the spirit guardian of this golden textual treasure, gave Smith permission to translate the plates into English with the help of the Urim and Thummim, stones in a breastplate that Smith found with the inscribed plates. Witnesses familiar with Smith's magical inclinations claim that the stones were actually "peepstones" of the type Joseph and his father had used to seek treasure. We will take a closer look at the Smiths and their alleged treasure hunting shortly.

From Smith's private translation of these plates—knowledge of this unusual Egyptian symbol system was limited to Joseph himself—came *The Book of Mormon*, a historical work cast in prose reminiscent of the King James Version of the Bible. *The Book of Mormon* describes several ancient immigrations to North America by Semitic peoples, some of whom are the lost tribes of Israel. Great battles on the North American continent between the Israelites, or Nephites, and other Semitic tribes called the Lamanites, resulted in the complete destruction of the former. This history is of vital importance to Mormonism, and yet its authenticity has always been a matter of great doubt. Jan Shipps, a leading student of Mormonism, comments that "in Mormonism, history has always been at one and the same time unusually significant and very problematic."[45]

Shipps is certainly right if Smith's historical accounts were intended as ordinary textbook history. But another reading is possible. *The Book of Mormon*, like Ilive's *Book of Jasher*, may reflect a disregard for ordinary history, presenting instead Smith's own mythic history or *gnosis*. Before considering Smith's unorthodox approach to history and history's relationship to his gnostic leanings, it is crucial to understand something of the singular social setting in which he was reared.

Magic and hidden treasures: the Smiths of Palmyra. Michael Quinn writes that the family in which Joseph Smith grew up was deeply immersed in legends and folk magic common on the American frontier of the early nineteenth century. Quinn notes that Smith's mother practiced divination of various kinds, "including palm reading."[46] Moreover, Smith's father, like many American men of his day, was "preoccupied with treasure-digging."[47] The Smith family owned "implements of ritual magic," which included a "magic dagger" and three ritual parchments "inscribed with signs and names of ceremonial magic."[48] It is perhaps not surprising, then, that as a young man Joseph Smith was associated with Luman Walter, a "conjurer and Smith's mentor."[49] Throughout his life, Smith was an ardent believer in astrology.[50]

Joseph Smith and his father and brother were well known for their treasure seeking activities.[51] According to a contemporary witness, Martin Harris, Joseph and his father "dug for money in Palmyra, Manchester, also in Pennsylvania, and other places."[52] Treasure seeking was a common activity among the rural residents of upstate New York in the early nineteenth century, fueled by legends about buried pirate loot and deposits of Spanish gold. The hills of some districts were pockmarked with the shallow mines of men desperate to find forgotten gold, silver and jewels. Treasure seeking typically involved the use of magical devices such as divining stones and rods, as well as astrological charts, talismans and other paraphernalia owned by the Smith family.

The idea that secret knowledge led one to personal advancement pervaded the atmosphere Joseph Smith breathed as a young man. Moreover, such notions were intertwined with spiritistic supernaturalism and magical practices. In such a setting, the youthful Joseph Smith claimed he had discovered a pearl of great price: ancient and mysterious golden plates buried in a hillside. It is also understandable why Smith would give the discovery a religious meaning, why spirit beings directed him to the plates, why they were written in a code and why magical stones were required to decode them.

The Book of Mormon: sources. Smith's story of his angelic visitations and subsequent translation of the golden plates has been contested from the beginning. However, the polemical nature of virtually everything written by or about the Mormons during the first decades of the organization makes it difficult to know which accounts to believe. It is thus perhaps more productive to focus on the one point of objective agreement between Mormons and their critics—that *The Book of Mormon* with its epic stories of North America's early residents is crucial to Mormon history and theology. What, then, are the most likely sources of Smith's mythic histories if one does not accept the story of angelically revealed ancient golden plates written in an unknown and unknowable hieroglyphic? Again, social milieu is important.

The origin of Native Americans was a topic of great controversy virtually from the moment Europeans set foot on North American soil. Speculation often focused on the ten mysterious lost northern tribes of Israel. Perhaps, somehow, members of these tribes had traversed the Mediterranean Sea and Atlantic Ocean and established a new life in the New World. As early as the 1650s published versions of this theory appeared in the English colonies. By the early nineteenth century, then, such speculation had known almost two centuries of development. It mattered little to a fascinated American public that legitimate historians dismissed such accounts, and it mattered not at all to the young backwoodsman Joseph Smith Jr.

In 1823, Ethan Smith—not related to Joseph—published a book entitled *View of the Hebrews*. Harry L. Ropp notes that Ethan Smith's *View of the Hebrews* presents a detailed theory that the American Indians are descended from the Israelites, suggests that a book of their early history in America is buried somewhere on the American continent, and discusses early Egyptian documents. In other ways as well *View of the Hebrews* is similar to Joseph Smith's *The Book of Mormon*.[53] *View of the Hebrews* was republished in 1825, both the first and second printings occurring in Poultney, Vermont. Poultney was the place of residence of one of Joseph Smith's early partners, Oliver Cowdery. In 1825 Cowdery moved to New York and met Joseph Smith.

Other possible sources for *The Book of Mormon* include an epic tale of ancient North American tribes in conflict by Reverend Solomon Spaulding. Spaulding's manuscript, never published, also developed the theory that Native Americans were descendants of the Israelites. Spaulding wrote his fictional work in 1809 while living in Conneaut, Ohio. Ropp writes:

In 1812, Spaulding and his family moved to Amity, Pennsylvania, near Pittsburgh, and there he turned his manuscript over to Robert Patterson, a local printer, to be published. Patterson had an employee, J. H. Harrison, who was a friend of Sidney Rigdon. Rigdon frequently lounged around the printing office, and when the manuscript came up missing, Rigdon was suspected of the theft.[54]

Rigdon was critically important to Mormonism's founding. In fact, some scholars speculate that Mormon theology owes more to Rigdon than to Smith.[55] According to this theory, "Rigdon reworked the [Spaulding] manuscript with the aid of Smith and Cowdery, and this we have as the *Book of Mormon*."[56] However, Harry Ropp entertains the possibility that Smith used several sources—the Bible, the Spaulding manuscript, Ethan Smith's *View of the Hebrews*—to prepare *The Book of Mormon*. The controversy surrounding Smith and Rigdon's sources will likely never be resolved to the satisfaction of all interested parties. That there are parallels between Smith's *Book of Mormon* and the ideas of both Ethan Smith and Solomon Spaulding is strongly suggestive but not conclusive. Both his cosmology and the fact that it was founded on a mythic *gnosis*, a secret spiritual history, places Joseph Smith in the tradition of ancient gnosticism. That remarkable cosmology has had enormous impact on the American religious mind.

Smith's cosmology. Like early Gnostic mythologies, *The Book of Mormon* represents a rhetorical revolt against the whole Revealed Word tradition. Smith's encoded golden plates and spirit visitations provided him private access to *gnosis* or liberating spiritual secrets.[57] The spiritual truths derived by these magical means were held as personal secrets, the full contents of which were shared only with a small inner circle.[58] Several components in Mormon cosmology reflect gnostic influences.

Mormonism finds humans to be embodied preexisting souls, with earthly life being an important step on a journey toward divinity that is directed by the teachings and rituals of the church, some of which remain secret to outsiders. The end of the process of one's progressive escape from mundane restraints is elevation to divinity itself. "You have got to learn how to become gods yourselves; to become Kings and Priests to God, the same as all gods have done, by going from a small degree to another," Smith taught his followers. Harold Bloom has written, "though many Mormons now are uncomfortable with their very human God, their prophet was emphatic in his insistence that God had begun as a man upon our common earth, and had earned godhood through his own efforts."[59]

According to Smith, God the father and his wife are continually engaged in the propagation of spirit children who in turn await birth into human bodies in order to begin their ascent toward divinity. Adam of the Garden of Eden is also understood as a god who had been assigned to earth by a higher deity. Jesus, like Adam, resides in a lower echelon of gods. Anthony Hoekema sums up some of the gnostic principles of Mormon theology in a fashion strikingly reminiscent of Ilive's accounts in the Joyner's Hall address. Hoekema writes, "all gods first existed as spirits, came to an earth to receive bodies, and then, after having passed through a period of probation on the aforesaid earth, were advanced to the exalted position they now enjoy in the heavenly realm."[60] The Revealed Word's sharp distinction between the Creator and the creature is lost in Smith's cosmic progressivism that renders God an evolved human being, and all human beings potential gods. The idea that humans evolve or progress toward divinity is central to Mormon cosmology. Reflecting the gnostic astrological interest in stars and planets as residences of ascended human beings, Smith also promised faithful followers lordship over celestial bodies. Harold Bloom has correctly noted that "Mormons have a Gnostic freedom from the world of nature, a necessary liberty for men who aspire to become gods, each with his own planet, a world altogether his own."[61]

Such astral speculation, like spiritual evolution, was crucial to Smith's worldview.[62] Smith was taken with the stars, finding them critical to human spiritual progress. As noted above, Quinn argues that Smith's visits with Moroni occurred at astrologically propitious times. Moreover, a great star called Kolob was the site, according to Smith, where a council of divine beings initiated the vast spiritual plan in which humans still participate. Earth is a planet created jointly by Jesus (called Jehovah) and his father (Elohim) for carrying out the plan. Also involved in earth's creation were Michael (Adam in preexistent form), maybe Noah and Enoch, and perhaps even Joseph Smith before he was born. "The creation of this earth," writes Hoekema, "was thus a kind of cooperative venture between the gods and the spirits of certain preexistent men."[63]

All of these elements in the Smithian cosmology are at odds with central commitments of the Revealed Word tradition, which teaches the earth's creation *ex nihilo*—out of nothing—by the one true God. Smith taught, on the other hand, the gnostic idea that the "creation" of earth was merely a reorganization of existing matter. Bruce McKonkie, a Mormon writer, argues that "to create is to organize." Thus, "it is an utterly false and uninspired notion to believe that the world or any other thing was created out of nothing." Another Mormon authority concurs, writing that God "cannot conceivably originate matter."[64] Thus, on Smith's interpretation the creative activity of the various gods was limited to reorganizing matter into various physical forms, one of which was the human body.

Joseph Smith embraced and taught a cosmology that more closely resembles gnostic thinking than the theology expressed in the Revealed Word. Smith affirmed spiritual ascent toward divinity through the combination of disciplined effort and *gnosis* or spiritual secrets. Joseph Smith conceived of himself as the human conduit of these secrets from the spirit world. Moreover, he viewed physical embodiment as a probationary condition temporarily endured for the sake of human spiritual advancement to higher realms of existence—from telestial through terrestrial to celestial. For all of these reasons, Smith can be understood as a potent advocate of gnostic spirituality in nineteenth-century America. In the last century and a half millions have embraced Smith's message, and many others who have not become Mormons have been influenced by his basic cosmology.

CARL JUNG AND THE GNOSTIC IMPULSE

Few writers or thinkers have had a greater shaping influence on contemporary thought than the Swiss-born psychoanalyst Carl Jung (1875-1961). Joseph Campbell refers to Jung as "a scholar in the grand style, whose researches, particularly in comparative mythology, alchemy and the psychology of religion, have inspired and augmented the findings of an astonishing number of the leading scholars of our time."[65] Major shaping influences in the development of Jung's own thoughts about religion include, among others, Nietzsche, Eastern religious thought and ancient gnostic writers.

Jung's principal role in the twentieth century may not have been the propagation of psychoanalytic theories. Rather, he has been a highly successful proponent of a closely related set of religious ideas, some of which are at the center of the New Religious Synthesis. He retrieved for modern Western readers many ancient Eastern, gnostic and occult ideas such as the divinity of the individual, the existence of spiritual *gnosis*, the reality of a spiritual elite and the legitimacy of parapsychological phenomena. He is famous for affirming that humanity's various divinities are generated from deep within the human psyche and that individual human minds are connected by a vast psychic force he termed "the collective unconscious." Moreover, Jung found the individual to be "the maker of history."[66] Jung disseminated these ideas in his many books and essays on psychoanalysis, religious psychology and mythology. A leading expert on Jung's spiritual ideas, Richard Noll, writes, "Such ancient ideas, ironically, are what Jung is best known for introducing as modern innovations." Indeed, Noll comments, these ideas "are so widely spread in our culture through their connections to psychotherapeutic practice, New Age spirituality, and neopaganism that they continue to be the subject of innumerable workshops, television shows, bestselling books, and video cassettes, and they form the basis of a brand of psychotherapy with its own trade name: Jungian analysis."[67]

A return to gnosticism. Jung grew up as part of a social elite in late nineteenth-century Switzerland. Consequently, "Nietzschean ideals of a new nobility were . . . grounded in Jung's personal and practical experience."[68] But from the time he was a young man, Jung also had a strong interest in spiritistic phenomena, also probably derived from his family situation. Whereas Jung's father was a Protestant pastor, his mother maintained a decided interest in the occult. Jung recalls his mother's involvement with a spiritual medium, and he was known to take notes at seances. His mother also "introduced him as a child to Hindu gods, for which he maintained a lifetime fascination."[69] He eventually rejected the Christian theology of his father, cultivating in its place an intense fascination with ancient mystery cults, especially the Roman cult of Mithra.[70] One commentator writes, "Jung's works abound in selections from Gnostics, mystics, and alchemists, all of whom pointed to the God within."[71]

Indeed, Jung came to affirm "mankind's native divinity" and called for "a return to the Gnostic sense of God as an inner, directing presence."[72] This required turning away from the external forces of both history and the wholly other God of the Bible, and toward the interior life of the soul. His vehement rejection of Christianity and the entire Revealed Word tradition was focused specifically on this point—that it had "emptied the soul of a native divine presence" and made God external.[73] Jung also held, in keeping with gnostic theories, that the soul experienced "imprisonment in the body" from which it could be led into unity with the divine through techniques of psychic magic.[74] Jung's effort to found a new religion based on gnostic thought was fueled by moral outrage against Revealed Word thinking and its enfeebling effect on the human psyche. A return to gnosticism was the true path to spiritual liberation for the Western world.

The Volk and the East. Perhaps because of his strong interest in gnostic and occult thought, Jung was drawn to the Volkish movement that Nietzsche helped to foment. Jung "undoubtedly felt himself to be part of the community of Germanic

Volk united by its faith in a field of life-energy, with all of its accompanying transcendent spirituality and pantheistic beliefs."[75] With its foundational concept of an
Aryan spiritual elite, the Volkish movement created some of the preconditions for
the rise of Nazism in Germany. Jung became an important proponent of Volkish
thinking, and many in Europe and America were influenced by his views. Historians have often obscured the connection between the widely admired Jung and a
movement with decidedly racialist tendencies. According to Jung biographer Richard Noll, Jungians "seem to place more value on preserving an image of Jung as a
divinely inspired human vessel for dispensing the eternal truths of the spirit."[76]

Jung was also a devoted student of Eastern religious thought, finding it superior
in many ways to the Western theology expressed in the Revealed Word. In his essay
"The Difference Between Eastern and Western Thinking" Jung wrote that "the
East" possessed "a superior psychic proficiency [which] is throwing our spiritual
world into confusion."[77] This was a spiritual confusion of which Jung most decidedly approved. The West was destined to jettison the outmoded spirituality of the
Revealed Word tradition in favor of a blend of ancient wisdom and modern psychological insight. Only in this way could it save itself from the destructive tendencies of
monotheism. In fact, Jung held that all religious traditions would be transcended by
"a religious consciousness much richer and more encompassing than any that had
yet been manifested."[78] This new and universal religion of humanity would arise
from within the human psyche itself.

Jung foresaw the advent of an Eastern inspired Religious Synthesis in the West,
albeit an advent largely hidden from direct view. "We have not yet hit upon the
thought," he wrote, "that while we are overpowering the Orient from without, it
may be fastening its hold on us from within."[79] Jung's vast study of religious systems convinced him that "the East is at the bottom of every spiritual change we are
passing through today."[80]

A new spiritual path for the West. Jung believed that the West was "at the threshold of a new spiritual epoch." He was himself a major force pushing Europe and
American toward that threshold. Noll writes that "Freud may still be the genius of
choice for the learned elite of the late twentieth century, but it is clear that, in sheer
numbers alone, it is Jung who has won the cultural war and whose works are more
widely read and discussed in the popular culture of our age."[81] While "practitioners
and theoreticians" advocate Jungian psychoanalysis, "far greater numbers" of
Westerners are drawn to Jungian "spirituality."[82] Jung is more important today as

a spiritual guide than as a clinical theorist, and the spiritual guidance he offers is fundamentally gnostic and esoteric in outlook. Jungian groups "sponsor programs and workshops related to New Age spirituality and neopaganism." Noll adds that "most Jungian analytic-training institutes" also provide "practical classes or programs on astrology, the I Ching, palmistry, and other practices associated with the occult sciences."[83]

At least one leading Jungian analyst, Edward Edinger, "openly acknowledges Jung's role as a prophet in the twentieth century," a voice ushering in a new religious age. Edinger terms Jung's *Collected Works* "a divinely inspired 'new dispensation' to succeed the Jewish and Christian dispensations of the Old and New Testaments." Jung's works are "read as part of the services of a New Age 'Gnostic Church' in San Francisco, as they are alongside the works of Emerson at some Unitarian services." Noll openly wonders if with the "Jungian movement and its merger with the New Age spirituality of the late twentieth century we are witnessing the incipient stages of a faith based on the apotheosis of Jung as a God-man." He concludes, "Only history will tell if Jung's Nietzschean religion will finally win its Kulturkampf and replace Christianity with its own personal religion of the future."[84] In the enormously influential works of Carl Jung, the confrontation between the New Religious Synthesis and the Revealed Word could not be more pronounced.

JEAN HOUSTON: GNOSTICISM AND THE NEW AGE

Bestselling author and sought-after speaker Jean Houston (b. 1941) is one of the leading proponents of the idea that new scientific discoveries are assisting a revolutionary understanding of human spirituality. Some of Houston's many books include *The Possible Human, Mind Games, The Search for the Beloved, A Mythic Life* and *The Hero and the Goddess*. Among the greatest influences on Houston's thought and writing are Carl Jung and Joseph Campbell. Houston focuses attention on mythology, spiritual evolution, and techniques for exploring the realm of the psyche including meditation and guided experiences. She offers courses in developing personal spiritual potential through her Mystery School in Oregon and Institute for Mind Research in New York.

Jean Houston affirms that the modern residents of the industrialized West stand at the threshold of a new religious era. In *A Passion for the Possible*, a popular book that resulted in a PBS television series, she sets out both the Darwinism and monism that underlie her own theories of unlimited spiritual evolution. "Our cells," she writes, "contain the memories of all things past—the birth of stars, the coming of life, the experience of being fish and amphibian, reptile and early mammal, monkey and human, and the lure now calling us from beyond the horizon to enter the next stage of our becoming."[85] Within each one of us lies latent an unlimited spiritual potential awaiting an awakening. Indeed, Houston contends that within each of us there exists deity itself.

Exploring of the inner realm of myth and mind will characterize the new spiritual age, much as exploring outer space characterized the scientific era of the late twentieth century. At the very core of the emerging religious paradigm shift is the monistic recognition that all things are one thing. "Eventually the worlds within and without," writes Houston, "are recognized as inseparable parts of the One Reality in which we live and move and have our being."[86] Houston urges her readers to follow her on a quest for the truths that this basic insight provides when taken to its logical, or spiritual, conclusion. Thus, she issues an exciting and winsome call to the new religious seeker to "whet your appetite for inner adventure."[87] This inner journey toward enlightenment is distinctly gnostic, with spiritual secrets important to one's progress being revealed during an interior passage through the psyche.

Going inside to find activating intelligence. Houston presents herself as a friendly, supportive and knowledgeable guide to the realm of the soul. The "inner adventure" begins with readers imagining that they are "climbing a spiral path up a small mountain."[88] On the ascent, various thresholds must be crossed, doorways entered and spirit beings confronted. Light plays a prominent role on this upward and interior journey. "Suddenly you see a light. Another doorway is before you. Its shiny surface is a mirror." This is the entrance "to the realm of the Psyche."[89] Once inside this new realm we realize that we are not alone, for within us reside many selves, in fact, "a vast crew."[90] Houston affirms that the members of this crew are simply expressions of the varieties of the self—a thinker, an artist, a psychologist.

This crew, however, is under the direction of its own Guide, an entity Houston draws attention to throughout this and other of her books. This being is "a presence that all the other selves regard with awe and respect." Houston identifies this dominant presence as the evolved self, the "you who has evolved into all that you could be." Houston acknowledges that "the presence is sometimes called the Daimon—the activating intelligence that guides your life."[91] This notion of a guiding daemon is central to much ancient gnosticism. She adds that when you "enter consciously into close relationship with this presence, your life takes on purpose and energy."[92]

This internal presence plays an enormously important role in one's spiritual evolution, the next step in which process is death.

Death, power and the Self. For all of her spiritual optimism in *A Passion for the Possible*, motifs of death play a major role in Houston's spirituality, as do exotic locations associated with death such as the Egyptian pyramids and coffins. The reader is encouraged to "walk on until you come to a pyramid." Opening a door, we "follow a long upward path into a chamber where there is an empty sarcophagus—the King's coffin." At this point, "something beckons you to lie down in it." The tomb becomes a place "from which you will be birthed to a richer, more complex life. Your gestation complete, you rise and continue your journey."[93] Thus, the reader is encouraged to embrace death in order to move on spiritually.

Following one's death experience, the spiritual guide is reintroduced as "the Beloved of your Soul—your angel, your divine other half, your life's spiritual partner." Once in "the Beloved's embrace," we find that "all yearnings are fulfilled" and experience "the wonder of unconditional love." At this point "you and your allies"—the Beloved and the crew—return across the threshold of amplified power." Though departing, they assure you that "they live forever within you to give you protection and guidance."[94] Various techniques have assisted some in reaching out to the inner crew, understanding spiritual advancement, and continuing the psychic journey, including "hypnosis, meditation, inward focusing and even electrical stimulation of the brain."[95]

Some readers may be reluctant to yield themselves to a spiritual friend accompanied by an "inner crew." Houston assures us, however, that this is nothing to worry about, that our fears reflect the remnants of Western thinking, specifically the notion of a persistent, unified self. "If the idea of having so many 'beings' within yourself seems strange, it's because our culture puts so much emphasis on each person having a single, consistent personality or role."[96] The Beloved is merely a manifestation of what each of us may become, provided we have the right guidance and the necessary courage to evolve spiritually. This daimon or activating intelligence is a trustworthy friend who "holds the totality of your life and memories" while at the same time offering you the opportunity to "contribute to the design of your life."[97]

Houston's role as a contemporary gnostic master emerges gradually in *A Passion for the Possible*. First, she is familiar with the spiritual realm and with the spiritual keepers of secrets residing there. Second, Houston has an acquired understanding of how one navigates the spiritual world, a knowledge or *gnosis* without which the wandering reader would be lost and perhaps even in danger. Finally, she possesses personal knowledge of the interior transactions with spirit entities that lead to spiritual release and development. For example, she knows how one ought to proceed through the pyramid scenario. Finally, as will become clear in a moment, Houston holds that human beings possess a divine spark waiting to be reunited with the larger divinity of the cosmos.

Myth and evolution. Gnostic systems always involve a myth of human origins, the *gnosis* itself. Jean Houston, like her mentor Joseph Campbell, is a devotee of mythology and its place in spiritual evolution. Myth as the carrier of the stages of ascent is crucial to individual spiritual progress, according to Houston and our spirit guides. The Inner Friend himself reveals that "most of the world's great myths" express that "imbedded in the human psyche" are the various "stages of our evolution."[98] The use of the qualifier "most" in this sentence is suggestive, perhaps implying that the Revealed Word tradition—which has resisted the idea of a purely interior spirituality—may not carry the knowledge necessary for one to "wake up to a higher destiny."[99]

A crucial role of myth in Houston's system, as in ancient gnostic theories, is to provide the knowledge important to overcoming the guardians who would prevent our spiritual advancement. "The Threshold Guardian," for example, "is a monster who guards the gateway to the larger reality we seek." Consequently, "one is required to prove oneself faster, wiser, and more ingenious than the Guardian in order to make safe passage."[100] And there are many such guardians in Houston's cosmos, just as there were in the cosmos of ancient gnostic masters. "As you feel the power of this Guardian fade, cross the threshold. Then return to confront another of the Guardians."[101] Once having conquered the various guardians, we "become aware of a Force within ourselves that links our life to Great Life."[102]

Commitment to the Inner Friend. A surprising passage occurs near the end of *A Passion for the Possible*. Here Houston leads her readers through what can only be described as a spiritual wedding ceremony. Readers are urged to "be acknowledged by the one who is known as the Beloved or Heavenly Partner." While insisting that "this glorious being" is actually "your other half," Houston adds that the Friend "dwells in the depth world" and is rightly referred to as "the Divine Other." The appropriate response to this Divine Other is, apparently, nothing less than total commitment and submission. "Go out in the evening or early morning," she writes, "when Venus is bright in the sky, and using the planet of love as the symbol of the

Beloved, say words such as these: 'From this moment forth I am with you always. From this moment forward, I am your partner in the human realm. From this moment forward, I will bring you, my Beloved, and your ways into time. I know you will ignite the fire in my mind.'"[103]

At this point, the last great barrier having been traversed, one finally achieves the gnostic realization that "each person is really 'God in Hiding.'"[104] The divinity of the individual human is the final great spiritual insight toward which all this inner journeying has been leading. This insight is only possible because of Houston's guidance into the realm of spirit and out of the imprisonment of "the habits of consciousness that sustain the brain's cataracts."[105] As ancient myths related repeatedly, "each person holds a Godseed, a divine essence that can be nurtured through spiritual practice into a fully matured expression of the Godstuff within."[106] Houston helps her readers to recognize this fact about themselves and to engineer their inner divinity's escape from time and ordinary existence.

In *A Passion for the Possible* the reader's spiritual advancement is achieved with the help of a person specially qualified to direct our path through her familiarity with the secrets of the spiritual realm. This process of spiritual evolution is accomplished with the assistance of one who knows well the guiding spirits. Houston thus plays the role of gnostic master, a knowledgeable pathfinder through the spirit realm and a guide to the secrets of spiritual growth and escape.

SCIENCE FICTION: THE FINAL GNOSTIC FRONTIER

Science fiction, among the most popular of literary and cinematic genres, has long been a carrier of religious ideas. This genre is particularly influential in shaping the thinking of its legions of young devotees, but always maintains a sizeable adult following as well. From the genre's inception, science fiction has embraced evolutionary thinking. Several prominent science fiction writers added to the basic Darwinian plot the idea that a small elite of the human race possess the special capacities required to master the secrets and techniques that enable the next step in mental or spiritual advancement. Adding a third factor to evolution and elites— namely, that the secrets of human ascent were delivered by entities from other planets or dimensions—launched hundreds of science fiction stories.

Gnostic thinking and space stories have often enjoyed a natural union. In fact, the two ideas have been almost inseparable in the modern period. Jacob Ilive imagined creatures thrown out of heaven (space) and falling to earth where they were given human bodies. While on earth they were to regain the knowledge that would allow their reentry into the cosmic realms. Other inhabited planets played a role in Ilive's cosmology as well, each performing a specific function in a vast scheme of cosmic ascent. It is also interesting to reflect that Joseph Smith's account of human origins involves an extraterrestrial being (Adam) from a distant star (Kolob) coming to earth to help the human race—embodied spirit entities from another realm—to begin the process of achieving its cosmic destiny of reattaining the celestial realm.

By the middle of the twentieth century—particularly following a series of well-publicized UFO sightings in 1947—many spiritual masters with gnostic leanings began to portray their spirit guides, not as Blavatskian Tibetan ascended masters, but as "space commanders" and "aliens."[107] Catherine Albanese reports that "from 1954 Englishman George King—a yoga adept long familiar with theosophical tradition—began, according to his own report, to have a series of unusual experiences." Specifically, King reported that "he had been designated by Venusian Master Aetherius as the 'Primary Terrestrial Mental Channel.'" By 1956, King's followers became "the Aetherius Society in London, and in 1959 he moved to Los Angeles, where his movement grew."[108]

With King we have a direct link between the fundamental building blocks of much science fiction and religious invention in the world of actual human affairs. Others have followed his lead. Marshall Applewhite's suicidal Heaven's Gate UFO cult, briefly described in the introduction to this chapter, is just one recent example of the phenomenon of fitting gnostic spirituality to a science fiction narrative. Another example of the apparently natural connection between science fiction and gnostic thought is the fiction of writer and religionist L. Ron Hubbard (1911-1986). Hubbard authored a series of pulp science fiction books in the 1940s. In 1950 he turned his attention toward religion, writing his now famous *Dianetics: The Modern Science of Mental Health*, the foundational work of a new faith.

Hubbard's gnostic leanings are evident in his account of human origins. According to Hubbard, humans are embodied alien beings called Thetans who were banished to earth 75 million years ago by a cosmic tyrant known as Xenu. Once this hidden truth about our nature is recognized, a process known as "auditing" can begin to undo the damage done by the Thetans within. In Hubbard, ideas first expressed in science fiction are seamlessly transformed into a worldwide religion with affinities to gnosticism.

"Star Wars" and "The Matrix." Several of the most popular science fiction movies in recent years have woven a gnostic cosmology into their narrative fabric. Two examples will suffice to illustrate the point. George Lucas's wildly popular *Star Wars* movie series introduced American audiences to Yoda, a diminutive master of spiritual secrets that allowed one to control and benefit from a vague spiritual force known as, well, The Force. Protagonist Luke Skywalker studies under Yoda's direction until he is able to control The Force and communicate with deceased individuals and spirit beings. In learning Yoda's secrets, Luke has taken an important step toward spiritual enlightenment. Another suggestion of the movie series is that Luke's special pedigree—he is the descendant of a select group known as Jedi Knights—enables him to master the secrets of The Force. Presumably an ordinary human might not have what it takes to control this potent spiritual force akin to Bulwer-Lytton's Vril.

More explicitly gnostic than *Star Wars*, *The Matrix* was one of the most popular films among America's teenage audience in 1999. Its protagonist, Neo, is selected by an ascended master named Morpheus to learn the grand secret—a mythic *gnosis*—behind all apparent reality. Morpheus reveals that the entire human scene is, in fact, an elaborate illusion. Embodiment is a trick played on the human mind by computers, the consequence of a cosmic struggle between evil intelligences and human beings that the humans lost. By learning the *gnosis* that unlocks the secret of human existence—something within the reach of only a select elite—Neo enters a special order of ascended spiritual adepts. Within this small community, life is monastically simple. All fleshly appetites are denied, rejected as elements of the deception of embodiment. The struggle with the evil intelligences—called Agents—for the souls of humanity is the central purpose of the small community of futuristic *pneumatikoi*.

In a detailed analysis of the film's gnostic message published in *Envoy* magazine, Steve Kellmeyer identifies a number of parallels between the movie's plot and ancient gnostic doctrine. *The Matrix* affirms that "we live in an illusion, creation is an evil prison in which we serve its creator, and we must be freed."[109] He adds, "Once we're acquainted with this worldview, we can see how *The Matrix* clearly unfolds as a modern retelling of the Gnostic version of salvation history."[110]

CONCLUSION

In his now classic 1969 work *The Teachings of Don Juan*, Carlos Castaneda relates his apprenticeship to a Sonoran Indian medicine man. Don Juan teaches Castaneda to become "a man of knowledge." But not just anyone can master the secret knowledge necessary to achieving such status. Moreover, the master himself must specially select the student of such secrets, albeit guided by spiritual entities. "Don Juan as a teacher," writes Castaneda, "selected [as] his apprentices" individuals possessing "a certain disposition of character, which [he] called 'unbending intent.'" Castaneda adds regarding the selection process, however, that "the final decision in matters of who could learn to become a man of knowledge was left to an impersonal power that was known to don Juan, but was outside his sphere of volition."[111] Like a true gnostic master, don Juan recognizes that spiritual insight and liberation are not attainable by all people. Unlocking the secrets of the spirit realm demands an arduous effort to acquire secret knowledge and great discipline to employ that knowledge correctly once acquired.

The gnostic impulse is at work in a variety of contemporary religious and spiritual movements. This impulse elevates a spiritual elite who, through secret spiritual knowledge, are enabled to transcend time, the body and conventional morality. Gnostic thinking seeks to shake off the restraints of Revealed Word thinking with its restrictive personal morality, its sovereign deity, its regard for time and history and its veneration of the physical as part of the good creation of God. Carl Raschke writes, "Through private, internal excursions into the spirit realm the Gnostic learns the secrets that bring mastery over the great mysteries of death and eternity." He concludes that gnosticism is thus a "'religion of revolt' against conventional religion, its symbols, and its terminology."[112]

For the gnostic, the human mind or soul possesses virtually unlimited capacity for expansion provided it apprehends *gnosis*. Knowledge of *gnosis* may come in the form of a myth about the human predicament—we are fallen angels or eternal souls trapped in bodies—as techniques of spiritual ascent or perhaps simply as a revelation about the power of one's own mind. However, modern gnostics remind us, as did their predecessors, that ordinary human beings limit their spiritual potential through adhering to various cultural constraints on thought and action. They thus can never achieve the breakthrough to spiritual self-liberation.

This chapter has considered several important religious, philosophical and literary works that have served to reintroduce the Western religious mind to gnosticism. The Enlightenment Deist Jacob Ilive had somehow absorbed and then replicated a pure strain of ancient gnosticism, advocating it in a series of public lectures in eighteenth-century London. Biblical history was for Ilive the product of a priestly caste, and he set about to rewrite Genesis history to comport with gnostic ideas. The surprising demonology of his Joyner's Hall address is inexplicable except when read as a return to an earlier gnostic tradition. In a similar fashion, Joseph Smith advocated that human beings were temporarily embodied preexistent souls working their way back to a more elevated cosmic realm and eventually to divinity. His own mythic *gnosis* was revealed by spirit beings and encrypted, rendering it inaccessible to anyone but Smith and an inner circle.

The early twentieth-century European intellectual Carl Jung also revived ideas at the heart of the gnostic impulse, including the reign of the powerful individual, the crucial role played by spiritual elites and the place of magic in unlocking spiritual secrets important to unlimited self-expansion. More recently the cluster of ideas that animates gnostic thought has shown up in writers in the spiritual self-help genre, including Jean Houston, and in the extraordinarily popular narratives of science fiction. Secrets are taught by knowledgeable adepts to those specially equipped to receive them, and spiritual elevation results from mastering techniques and apprehending *gnosis*.

The contrast between gnostic and Revealed Word spirituality could not be starker. The Revealed Word has always been radically public in nature. It is a proclaiming perspective, a disclosing faith view devoid of secrets. Moreover, the Revealed Word affirms history as ardently as gnosticism denies it, and elevates the physical as determinedly as gnosticism demotes it. The creating God of Genesis creates both humanity and history, treating the former as good and the latter as a serious fact. Finally, the Revealed Word eschews the notion of an inner circle of adepts learning spiritual secrets from an ascended master, repudiating the very idea that salvation comes by way of apprehending secrets of spiritual ascent.

As the following chapter reveals more clearly, gnosticism is often closely aligned with occultism—the pursuit of spiritual power through ritual magic and spirit communication. Theodore Adorno writes, "the tendency to occultism is a symptom of regression in consciousness" toward a "metaphysics of dunces."[113] Nevertheless, the gnostic affirms that the liberating use of *gnosis* depends on the work of a few rationally gifted and spiritually advanced individuals. Under the influence of the gnostic impulse "the rescue of society and culture" is brought about by "great, gifted, powerful and autonomous individuals" under the direction of a leader "whose vision traverses and transcends time and space, and who sings of the return of a golden age."[114] So, which assessment of the gnostic master—metaphysical dunce or spiritual genius—is correct?

The New Religious Synthesis has revived the ancient gnostic tradition, so long opposed by the Revealed Word. *Gnosis* is on the rise, and spirituality is again being construed as a matter of mastering secrets that make self-deliverance possible. The path back to *gnosis* from grace was opened by writers like Ilive, explored by Smith, celebrated by Jung, popularized by Houston and rendered in winsome narratives by the writers of science fiction. Gnosticism is now a crucial building block in the New Religious Synthesis, a foundational complement to components such as spiritual evolution and pantheism in the formation of a contemporary Western religious mind. The Revealed Word with its images of redemption, faith and universally available grace has been displaced in that mind by a vision of the spiritual struggle of an ever-ascending elite in possession of secret knowledge. The following chapter explores the alleged source of some of these spiritual secrets, and it examines the private conversations of several leading spiritual masters with voices from beyond the physical realm.

9

MODERN SHAMANISM

Spirit Contact and Spiritual Progress

Since I wished to know what the people of Mercury were like in face and body . . . a woman was displayed to my gaze, who was very much like the women on earth. She had a comely face, but one smaller than women on earth have.

EMANUEL SWEDENBORG, The Worlds in Space

It was absolutely astonishing. I saw the form of a very tall, overpoweringly confident, almost androgynous human being. A graceful, cream-colored garment flowed over a figure seven feet tall, with long arms resting calmly at its side.

SHIRLEY MACLAINE, Dancing in the Light

As we approached the door we encountered two taller, thin men with gigantic, black, almond shaped eyes. . . . It was hard to be in their presence. One of them said, "He isn't ready yet."

WHITLEY STREIBER, Transformation: The Breakthrough

This experiment seemed to show that scientists can learn a good deal by working with Amazonian shamans. Some observers have suggested that shamanism, as classically defined, is reaching its end. But bringing scientists and shamans together seems more like a beginning.

JEREMY NARBY, Shamans Through Time

The term *shaman* originated among the Tungus-speaking people of Siberia, and it described an individual who professed to have healing powers and the ability to see the future and to summon demons.[1] Sixteenth- and seventeenth-century European explorers in South America also observed local healers who claimed to communicate with spirits, often with the aid of tobacco, hallucinogenic drugs and self-inflicted wounds. Exorcised by Catholic monks and debunked by Enlightenment philosophers, shamans eventually became a curiosity that Westerners associated with new worlds and exotic lands.

However, if the essence of shamanism is to gain hidden knowledge through contact with spirits, demons, the dead or beings from other worlds, then the practice of shamanism has its own long and vigorous tradition in the Western world as well. Magicians, witches, mediums and alchemists have claimed for centuries to receive information or direction from spirits. Moreover, in recent times shamanism has experienced a surprising resurgence of public interest and is today complementary to the spiritual outlook I have termed the New Religious Synthesis, particularly as a source of the secrets that assist spiritual evolution. How, in an allegedly scientific and rationally enlightened age, has shamanism managed to reassert itself? As with other components in the Other Spirituality, persuasive public texts have played an important role.

Philip Jenkins underlines the importance of the 1932 publication *Black Elk Speaks*, which "introduced a White audience to the riches of Native American spirituality and shamanism," adding that "Black Elk's words proved a major inspiration to many hopeful White imitators in the 1960s and beyond."[2] Jeremy Narby and Francis Huxley write that in the 1950s "western observers began participating in shamanistic sessions involving hallucinogenic plants, [and] found, to their astonishment, that they could have experiences similar to those described by shamans." A major story in *Life* magazine in 1957 popularized the idea of shamanism for many American readers. "In Mexico, American banker Gordon Wasson ate psilocybin mushrooms in a session conducted by Mazatec shaman Maria Sabina." Wasson described to *Life*'s readers "flying out of his body." Narby and Huxley report that "hundreds of thousands of people read Wasson's account, and many followed his example."[3]

In the 1960s Carlos Castaneda described his apprenticeship with a Yaqui Indian shaman named don Juan in an enormously popular series of books that were read by hundreds of thousands of university students. *The Teachings of Don Juan: A Yaqui Way of Knowledge* and its sequels "became worldwide bestsellers."[4] Castaneda's training involved in part the use of the hallucinogen peyote and techniques for conjuring spirits. "In the wake of Castaneda's books, millions of people became interested in shamans in a hands-on way," write Narby and Huxley. "There was a great flowering of neo-shamanism in the New Age movement, concentrated in the United States, but increasingly spreading around the world."[5] The 1980s and 1990s saw the publication of dozens of New Age accounts of messages channeled from spirit beings and direct contact with a host of otherworldly entities.

This chapter explores the reemergence of shamanism in the modern Western world and its place in the New Religious Synthesis. That members of a spiritual elite can garner important information from beings in another realm or on another planet is now a widely accepted component of religious thought. Spirit contact, once limited to occult works, surfaces today in popular fiction, the personal accounts of New Age aficionados, the literature of the UFO movement, spiritual biographies, the literature of angelic visitation, countless movies and in a variety of other genres.

This chapter examines several important documents that have assisted in again popularizing the ancient practice of communication between human and intelligent nonhuman entities. We shall begin by considering an early modern proponent of human-spirit contact, the famous religious writer Emanuel Swedenborg, who claimed to have been instructed by beings on other planets as well as by angels. We will then take note of the explosion of occult interest that occurred in Victorian England and America, a social phenomenon that radically altered public attitudes about spirituality while at the same time undermining Revealed Word prohibitions on the practice of mediumship or shamanism. Twentieth-century advocates of shamanism and related practices to be considered include the Harvard psychiatrist John Mack and his surprising accounts of sessions with UFO abductees, as well as spiritual counselor Paul Ferrini and his conversations with Jesus.

EMANUEL SWEDENBORG

Eighteenth-century Swedish scientist, engineer, artisan and mystic Emanuel Swedenborg (1688-1772) had an important influence on a variety of nineteenth-century writers and thinkers including Ralph Waldo Emerson and Joseph Smith. Swedenborg's theology is complex and difficult to apprehend due to his tendency to mask heterodox ideas with Christian terminology. What is particularly striking about Swedenborg's theology is his claim about its ultimate source. He insisted that virtually everything he wrote on spiritual matters after 1744 was revealed to him directly by spirits in almost daily episodes of direct spirit contact.

The corpus of Swedenborg's work is massive, and I have chosen here to focus on one particularly unusual and popular short book in which he claims to have traveled among various planets and learned from their inhabitants a variety of spiritual secrets. The original Latin title of this book was *Telluribus in universo*, and it was first published in 1758. The first English translation, *The Worlds in Space*, appeared in London in 1787. The book has maintained a readership for more than two hundred years and is still published by the Swedenborg Society.

Though others had speculated about the possibility of life on other planets prior to the 1750s—Bernard Bouvier de Fontenelle wrote *Conversations on the Plurality of Inhabited Worlds* in 1686—Swedenborg likely invented the genre of the first-hand account of alien contact. This rhetorical invention, an early version of science fiction, proved irresistible to many readers then as now, and the space alien narrative remains a highly persuasive carrier of religious ideas.

Talking with alien spirits: questing for knowledge. Swedenborg opens *The Worlds in Space* by claiming, "I have been enabled to talk with spirits and angels, not only those in the vicinity of our earth, but also those near other worlds."[6] These other worlds include Mars, Venus, Saturn, Mercury and Jupiter, planets well known to eighteenth-century astronomers. Swedenborg's "space" travel is, however, a strictly interior, spiritual journey in which he encounters beings he terms "spirits" who belong to the planets of our solar system. He writes, "as I have said several times before, a spirit is taken from place to place by nothing but changes in his inner state."[7] Swedenborg journeyed in a similar fashion, entering an altered mental state in order to achieve the spirit contact he alleged was a daily experience for him for more than twelve years.

Many of the planetary spirits whom Swedenborg encountered desire human contact because of their great thirst for knowledge, which is the key to their own spiritual attainment. When happening upon a knowledgeable human being, "they review everything in his memory, calling up from it whatever suits them," a technique reminiscent of the aliens in Sagan's *Contact* as discussed at the end of chapter five.[8]

The point of Swedenborg's quest for alien contact is to increase his own knowledge of the true spiritual nature of the universe. In fact, much of *The Worlds in Space* is taken up with passages in which planetary spirits correct the false teachings of Christian orthodoxy on such issues as the Trinity and the incarnation and resurrection of Christ. One of the principal lessons conveyed in this unusual book is that the literal sense of the Revealed Word is insignificant when compared to the true or spiritual meaning of the Christian Scriptures. "Everything in the literal sense of the Word corresponds to Divine things in heaven," and it is these things in heaven, or space, that are preeminent.[9] Just as the Deist Thomas Woolston claimed that only the spiritual sense of Scripture mattered—an idea he occasionally attributed to spirit contact as well—so Swedenborg is at pains to instruct his readers that planetary spirits have conveyed to him undiluted spiritual truth.

"Correspondence" is a key component in Swedenborg's cosmology in *The*

Worlds in Space, an idea he borrows from Hermeticism and the occult tradition. The familiar phrase from the world of magic states "as above, so below." That is, the microcosm of the visible world and nearby worlds is a miniature representation of the macrocosm that is the vast system of an invisible spiritual universe. For Swedenborg, each planet and its spirits correspond to a particular part of something he calls "The Grand Man," a gigantic cosmic entity that is the sum of the many parts of a vast, invisible world. "The whole of heaven corresponds in every part to a human being," he writes.[10] This notion was also common to earlier works on alchemy and the occult: the elements of the zodiac were thought to correspond to parts of the human body, and the cosmos itself was understood as fashioned on the model of an enormous man.

For Swedenborg, to understand the spirits and planets and their various places in the cosmic scheme of things is to achieve potentially great spiritual power. As Swedenborg admits, however, there are certain risks associated with the work of acquiring cosmic knowledge through direct spirit contact.

Alien abuse. Swedenborg as modern shaman is a conduit to humans of secret spiritual knowledge. Yet he is also at the mercy of alien beings who themselves wish knowledge from him. Oddly, though in keeping with contemporary alien contact literature, Swedenborg frequently mentions the physical abuse these planetary spirits are more than ready to inflict on uncooperative hosts. For instance, when Swedenborg fails to comply with an alien request for information, he reports: "So as to show their annoyance they brought a kind of painful contraction of the right side of my head as far as the ear."[11]

Similar incidents are frequently reported in *The Worlds in Space*. Some of his alien acquaintances from Jupiter reveal to Swedenborg how they "draw out from a person's memory all he has done and thought." If they "find fault with his actions or thoughts," their response is to "chastise him by means of pains in the joints, the feet or the hands, or around the epigastric region."[12] Another punishment for bad thinking was "spells of choking until the victim was very distressed . . . and finally a death sentence."[13]

More than once Swedenborg mentions that the abuse aliens inflict on humans or on their own kind extends to the sentence of death. Bad theology—such as accepting the historical accounts of Jesus' life—might bring such a harsh penalty. Swedenborg suggests that planetary spirits often inflict the penalty of death on anyone or any family on their planet holding to false theological ideas. It is the aliens' practice "to get rid of any family so infected . . . by spirits suppressing their breathing and so taking their lives, after they had passed sentence of death on them."[14] It is an inescapable feature of Swedenborg's account that alien entities are inclined toward violence, a characteristic that attends shamanistic practices both ancient and modern.

Alien advances: the body and science. Many of the alien spirits Swedenborg encounters resemble humans, but are smaller and of slighter build. In keeping with racialist notions of physical and spiritual evolution, the aliens' faces "resembled the faces of people of our world, white and handsome, with a look of sincerity and modesty shining from them."[15] Imperfections are not allowed among these advanced races from space. Faces with "warts and spots, or otherwise disfigured . . . were never to be seen among them." However, "they did approve of some faces, the ones that were cheerful and smiling, and had slightly pouting lips."[16] Of a later alien encounter, Swedenborg writes, "their faces were not unlike those of people in our world, except that the eyes are smaller, and so were the noses."[17] Implicit, then, in alien encounter is the notion of physical perfection—including white skin, beautiful faces and delicate facial features—as characteristic of more advanced humanoids.[18]

The advances enjoyed by aliens—physical and otherwise—are the result of scientific researches. Among some of the alien spirits with whom Swedenborg communicates, the "sciences" are treated as "spiritual riches" that may be used to open the "path to the light of heaven."[19] In a later episode, he proudly explains "various achievements of our world" to some planetary spirits, "especially about our possession of sciences unknown elsewhere, such as astronomy, geometry, mechanics, physics, chemistry, medicine, optics, and philosophy." Through science and technical advances such as printing, "there was a revelation permanently operating in our world."[20] Science, then, had important spiritual significance for Swedenborg, who began his circuitous public career as a highly regarded scientist. Of all human achievements it is science that he is most eager to explain to the spirits, and in which they take the most interest.

History, on the other hand, does not fare so well. When informed about the earthly and historical life of Jesus Christ, the spirits reply that this is "of no interest to them," though Jesus' spiritual nature and authority were deemed important.[21] Other historical details of Jesus' life such as "that he was born as a baby, lived as a man, looked like any other man, was crucified and so forth" were considered among enlightened spirits to be "scandalous ideas."[22]

The qualities of a shaman. To be a shaman, to communicate with spirits, one must possess special qualities. "Only those whose interiors are open," writes Swedenborg, "can hear those speaking from heaven." Special faith and a great capacity for love are important to this capacity for contact. "No one is allowed to talk with spirits and angels . . . unless he is, as regards faith and love, capable of associating with angels." Because so few meet these criteria "there are few today allowed to talk and converse with angels."

Of course, crucial to this process is "belief in spirits and angels" as well as the belief that "these put a person in touch with heaven."[23] Being in touch with heaven means "travelling . . . in spirit" as one is "guided through varying states of inner life, which appear . . . like travels through space." Both "the outward and return journeys" require "continuous guidance" from spirits.[24]

This is the essence of shamanism—to be found qualified to speak with spirits and to be guided by them on an inner journey that involves risks, pain, ecstatic experience and vast personal knowledge. Swedenborg helped to reintroduce this ancient spiritual practice to the Western world. Through his influence and that of a host of other public advocates, the notion of spirit contact has made its way into the New Religious Synthesis. The following section explores shamanism's tremendous appeal in England a century after Swedenborg's death.

VICTORIAN SHAMANS: OCCULTISM, THEOSOPHY AND SPIRITUALISM

The late nineteenth-century occult movement was vast, complex and somewhat surprising in a nation engaged at that time in creating the modern Christian missionary movement. Through books and especially cheap periodicals, the mysteries of the occult, witchcraft, magic and Satanism became matters of public curiosity and even devotion in the British Isles. Shamanism was at the center of this wildly popular spiritual phenomenon. I want to take note of a few of the major characters and characteristics of Victorian occultism and shamanism, as this movement played a major role in shaping the public religious mind in the direction of the New Religious Synthesis.

Bulwer-Lytton and Crowley. In the 1830s and 1840s a series of popular novels by authors such as the Rosicrucian and occultist George Edward Bulwer-Lytton popularized occult practices and familiarized the European and American reading public with the idea of contacting spirits, demons and ascended masters using secret techniques. Bulwer-Lytton, a nineteenth-century Stephen King, churned out spine-tingling page-turners at an astonishing rate, each one finding a waiting audience. His novels incorporating occult themes include *Godolphin* (1833), *Asmodeus at Large* (1833), *Pilgrims of the Rhine* (1834) and *The Last Days of Pompei* (1834).[25] Bradford Verter calls Bulwer-Lytton "a fictive popularizer of esoteric philosophy" who published almost without a break from 1828 through 1873. "Through collected editions and cheap reprints," writes Verter, "his work would continue to find an audience into the early twentieth century."[26]

But Bulwer-Lytton's most famous and influential occult novel was without doubt the 1842 bestseller *Zanoni*, the story of a five thousand year old alchemist and his student, set during the French Revolution. Such was the demand for *Zanoni* in America that "readers could buy pirated editions for as little as six cents."[27] Philip Jenkins writes that "characters like Zanoni . . . exercised a powerful spell on the esoteric subculture on both sides of the Atlantic."[28] Reading *Zanoni* amounted to taking an introductory course in magic and spiritism. The most riveting element in the novel, however, was the young hero's encounter with spirits from another realm who imparted to him esoteric knowledge. The book attracted the attention of occultists, religious opponents, social reformers and the simply curious. One effect of the novel, however, was to assist in popularizing the traditional practices of shamanism, a fact that did not escape the notice of the subject of the next section, Madame H. P. Blavatsky.

Bulwer-Lytton's works were among the required reading for students of the greatest English occultist of the first part of the twentieth century, Aleister Crowley.[29] It would be impossible to exaggerate the scandal, controversy and general social alarm that attended the man who called himself The Beast, or to overstate his influence. Crowley more than any other figure popularized ritual magic for Westerners. He was instrumental in developing the highly influential occult organization known as the Order of the Golden Dawn. Crowley authored dozens of books and pamphlets between 1911 and 1940, and he managed to keep himself almost continuously before the public eye. He saw himself as "the prophet of a New Aeon that would supplant the Christian Era" and the developer of "nothing less than a full-fledged successor religion" in which humans would "become the gods" we had previously "merely worshipped."[30] A self-professed occultist, Satanist and magician, Crowley created intense pubic interest in the occult with books such as *Magick* (1911), *The Book of Lies* (1913), *Confessions of a Drug Fiend* (1922) and *The Confessions of Aleister Crowley* (1929). Biographer Lawrence Sutin writes that Crowley "anticipated the spread of Eastern spirituality in the West."[31]

A master rhetorician, Crowley recognized the persuasive power of a sensational novel as well as did Bulwer-Lytton. "The publication of *Confessions of a Drug Fiend*," his most popular novel, "garnered Aleister Crowley more press coverage than his mystical texts ever received."[32] Occult novels, according to Verter, "proved to be an effective means of expanding the readership base for occultist literature, and thus served as a method of propaganda and recruitment."[33] The shamanistic elements in these novels—their instruction in conjuring spirits, seeking secret knowledge from departed individuals or lashing out at enemies with demonic assistance—provided their greatest intrigue. Public thirst for stories of the occult knew no bounds from the late eighteenth century through the early twentieth.[34] Throughout this period, popular fiction and nonfiction advocating contact with spirits, ghosts and demons helped lay the groundwork for a new religious outlook that would compete with the Revealed Word perspective.

Nineteenth- and twentieth-century occult shamanism combined several elements associated with the New Religious Synthesis—rejection of biblical theology, the elevation of reason and science, and a pantheistic belief in a divine energy permeating the cosmos. Particularly prominent was the notion of spiritual evolution, for "great mystics or prophets might represent souls in a very advanced state of spiritual progress, who should be regarded as the rightful teachers of humanity, Masters or Secret Chiefs."[35] Among the most influential of these "advanced souls" was the great Victorian occult leader Madame Blavatsky.

Madame Blavatsky. Evolutionary progression was a central component in Theosophy, founded in America by Madame Helena Blavatsky and others in the last third of the nineteenth century. Her spiritual system is eclectic in its sources, but fundamentally occult and shamanistic in orientation. She, like Joseph Smith, saw herself as a human conduit of secret spiritual truths from another realm. In several lengthy books Blavatsky argued strenuously that mystical, astrological, gnostic, Hermetic and magical teachers of old understood the cosmos correctly. She rejected the Revealed Word tradition out of hand. No less a student of spiritual culture than Carl Jung noted in the 1930s that Madame Blavatsky and Theosophy were the harbingers of a completely new spiritual orientation for the Western world.[36]

Madame Blavatsky traveled extensively in search of hidden spiritual knowledge. She claimed that much of her knowledge had been obtained in the lamaseries of Tibet and other exotic sites. Her 1877 publication, *Isis Unveiled*, denounces conventional Western science—though not true Science—and argues for spiritual

insight through mysticism and occultism. "Science finds herself in a very disagree-
able dilemma," Blavatsky wrote in 1877: "She must either confess that the ancient
physicists were superior in their knowledge to her modern representatives, or that
there exists something in nature beyond physical science, and that *spirit* possesses
powers of which our philosophers never dreamed."[37]

Despite such criticism of empirical science, Blavatsky fancied herself a determined advocate of true Science—the systematic study of a cosmos charged with
occult energy. A friend and associate, Colonel Henry Steele Olcott, wrote at the
time of her death that she "desired that science should be brought back to the true
ground where life and intelligence are admitted to be within and acting upon and
through every atom in the universe. Hence her object was to make religion scientific and science religious."[38]

Helena Petrovna Blavatsky (1831-1891) was born in Russia on August 12.[39] At
the age of seventeen she was married to a Russian nobleman named General Nice-
phore Blavatsky. After a year she fled from her husband, disappearing "from an
English ship bound for Constantinople."[40] This episode began nearly twenty years
of travel, the numerous contradictory allegations about this lost period of her life
becoming part of the extensive Blavatsky legend. During her travels she claims to
have carefully studied firsthand the religious, spiritualist and magical traditions of
Europe and the East.

The period of her life from 1850 to 1875 was a closely guarded secret, and Blavatsky forbade friends and biographers alike from inquiring about it.[41] She did intimate late in life that during an 1851 visit to London with her father (which
contradicts the claim that she traveled alone) she was directed by a mysterious "tall
Hindu" to form the Theosophical Society, "and shortly afterwards left London for
India."[42] Rumors of numerous illicit love affairs and equally numerous illegitimate
children, egregious deceptions of her many followers, and a host of other scandals
haunted Blavatsky throughout her life.

Theosophy. Along with Colonel Olcott (1832-1907) and William Q. Judge,
Blavatsky founded The Theosophical Society in New York in 1875. In 1878, Olcott and Blavatsky traveled to India, where they settled. Eventually the headquar-
ters of The Theosophical Society was established in Madras where local Christian
missionaries feverishly opposed its work. In December of 1878 Blavatsky made a
visit to England where she was welcomed by a number of spiritual explorers. From
1879 through 1888, Blavatsky edited *The Theosophist*. She wrote incessantly on

magic, the occult and spiritualism, her collected works running to fourteen volumes. Blavatsky was involved in an extensive and widely publicized scandal in 1884 when the British press accused her of faking dramatic spiritual phenomena. She was forced to go into seclusion and wrote her most famous work, *The Secret Doctrine* (1888), shortly before her death.

Theosophy did not develop a significant following until Blavatsky and Olcott moved to India, where the native population was quite receptive to a system that incorporated many Hindu teachings, including reincarnation. At the height of its influence, "the Theosophical movement directly involved hundreds of thousands, if not perhaps millions, of individuals."[43] Eventually, Blavatsky's influence was felt strongly in the West. Some adherents of Blavatsky's gnostic shamanism were famous and influential: "Prominent among these were poets Lord Tennyson and W. B. Yeats; the young Mahatma Gandhi; the Goethe scholar, spiritualist medium, and founder (in 1913) of the rival occultist tradition Anthroposophy, Rudolf Steiner; and Thomas Edison, who was busy in the 1890s trying to invent a phonograph-like device to speak to the spirit world."[44] The rapid rise and surprising influence of Theosophy further illustrates how occult spirituality achieved great popularity in nineteenth-century America and Europe.

Ascended masters, secret doctrines and lost races. Blavatsky built Theosophy out of various elements including occultism, spiritism, mysticism, her peculiar understanding of world religions and what she accepted as advances in science. A committed spiritualist, Blavatsky "chose the name *theosophy* ('knowledge of God' or 'divine wisdom') for her doctrine, which was based on the idea that all of the world's religions and spiritual traditions down through history were derived from a long-lost 'secret doctrine' that had been revealed to her by . . . divine beings." Blavatsky referred to these divine beings as the brothers, the Mahatmas or the Masters, and alleged that they resided in Tibet and communicated with her telepathically and in visions.[45]

The knowledge Blavatsky claimed came to her by shamanic means was of ancient origin and had been carefully preserved to be revealed at the appropriate time and to carefully selected individuals. At various times Blavatsky allegedly received secret information from a host of spirits, masters and departed spiritual leaders. Philip Jenkins writes that she "relied on material channeled from great spiritual Masters, members of the Great White Brotherhood, a select club that included Jesus, the Buddha, Confucius, Mesmer, and Cagliostro, as well as real-life occultists she had consulted over the years."[46]

"Isis Unveiled" and the sources of Theosophy. Blavatsky's first major work was her massive polemical survey of ancient magical and occult sources entitled *Isis Unveiled.* Originally published in 1877, *Isis Unveiled* provided the philosophical groundwork for Theosophy, and is still published by the Theosophical University Press in Pasadena, California. Encyclopedic in its coverage of the magical tradition, this two-volume, 1,200-page work reflects throughout Blavatsky's preoccupation with Indian thought. She embraced the pantheism advocated by European writers from Pythagoras to Spinoza, a perspective consistent with Hindu cosmology. "The universe is itself Brahman," she wrote. "This is the philosophy of Spinoza which is derived from that of Pythagoras; and it is the same for which Bruno died a martyr."[47]

Like many public advocates of the New Religious Synthesis from the late seventeenth century onward, Blavatsky labeled Christianity and the Revealed Word tradition a spiritual aberration that deviated from its ancient mystical and pantheistic sources. Blavatsky adhered to the idea, advocated by the Deist Woolston and recently resurrected by several prominent scholars including Marcus Borg, that Jesus was a mystic and a magician who practiced the *"divina sapientia."*[48]

Theosophical thought draws heavily on standard gnostic sources such as Simon Magus and Valentinus, the medieval mystic Meister Eckhart, Renaissance writers in the school of Bruno, the German mystic Jacob Böhme and some Romantic philosophers. However, with Indian cosmology being so important to Blavatsky, Olcott and Annie Besant, the Hindu Vedas, Upanishads and Bhagavad-Gita are perhaps the richest source of theosophical ideas. The tributary of Buddhism also flowed into the stream of theosophical speculation. Olcott himself authored the highly successful *Buddhist Catechism* in 1881, a book translated into several languages.

Spiritual evolution and racial superiority. Blavatsky contended that modern science supported her spiritual system. She was especially intrigued with Darwinian evolution, so powerfully present in late nineteenth-century religious speculation. According to Blavatsky, human evolution would eventuate in a *spiritually* perfected human race, a theme repeated by numerous Victorian writers. She maintained that a lost continent, which she dubbed Lemuria, was once home to a master race. "Historical accounts of this lost society," according the Philip Jenkins, "were mainly derived from mediumship and channeling."[49] From this now lost race, a variety of races have descended. Blavatsky and the other developers of Theosophy used Darwin's evolutionary theory as the basis for a racialist scheme featuring seven "root" races. The fifth of these root races included the Aryans.

Linguistic analysis featured among the various approaches Blavatsky employed to determine which current races were intellectually and spiritually the most advanced. Highly evolved races, it was argued, spoke highly evolved languages. She employed the analytic work of linguists such as August Schleicher (1821-1868) to support her case that Europeans represented the human spiritual vanguard. Richard Noll writes that Schleicher's diagrams were "widely adapted by Blavatsky and the Theosophists to give the appearance of seriousness and scholarly legitimacy" to their racial theories. On such linguistic grounds, Blavatsky argued that the Aryan race "contained the highest spirituality of all mankind."[50] Philip Jenkins notes that occult groups often "drew on the scientific findings of the era, at least as far as they understood them, and this apparent ultramodernity was part of their appeal."[51]

In true shamanic fashion, however, Blavatsky augmented her scientific argument for racial superiority with messages from two of the Mahatmas—Koot Hoomi and Morya—who conveyed their views by means of "spiritual communication from beyond" to Blavatsky's associate A. P. Sinnett.[52] In addition, she posited that Maitreya Buddha, "the Buddha of the final age" would inaugurate "a new stage in the human evolutionary cycle."[53] This "evolutionary cycle" was something Blavatsky found taught in many of the world's magical traditions. The Hermetic writers, for instance, maintained that the human race must "inevitably and collectively . . . in accordance with the law of evolution . . . be finally *physically* spiritualized."[54] This eventuality—physical spiritualization—represents the final stage in human evolution. But, despite her apparently inclusive language—"inevitably and *collectively*"—this apogee of human evolution is not to be achieved by all members of the human race.

Blavatsky endorsed spiritual racism, for some races were simply spiritually superior to others. Blavatsky had imbibed this view from the eminent scientist Alfred Russel Wallace, who arrived at the theory of natural selection at the same time as did Darwin. Blavatsky writes, "In his lecture on *The Action of Natural Selection on Man*, Mr. Alfred R. Wallace concludes his demonstration as to the development of human races under that law of selection by saying that, if his conclusions are just, 'It must inevitably follow that the higher—the more intelligent and moral—must displace the lower and more degraded races.'"[55] Wallace, like Blavatsky, was a spiritist who held that the course of the human race was being directed by "higher intelligences." Eventually, Wallace set about "revamping evolution to take account of unseen spirits."[56]

Blavatsky held, along with many Victorian intellectual figures, that the evolutionary juggernaut leaves behind the "lower and degraded" human races, while a homogenous, perfected race gradually but inexorably emerges. The perfected humans' "mental constitution may continue to advance and improve, till the world is again inhabited by a single, *nearly homogenous race, no individual of which will be inferior to the noblest specimens of existing humanity.*"[57] Blavatsky, the notorious spiritual charlatan of Victorian London, apparently included herself among these "noblest specimens." Moreover, Blavatsky noted that such a racist and evolutionary view was fully consistent with the magical tradition generally. She writes, "What he [Wallace] says" about evolution and the rise of a superior race "clashes in no way with our kabalistic assertions."[58]

Interestingly, Blavatsky had read with approval the work of Bulwer-Lytton, especially *Zanoni* and *The Coming Race*. She apparently derived her idea of ascended masters "from the novels of Bulwer Lytton, which were enormously influential in the English-speaking world as well as in Europe."[59] *Isis Unveiled* was published in 1877, just six years after the appearance of Bulwer-Lytton's *The Coming Race*, and at the height of Vril excitement in Europe. When "ever-progressing nature" follows "the great law of 'survival of the fittest,'" she wrote, then we will see in the "future the possibility—nay, the assurance of a race, which, like the Vril-ya of Bulwer-Lytton's *Coming Race*, [and] will be but one remove from the primitive 'Sons of God.'"[60] Similar racialist-evolutionist ideology is one of the most disturbing aspects of a large number of new religious groups as well.[61]

JOHN MACK AND UFO ABDUCTION

John Mack is a professor of psychiatry at Harvard Medical School. Thus, he is perhaps an unexpected expert on the experiences of individuals who claim to have been abducted by aliens. Nevertheless, Mack's bestselling book *Abduction: Human Encounters with Aliens*, reports his interviews with several persons who allege that beings from another dimension or another planet have contacted and even kidnapped them.[62] Other books in this genre by Mack include *Secret Life: Firsthand, Documented Accounts of UFO Abductions* (with David M. Jacobs, 1993) and *Passport to the Cosmos: Human Transformation and Alien Encounters* (1997).[63] Mack's unusual clinical work finds a place in this chapter because of his suggestion that abductees are themselves modern shamans with important spiritual messages from beyond.

Mack addresses his readers from the perspective of a medical expert in search of the facts behind his clients' curious reports and the explanations for their bizarre experiences. As a trained psychiatrist and member of the Harvard faculty, he carries unusual credibility. Mack's book recounts clinical sessions in which clients are encouraged to remember the details of their abductions, often after being placed into a hypnotic trance to assist their recall. But he is quick to point out that he may be dealing with something other than actual memory in his interviews with the abducted. To think of memory "as 'true' or 'false,'" he writes, "may restrict what we can learn about human consciousness" from abductees.[64] Mack's curious qualification—that thinking of memory as true or false is restricting—makes sense if one considers his clients not victims of abductions but mouthpieces for guiding spirits, that is, shamans.

A cosmos filled with intelligences. Mack's extensive experience with UFO abductees has convinced him that the cosmos, like Swedenborg's planets and Houston's realm of the psyche, is filled with "intelligences." He writes, "What the abduction phenomenon has led me (I would now say inevitably) to see is that we participate in a universe or universes that are filled with intelligences from which we have cut ourselves off, having lost the senses by which we might know them."[65] Surrounded by intelligences with whom we no longer know how to communicate, the need for shamanic intermediaries between humanity and these higher minds is clear. The alien intelligences can guide us into truths unknown to us, Mack contends, teaching us to stop war, ecological disaster and racial conflict.[66]

Apparently we have been in contact with such beings for a very long time indeed. Mack writes of the "long story of humankind's relationship to vehicles and creatures appearing from the heavens that goes back to antiquity."[67] Moreover, mythology traditionally has provided a language for communicating the essence of these encounters. This "connection between humans and beings from other dimensions has been illustrated in myths and stories from various cultures for millennia."[68] Thus, myth is as central to Mack's explanation of the alien abduction phenomenon as it is to Houston's understanding of the encounters of inner journeying.

But the West's understanding of consciousness has prevented Western people from recognizing the true nature of contacts with the other side. "Throughout history, many societies have acknowledged consciousness as something more potent than we have in the west—as a sieve or receiver and transmitter of communication with forces, not always visible, other than ourselves."[69] Thus, Mack concludes, "It would seem that today's UFO abductees are continuing an amply documented tradition of ascent and extraterrestrial communication." The meaning of "extraterrestrial communication" is relatively clear, but what does Mack mean by "ascent"? Apparently a spiritual issue comes into play here, with abductees taking a step up spiritually through their experiences with alien beings.

As support for the view that abductees are on a spiritual journey, Mack cites folklorist Peter Rojcewicz, who "has compared the experience of today's abductees" with "aerial and abduction phenomena" in earlier times and other cultures. Rojcewicz finds "the possibility of the existence of an intelligence, a spirit, an energy, a consciousness behind UFO experiences and extraordinary encounters of all types, that adapts its form and appearance to fit the environment of the times."[70] Thus, Mack believes that, in addition to UFO abductees, "contemporary examples of such entities in the West might be the spirit guides that are reported by many individuals."[71]

The shamanic connection. In *Abduction,* John Mack entertains the idea that consciousnesses from another dimension are actively seeking to contact and influence the human race. But in order to receive the benefits of such contact, one's worldview must include openness to these cosmic conversations. Religions and worldviews that allow for such a possibility are commended. Those that limit the view of consciousness or that demonize contact with spirits are to be censured, for we are on the verge of a new, shamanic religious consciousness.

"What function," he asks, "do events like UFO abductions and various mystical experiences play in our psyches and in the rest of the cosmos?"[72] His answer to this question appears to be a religious one: "The UFO abduction experience, while unique in many respects, bears resemblance to other dramatic, transformative experiences undergone by shamans, mystics, and ordinary citizens who have had encounters with the paranormal."[73] The abductee takes on the crucial role of providing a bridge between mundane experience and the spirit world beyond, and she does this in much the same way as the mystic or shaman of lore. "The mystic or shaman, like the abductee, makes a pilgrimage, usually with ardor, to receive a new dimension of experience or knowledge."[74]

Mack even finds that abductees often perceive their alien visitors as animals—"owls, eagles, raccoons, and deer"—which he quickly points out is remarkably similar to the reports of tribal shamans regarding their encounters with beings from the spirit world. "The connection with animal spirits is very powerful for many abductees." Mack believes that "this shamanistic dimension needs further study" because such events "cannot be understood within the framework of the laws of Western science," even though "they are fully consistent with beliefs developed thousands of years ago by other non-Western cultures."[75] Joseph Campbell also noted that the Hindu term *marga* "means 'path or track, trail of an animal, to be followed,' and this is precisely what is implied by C. G. Jung's term 'the archetypes of the unconscious.'" Following these animal guides "we are led—if we can follow—beyond maps, according to the Indian view, to the seat from which all the gods have sprung, which is the revelation of the deepest source and being of ourselves."[76]

Mack notes that abductees, like all shamans, possess a peculiar openness to diverse spiritual experiences. "I have the impression that the abductees as a group are unusually open and intuitive individuals, less tolerant than usual of societal authoritarianism, and more flexible in accepting diversity and the unusual experiences of other people."[77] Abductees may, in fact, be of an entirely different species than the rest of us. Mack writes about some abductees "being told by an alien female that she was their true mother." The abductees felt that "in some vague but deep way that this is actually true, i.e., that they are not 'from here' and that the Earth mother and father are not their true parents."[78] Mack suggests in *Abduction* that such accounts of alien parentage, as well as of strange sexual experiments reported on some abductees, are related to alien efforts to prepare the human race for the next stage in its physical and spiritual evolution.

The abductee is for Mack, then, a uniquely spiritual being, a religious seer, a shaman bearing messages from another realm and the harbinger of a new human race. Many other modern day shamans have claimed that beings from other planets were trying to contact and educate the human race, usually on the rationale that our spiritual and social progress would thus be enhanced. Sometimes the initial contact is more spiritual than physical. Thus, Wilfred Kellogg claimed that his massive *The Urantia Book*, a "history of the galaxy and the solar system," came to him through channeling messages from aliens.[79]

Mack's work with UFO abduction claimants is remarkable, both in the fact that his own status lends credence to the reports of abductees and in his tendency to view the abductees as contemporary shamans. In a fashion typical of New Religious Synthesis efforts to appropriate science to spirituality, Mack argues that Western science is currently undergoing "spectacular advances in physics, biology, neuroscience, and psychology," which may "shed light on" abduction experiences and other mystical or shamanistic phenomena.[80]

In a similar vein, Whitley Streiber has written about his experiences with aliens in enormously popular books such as *Communion* and *Transformation: The Break-*

through. He has also collected various evidences for alien contact in *Confirmation: The Hard Evidence for Aliens Among Us.*[81] As the titles of these books imply, Streiber finds a virtually religious significance in human encounters with aliens, which he terms the "visitor experience." He writes, "The 'visitor experience' is old. Two hundred years ago a farmer might have come in from plowing and said, 'I just saw fairies dancing in the glen.' A thousand years ago he might have seen angels flying." Though the experience is ancient, it now has a new dimension. "That we could ever conceive of being in relationship with this force is what is new about the visitor experience in modern times." This is possible because, "thankfully, the very way we think and perceive our universe may be changing."[82]

As we shall see in the next section, sources of spiritual wisdom from nonhuman entities are not limited to UFO abductees. In fact, Jesus himself has recently been transformed into a spirit guide.

PAUL FERRINI AND THE JESUS PHENOMENON

Paul Ferrini, a "spiritual counselor" from Massachusetts, has written a number of books advocating a new approach to religion, one with shamanic overtones. In one of his most influential books, *Love Without Conditions: Reflections of the Christ Mind*, Ferrini claims to bring a message directly from Jesus Christ.[83] He urges his readers to cultivate their own capacity to make direct contact with a consciousness existing beyond ordinary experience. Moreover, the Jesus to whom Ferrini introduces his readers shares similarities with the "Inner Friend" described by Jean Houston—an interior guide to spiritual truth, perhaps another name for the self. "To think of Jesus as being outside of and independent of your mind," Ferrini writes, "is to miss the point. For it is in your mind that Jesus addresses you." Ferrini even describes his Jesus as "your most intimate friend speaking to you, sometimes in words, often beyond words."

Ferrini's Jesus makes no unique claims to divinity or spiritual authority and, in fact, advocates religious pluralism. Jesus is merely the mouthpiece of something called "the Christ Mind," a universal consciousness expressed in varying ways in many religious traditions. Thus, Jesus is not unique; he is simply one among many spirit voices of universal truth. "Let us be clear," writes Ferrini in his role as shaman, "that Jesus has no exclusive place or position in the Christ Mind." Rather, "Krishna, Buddha, Moses, Muhammad, Lao Tze, and many others are consciously joined with him there, or perhaps I should more accurately say 'here.'" Thus, we

may address Jesus by any number of names. "If you feel more comfortable address-
ing yourself to Buddha or Krishna, please do so. Jesus will not be offended. Indeed
he will be pleased because you are following his teaching of non-separation."[84] All
people "commune and communicate with the Christ Mind (you can say Buddha
Mind or Brahman or Holy Spirit if you prefer)." This is because "we are all joined
with the mind of God."[85]

Ferrini advocates an essentially gnostic spirituality in which this One Mind
shows up as a divine spark in all people. "Each of us has a tiny spark of light that
illuminates the darkness of our unconsciousness." This "divine spark of awareness"
keeps our "connection to God alive."[86] With these framing considerations in mind,
what does Jesus have to say to us through Ferrini?

Jesus speaks: lessons from the Christ mind. Ferrini insists in *Love Without Conditions* that he is not "channeling" Jesus. He does claim, however, shaman-like contact
with a being he labels Jesus, and this spiritual contact becomes a source of authority
for a wide range of teachings. One of the first lessons we learn through Ferrini's
Jesus is that religious division is wrong, that "divisions into religions are relics of
this world." Jesus informs Ferrini that "such boundaries do not exist in the Christ
Mind, where all beings join in a single goal."[87] Thus, the foundational Revealed
Word notion that Christianity is uniquely true is categorically false; Jesus himself
says so. Ferrini assures us that "Jesus does not ask us to convert to Christianity, for
there is no such thing." For the Jesus with whom Ferrini communicates, "Christianity is a myth of separation. It divides the Christian from the Jew or the Muslim
or the Buddhist." Ferrini asks rhetorically, "Do you think that Jesus would advocate such an idea? Of course not."[88]

There is more to learn from Jesus than the message of religious pluralism.
Among other things, Jesus is *not* concerned about sin, in fact, he does not even believe in the concept. "My teaching is a simple one: I teach the forgiveness of sins. I
teach that sin itself is not real."[89] It follows that human evil is also an illusion. Moreover, the body is not important, for the true individual is a spirit that experiences
neither birth nor death. "You are not the body, for the body is born and dies, and
you are not born, nor do you die."[90] The Revealed Word teaching that the body *is*
significant is an unhelpful thought, and "unhelpful thoughts must be eliminated.
This is the essence of mind training."[91]

Ferrini demotes the Jesus of history—whose teachings have been twisted by
Christians—and elevates the *spirit* Jesus who can inform us directly and accurately.

The latter states through Ferrini that "my teaching has been and will continue to be distorted because it threatens every thought which is false."[92] At the heart of Jesus' true spiritual teaching is a central tenet of the New Religious Synthesis— that we are embodied for a time, only to be released eventually through a process of spiritual evolution. Feelings of guilt are themselves just part of an evolutionary process taking place while we remain in our embodied stage. In this way "unresolved issues of self-worth" are being worked out as we progress spiritually. Oddly, Jesus teaches that each of us "selected" our parents in order, he tells us, to "exacerbate your guilt so that you can become conscious of it."[93] Once conscious of guilt, it can be eliminated as a false concept. Conversely, feelings of guilt are not the result of any actual wrongdoing on the reader's part.

Paul Ferrini's performs a shamanic function in *Love Without Conditions*, making contact with a spiritual entity named Jesus who speaks truth derived from a diffuse divinity called the Christ Mind. Ferrini's Jesus has much to say that assists the reader in making spiritual progress, much of it in direct contradiction to the Revealed Word tradition as expressed in the New Testament. Ferrini's message of a unity at the heart of all faiths will be taken up in the next chapter when we consider how, in the New Religious Synthesis, the shaman's experience of a direct encounter with the realm of the spirit has now become a crucial argument for religious pluralism.

CONCLUSION

In his bestselling book *The Seat of the Soul* (1989), frequent Oprah Winfrey Show guest Gary Zukav takes for granted the existence of "nonphysical Teachers" who come to us from "levels of Light" that are beyond our immediate perception.[94] These "impersonal consciousnesses" are often involved in instructing human beings in the higher spiritual truths, such as the evolutive nature of the cosmos and the fundamental unity of all things. In other words, these spirit beings accept some of the basic tenets of the New Religious Synthesis and are here to teach them to us. "This is not their home, so to speak. They are teachers to our plane. They are free to teach in our plane without being of our plane." That these Teachers can come to us in our plane without becoming one with our plane is a result of their having transcended duality altogether. They live in the plane of the ultimate unity of all things, and this "is simply the natural dynamic of evolution." Zukav assures his readers that "as you evolve beyond [duality], and also when you leave your physical body and journey home to your nonphysical plane of reality, you will not exist in dualism."[95]

Zukav takes for granted several foundational elements of the New Religious Synthesis: the fundamentally evolutive nature of the universe, the spiritual evolution of human beings and the essential unity and divinity of all things. Compatible with these is the presence of spirit teachers to guide us on in our evolutionary progress. Moreover, these entities and "advanced human souls" go on to inhabit "millions, indeed, billions of life-filled planets."[96] In fact, he asserts that "there is not one planet that lacks a level of active consciousness, some of it akin to our human form, and some of which does not come close to our form." These members of "the Angelic kingdom" are here to "guide and interact with us" in order to assist our evolution. Moreover, they have assisted with "the evolution of other galaxies and Life forms there."[97]

Zukav's fundamental thesis is compatible with the position outlined by Emanuel Swedenborg more than two hundred years ago and has been reiterated in innumerable popular religious texts in the modern period. It is present not only in Madame Blavatsky's treatises, but also in John Mack's alien abductee accounts. Other examples of this position appear in contemporary popular religious writing. For example, Neale Donald Walsch affirms in his *Conversations with God* that there is life on other planets, that human beings have been visited by aliens and that we currently are being observed.[98]

In the cosmos of the New Religious Synthesis there is no sovereign deity, though minor deities abound. They may be identified as spirits or aliens, inner guides or higher selves, ascended masters or highly evolved intelligences. Whatever the name they are called, they have something of profound spiritual significance to tell humanity. Often they seek to instruct us through their human mouthpieces in proper theology, or at the very least to correct theological misconceptions.

The theological perspective articulated by spirit guides contradicts that of the Revealed Word. Swedenborg's planetary spirits repudiate the historical details of the Christian gospel, while Blavatsky's ascended masters reveal ancient spiritual secrets that prove Christianity to be a spiritual aberration. And so it goes right down to the present—Paul Ferrini's Christ proclaims a distinctly unchristian religious pluralism.

Lacking a sovereign deity, the Other Spirituality's evolutive universe yields up its secrets by two means—scientific enquiry and spirit contact. And, as it turns out, both sources say complementary things. Similarly, Jeremy Narby reports experiments in which shamans help research scientists resolve difficult experimental issues. Of one such collaborative effort he writes, "This experiment seemed to show that scientists can learn a good deal by working with Amazonian shamans." Thus, he concludes, "Bringing scientists and shamans together seems more like a beginning."[99] In the Other Spirituality, shamanism and science embrace. The next chapter explores in detail the case for religious pluralism embedded in the shaman's mystical experience.

10

THE MYSTICAL PATH
TO PLURALISM

Discovering That All Is One in Religion

It is striking how similar the analysis of human "interior life" reads among mystics of all the great religions, be the individual Jewish, Zen-Buddhist, Sufi, or Christian.

RICHARD ROHR, The Enneagram

There is a unity at the heart of all religions. More than moral it is theological, but more than theological it is metaphysical in the precise sense of the word. The fact that it is thus transcendent, however, means that it can be univocally described by none and concretely apprehended by few.

HUSTON SMITH, *introduction to*
The Transcendent Unity of Religions

Evidence suggests that the deepest origins of religion are based in mystical experience.

ANDREW NEWBERG AND EUGENE D'AQUILI,
Why God Won't Go Away

Is Jesus Christ the unique mediator of salvation? I was one of five panelists assigned to address this question at a recent meeting of Catholic theologians. I was the first to speak and, as it turned out, the only panelist prepared to advance an unqualified affirmative response to this question.

J. A. DI NOIA, *in* First Things

In his recent book *The Mystic Heart*, Catholic lay brother Wayne Teasdale has written that mystics and "some enlightened philosophers" have long "known and proclaimed the essential interconnectedness of all things," which is "consciousness itself!"[1] Human consciousness is, for Teasdale, simply our participation in "*a community of consciousness*" that is present everywhere.[2] Science, for Teasdale, supports this spiritual insight. He invokes Amit Goswami, "one of the most eloquent voices in physics today," to confirm "a familiar new paradigm: that consciousness is the basis of reality."[3] That is, science proves that consciousness, not the Revealed Word's personal God, is "the basis of reality."

According to Teasdale, "the real religion of humankind can be said to be spirituality itself, because mystical spirituality is the origin of all the world's religions." He predicts that "the religion of the third millennium" will be pluralistic in nature—"the sharing of ultimate experiences across traditions."[4] Mystical experience, then, is the common core of all religious traditions, and as such the basis of a new spiritual paradigm to replace the Revealed Word. Mysticism "points to the realization that although there are many spiritual paths, a universal commonality underlies them all."[5]

Teasdale acknowledges that some mystics are seeking contact with a personal God. However, these "mystics" are in the minority and misunderstand the nature of the mystical experience. The "mystery and reality known for tens of thousands of years by mystic sages" includes the truth that "we are all already divine, and we simply have to wake up and realize it."[6] Despite theological differences that tend to divide people of different faith traditions, mysticism unites the various faiths through a common experience of Ultimate Reality. Through mystical experience, the human race will learn to transcend the restraints of differing theologies.

Teasdale also acknowledges that in Buddhism and Christianity one finds an apparently irreconcilable contradiction between atheism and theism. As he articulates the point, "the basic contradiction lies between the Buddhist concept of no god, and the Christian commitment to God."[7] Nevertheless, he writes that "Buddhism and Christianity have a historic mission to create, together, a new vision for the world." These two historic faiths will lead the way to religious unity by making "a precious contribution toward the evolution and communication of a new consciousness all around the world."[8] Such a "breakthrough" will take us to "a higher level of awareness."[9] For Teasdale, the awareness that transcends theological contradictions will come not through theology but through "mystical practice and a new spirituality." He adds, "The resulting spirituality or mystical practice will embrace the totality available from the vast deposit of humankind's inner experience."[10]

Pluralism has come to dominate the Western religious scene in the past thirty or so years. The pluralistic perspective affirms that all religions provide unique insights into the transcendent and reflect a similar human longing for the divine. In addition, pluralism insists that no single faith can make an exclusive claim to truth and that there is no superior spiritual perspective from which other perspectives can be assessed.

The presence of a strong and apparently inextinguishable human religious impulse has itself been advanced to support pluralism, and the goal of much scholarship over the past two centuries has been to discover the common origin of all religions. The project of discovering what Mircea Eliade has called "the *fundamental unity* of all religious phenomena," then, has been at the center of religious research and speculation in the modern period.[11] Though this is a long and complex chapter in Western intellectual history, an overview of some important developments provides us with a sense of the project's history.

English Deists of the seventeenth and eighteenth centuries believed that Reason was the source of an early and universal religion. In *De religioni laici* (1645), Lord Herbert of Cherbury (1583-1648) observed that each faith shares many points in common with the others.[12] In *Of Truth* (1624), he argued that the universal practice of worship and sense of repentance indicated that human reason apprehended a common spiritual truth in the cosmos. In 1794, a French writer by the name of Dupuis published a three-volume treatise entitled *On the Origin of all Forms of Worship*, in which he maintained that all human religions could be traced back to astrology and the worship of the stars.[13]

In the early nineteenth century, the great theologian Friedrich Daniel Ernst Schleiermacher (1768-1834) contended that Jesus Christ represented a starting point in a new phase of human spiritual progress. Just as biological life progressed, so spiritual progress followed a similar path. Jesus Christ represented this "first point" in an ongoing spiritual process, a man "entirely unique in that he was dominated by the consciousness of God as no man had been before and no man has since been."[14] Christ reflected "absolute dependence upon God," an experience noted in all faiths, each expressing the concept in differing but legitimate fashions.

By the middle of the nineteenth century, psychological theories emerged that placed the origin of religion within the human mind. In *The Essence of Christianity* (1841), Ludwig Feuerbach (1804-1872) argued that human beings possess an innate desire to create an ideal humanity, really an ideal self. This overwhelming desire for personal perfection leads us to create gods who embody the virtues we would like for ourselves. Thus, Feuerbach "reduced religion to unconscious self-projection."[15]

The twentieth century produced additional explanations of religion's universality. Rudolf Otto's book *The Idea of the Holy* (1917) found a human encounter with "the numinous"—something divine and awe inspiring—to be at the heart of all authentic religious experience. Religious feeling arises from "that strange and profound mental reaction to the numinous," which Otto referred to as "'creature feeling' or creature consciousness." This awareness of a divine reality, even of a divine person, beyond our sensate comprehension leads to "the diminution of the self into nothingness."[16] Even the early "Religion of Primitive Man" reflects such a "numinous dread" that later matures into "more highly developed forms of numinous emotion."[17] Otto saw Christianity as the highest and most fully developed expression of what he took to be an authentic human encounter with the divine. In Christianity, the primitive dread of the numinous "invades the mind mightily . . . with the words: 'Holy, holy, holy.'"[18]

Not all twentieth-century explanations were so complimentary of the religious believer, however. Sigmund Freud (1856-1939), in his 1927 work *The Future of an Illusion*, advanced the now famous hypothesis that early human beings personified nature in order to gain a sense of control over its forces.[19] Thus were created gods responsible for rain, fire, sun and wind. These gods helped to ameliorate human fear in the face of the extraordinarily powerful forces at work in the natural world. Nature gods eventually became supernatural parents who were at once feared, appeased, petitioned and worshiped. The Jews invented the notion of a single parent-God.[20]

Freud's associate and disciple Carl Jung developed a theory of his own as to the origins of human religions. Jung had an abiding interest in religion and was particularly taken with gnosticism. Like Freud, he maintained that all religious ideas, including the idea of God's existence, are generated within the human mind. Unlike Freud, he affirmed the existence of a source of religious ideas common to all human minds, which he dubbed the "collective unconscious." The collective unconscious is a kind of deep and common memory that binds human beings to one another and to their ancestors. Thus, religions are the products of "a deity-engendering faculty within the human psyche."[21]

Other explanations of religion have turned upon a society's need for a mutually binding moral code, the search for meaning in human experience, the structure of the human mind, the devious efforts of a priestly caste to gain social dominance, and human wonder in the presence of great power such as that of the sun. The famous primatologist Jane Goodall suggested in 1970 that the exuberant reaction of apes watching a waterfall revealed the evolutionary origins of the sublime feelings in humans that were the source of the first religions.[22] Recent speculation about the evolution of the brain, however, has turned increasingly to a hypothesis close to the center of New Religious Synthesis thinking. In *The Mystical Mind: Probing the Biology of Religious Experience*, psychiatrist Eugene G. D'Aquili and physician Andrew B. Newberg argue that the brain's evolution has equipped it specifically for the mystical experience.[23] Moreover, this universal mystical encounter with a realm beyond the physical accounts for the variety of human religions. Thus, at least some scientific research is moving in the direction of a particular argument for religious pluralism.

This chapter explores one of the "common source" arguments for religious pluralism that advocates of the New Religious Synthesis have endorsed with remarkable consistency. This approach finds mystical experience or the experience of spiritually sensitive individuals to be the source and center of human spirituality throughout the ages. Historian Roland Bainton has noted that "mysticism is actually found in all religions, and can very readily conceive of Christianity as simply one among many valid approaches to God."[24] This effort to bring the Revealed Word under the mystical umbrella runs contrary to its two most foundational and controversial claims about itself—that it is directly revealed by a personal and wholly other God and that it is uniquely true among the world's religious traditions. This chapter considers several important efforts to render mysticism the essence of human religious experience, and in this way to make it the basis of a powerful argument for religious pluralism emerging out of the New Religious Synthesis.

The chapter begins by considering some important early efforts to discover a common source of the human religious experience. We will then turn our attention to the specific effort to ground an argument for pluralism in mysticism. One major proponent of this view is the nineteenth-century Canadian physician R. M. Bucke, who argued that mysticism was an essential stage in the evolution of the human spirit. Frithjof Schuon is another prominent voice in the effort to place mystical or "esoteric" experience at the center of human spiritual life, and we will consider both his argument in *The Transcendent Unity of Religion*, as well as comparative religions scholar Huston Smith's endorsement of Schuon's ideas. One of the more persuasive voices for religious pluralism in the last fifty years has been Joseph Campbell. We will consider how mysticism plays an important role in his arguments for a new approach to accommodating religious diversity. The chapter concludes by exploring Marcus Borg's argument that Jesus himself should be understood as a mystic whose experience of the realm of the spirit has been shared by many founders of religions.

AN ORIGINAL RELIGION

As noted in chapter two, several prominent European scholars of the Renaissance period advocated an undifferentiated view of religion. Bainton notes that Renaissance mystics in particular "sought to discover the same set of truths beneath the symbols of many systems: in the lore of Zoroaster, the mysteries of Hermes Trismegistus, in the alluring number speculations of the Jewish cabala." Some sought to establish a World Parliament of Religions based on mystical insights.[25] Fifteenth-century scholar Nicholas of Cusa argued in 1453 for "a fundamental harmony linking all faiths to the worship of a common hidden God," not the self-revealing God of the Revealed Word. Bradford Verter notes that in Nicholas and other similar thinkers we find "seeds of both esoteric mysticism and theological unitarianism."[26] The important Renaissance writer Pico della Mirandola blended Neo-Platonism, Hermeticism, Christianity and the kabbalah as part of his search for a mystically based religious unity.[27]

European colonial expansion provided additional impetus for pluralistic theories. Religious documents from the Eastern world in particular contributed to the sense that a single, unifying source lies at the foundation of all religions. Some European scholars concluded that "all of Eastern religion must have been reducible to a single pattern," which might be considered "a gentile approximation of Christianity," albeit with an important difference.[28] Eastern faiths tended to posit a diffuse divine essence rather than the personal God of the Revealed Word, an essence best understood through mystical experience rather than rational apprehension.

Not until the seventeenth century did pluralistic arguments begin to achieve genuinely popular acceptance. Charles Blount (1654-1693) was the first successful proponent of a religious pluralism based on comparing various faiths. Blount collected the views of ancient religions on an afterlife in his work *Anima mundi (World Spirit)* (1678).[29] This work introduced British readers to several religions of the Near and Far East, advocating in the process their underlying pantheism and direct experience of the divine. Blount systematically compared a number of religions in order to demonstrate that there exists in each an irreducible pantheistic core, the fundamental element, he argued, of a natural human religion. Personal experience of a divine essence and a corresponding religious pluralism rooted in such experience were already being advocated in tandem as components in a new religious understanding.

In *Oracles of Reason* (1693), Blount compared various ancient religious sources and examined the foundational doctrines of Islam, Hinduism and Zoroastrianism.[30] In his search for an argument supporting pantheism and condemning Revealed Word exclusivity, Blount scoured classical and contemporary religious texts including works by early Christian heretics such as Philostratus, Porphyry and Celsus. He also examined classical writers such as Lucian, Seneca and Cicero, the Arabian philosopher Averroes and European Humanists and skeptics such as Erasmus, Montaigne, Bacon, Spinoza, Hobbes and Locke.[31] The result was a catalog of religions and religious philosophy, initially intended as a sourcebook for skeptics.[32] Blount's efforts to discover a common basis for human religions, however, inspired a generation of writers seeking an argument for religious pluralism as an antidote to Revealed Word exclusivity.

True religion that recognized the divine in nature was universal. So how did the misleading Revealed Word tradition arise? The notion of a personal God who demanded a particular kind of belief for salvation, it was argued, grew out of the efforts of a priestly caste to overturn natural religion. The Deists' name for this error was "Priestcraft." Blount argued that the conspiracy against direct experience of the natural divinity started when a priestly class began exploiting the fear of death. The original priest was a "crafty discerning person, who having observed what is most dear to Mankind" pretended that he was "able to assist in the preservation of life." This proto-priest's goal was purely self-serving; he sought "esteem and credit in the world."[33] From such common ancestors the whole class of priestly types descended, seizing spiritual power by exploiting primal fears.[34] Freethinkers throughout history, however, employed reason to cut through the thick fog of fear and priestly deception, keeping alive the native human religion.

An intriguing eight-page pamphlet appearing on the streets of London in 1753 advanced anthropological evidence for an original and natural human religion. Its title, *A Speech Delivered by an Indian Chief in Reply to a Sermon Preached by a Swedish Missionary*, did not suggest the pamphlet's true intent—to affirm a universal religion still known to primitive people. Presented with the Christian gospel, a Native American tribal chief asserts that "every Man is possessed with sufficient Knowledge for his own salvation," and that this saving knowledge comes through "natural religion." Moreover, the chief was adamant that the missionary's Bible "can't add to natural religion."[35]

The argument for a universal religion of humanity received a boost in eighteenth-century Europe with the diligent work of the French scholar Anquetil du

Perron (1731-1805) to introduce Westerners first to Zoroastrianism and then to Hinduism. In 1754, when only twenty-three, du Perron visited India, where he became acquainted with the members of the Parsee sect, descendants of ancient Zoroastrians. A scholar named Dastur Darab introduced du Perron to the teachings of Zarathustra. In 1771, du Perron presented his French translation of the Avesta, the sacred book of Zoroastrianism that had shaped the religious thinking of the entire Eastern world. The book created an immediate and heated controversy when Christian missionaries and scholars challenged it, a controversy that only contributed to its readership.

Throughout his life du Perron published papers and books for a Western audience on the religions of the East. In the opening years of the nineteenth century du Perron returned from India with "a translation of the *Oupnek'hat*—a collection of fifty *Upanishads*—which gave the Western world its first deep insight into the baffling mind of the East." Carl Jung wrote that du Perron "brought the Eastern mind to the West, and its influence upon us we cannot as yet measure." Jung, ever the student of mystical experience, held that du Perron's work introduced to the West "the secret, spiritual influence of the East," and thus threw the Western spiritual mind into "confusion."[36] Mystical experience and the interior psychic life were now elevated in a fashion that permanently changed how Europeans and Americans thought about both the spiritual world and the origins of religion. The Revealed Word perspective with its external and personal God could no longer claim unchallenged dominance of Western religious thought. Moreover, the foundation of a new religious pluralism was in the making.

R. M. BUCKE

At the end of the nineteenth century, a Canadian physician advanced a surprisingly durable theory regarding the biological and religious evolution of the human race. Richard Maurice Bucke (1837-1902), in *Cosmic Consciousness: A Study in the Evolution of the Human Mind*, argued from historical evidence that certain individuals in the human family had already taken the next step in spiritual evolution and that this step involved mystical awareness or what he termed "Cosmic Consciousness." Bucke wrote that "this consciousness shows the cosmos to consist not of dead matter governed by unconscious, rigid, and unintending law; it shows it, on the contrary as entirely immaterial, entirely spiritual and entirely alive." Thus, Cosmic Consciousness opens one to the fact of pantheism, revealing that "the universe is

God and that God is the universe, and that no evil ever did or ever will enter into it."[37] The experience of Cosmic Consciousness also "shows that death is an absurdity, that everyone and everything has eternal life." The experience of Cosmic Consciousness is "called in the East the 'Brahmic Splendour,'" while in "Dante's phrase," the experience is "capable of transhumanizing a man into a god."[38]

Cosmic Consciousness is, for Bucke, the third stage in the evolution of human consciousness. It follows simple consciousness or awareness of one's basic existence, and self-consciousness or awareness that one exists as a self distinct from others. In keeping with the New Religious Synthesis emphasis on science as a source of spiritual insight, Cosmic Consciousness will lead humankind into a scientific study of the divine that will enhance the human capacity to continue its spiritual evolution toward even greater consciousness. Developing an adequate science of God will take a great deal of time, according to Bucke, but is an important component in the spiritual destiny of the human race. Bucke writes, "If it has taken the race several hundred thousand years to learn a smattering of the science of humanity since its acquisition of self-consciousness, so it may take it millions of years to acquire a smattering of the science of God after its acquisition of Cosmic Consciousness."[39] Bucke, then, turns science in the direction of an ultimate theology, much like contemporary authors in the New Science genre.

Cosmic Consciousness is already known in some religions, though certainly not in all. It is the foundation of "the higher religions and the higher philosophies and what comes from them, and on it will be based, when it becomes more general, a new world of which it would be idle to try and speak today."[40] This next evolutionary step comes when our present minds are "overcrowded" with increasingly "larger, more numerous and more and more complex" concepts. Eventually, "the chemical union of several [such concepts] and of certain moral elements takes place," resulting in "cosmic consciousness."[41] That is, chemical pressures in the advanced human minds cause an eruption into the next level of consciousness. Thus we continue our "beginningless and endless ascent" toward a "higher life than any heretofore experienced or even conceived."[42]

Evolving consciousness, the moral nature and lunacy. In Bucke's late nineteenth-century theorizing, the "savage" represented an early stage in human mental development, as did the human child. Thus he could write that "as the individual physical man begins at the very bottom of the scale as a unicellular monad, so does the physical man begin on the bottom rung of the ladder of mind." For Bucke, the "lower minds" of savage races lack important spiritual qualities such as "faith, cour-age, personal force, sympathy, and affection."[43] Only higher minds would be capa-ble of advancing to Cosmic Consciousness, while lower human minds represent an evolutionary dead-end.

Something Bucke called "the moral nature" guides the evolution of higher minds. This "moral nature" determines "for the race at large" and "from age to age" what sort of place we experience the cosmos to be.[44] The general direction of the "moral nature" is to create a cosmos that is increasingly friendly and accepting. Already the whole world is better than it once was. "The whole human race and all living things have put on," writes Bucke, "a charm and sacredness which in the old times they were far from possessing." Our view of the divine is more sanguine under evolution-ary pressures as well. "The governing powers of the universe (obedient to the same beneficent influence) have been gradually converted from demons into beings and forces less and less inimical, more and more friendly to man."[45] All of this is proof of our spiritual evolution, which "is a simple matter of growth strictly analogous to the unfolding of the branch from the bud, or the plant from its seed."[46]

Some races are evolving rapidly toward Cosmic Consciousness; others are mov-ing more slowly. But there is hope, for spiritual evolution begins in individuals and spreads to larger groups. "When a new faculty appears in a race, it will be found, in the very beginning, in one individual of that race; later it will be found in a few in-dividuals."[47] Still, evolved faculties appear only in those members of a race "*who have reached full maturity,*" for the spiritually immature "cannot over-pass or go beyond a mature individual of the same race."[48] Such spiritual maturity is often found in those we call mystics, and mystics may appear to us at first as lunatics.

For Bucke, a psychiatrist, "the large number of mental breakdowns, commonly called insanity, are due to the rapid and recent evolution of those [new] faculties" in the human race.[49] Some true mystics are taken to be insane only because they demonstrate abilities the rest of us do not yet have. However, "cases of cosmic con-sciousness should become more and more numerous" as well as "more perfect, more pronounced." Bucke was even willing to assert that "at least thirteen cases are so great that they can never fade from human memory—namely Gautama, Jesus, Paul, Plotinus, Muhammad, Dante, Las Casas, John Yepes, Francis Bacon, Jacob Behmen, William Blake, Balzac, Walt Whitman."[50]

Evolution toward pluralism. Cosmic Consciousness occurs with increasing fre-quency as history progresses. Bucke counts "five cases" in the eighteen-hundred-year period from Gautama the Buddha to Dante, or "one case to every three hundred and sixty years." However, "from Dante to the present day" there have been more than six hundred cases. This means that "cosmic consciousness has been 4.8 times more frequent during the latter period than it was during the former."[51] Eventually, it will be a common experience, and finally, one spread throughout the human race. Thus, in the distant future distinctions among religions will disappear because every human being will share Cosmic Consciousness. For now, however, the rest of us must look for religious guidance to "the few who have been illumined."[52]

Cosmic Consciousness produces harmony among religious teachers, even ones whose followers mistakenly think they are at odds with the adherents of other faiths. Bucke states categorically that "there is no instance of a person who has been illumined denying or disputing the teaching of another who has passed through the same experience."[53] Thus, if Jesus' followers took him to be claiming that he was unique in some way, they misunderstood his message. According to Bucke, Jesus was "a Specialist—that is, he had Cosmic Consciousness."[54] But he was not the Son of God in the sense that the Revealed Word tradition means that term to be understood. He did, however, "have the earnest temperament" from which "the Cosmic Sense springs."[55]

Despite the coming religious egalitarianism, the Cosmically Conscious currently constitute a spiritual, emotional and physical elite. Bucke affirms that "in order for a man to enter into Cosmic Consciousness he must belong . . . to the top layer of the world of Self-Consciousness." The candidate for Cosmic Consciousness "must have a good physique, good health, but above all he must have an exalted moral nature, strong sympathies, a warm heart, courage, strong and earnest religious feelings."[56] Bucke's opinion as to whether a woman could take this next evolutionary step is uncertain.

The experience. Bucke gathered from the works of various mystics and visionaries their accounts of the initial leap into Cosmic Consciousness. The experience itself involved the sense of "suddenly, without warning . . . being immersed in a flame, or rose coloured cloud, or perhaps rather a sense that the mind is itself filled with such a cloud or haze."[57] At the very same time the Cosmically Conscious person is "bathed in an emotion of joy, assurance, triumph, 'salvation.'"[58] Following this "like a flash there is presented to his consciousness a clear conception (a vision) in outline of the meaning and drift of the universe."[59]

Insights arising from this mystical experience are almost doctrinal in nature, and often contrary to the Revealed Word. They include the sense that "all life is eternal," that the universe is "a living presence" and an "infinite ocean of life," that "the soul of man is as eternal as God is" and that "the happiness of every individual is in the long run absolutely certain."[60] On the difficult issue of sin, which clearly and irreconcilably separates the Revealed Word from Cosmic Consciousness, Bucke is unyielding—the concept is false and misleading. "It is not that the person escapes from sin; but he no longer sees that there is any sin in the world from which to escape."[61] The work of drawing the human race out of error and toward Cosmic Consciousness "has been going on within us since the dawn of life on this planet."[62]

FRITHJOF SCHUON AND TRANSCENDENT RELIGIOUS UNITY

Perhaps the foundational text for all subsequent discussions of mysticism as the essence of pluralism is Frithjof Schuon's (1907-1998) classic *The Transcendent Unity of Religions*. In this dense polemical work, first published in 1957, the Swiss comparative religions scholar sets out his now famous distinction between exoteric and esoteric approaches to faith. Schuon argues that the latter takes a more open approach to religion, emphasizing experience over the exoteric's doctrine. Esoterics, for Schuon, represent a more advanced stage of religious attainment, as well as a path to religious enlightenment.

Born in Basel, Switzerland, on June 18, 1907, Schuon eventually immigrated with his family to France. From an early age he was drawn to the texts of Indian religion, especially the Upanishads and the Bhagavad-Gita. An avid student of Arabic, Schuon traveled in North Africa in the 1930s, becoming familiar with Islam. In 1939 he visited India, returning to Switzerland where he lived for forty years following World War II. On visits to America in the late 1950s, he lived with members of the Sioux and Crow tribes and studied their religious practices. The author of more than twenty books, Schuon was a world-renowned scholar in religion. In 1980 he took up residence in the United States, where he continued to write until his death in 1998.

Schuon's distinction between the exoteric and the esoteric religious believer has been widely adopted.[63] The exoteric believer demands literal understandings of external and accessible religious symbols, thus insisting, for example, that the Bible is to be read literally and historically rather than symbolically or allegorically. This leads to conclusions such as that Jesus actually *is* God in some literal sense, rather than recognizing that a phrase such as "Son of God" is to be taken as a symbolic expression of a spiritual reality. The esoteric seeker, on the other hand, recognizes that religious symbols are just that—representations of something incapable of linguistic description or of historical manifestation. The esoteric thus possesses a more sophisticated and flexible understanding of spiritual matters than does the exoteric.

For Schuon, a single divine reality lay behind various religious experiences and expressions. As renowned religions scholar Huston Smith explains, "Intimations and realizations of this supreme identity appear in varying degrees of explicitness in all revealed religions and constitute the point at which they are one."[64] Schuon found that the exoteric was "anchored" to a particular spiritual spot, believing in a single, uniquely true revelation. The esoteric, on the other hand can accept that "revelation has multiple and equal instances" and thus that "no single instance can be absolute." Smith notes that for Schuon, religious unity can only be realized "on the esoteric plane," even though esoterics constitute a "minority" of religious believers "who realize that they have their roots in the Absolute."[65] Exoterics are "less supple in their capacity for 'spiritual abstraction'" and are thus unlikely to realize commonality with members of other faiths.[66] The esoteric would be, in R. M. Bucke's terms, ready to take the next step toward Cosmic Consciousness.

Schuon sought to liberate religion from the Revealed Word notion of personal salvation rooted in exoteric doctrines such as the uniqueness of Jesus Christ and his atoning death.[67] Schuon found the exoteric's self-interested emphasis on personal salvation to deflect attention from Ultimate Reality, the true source of spiritual experience. "Exoteric ideology," he writes in The Transcendent Unity of Religions, is "limited to a relative point of view, that of individual salvation" which constitutes "an interested point of view."[68] "The exoteric point of view," he writes, "cannot comprehend the transcendence of the supreme Divine Impersonality. . . . Such truths are of too high an order, and therefore too subtle and too complex . . . to be accessible by the majority or formulated in a dogmatic manner."[69]

Schuon thus rejected the uniqueness of Jesus Christ as a manifestation of the divine Logos, albeit on a rather strange argument. "If Christ had been the only manifestation of the Word . . . the effect of His birth would have been the instantaneous reduction of the universe to ashes."[70] This is because "a universal Reality cannot have only one manifestation to the exclusion of others, for in that case it would not be universal."[71] In other words, Jesus Christ cannot be the one manifestation of the Divine, for then the Divine would not be universal.

Schuon finds "the Divine Authority" to be "inherent in every Revelation."[72] He posited an early, unified and unsullied religion, which he termed "the Primordial Tradition" and which is "the only unique religion possible."[73] Under this Tradition, humankind experienced "thousands of years of sane and balanced existence," but then went astray. But the idea that God would save humanity through "a means so materially and psychologically ineffective as a new religion" like Christianity would render the Divine "monstrous."[74] The "ideology of 'the believers'" in a single, unique revelation is "nothing but an intentional and interested confusion between the formal and the universal."[75]

"Indispensable" religious ideas are not owned by one faith. "Indeed, the more important and indispensable any particular means of grace may be, the more certain it is that it will be found in all the orthodox forms in a mode appropriate to the environment in question."[76] In a famous formulation he affirmed that "the Divinity manifests Its Personal aspect through each particular Revelation and its supreme Impersonality through the diversity of the forms of Its Word."[77] Consequently, perceptive thinkers will recognize that Christ was one among many "God-men," individuals specially gifted both to experience and to express the inexpressible ultimate reality behind all religious symbols.[78] These are the most advanced esoterics, humanity's spiritual guides along the path to religious unity.

Prophets, inner reality and esoteric elites. Esoterism is not the religious view of most people, nor does it seek to explain the religious experience of the majority. In fact, Schuon held that "esoterism is reserved, by definition and because of its very nature, for an intellectual elite necessarily restricted in numbers."[79] Certain specially endowed individuals throughout human history—including both Christ and Muhammad—reflect an "inner reality" in which they are "identified with the Word," Schuon's term for an ultimate divine reality.[80] Indeed, "every being who has achieved metaphysical reality" is identified with Ultimate Reality or the Word.[81] Thus, Jesus of the Revealed Word represents but one among many expressions of the divine Word.

These spiritually attuned individuals are the God-men among us, and "without the idea of the 'God-man' esoterism would be deprived of an aspect of its very existence."[82] The fact that God-men experience Ultimate Reality in an extraordinary way undergirds statements such as Jesus' famous remark, "I and the Father are one." Such a man will join "his essential identity with the divine principle that alone is real."[83] On the other hand, those not so equipped for special spiritual experience are relegated to the status of "the collective average" who become "passive and unconscious transmitters of the symbols."[84] Thus, though Schuon's theory accommodates religious pluralism by finding the special experience of the esoteric at the heart of all legitimate spiritual expression, it may, like Bucke's account, result in a kind of spiritual elitism.

JOSEPH CAMPBELL: THE PERENNIAL PHILOSOPHY AS PLURALISTIC HOPE

Joseph Campbell (1904-1987) was one of the most famous intellectual figures of the twentieth century. His public fame was due to his many publications that clearly presented the history, geography and theory of myth. Campbell was the author of such widely read works as *The Hero with a Thousand Faces* (1949), the four-volume work *The Masks of God*, the five-volume *The Historical Atlas of World Mythology*, and innumerable book chapters, published lectures and essays. But Campbell was perhaps best known and remembered for his enormously popular television specials, *The Power of Myth*, with Bill Moyers on Public Broadcasting System, and *Transformations of Myth Through Time*, a televised series of lectures produced by Stuart Brown and William Free. The lectures from *Transformations* were published in book form in 1990, three years after Professor Campbell's death. Campbell contributed significantly to public acceptance of a religious pluralism rooted in myth and mystical experience.

Campbell popularized the idea that myths reflect recurring themes in human experience of the transcendent. He writes, "Throughout the mythologies and religious systems of the world, the same images, the same themes are constantly recurring." These he referred to as "elementary ideas," following the work of Adolf Bastian.[85] Campbell was a devoted student of Bastian's work and cites it frequently. Bastian's concept of *Elementargedanken* or elementary ideas is of particular importance to Campbell's theory of myth. Elementary ideas "characterize the recurrent themes and motifs that [Bastian] was everywhere encountering." Bastian also recognized that "wherever and whenever they appeared it would be in costumes local to that region."[86] Thus, basic religious ideas recur throughout the world, albeit dressed in native mythic costume.

Myths, power and pluralism. Campbell emphasized those myths conveying what he, like Aldous Huxley, liked to call the Perennial Philosophy, particularly "the mythologies and the interpretations of the myths in India."[87] The Perennial Philosophy posits an undifferentiated Ultimate Reality of consciousness in the universe, elevates mystical experience as contact with this Ultimate Reality, and venerates the special spiritual knowledge of mystics. Campbell took the Indian Vedas, for example, as records of this experience of Ultimate Reality, literally as what has been *heard* by those who experience the Reality. He writes, "the word *veda* is from a Sanskrit root, *vid*, which means 'knowledge.'" Thus, "the Vedas are the manifestation of a specific kind of knowledge. It's called *sruti*, which means 'heard.'" In the Indian tradition, "the Rhishis, or saints, were people who did not invent the poems, the hymns of the Vedas. They heard them, just as anyone who listens to the muse will hear." The special knowledge of the Vedas can be employed to summon the gods. "Those who have heard deeply the rhythms and hymns and words of the gods can recite those hymns in such a way that the gods will be attracted." The Vedas, then, convey spiritual power to those who know them well. "The Vedas form the substance of the rituals by which the powers of nature, personified as gods, are invoked to support the intentions of Aryan society. You invoke the gods to do your will."[88] Those who control such power are "stronger than the gods." Thus, "an illuminated man is stronger than any deity. This is the great thing in the universe, and this is what the Brahman is."[89]

A component in the Perennial Philosophy, then, is that divine power is present in anyone who learns how to "turn in" and discover the deity within himself or herself. "All those gods that you are invited to worship through public sacrifice are projections of the fire of your own energy." This belief supports a kind of religious pluralism, for regardless of the god one says one is worshiping, one is worshiping oneself. "There's a wonderful passage in the Chandogya," writes Campbell. "Worship this god, worship that god, one god after another; those who follow this law do not know. The source of the gods is in your own heart. Follow the footsteps to that center and know that you are that of which the gods are born."[90] This idea, writes Campbell, is "the basic idea of the Perennial Philosophy. Deities are the symbolic personifications of the very energies that are yourself."[91]

The deep well of the human psyche. Campbell supported his case for the Perennial Philosophy, and for the religious pluralism that is its byproduct, with passages from the Tibetan Book of the Dead, a manual of instructions to help the spirits of the recently deceased find heaven. Though the full content of Campbell's description of this book need not detain us, one of its instructions is particularly relevant to the question of pluralism. The lama guiding a departed soul by the Book of the Dead tells it the following: "Try to bring into your consciousness the image of the lord that has been of your worship throughout your lifetime." Campbell adds, "this may be any god, so long as that god has been understood as the supreme image of the powers of the energizing energies of the universe as they have operated in your lifetime. ... Any deity that's been your top deity, this is the place to contemplate it."[92]

But even this deity must be released as the soul attempts union with Ultimate Reality by letting go of itself. The departed soul seeks "absolute Brahma, undifferentiated consciousness; that's what we're intending all the way here. You may speak of it as the Void, you may speak of it as the abyss, you may speak of it as mother light."[93] Undifferentiated consciousness is the ground of all genuine religious experience and thus a unifying factor in the case for religious pluralism. It is also the source of the universal myths arising from the "bottomless, deep and dark" well of "the human psyche itself."[94] These myths give voice to the unspeakable experience of direct contact with the unknowable, the "sphere of the intelligible," Ultimate Reality, or god. But Ultimate Reality clearly is not the personal and transcendent God of the Revealed Word whose consciousness is differentiated from that of human beings.

Funerals and hallucinogens. Ancient funerary rituals are, for Campbell, an important source of human mythology and thus of the Perennial Philosophy. These rituals often were efforts to make contact with Ultimate Reality in which hallucinogenic drugs played an important role. Campbell writes that "at one important site, at Shanidar in northern Iraq, there has recently been discovered a cave containing a number of burials, in one of which the body had been laid to rest on a bier of evergreen boughs overspread with flowers, the pollens of which could still be traced, and all of which have turned out to be plants with hallucinogenic properties. Some sort of belief in a life beyond death is here indicated, inspired perhaps by visions."[95] At least some early human mystical experiences implanting the idea of an Ultimate Reality, then, were drug-induced.

Huston Smith has recently made a similar observation about early human religious experiences and hallucinogenic drugs. In his most recent book, *Cleansing the Doors of Perception*, Smith writes that shamans, the "Native American Church" and some mystics employed "virtually nonaddictive mind-altering substances that are approached seriously and reverently," and suggests the word "entheogens" as a substitute for psychedelic in this regard.[96] For Smith "a connection exists" between entheogens and some human encounters with "God and the Infinite," a connection that he finds too often underestimated and insufficiently appreciated.[97]

In addition to the visions inspired by sacred drug use, traditions once vibrant in the West reflected the Perennial Philosophy, in Campbell's estimation. However, the West endured "a gradual attack on the mythological ideas," which separated its religious thought from "the elementary ideas." Nevertheless, Campbell notes that the elementary ideas endured in fringe traditions such as "Gnosticism, alchemy, and many of the discredited manners of thought that carry on this interest in what might be called the perennial philosophy."[98] Primitive people did not approach religion in an analytic fashion, and thus maintained a purer contact with the Perennial Philosophy. Campbell repeats Smith's point that the loss of primal religion is due to confusing concrete religious symbols with their abstract referents such as Ultimate Reality. "One of the great dangers to be avoided in the interpretation of *all* symbolic systems is that of mistaking the symbol for its reference—which, curiously, seems to be a mistake more likely to be made by teachers and students of our own symbolic heritage than even by illiterate hunters."[99] Thus, to make particular historical claims central to a religious system—as the Revealed Word does—is a mistake of this type.

Tribal hope. According to Campbell, the best hope for Westerners to retrieve the Perennial Philosophy is to return to tribal wisdom. Campbell finds such wisdom to parallel the aforementioned European traditions that were eventually abandoned. For instance, a twelfth-century translation of the Hermetic work *The Book of the Twenty-Four Philosophers* includes a statement "very much like his [Sioux medicine man Black Elk], which has been quoted, through the centuries, by a number of significant Western thinkers . . . and which is a wonderfully apt epitomization of the mystery that speaks to us everywhere through mystic vehicles: 'God is an intelligible sphere, whose center is everywhere and circumference nowhere.'" Campbell adds that "that is the elementary idea, and the function of all ethnic ideas is to link, as by a flexible tethering, all the acts, thoughts, and experiences of our daily lives—individual and social—to this realization."[100]

The true and central religious idea at the core of myth, mystical experience and the Perennial Philosophy, then, is the mystic's insights that God is "an intelligible sphere, whose center is everywhere and circumference nowhere." Religious systems adhering to this assertion are true and unifying, while those not recognizing such a theology are false and divisive. It follows that shamans and mystics are right to teach that God is a consciousness to be experienced, and that Revealed Word advocates are wrong to insist that God is a divine person to be worshiped. Clearly the latter perspective does not square with Campbell's notion that the individual is divine, the "source of all gods."

MARCUS BORG AND JESUS THE SPIRIT PERSON

Founding director Robert W. Funk of the University of Montana first convened the Jesus Seminar in 1985 under the auspices of the Westar Institute. The stated purpose of the Seminar is to investigate the figure of the "historical Jesus"—a term the group's website also puts in quotes—using the best scholarship and sources available. The Jesus Seminar has published a large number of books and other materials through Polebridge Press and has achieved a level of fame and generated a degree of controversy unusual for academic study groups. The Seminar's participants have not limited their public comments to biblical criticism, but also have advocated positions on a variety of religious issues including religious pluralism.

Marcus J. Borg is perhaps the most widely read member of the Jesus Seminar. Borg, a graduate of Oxford University, teaches in the Department of Religion and Culture at Oregon State University. The author of nine books, Borg has been both a provocative and persuasive voice in the recent Western religious conversation. In one of his bestselling books, *Meeting Jesus Again for the First Time*, Borg writes, "I agree with those who speak of each religious tradition as a 'cultural linguistic world.'" Though the religions of the world are "clearly not all the same," Borg is convinced that "the impetus for creating these cultural-linguistic worlds" of the different religions "comes out of certain kinds of extraordinary experiences that are cross cultural."[101] In *Meeting Jesus*, Borg seeks to redefine the historical character of Jesus as a mystic, a person in touch with the spirit world, a conduit of truth from another realm. As a mystic, Jesus becomes for Borg part of an argument for religious pluralism that complements the New Religious Synthesis.

Reconceptualizing God as "holy mystery." Borg's personal quest for a path to religious pluralism started with the realization that "*God* does not refer to a supernatural being 'out there' (which is where I had put God ever since my childhood musings about God 'up in heaven')." Rather, he writes, "I began to see, the word *God* refers to the sacred at the center of existence, the holy mystery that is all around us and within us."[102] God, for Borg, is transformed from the Revealed Word's wholly other and personal being—a view Borg associates with childhood—to a "holy mystery" that is everywhere and even in each one of us. "God, was no longer a concept or an article of belief, but had become an element of experience."[103]

Borg argues that traditional Revealed Word conceptions of a historical Jesus and a personal God reflect a "precritical naivete," which one grows beyond in the "critical thinking of adolescence and adulthood" when it is no longer necessary to demand that the Bible's accounts be "literally true."[104] An evolution of theological thought occurs as the believer leaves literalism behind and moves on to find truth in the "extraordinary experience" of the God that is "all around us and within us." That is, mature theology is more clearly represented in the mystic's direct experiences of the spiritual realm than in the church's historical creeds and biblical literalism.

Jesus, spirit people and the mystic experience. Borg's research into the life of Jesus of Nazareth and the origins of religion leads him to classify Jesus as a "spirit person" rather than as the Revealed Word's Messiah or God incarnate. Indeed, Jesus the spirit person is difficult to distinguish from a mystic. Borg argues that the insight that Jesus was a spirit person is "foundational to everything else Jesus was." He continues, "the most crucial fact about Jesus was that he was a 'spirit person,' a mediator of the sacred, one of those persons in human history to whom the Spirit was an experiential reality."[105]

Borg indicates that it took him "a long time" to come to this realization about Jesus' true mystic nature. "The process began," he relates, "with the realization that there really are such phenomena as experiences of Spirit and spirit persons." Religions that recognize mysticism as the foundational human spiritual experience were the source of this insight for Borg. "The realization came to me initially not from the study of the Bible of the Christian tradition, but from the study of non-Western religions and cultural anthropology." When Jesus' mystic role is recognized, a new vista is opened on his life and ministry. "This illuminating category helps us see much about Jesus that we otherwise might miss," writes Borg.[106]

Borg explains that "spirit persons are known cross-culturally." They "have vivid and frequent experiences of another level or dimension of reality," experiences that "involve momentarily entering into nonordinary states of consciousness and take a number of different forms." These different forms include "visionary experiences" and "journeying into another dimension of reality" which is, to quote Borg, "the classic experience of the shaman."[107] This "other dimension of reality" that the spirit person, mystic or shaman enters is known by many names, such as "Yahweh, Brahman, Atman, Allah, the Tao, the Great Spirit, God."[108] Thus, making Jesus a shaman becomes for Borg both a source of great insight about Jesus and a step toward religious pluralism.

Borg renders mystic experience a defining quality of religious leaders; then he brings Jesus into the category of spirit person or mystic. The implication of such a maneuver is clear—all spiritual pioneers experience mystical entrances into the spirit world, a world parallel to our own, which is incapable of any genuine description in language and which must be experienced by the mystic directly. Thus, John Mack's comparison of his clients' ordeals with the experience of the mystic fits with Borg's understanding of the spirit person. "The mystic or the shaman," writes Mack, "like the abductee, makes a pilgrimage usually with ardor, to receive a new dimension of experience or knowledge."[109] Western science may eventually help us to understand these experiences, if it can accept dramatic changes in its presuppositions about the universe.

The spirit world of the mystic, the other reality that the spirit person experiences, is directly adjacent to our own. "This other reality it is important to emphasize," he argues, "is not 'somewhere else.' Rather, it is all around us, and we are in it."[110] Borg insists that Jesus was just another person capable of making the short passage to the Other Reality and then telling us about it. "Jesus was clearly a spirit person," he writes. Specifically, Jesus was a Jewish mystic: "The more we realize that there was a form of Jewish mysticism in first-century Palestine, the more likely it seems that Jesus stood in that experiential tradition."[111]

Moreover, Jesus is not unusual in this regard, for prophets, seers, mystics and shamans have always grounded religion on experience. Thus, the Revealed Word understanding of Jesus as unique mediator of human salvation, as revealer of the character of God himself, must be set aside in favor of a new perspective. "The image I have sketched views Jesus differently: rather than being the exclusive revelation of God, he is one of many mediators of the sacred." Borg adds, "Even as this view subtracts from the uniqueness of Jesus and the Christian tradition, it also in my judgment adds to the credibility of both."[112] Thus, he reasons that capitulating to the Other Spirituality actually strengthens the Revealed Word tradition.

Promoting Christianity by demoting Jesus. As I have indicated, embedded in Borg's account of Jesus as spirit person is an argument for religious pluralism. A single communication of divine truth in human history is highly unlikely. "What are the chances that God would speak only through this particular groups of people [the Jews]"?[113] Borg does not answer his rhetorical question, but clearly he is bothered by the logic of theological exclusivism. Mysticism thus becomes an important argument for religious pluralism—each tradition advances individuals who have experienced the "other reality," and Jesus is but one of these. Jesus had an "enlightenment experience similar to such experiences reported of other great sages."[114]

Jesus as spirit person is no longer understood as Son of God in the unique Revealed Word sense of the phrase. He is, rather, one among many sons and daughters of god, mystics who have traveled from this dimension to another and returned with a life-giving message. Borg writes, "This recognition subverts the common impression that Christian faith involves believing that Jesus was *literally* 'the Son of God.'" But this "is a helpful subversion," because "the literalist reading of 'Son of God' narrows the scope of Christology by giving primacy to one image."[115]

Borg overturns traditional understandings of the life and ministry of Jesus Christ, moving him outside of the frame of history and redefining him as a 'spirit person' in the mystic tradition. As a witness in support of this position, Borg brings Jesus himself. "His own self-understanding," Borg writes of Jesus, "did not include thinking of himself and speaking of himself as the Son of God whose historical intention or purpose was to die for the sins of the world, and his message was not about believing in him." Instead, Jesus cast himself in the role of "a spirit person, a subversive sage, social prophet, and movement founder who invited his followers and hearers into a transforming relationship with the same Spirit that he himself knew."[116]

The New Testament as myth. Consistent with New Synthesis constructions of the Bible, Borg's view of Jesus and his consequent reduction of Christianity to a mystic faith founded by a spirit person depend upon reading the Gospel accounts as narrative or myth. "The centrality of narrative in the Bible is also pointed to by the fact that it contains literally hundreds of individual stories." Moreover, "at the center of Scripture are a small number of 'macro-stories'—the primary stories that shaped the religious imagination and life of ancient Israel and the early Christian movement."[117]

Borg's point is reminiscent of David Strauss's search for mythi, recurrent mythical themes in the New Testament. Again the biblical account of Jesus is read, not as history, but rather as myth, as a narrative about the journeys of a spirit person to another reality. In this way, Jesus the spirit person is to be understood as similar in kind to many hundreds of such mystics and shamans throughout human history.

CONCLUSION

Religious pluralism rooted in the twin concepts of the divine as an Ultimate Reality and mystical experience as an encounter with that Reality is an important component of the New Religious Synthesis. Closely connected to spiritual evolution, mystical pluralism sees belief in concrete religious images and fixed revelations as an early stage in religious development, and thus as an impediment to the coming age of religious unity. An obstacle in the road toward that new day is the historically grounded Revealed Word tradition. In the Other Spirituality, all human religions are inadequate human attempts to express the inexpressible truth of a divine essence or consciousness beyond ordinary human experience.

Renaissance scholars in the Hermetic tradition hoped to discover the common core of all religious experience. The goal of their researches into the occult traditions of the ancients was a single world religion centered on mystical experience, guided by secret teaching and led by a priesthood of *magi* or enlightened spiritual masters. As John G. Burke, a leading expert on Renaissance Hermetism, has written of the notorious Dominican monk Giordano Bruno, "Bruno shared the feelings of his contemporary Hermetists that there should be one universal religion, but it was not a reformed Christendom that he desired. Instead, it was a return to the worship of ancient Egypt as described in the Hermetic literature."[118]

In the modern period, the ancient hope of a single world religion has had numerous advocates. At the end of the seventeenth century, Charles Blount affirmed an original, natural faith that began with the human race itself.[119] More recently, advocates of a new approach to religion have focused much attention on mystical experience as the likely source of that primordial human religious sense. We have noted how R. M. Bucke found mysticism to be a step along the path to spiritual maturity for the human race. More recently, Frithjof Schuon and Huston Smith have claimed the presence of an esoteric and mystical core at the heart of all faiths. Joseph Campbell, in apparent agreement, calls us to affirm the centrality of a direct experience of the spiritual realm to the world's great faiths. Finally, Marcus Borg makes Jesus a "spirit person," an individual with a peculiar capacity for encountering that realm. In this way, Jesus resembles the founders of other world faiths. These writers affirm a potent source of religious unity in the experiences of these spiritually gifted individuals. Similarly, Wayne Teasdale writes that "the real religion of humankind can be said to be spirituality itself, because mystical spirituality is the origin of all the world's religions."[120] He adds that "the religion of the third millennium" will be "the sharing of ultimate experiences across traditions."[121]

Mystical experience is the common core of all religious traditions, and as such the basis of a new spiritual paradigm, another spirituality to replace the Revealed Word. Mysticism "points to the realization that although there are many spiritual paths, a universal commonality underlies them all."[122] Similarly, Gary Zukav suggests that the special spiritual experiences of evolving human masters, "such as those after whom religions have been named on earth," accounts for the multiplicity of religions.[123] However, the argument for a new pluralism via mysticism runs dramatically at cross-purposes to the internal logic of the Revealed Word. That logic states that God entered human history one time in the person of Jesus Christ, that Christ's atoning death occurred at a particular historical moment, and occurred but once, and that personal knowledge of God is available through faith rather than through mystical experience.

11

CONCLUSION

A New Spirituality for a New Age

In the beginning God created the heavens and the earth.
GENESIS 1:1 NIV

I have invented the world I see.
HELEN SCHUCMAN, A Course in Miracles

If a kingdom of heaven is desired, it must be synthesized from the available stuff.
JOSEPH CHILTON PEARCE, The Crack in the Cosmic Egg

We do not realize that while we are turning upside down the material world of the East with our technical proficiency, the East with its psychic proficiency is throwing our spiritual world into confusion.
CARL JUNG,
"The Difference Between Eastern and Western Thinking"

A dramatic shift in popular Western religious assumptions has occurred during the modern period, starting around 1700, and public religious advocates have played a central role in bringing about this fundamental alteration in spiritual outlook. We have surveyed the component parts of what I have called the New Religious Synthesis, a comprehensive religious view now successfully contesting the dominance of the Judeo-Christian tradition, or Revealed Word. The Revealed Word had affirmed a sovereign and personal God intervening continuously in human history, a single uniquely true revelation, a fallen humanity incapable of correcting its spiritual predicament, a central and historical act of atonement and the open proclamation of a message of forgiveness grounded in that divine act of redemption.

The New Synthesis reverses each major tenet of the Revealed Word. The Word's insistence on history as faith's foundation gives way to myth as the universal mode of spiritual expression. Salvation through faith in God's grace yields to the mystical episode as the elemental religious experience. An evolving universe infused with divine consciousness supplants a wholly other God, while human beings evolving toward a divinity of their own are no longer created in the image of such a God. Our rational self-awareness—Reason, Mind, Consciousness, Intellect—is the first inkling of our own latent divinity.

Science, Reason's instrument, provides theological insight to guide our quest for spiritual awareness and attainment. Among science's greatest revelations—second only to its confirmation of evolution as the operative principle of the cosmos—is that monism and pantheism are proven by deep inspection of physical matter. This massively significant discovery confirms ancient ideas about universal unity originally delivered through shamans and mystics and still reflected in tribal spirituality.

The New Synthesis affirms a new *gnosis* consisting of spiritual and scientific secrets. These keys to our spiritual advancement are available first and most clearly to a knowing elite of shamans and scientists—the new gnostics. Moreover, in spite of its foundational pantheism, the New Religious Synthesis embraces a host of minor divinities—spirit guides, teaching angels and alien visitors. A consistent message of these voices, delivered via a new class of seers, prophets and magical scientists, is that all faiths express the presence of the numinous sphere just beyond ordinary experience. In addition to advocating religious pluralism, the same entities can usually be counted on to confirm evolutionism and monism. In these ways the New Science and the New Shamanism are completely in sync, their collaboration providing a virtually irrefutable double-barreled argument for the New Religious Synthesis. When angels and scientists agree, who are mere humans to doubt their word?

It has often been noted, and succinctly expressed by Richard Weaver, that ideas have consequences. And no ideas have greater consequences than our religious ideas. As the West moves steadily in the direction of a new spirituality, it becomes imperative to ask whether the New Religious Synthesis provides an adequate account of our human condition and of our spiritual destiny. For instance, what does the resuscitated ancient wisdom have to tell us about who we are as human beings and about our destiny? What is gained and lost in embracing its conception of divinity? Does the New Synthesis adequately address the problem of evil? These are fundamentally religious questions, and the adequacy of the answers they receive from the Other Spirituality will affect every aspect of our existence. By the same token, does our previous spiritual perspective, what I have termed the Revealed Word, provide better answers to these basic religious questions? Returning briefly to the topics addressed in previous chapters, I would like to offer several implications of our present spiritual direction.

TAKING LEAVE OF HISTORY

In a 1916 interview with Charles N. Wheeler of the *Chicago Tribune,* Henry Ford made the famous statement "History is more or less bunk." While proponents of the New Religious Synthesis do not typically approach history quite so dismissively, they often either express a discomfort with history as a source for spirituality or treat history as an infinitely malleable concept with no grounding in actual events. Instead, personal experience in the realm of the spirit and the insights of experimental science are presented as the fountains from which flows spiritual truth. By contrast, while not denying the validity of individual spiritual experience, advocates of the Revealed Word perspective have always insisted on history—not individual experience—as the ground of religion.

The apostle Paul, by his own account, experienced something that can only be classified as a direct, personal encounter with the divine. A blinding light so powerful that it knocked him to the ground and a voice instructing him about the subsequent course of his life transformed Saul of Tarsus into Paul the apostle. However, despite his own arresting experience, Paul made the physical and historical resurrection of Jesus Christ the sine qua non of Christian theology. "If Christ has not been raised," he wrote in his first letter to the Corinthian church, "our proclamation has been in vain and your faith has been in vain" (1 Cor 15:14). Similarly, the evangelist Luke began his Gospel by insisting that he was writing "an orderly account" of actual events, in order that the reader would "know the truth concerning the things about which you have been instructed"(Lk 1:1-4). Jesus' disciple Peter also insisted that he "did not follow cleverly devised myths," but that he was an "eyewitness" of Christ's "majesty" (2 Pet 1:16; cf. 1 Cor 15:3-4). By the same token, the apostle John affirmed that he and the other disciples "have heard . . . have seen . . . and touched with our hands" the living Jesus (1 Jn 1:3).

This same insistence on the centrality of history to spiritual truth is evident today in Revealed Word proponents. For instance, the Reverend John Stott, a leading contemporary advocate of the perspective, writes that Christianity "does not rest only on a historical person, Jesus of Nazareth, but on certain historical events which involved him, especially his birth, death, and resurrection."[1]

Should history ground spirituality, as the Revealed Word tradition has insisted? Or should myth, allegory and private spiritual experience—each cut free from external events—provide the basis of our religious commitments? We might say that the advantage and the risk of basing spirituality on history are the same—the possibility of proof and disproof. Vulnerability to historical scrutiny imports openness and candor. When a religious claim can be examined, tested, subjected to critical review, the public being asked to accept the claim is at the very least invited to participate rationally in a process of choice. When, on the other hand, a claim cannot be tested or subjected to any of the ordinary tests of truthfulness, we are left with no recourse but to trust the probity of the claimant.

Two cases may help to illustrate this point. The first occurred more than two hundred and fifty years ago. When the New Testament narratives initially came under sustained public scrutiny in England during the opening years of the eighteenth century, the evidence for the resurrection of Jesus Christ became the focus of particularly intense examination. The Church of England chose not to simply stifle the historical critics, but rather to meet their criticism head on in the public arena. The most famous and successful defense of the resurrection evidences was Bishop Thomas Sherlock's *Tryal of the Witnesses to the Resurrection of Jesus Christ*, first published in 1729. Imagining a trial at which the evidence for and against the resurrection of Jesus was systematically examined, Sherlock masterfully presented the *historical* case for the central Christian miracle in a surprisingly accessible and thorough fashion. Sherlock's book was generally considered an unqualified success, and, remarkably, was not seriously answered in print for nearly fifteen years. Of course, a risk attended Sherlock's efforts, for the church was allowing members of the public to make up their own minds about Christianity's historical evidences. And, predictably, not everyone in the British reading public was convinced by the Bishop's argument.

The famous skeptic Peter Annet proved this point in an especially compelling way in 1744. That year, the first of many editions of Annet's skillful and persuasive response to Sherlock's *Tryal of the Witnesses* appeared in London. Titled *The Resurrection of Jesus Considered by a Moral Philosopher*, Annet's book set out to answer Sherlock argument for argument and to overturn every piece of evidence the Bishop advanced. Like Sherlock's *Tryal*, Annet's *The Resurrection Considered* was wildly popular and controversial. It is impossible to say with any certainty which author carried the day, but it is possible to say that the public was allowed to consider the evidence and arguments on each side of a crucial historical question: Did the available evidence suggest that Jesus Christ died and then returned to life? The tradition of arguing the historical evidences for and against the Revealed Word's central claims, perhaps launched by Paul's bold statement in his letter to the Corinthians, continues unabated.

My second case is more recent. Shirley MacLaine is famous for describing several of her past lives in the 1985 bestseller *Dancing in the Light*.[2] Among other lives, MacLaine suggests that she was a male actor in ancient Greece and that she was present at the writing of the Constitution and the Declaration of Independence. But perhaps her most riveting and detailed account of a previous existence involves her life as a twelve-year-old orphan girl named Asana who lived with wild elephants "thousands of years ago." "I became known as the princess of the elephants," writes MacLaine. MacLaine/Asana also realizes that she can "communicate with them [the elephants] telepathically."[3] As the elephant princess, MacLaine/Asana "presided over the births of the young, and if one of my friends injured herself, I used more sophisticated human healing techniques to nurse her back to health." MacLaine and the female elephants of the herd also dissuaded a group of male elephants from their plan to kill a man who had murdered a friend of Asana.[4]

It is important to note that MacLaine's "past life incarnations" are not mere diversions related for the sake of entertaining the reader. Rather, they become the factual and experiential basis on which MacLaine develops spiritual principles and techniques that she freely terms "spiritual conjectures."[5] Many of these "I came up with just by being by myself," she writes, though some also involve the assistance of other human beings and a variety of spirit entities.[6] But the past life experiences are particularly important to the spiritual perspective that emerges from the pages of MacLaine's books. For instance, from her time as an elephant princess, MacLaine learned that "we humans should never forget our capacity to connect with the collective spirit of animals."[7]

But unlike Sherlock's claims in *Tryal of the Witnesses*, based as they are on historical documents and developing from allegedly historical events, MacLaine's claims cannot be subjected to any imaginable historical verification. No one can play the critical role of Peter Annet in MacLaine's spiritual cosmos. MacLaine writes within the context of the New Synthesis, a spiritual movement that has taken leave of history, that has severed the spiritual from the physical, the subjective from the objective and has thus rendered irrelevant any effort to prove or disprove experiential claims as "historically accurate." By the same token, spiritual claims no longer stand or fall on the merits of their attending historical claims. Such a division between claims about events in space and time, on the one hand, and claims about spiritual truths, on the other, is unknown to the Revealed Word. Attending the risk of the Revealed Word's commitment to history is a refreshing honesty before a public being asked to embrace its worldview.

Revealed Word proponents have long argued that history provides their perspective with an objective foundation that serves to ground spiritual claims in verifiable events, a commitment that also serves to limit theological speculation. By contrast, the movement of the New Synthesis away from history and toward myth, away from physical events and toward transcendent symbols, away from verifiable occurrences and toward imaginative narratives, is attended by no commensurate promise to the potential convert. The only promise of spiritual authenticity is that myth somehow conveys timeless and universal religious truths, while history is mired in local events and parochial values. But this dramatic shift in perspective regarding spiritual truth leaves us in an untenable position where the teachings of the historical Jesus recorded in the four New Testament Gospels carry no greater weight than an imagined conversation with Jesus (or an elephant) in one's living room.

I have argued that the Revealed Word tradition's insistence on historical grounding for spiritual truth renders this perspective vulnerable to historical criticism by laying open all of its foundational claims to public scrutiny. Having said this, it is worth noting that arguments against Revealed Word history often reflect, not compelling historical criticism, but an author's more or less personal objections to elements in the historical narrative. Thus, John Shelby Spong asks his readers, "Are we drawn to a Lord who would destroy a herd of pigs and presumably a person's livelihood in order to exorcise a demon (Mark 5:13)?" And again, "Are we impressed when the one we call Lord curses a fig tree because it did not bear fruit out of season (Matt. 21:18, 19)?" The implied criteria for rejecting these stories are not historical, but strictly subjective—the stories do not draw us, do not impress us, by which Spong must mean himself and others already inclined to agree with him.

But do such subjective measures count as tests of the truthfulness of the accounts in question? After all, if Jesus is God incarnate—a central Revealed Word claim—is it reasonable to expect that his actions would consistently strike us as appealing, impressive or even fair? Similarly, Spong rejects the historical Jesus as someone who "seems to have accepted without question the language of hell employed by his religious contemporaries."[8] Again, this is less an argument against the teachings of the historical Jesus than it is a statement about Spong's revulsion at the idea of hell. Spong's claim says nothing about whether Jesus and his "religious contemporaries" were right or wrong in their views of hell, though it tells us a great deal about Spong's attitude toward such views. Spong's claim is thus better understood as autobiography than as argument.

The New Religious Synthesis dispenses with history, or so its proponents claim, as a means of opening the way to universal religious insights. When obsolete or parochial historical claims are jettisoned, the obstacle to spiritual progress created by a personal and local God is also removed. Biblical narratives can be understood for what they are—metaphors for understanding God. Jesus need no longer be seen as the literal Son of God but rather as a religious philosopher, a mythic hero, a mystic or a symbol for human spiritual aspiration. Religious belief is no longer dependent on outward and historical events in particular locations at remote times, but now finds its source in the ever-contemporary interior life of the spirit, the unfathomable human psyche, the myth-generating subconscious self.

However, may it not also be the case that to sever history from spirituality opens the gate to the self-styled mystic, the spiritual charlatan, the religious expert or just the self-deceived neighbor, each operating in a realm of private interpretation of elusive evidences largely inaccessible to their followers or to any would-be critic? Under the New Religious Synthesis, no longer is the test of actual historical occurrence also a test of truth in religion. Other standards now take history's place as spirituality's foundation, including channeled advice from spirit guides, mystical and hallucinogenic experience, an expert's take-my-word-for-it code-breaking or myth-interpreting, narrative cleverness or the spiritual imagination run amok. History's relative accessibility to the ordinary reader is lost in the mythic mists, tall tales, clouded code and alien advice. Shamans, gurus, scholars of religion and even laboratory scientists now intervene between the public and the divine as a new class of priests. Clearly, the movement away from history has not served to democratize spirituality. Rather, the opposite has occurred. Under the New Religious Synthesis an asymmetrical relationship develops between the gifted few with unaccountable access to spiritual truth and the dependent many incapable of evaluating that truth.

Finally, elevating myth, allegory or narrative turns spirituality inward, inviting us to explore, not the objective external events of human history, but the depths of our own minds and imaginations. Rather than navigating life's seas by the fixed stars of recorded events, we dive into the "deep well of the psyche" and in these dark waters find, according to our spiritual Jacques Cousteau, Joseph Campbell, "deities [that] are the symbolic personifications of the very energies that are yourself."[9] Because "the symbols of mythology" are "spontaneous productions of the psyche," they are better experienced within our own heads than out in history.[10] Thus, as we saw, Jean Houston led her readers on an interior journey up an imaginary mountain of the psyche where, as in Campbell's well, deities aplenty flourish. But Houston must be trusted as our guide up this mountain, for what we encounter there will never be brought out into the light of external events.

It is interesting to note that the shift from history to myth as the basis for spirituality may find a ready audience among the diverse, far-flung residents of cyberspace. Brenda Brasher writes that "one of the best-kept secrets of cyberspace is the surprising amount of religious practice that takes place there." She adds, "my own explorations have revealed more than a million online religion websites in operation." Mythic forms of spirituality suit the cyberspace experience better than do historical accounts. Brasher writes, "among the genres of human fantasy, cyberspace most closely resembles myth. It is a public story that expresses widely held values and beliefs."[11] Thus, the translation of spiritual truth to a mythic experience may be readily embraced by a new generation of online seekers.

Does spirituality need history? The Revealed Word tradition has always answered *yes;* the New Religious Synthesis says *no.* In the Revealed Word tradition, history has been the scene of God's acts of intervention and ultimately of redemption. A perhaps unrecognized or at least underappreciated fact about this historical grounding is that it has provided an objective, accessible, external foundation for human spiritual experience and religious teaching. As such, appeal to history has tended to restrain theological speculation, and perhaps even the spiritual abuses of leaders inventive enough to manufacture their own internal experiences and clever enough to devise their own myths. The restraint of objective history, however, seldom exerts control over religious thinking or the exercise of spiritual leadership any longer.

THE ADVENT OF REASON

The Revealed Word tradition consistently imbues the human being with extraordinary value, while at the same time reflecting a noteworthy ambivalence about human reason. Clearly, humans are different from the other animals, and much of this difference has to do with their capacity to think rationally. However, this an-cient tradition also cautions against sole reliance on reason for spiritual guidance. The book of Proverbs, for instance, warns the reader to "trust in the LORD with all your heart, and do not rely on your own insight" (Prov 3:5). The mind and rational thought are valued, but nowhere are they presented as adequate to fathom the depths of the human soul, let alone the nature of God.

It is recorded that Jesus himself prayed, "I thank you, Father, Lord of heaven and earth, because you have hidden these things from the wise and the intelligent and revealed them to infants," that is, to those of humble and untrained rational abilities (Lk 10:21). Similarly, the apostle Paul asks the members of the church in the Greek city of Corinth, "Where is the one who is wise? Where is the scribe? Where is the debater of this age? Has not God made foolish the wisdom of this world?" (1 Cor 1:20). This "making foolish" of human wisdom occurs as God sur-prises the church with a tendency to "reveal to infants" the profoundest of spiritual truths. One wonders how such statements must have sounded to the Greeks, who were prone to find in reason the highest expression of human nature.

Under the New Religious Synthesis, however, this God who reveals profound truths to the simple has been excised from the cosmos and replaced by a very dif-ferent deity variously described as Reason, Mind, Consciousness or Divine Intel-lect. This impersonal force that drove the universe's evolutionary destiny was referred to centuries ago in the European magical tradition as the divine *Mens*, or Mind. It was cosmic in scope, and through careful study and practice the magus or magician could control and channel its power. The goal of magical studies was to recreate the cosmic *Mens* within the human mind. Renaissance magi spent their lives training the intellect and the imagination in order to control *Mens* and so transform themselves into virtual deities.[12] Thus, then as now this elevated Reason or Mind is difficult to distinguish from the radically autonomous self seeking its own spiritual advancement. It was always understood that very few members of the human race possessed the discipline, mental capacity and, importantly, spiri-tual secrets that rendered possible this transformation from human to divinity.

The tension between a spirituality that finds a creating and personal God as the universe's foundational fact, and one that finds that fact in undifferentiated Reason or Consciousness could not be greater. Whereas the apostle John advocated the Revealed Word perspective that "the Word became flesh and dwelt among us"— referring to Jesus as the unique human manifestation of the personal and wholly other deity—the Deist Peter Annet responded on behalf of a new spirituality that "Reason is God incarnate." In his first epistle, the same John affirmed that "God is light" (1 Jn 1:5). Thomas De Quincey countered for an emerging religion by composing a hymn to "the light of the majestic intellect." The unknown New Testament writer who penned the epistle to the Hebrews urged that "without faith it is impossible to please God" (Heb 11:6). Ayn Rand scolded in *Atlas Shrugged* that the incompetents of the earth had "sacrificed reason to faith."

The New Religious Synthesis calls us to self-adoration as spirituality, to the exaltation of our own rational self-awareness—"the divinity operating within us," according to Annet—as an act or worship. The Other Spirituality's journey away from submission to a personal and sovereign deity, away from moral responsibility before a Creator God, away from community built on worship of the Wholly Other, arrives at no more interesting destination than spiritual narcissism. In Rand, such self-worship is revealed for what it truly is—ruthless self-interest masquerading as rational self-liberation. The less mentally gifted among us—the "incompetents of the earth"—that is, the poor, are punished for the sin of having not enough of the new god.

Perhaps something like Rand's hard-edged elitism is inevitable when Reason becomes a god, particularly in an evolving cosmos. Annet and the Deists argued that Reason was universal. However, they also admitted that most of us never gain sufficient mastery of this internal power to free ourselves from the restraints of conventional morality and the errors of the Revealed Word. Voltaire maintained that a single clear thinking follower of Reason—exemplified in the character Zadig—understood more about true religion than did the masses of the religiously devout. His followers held to the same prejudice; the altar to Reason in Notre Dame bore the busts, not of ordinary citizens, but of four advanced thinkers—Franklin, Rousseau, Montesquieu and, of course, Voltaire himself. Thus, this was not an altar to human reason understood as universal rational ability. Rather, it was an altar to Reason Triumphant, a monument to the rationally gifted members of the human race, the new spiritual vanguard.

Interestingly, De Quincey did not find even the dreams of opium to be available to all. Ordinary existence, "this too intense life of the social instincts," destroys the capacity for great dreams in most people. Only an elite can understand "the mystery of darkness" and "the profound philosophy" that allows Majestic Intellect to escape mundane existence and even history itself. Similarly, the advocates of New

Thought suggested that particular rational gifts and carefully studied techniques are necessary to harness and direct the energy of Mind. Even prayer, that most democratic of spiritual exercises in the Revealed Word, is transformed in New Thought into a rational technique to be mastered. Only the skilled practitioner, not the simple person of faith, can through prayer concentrate mental energy or Mind in such a way as to unleash its healing, life-giving powers.

Reason, it appears, is no egalitarian divinity. But then, an evolving universe cannot afford such a god. Progress in such a universe depends on a determined weeding out of the weak. In this regard, Rand read the face of the future with precision and prescience. The mechanism of evolution always recognizes and rewards the superior members of a species, and, according to the New Synthesis, the most rationally advanced members of the human race are currently being so recognized and so rewarded. The Revealed Word proposed an impartial God, a deity who was, in the biblical phrase, "no respecter of persons" (Acts 10:34 KJV).

Even as sanguine and friendly an analyst of our spiritual destiny as Gary Zukav cannot bring himself to believe that all human beings are equally endowed of the potential for rational advancement. He is aware of the elitism inherent in the idea of self-awareness as the basis of spirituality, and his discomfort with the fact is palpable. "Not all humans are equally aware of their souls." This raises the obvious question, "do all human beings have equal potential?" to which Zukav provides the apparently contradictory answer, "yes and no." Admitting that "this question is complex," he adds that "an individual that is not quite as expanded in his or her awareness is not equal in the sense that we usually mean equal to someone of greater awareness. There is an inequality. Yet it is not an inequality that remains unequal. It is just a temporary level of momentum in the flow of evolution."[13] An unequal equality certainly would be an equality that is not what is usually meant by the term. And yet, this is the best answer the New Religious Synthesis has to offer to the troubling questions raised when any human "potential" is set out as a spiritual hope in a fundamentally evolutionary scheme in which potential or fitness is everything.

It appears, then, that we face a dilemma in the spiritual realm: either all of us are submitted to the uniquely perfect Reason of a personal creator God, or most of us must defer to the more highly evolved reason of some of us. Much science fiction advocates the second option. Time and again space delivers to us our highly evolved alien saviors, advanced intellects whose mission is to enlighten the human race and in this way to help us on to our ultimate destiny—a virtual divinity akin to their own. By contrast, the Revealed Word proposes the descent from heaven of a single incarnation of the one true God, a single divine person offering salvation universally through grace rather than selectively through rational potential.

THEOLOGICAL SCIENCE

During the modern period, science has taken on greater and greater religious significance. Scientists have become outspoken advocates and devotees of new spiritual systems, while at the same time science has increasingly been employed to prove theological and spiritual propositions. As one writer recently stated the point, the "discoveries of science illuminate both inner and outer experiences," that is, both "physical and nonphysical dynamics."[14] Science, which had always taken the observable world as its only domain, now informs us about the unseen world as well.

The use of scientific experiment to achieve spiritual insight has had a variety of fascinating manifestations in the twentieth century. For instance, at Duke University in 1927, Professor J. B. Rhine created "the first parapsychological lab."[15] Rhine's experiments were intended "to establish the existence of ESP—clairvoyance, precognition, telepathy—and psychokinesis, using experimental methods."[16] He was nurturing a new view of science, one that would have profound implications for a wide range of spiritual thought by the end of the twentieth century.[17] Rhine was not himself an objective scientific observer, but rather "believed that parapsychology was relevant to religion and that it offered a way to reconcile the claims of religion with the principles of science."[18]

Rhine pursued his "seven years of patient work" with a virtually religious commitment to establishing on scientific grounds various unobservable powers of the human mind. Other scientists scoffed, but Rhine countered prophetically that "the stone which a hasty science rejected has sometimes become the corner of its later structure."[19] Rhine hoped to overturn the "psychological dogma" that "*nothing* can enter the mind except through the gateways of the recognized senses" through scientific experiments alone. And he felt he succeeded and that a "new frontier" had been opened "by years of testing and hundreds of thousands of trials." Rhine found in his results nothing less than a revolutionary view of the mind that would displace traditional psychology in the same way that relativity theory had displaced Newtonian mechanics.[20] Science had shown that the human mind has a spiritual dimension.

The tendency to see science as pregnant with spiritual insight is a commonplace of the new spirituality. Thus, dancer and actress Shirley MacLaine bases her belief in reincarnation in part on an appeal to science. She writes in her bestselling *Dancing in the Light*, "If, as science says, energy never dies, it merely changes form, then life, which is also energy, never dies. It, too, merely changes form." She continues, "Since energy is never still, because nothing remains inert, then energy must continually have a changing form." What does MacLaine conclude from this scientific observation? "There was no doubt in my mind that the life energy simply changed its form from lifetime to lifetime, just as nature did from spring to spring."[21] Thus, the law of the conservation of energy proves reincarnation and past life experiences. In many similar cases science is now a taken-for-granted source of a new theology.

To view science as a religious hope is not new. Nineteenth-century Biblical critic David Strauss prophetically proclaimed that "he embraced 'the Universe' as revealed by science, in which he purported to find an all-pervasive spirit of love."[22] Similarly, Wayne Teasdale has written recently that mystics have long "known and proclaimed the essential interconnectedness of all things."[23] This spiritual insight is for Teasdale himself also supported by science. According to Teasdale, science proves that "consciousness," not a personal God, is "the basis of reality."[24]

Science has birthed a new theology, or, more accurately, rebirthed an old one. "The most powerful transformative ideas from modern science," writes Ferguson, "connect like parts of a puzzle" and "support each other," thus forming "the scaffolding for a wider worldview." This apparently new worldview is really a primitive one that mystics have articulated for centuries. The great scientific discoveries of our own day have "uncanny parallels to ancient poetic and mystical descriptions of nature," she writes. "Science is only now verifying what humankind has known intuitively since the dawn of history."[25]

Throughout the modern period, science has been employed to confirm spiritual truths that hearken back to earlier traditions. Thomas Paine argued that science supported, not the theistic religion of the Revealed Word, but the pantheistic religion of nature and reason. Madame Blavatsky's Victorian occultism—a social movement that paved the way for the revival of shamanism—was founded on the idea that scientific discoveries confirmed occult practices. According to David Strauss, scientific biblical criticism opened the way to mythological readings of the Bible. The naturalist Ernst Haeckel asserted that science proved both pantheism and monism. And by pursuing the science of psychiatry, John Mack concluded that alien entities were seeking contact with a new class of shamans—UFO abductees.

The trend toward confirming ancient spiritual systems through modern science continues today. Again, Shirley MacLaine affirms the close connection between discoveries in quantum physics and new spiritualities that resemble old ones. She writes, for example, "J. Robert Oppenheimer said that the general notions about human understanding which are illustrated by discoveries in atomic physics were not wholly unfamiliar. They had a history not only in Buddhist and Hindu thought, but also in our own culture. 'What we are finding,' he said, 'is a refinement of old wisdom.'"[26] A characteristic passage in her *Dancing in the Light* moves effortlessly from contact with spiritual entities to a vision of the lost civilization on Atlantis to a discussion of quantum physics.[27]

And this purposeful blurring of the line between science and spirituality is not limited to nonscientists such as MacLaine. David Gergen, editor-at-large for *U.S. News & World Report*, profiled Severino Antinori for his magazine on August 20, 2001. Antinori, one of the leading scientists in the race to clone the first human being, is a man "who suggests that Napoleon and Galileo are his role models." Gergen points out that "one of Antinori's key supporters in his cloning effort is linked to a group that believes that humans are clones in the image of aliens from another solar system."[28] The group referred to is the Raelian UFO religion, which now claims to have cloned two human beings. According to their leader—a Frenchman calling himself Rael who asserts that he was once abducted by aliens—the goal of their cloning experiments is to achieve immortality through continuous cloning of the individual with the mind transferred from one body to another ad infinitum.

At this juncture in Western history, it is perhaps especially important to recall that spiritual values have long guided scientific endeavors, a fact that is clear from the history of alchemy, eugenics and more recent efforts to clone a human being following the religious tenets of the Raelians. And now science is being employed to "prove" spiritual theories as well. In a culture that has trained itself for three centuries to trust the findings of science, such a procedure will certainly lend an advantage to the religious view that could enlist the largest number of scientists, or at least the most persuasive, in its support.

SPIRITUAL EVOLUTION

According to Teilhard de Chardin, the universe operates on the principle of evolution, and reality itself is, to use his term, "evolutive." Matter has, at this point in time, organized itself into consciousness, and consciousness, driven forward by the

force of evolution, is moving inexorably toward the "Omega Point" of pure consciousness.[29] Scientific discoveries are currently providing insights into our "spiritual evolution," as are tribal spiritual traditions steeped in ancient wisdom often
ignored in the West.[30]

At the very core of the New Religious Synthesis is a hope in human advancement through evolution. As George Bernard Shaw phrased the point in 1903, reflecting ideas he borrowed from Friedrich Nietzsche, "Our only hope, then, is
evolution. We must replace the man by the superman."[31] This fundamental tenet
shows up anywhere one cares to look in the literature of the Other Spirituality.
Human spiritual transformation via evolution is the promise of Darwin's heirs
from the biologist Huxley to the occultist Blavatsky to New Age novelist James
Redfield. As we enter a new era of awareness, or so the argument goes, we are taking an inevitable and unprecedented step in human evolution. Marilyn Ferguson
calls evolution "the mandate of nature" and the mechanism by which human beings
will achieve the great "leap forward" into a new spiritual age. Is this a consumma-
tion devoutly to be wished?

Francis Fukuyama, author of the recently published *Our Posthuman Future*, has
said in a recent interview that biotechnology may soon be used to "to consciously
take an otherwise normal human being and make him or her into something very
different." Calling this "the single greatest danger" of advances in biotechnology,
Fukuyama foresees "a period completely unprecedented in human history, where
human beings will consciously be able to take over the evolutionary process."[32] But
"conscious evolution" is not seen as a danger in all quarters. Psychologist Robert
Ornstein, today's leading expert on the evolution of consciousness, believes that
directed evolution affords a future to be embraced. The time has come for human
beings to seize control of evolution, albeit through education rather than biotechnology. Conscious evolution "may be easier, closer at hand, and more liberating
than we might normally think."[33] "Conscious selection," as opposed to natural selection, would be employed to "take our evolution in our own hands."[34] A program
of conscious evolution should be moved "to the top of the human agenda."[35]

Such assisted progress was clearly the hope of the first generation of evolutionary
scientists. T. H. Huxley envisioned a morally improved human race as the result of
guided evolution. Thus, the "social progress" of human beings meant "checking the
evolutionary process at every step" and encouraging moral evolution from one level
of moral attainment to another. But this possibility is precisely what has Fukuyama

worried, particularly if such occurs in the absence of an adequate conception of human nature. "A better cognitive neuroscience," he writes, "will lead to a much better understanding of the biological basis for human behavior, and thus will offer the potential to manipulate human behavior in ways that we haven't been able to do before." For Fukuyama, this greater control of human behavior, this hastening of humanity's moral evolution, "suggests experiments in social engineering—which are likely to be more successful than our previous efforts at social engineering."[36]

Fukuyama's concerns are reminiscent of those expressed prophetically by C. S. Lewis in his 1947 book *The Abolition of Man*.[37] Lewis argued that one generation could wield power over every subsequent generation by altering human nature through psychological conditioning and genetic engineering. In Lewis's own day this was a very remote possibility, but, as Fukuyama and others have noted, today it is not so remote. With an evolutionary understanding of human nature and destiny before us courtesy of the New Synthesis, the basic genetic makeup of the human race may be altered according to the insights of a spiritual and scientific elite. Lewis wrote, "If any one age really attains, by eugenics and scientific education, the power to make its descendants what it pleases, all men who live after it are the patients of that power." As a result of scientific advances, our "conquest of Nature, if the dreams of some scientific planners are realized, means the rule of a few hundreds of men over billions upon billions of men."[38] Advocates of the Revealed Word have been publicly exercised over the biological implications of Darwinian thinking. However, the evolutionary vision animating current scientific and spiritual movements is more moral than biological, more spiritual than physical, and more likely attained by artificial rather than natural means.

The New Religious Synthesis views human spiritual advance as a matter of incremental evolutionary change over time, and not the result of instantaneous rebirth or spiritual transformation described in the Revealed Word tradition. Zukav, for instance, contends that the human soul is continuously engaged in the process of "evolution toward authentic power."[39] New Synthesis writers hold that the cosmos is a place of increasing complexity and that evolution is its omnipresent operative principle, the organizing and complexifying force at the very center of being. As Ferguson puts the point, "All wholes transcend their parts by virtue of internal coherence, cooperation, openness to input." Moreover, "The higher on the evolutionary scale, the more freedom to reorganize. An ant lives out a destiny; a human being shapes one." So human beings are the only entities free to actually choose their evolutionary destiny because we are the only evolving entities consciously aware of our own existence. "Evolution is a continuous breaking and forming to make new, richer wholes," she writes. "If we enlarge our awareness, admit new information, and take advantage of the brain's infinite capacity to integrate and reconcile, we can leap forward."[40]

But, as I have noted more than once, spiritual evolution in the New Synthesis is not particularly democratic, and so there is reason for caution about this hope of the New Synthesis as well. Recall that Sir Julian Huxley finds that "transhumanist" evolutionary advancement takes place in "the best ten-thousandth" among us. The Revealed Word insists that its central principle—spiritual transformation through grace—is available to all. Herbert Spencer and Charles Darwin both recognized that evolutionary theory made advancement the domain of a few survivors. A vanguard, a capable elite, has always been a component of spiritual evolutionary schemes, even before the publication of *On the Origin of the Species*.

Contemporary writers would never embrace spiritual evolution's more sinister consequences, though earlier proponents of the idea happily advocated them as necessary deductions. For instance, racialism is clearly present in such influential works as Houston Stewart Chamberlain's *Foundations of the Nineteenth Century* (1899), in which the author looks forward to a "new era dominated by Aryan spirituality."[41] Aryan spirituality—the persistent notion that northern Europeans are a more *spiritually* advanced people destined to dominate the other peoples of the world in a new spiritual order—was a common theme of spiritual speculation in the nineteenth century. This impulse is far removed from the Revealed Word notion of the kingdom of God consisting of members from "every people, tribe and nation."

Even the embarrassment of eugenics has not been entirely purged from New Religious Synthesis thinking, though most contemporary writers would repudiate the practice. The Other Spirituality often openly advocates the notion that a small vanguard of the human race possessing the necessary capacities will help the race to advance. The Other Spirituality has at times looked back into human history to discover the evolving ones and then traced a trajectory to those presently among us who are specially fitted for spiritual evolution. Jesus may enter the picture at this point. As Joseph Pearce writes, "Jesus [was] a genius with radically new ideas, an evolutionary *Eureka!* development by which life tried to develop a new aspect of potential."[42] R. M. Bucke was also interested in discovering those members of the human race who had taken the next step of spiritual evolution, and also identified Jesus as a member of this elite group.

In his important apologetic work *Mere Christianity*, C. S. Lewis noted that the further evolutionary development of the human race is an idea most clearly represented in the literary genre now called science fiction. He identified the pervasive hypothesis as a rival to, perhaps a counterfeit of, the Christian idea of spiritual transformation. Lewis writes, "The Christian view is precisely that the Next Step has already appeared. And it is really new. It is not a change from brainy men to brainier men: it is a change that goes off in a totally different direction—a change from being creatures of god to being sons of God."[43] Lewis was prophetic in his realization that human evolution to higher moral and spiritual levels would be a theme of religious speculation in the second half of the twentieth century. He was also emphatic that the biblical vision of a human race spiritually redeemed and transformed through Christ was a vastly superior vision of the human future.

PANTHEISM

Recently, Americans were surprised to hear news reports that followers of the Wicca religion had petitioned the army to allow them to use space at an army base for a religious ceremony. It turned out that groups of Wiccans were meeting at American military bases around the country and in Europe. The rise of Wicca, an updated version of pre-Christian European pantheistic spirituality, corresponds to widespread interest in a variety of similar traditions including Druidism and various forms of witchcraft. The revived nature-worshiping religions have in common an underlying pantheism, a belief in the divinity inherent in all things.

Pantheism is not limited, however, to neo-pagan religions and witchcraft. Many contemporary spiritual movements are fundamentally pantheistic, and pantheism is crucial to the New Religious Synthesis. Pantheism rejects the notion of God as personal and sovereign, instead finding divinity to be an impersonal force, energy, spirit, consciousness or mind in all things. Contemporary Western interest in witchcraft, kabbalah, neopaganism, gnosticism, Theosophy, the occult, astrology, the New Age movement, the New Physics and Eastern religious thought all suggest that pantheistic assumptions are rapidly displacing the theology of a rational, sovereign, personal and moral divinity.[44] Interestingly, in Neale Donald Walsch's alleged conversations with "God," Walsch concludes, "if there is no end to bigness, then there is no *biggest*. This means there *is no God!*" To this notion, "God" replies, "Or, perhaps—*all of it is God*, and *there is nothing else.*"[45]

The Other Spirituality's god is a force to be managed, a potential to be tapped, a consciousness to be experienced. As Ferguson affirms in *The Aquarian Conspiracy*, God is now "the organizing matrix we can experience but not tell, that which enlivens matter."[46] Similarly, John Shelby Spong has recently stated that "god is the ground of being," something best understood by recourse to "non-personal images." Thus, "the theistic understanding of god no longer works."[47] As something "we can experience but not tell," this new god is perhaps best known by mystics or psychics, regardless of the religious or cultural tradition within which they operate.

Science—one of two great sources, along with spirits, of theological insight in the New Religious Synthesis—provides a basis for seeing God as diffuse and within the physical universe rather than as personal and external to that universe. Dana Zohar and Ian Marshall write that "for some people the idea of a transcendent God who creates, and possibly controls, the universe from a vantage point outside the laws of physics, from beyond space and time, will always remain appealing." However, belief in such a Revealed Word God, albeit "appealing," has no scientific support. A more scientifically justifiable theology understands God as "a basic sense of direction" in the universe that is moving everything that exists "towards further and greater ordered coherence." God is "embodied within . . . the laws of physics" and is "an evolving consciousness within the universe."[48] If, in fact, we inhabit a cosmos that is evolving, and if God is a consciousness contained within the very matter of that cosmos, then it stands to reason that God is an evolving consciousness within that cosmos.

What are the consequences of this new, pantheistic conception of God? Perhaps the principal and most dramatic spiritual change as we move from Revealed Word theism to the pantheism of the New Synthesis occurs precisely here—in the fundamental human-divine relationship. An energy, a Life Force, a spirit in all things, an evolving Consciousness, a Divine Intelligence, even an awe-inspiring spiritual-physical universe, are not a divine Person with whom one may enter a living relationship. Nor is the pantheistic deity of the New Synthesis the kind of god who places moral requirements on one's life. On the moral plane, pantheism allows us to create the god we wish—a god incapable of an opinion about human morality.

This last point brings us to the question of what the Other Spirituality's pantheistic theology has to say to the problem of evil. Gary Zukav writes that the highly evolved or "multisensory personality" will understand God as "Divine Intelligence" or "Conscious Light." Evil, then, is simply the absence of such Light. Thus, "understanding evil as the absence of Light requires you to examine the choices you make each moment in terms of whether they move you toward light or away from it."[49]

But this conception of evil as an "absence of Light" provides neither clear direction for avoiding evil, nor a strong mandate for opposing it. "Do you know the meaning of evil?" asks Shirley MacLaine's Spirit Guide. Answering its own question, the Guide comments that "evil is nothing but energy flowing backward rather than forward. . . . Allow all of your energy to flow back to the God source."[50] If God and we are energy, then there is no moral law at all, only correct or incorrect relationships to this divine energy. Thus, evil properly understood is simply an energy flow problem easily corrected through appropriate techniques.

Such accounts of evil hardly seem adequate to either explain or address the evil expressed in even a single act of murder, let alone wickedness on the scale of the Holocaust or the Rwandan massacres. Perhaps this is why Robert Green Ingersoll, a man whose Civil War experience had sharpened his understanding of the human moral predicament, recognized the need to attempt a serious response to the problem of evil. His "Creed of Science" called on each person to act by a rule of love somehow derived from science. But in the absence of a sovereign and personal God whose own ultimate goodness grounds all adequate conceptions of good and evil and who holds us accountable for our actions, even this call to act voluntarily in love is unlikely to serve as a preventative to human evil.

Ultimately the New Synthesis leaves us looking to ourselves for moral guidance, and thus for the spiritual authority to condemn evil and commend good. A god who cannot hold us accountable for our actions and who cannot reveal to us a moral standard grounded on ultimate goodness is a god whose nature provides no answer to the problem of evil. "Identifying God with everything," writes theologian Peter Jones, "effectively removes from God any real and specific identity."[51] Without that personal, sovereign divine identity as ultimate moral guide and judge, that is, without a God active in the universe and yet separate from it, human beings are in the cosmic driver's seat as minor deities. In New Religious Synthesis writers, Pantheism leads repeatedly to the notion of human divinity. Neale Donald Walsch asks his spirit guide, "You mean, I can even become—dare I say it?—a God?" The guide replies, "You are already a God. You simply do not know it."[52] Even a cursory review of human history would lead a reasonable person to question whether we have proven ourselves morally worthy of this great responsibility.

THE NEW GNOSIS

Artist Alexis Smith's striking Snake Path, part of the Stuart Collection, fascinates visitors to the campus of the University of California, San Diego. The Snake Path is a 560 foot long, 10 foot wide tiled walkway in the shape of a serpent. The snake's head rests on the terrace of the university's Central Library. Along the path one encounters an enormous granite book with a quotation from John Milton's *Paradise Lost:* "Then wilt thou not be loth to leave this Paradise, but shalt possess a Paradise within thee, happier far." The snake's body wraps around a tropical garden intended to represent the Garden of Eden. The snake leading to the library is said to represent both the loss of innocence and the liberation of the self through the acquisition of knowledge. Smith has said that the idea came to her in a dream. The Snake Path reflects the foundational myth of ancient Gnosticism—that the Edenic serpent was a heroic figure bringing spiritually liberating knowledge to the benighted Adam and Eve, trapped in physical bodies and the space-time dungeon of earth by an incompetent and vindictive deity.

Gnosticism teaches the soul's escape from the world, the body and time by means of secret insights into the nature of spiritual reality. Only the individual possessing hidden spiritual knowledge or *gnosis* has any hope of understanding the truth about our human predicament, and thus of being saved from spiritual darkness and the limitations of the physical. In both its ancient and more modern manifestations gnosticism questions the goodness, often even the reality, of physical existence. The soul is eternal and evolving, a manifestation of the divine essence in the highest realm of reality. The body, on the other hand, is merely the vessel of our entrapment to be escaped by means of the secrets of spiritual ascent.

"A soul has no beginning and no end," writes Gary Zukav, adding that "all souls come directly from the Godhead." Moreover, "not all humans are equally aware of their souls."[53] And yet, "the soul is the individual unit of evolution."[54] The body is simply a means of achieving certain ends that heighten awareness of the soul and its evolution, and once the body has served its purpose, the soul moves on to another location, another body or perhaps another planet, to continue its migration back to the Godhead. Here is Neale Donald Walsch on the same point: "The soul has come to the body, and the body to life, for the purpose of evolution."[55] In response to the question, "Where do advanced souls go?" Zukav answers, "There are many forms of life that exist as advancements of this one. There are literally millions of options. There is life in numerous galaxies. There are millions, indeed billions of other life-filled planets."[56]

"The body," writes Zukav, "is the instrument of the soul," the two standing in the same relationship as a piano and piano player.[57] The soul, then, is the body's animating intelligence, its "daemon," to use the ancient gnostic term. Without its activating intelligence, the body is a barely living drone. Possessed by a daemon, however, the body takes on life and intelligence. The notion is captured well in the popular *His Dark Materials* trilogy for young adults by Phillip Pullman. One exchange between the two principal characters, Will and Lyra, illustrates the point: "'You *have* got a daemon,' she said decisively, 'Inside you.' He didn't know what to say. 'You have,' she went on, 'You wouldn't be human else. You'd be . . . half dead.'"[58] Moreover, the *daemon* has access to the spirit world and the secrets of advancement to be found there.

The gnostic view of the body and physical existence runs consistently against the grain of the Revealed Word, a spiritual outlook that elevates both. According to the Word, a personal God intentionally created the physical universe, and it was from the beginning essentially good. Human physical existence—our embodiment—is purposeful and meaningful, not a cosmic accident. Christian writer Dallas Willard affirms that "people have a body for one reason—that we might have at our disposal the resources that would allow us to be persons in fellowship and cooperation with a personal God."[59] The Other Spirituality's relative disregard for physical experience challenges this view of the body, as well as the possibility of the individual's "fellowship and cooperation with a personal God." Fukuyama's caution about our view of human nature becomes crucial at this point, for if the soul is important and the body merely its dumb instrument, research that advances the soul, the moral component of the human, may be warranted. However, such experiments would, in effect, alter human nature itself. "My own preference, 'Hands off human nature.' You don't want to do things that really change core human behaviors. . . . [Y]ou don't want to do things that turn people into gods, or subhumans, in effect."[60] However, if the ultimate destiny of the human soul is to evolve to divinity, a core tenet of the rapidly advancing New Religious Synthesis, then where will the ethical principle to prevent such genetic alteration in human nature come from?

Gnostic thought is also committed to the notion that spiritual truth is purposely hidden and either unattainable or indecipherable without special assistance. The secrets that comprise *gnosis* must be learned from spiritual masters, spirit guides, super-intelligent aliens, secret texts, scientific experimentation or arduous exploration. Madame Blavatsky claimed direct instruction by ascended Tibetan spiritual masters like Koot Hoomi; Shirley MacLaine is educated by a spirit guide called the Higher Self; and John Mack's clients receive their higher truth from

aliens. Joseph Smith discovered a secret text that could be read only with the assistance of special lenses, while it takes a scanning electron microscope and a Ph.D. in
physics to read the hidden spiritual meanings in subatomic particles. Similarly, a
mathematician and high-speed computers were required for Michael Drosnin to finally crack "the Bible Code." The hero of James Redfield's *The Celestine Prophecy*
must travel to South America and endure various hardships before acquiring his
own secret text—the Manuscript—that reveals the hidden knowledge necessary
for spiritual deliverance. And it should also be noted that even more arduous trials
must sometimes be endured to acquire the new *gnosis*. John Mack's alien abductees
often endure what can only be called torture before they are spiritually qualified to
convey the messages the rest of us need to hear. Planetary spirits also found it necessary to mistreat Emanuel Swedenborg before he could absorb spiritual wisdom.

Secret arenas into which the New Religious Synthesis leads the spiritual seeker
include the subconscious mind, subatomic space, the world of spirits, the realm of
myth, the province of dreams, the domain of magic, the system of the stars, and
planets beyond earth. Spiritual secrets from such sources promise limitless potential for personal power. Modern practitioners of *gnosis* will claim the capacity to affect the nature of reality, as well as the certainty of eventual divinity. Such mastery
is, however, beyond the reach of all but the most capable and determined. The
"Way of knowledge" is for those possessing, according to Joseph Pearce, "dramatic
abilities and knowledge."[61] Why such effort, such extraordinary gifts and such unusual capacities? Because "extraordinary effort [is] needed to break with the broad
stream that makes up the . . . world of the ordinary." That is, lifting oneself beyond
the constraints of the body and conventional morality takes great strength of
will—a gift most of us do not possess. However, such massive spiritual exertion is
worth whatever it costs, for it opens the way to "ever greater levels of growth and
power" for the spiritual master.[62] At the same time, however, such secrecy in the
spiritual realm always invites the formation of hierarchies of authority and their attendant potential for spiritual abuse.

By contrast to the esoteric media and elusive masters of gnosticism, Jesus Christ
was a remarkably open spiritual teacher. "What I say to you in the dark," he is recorded as having said, "tell in the light; and what you hear whispered, proclaim
from the housetops"(Mt 10:27). The general openness of the Revealed Word tradition sets it apart from any spiritual system officially embracing secrecy or subtly
suggesting that spiritual knowledge is the private domain of the knowing few. In

Revealed Word thinking, the spiritual knowledge necessary to salvation must be made available to everyone regardless of personal circumstance or ability. Regardless of how one feels about Christian missionary endeavors, it is at least clear from these efforts that the Christian message of salvation by grace is to be broadly proclaimed, and it requires for its complete understanding no ascended masters, secret texts or remarkable devices.

Early Christians contended with a spiritual tradition teaching that the path to spiritual enlightenment ran through a maze of carefully guarded secrets known collectively as *gnosis*. Paul wrote against gnosticism in his epistle to the Colossians, while John tackled the problem in his first epistle. These Christian teachers offered a radically different way into spiritual truth. To *gnosis* they responded with *Logos*, a Revealed Word, literally a divine Person who was the eternal Word. Through this Person, salvation was open to all by grace, a divine gift. Such was the message of the Christian gospel, the openly proclaimed message of spiritual deliverance that eschewed the secrets of the gnostic inner circle, that saw the body as redeemable and that venerated the God of the Jews as both Creator and Redeemer.

The New Religious Synthesis has revived several elements in the ancient Gnostic tradition, so long opposed by the Revealed Word. With *gnosis* on the rise, spirituality is again construed as a matter of mastering secrets or techniques that make possible self-deliverance. Because of its commitment to secrets known only by a few, gnostic thinking breeds spiritual elites. Love of secrecy may seem a harmless endeavor in creative religious thought, but such ideology has had its tragic historic consequences. Richard Noll has pointed out that prior to the Nazi era in Europe there were "cries for new spiritual and political elites to lead the Germanic peoples of Central Europe to new 'awakening' through reliance upon the more highly refined 'intuitive' faculties of such specialists."[63] Historically it has often been a short step from the notion of a spiritual elite to the idea of an elite race. As William Covino writes, "The Great Mind" behind the cosmos can be "invoked" by the spiritual master "to restore truth, beauty and justice to humankind," but also to "ordain a master race."[64] Such a spiritual-racial elite may create a perfectly ordered and enlightened society, may "transform the world with its 'higher' values of community and truth," but at what cost?[65]

Nevertheless, because the retrieval of allegedly lost spiritual secrets places their possessors in a commanding spiritual position, the revival of gnosticism is now advocated as an advance beyond the Revealed Word. But gnosticism represents spiritual progress only if secrecy is valued over openness, elitism preferred to egalitarianism, and hierarchy deemed superior to community. For all of the intrigue associated with gaining insight into the machinery of the cosmos, for all of the ego-elevation that attends belonging to an inner circle of spiritual adepts, a spirituality based on *gnosis* reintroduces dubious spiritual tendencies into the mainstream of Western spirituality.

SHAMANS AND THE SPIRITUAL FUTURE

That spiritual advancement is aided by nonhuman spiritual guides is simply assumed in many contemporary spiritual works. Bestselling author Neale Donald Walsch, for instance, claims that in 1992 he began receiving direct answers from a spirit source to a series of perplexing moral and religious questions.

> To my surprise, as I scribbled out the last of my bitter unanswerable questions and prepared to toss my pen aside, my hand remained poised over the paper, as if held by some invisible source. Abruptly, the pen began *moving on its own*. I had no idea what I was about to write, but an idea seemed to be coming, so I decided to flow with it. Out came ... "Do you really want an answer to all these questions, or are you just venting?"[66]

The result was a three-year dialogue between Walsch and "God"—a spirit interlocutor—that appears in his three-volume *Conversations with God*, which purports to offer direct instruction from God on a large number of topics ranging from reincarnation (it occurs) to the ultimate source of morality (the individual human being). As noted above, however, the "God" with whom Walsch communicates is not the uncreated and eternal God of the Revealed Word, but apparently only a more advanced soul that was once also a human.

Much Western spirituality now embraces the shamanic tendency strongly repudiated by the Revealed Word tradition. In the ancient world *daemons*, angels and minor gods guided spiritual seekers. Centuries later, disembodied voices advised medieval and Renaissance alchemists, while in the nineteenth century otherworldly visitors in the form of ghosts and spirits instructed guests in the parlors of Victorian mediums. Tribal shamans around the world have for millennia claimed to have contact with demons and spirits offering a wide range of instruction and, importantly, power over one's enemies. This interest in guidance by spirit entities has recently reasserted itself with surprising success. Today one reads of alien advisors, Inner Friends, Higher Selves, supernatural teachers and spirit helpers in a vast and popular spiritual literature.

The Other Spirituality is frequently backward looking, as is clearly illustrated in this reintroduction of shamanism into the mainstream of Western religious experience. According to anthropologist Gerardo Reichel-Dolmatoff, it is the shaman in primitive cultures who "establishes contact with the supernatural powers and who, to the mind of his people, has the necessary esoteric knowledge to use this contact for the benefit of society."[67] This idea of human bridges between the spiritual and material worlds is flourishing again, as is the attendant idea of the inevitable benefit of such contact. Reliance on esoteric knowledge (*gnosis*) to achieve spirit contact is also evident in the new shamanism, as is the notion of a spiritual elite possessing such knowledge. "The shaman's satisfaction," writes Reichel-Dolmatoff, comes from "'knowing' things which others are unable to grasp."[68]

Several potential liabilities attend this recent revival of shamanistic practices, however. First, the shamanism of the New Religious Synthesis substitutes contact with spirit entities for a living relationship with the Revealed Word's creating and redeeming God, a relationship that the Revealed Word has always contended brings ultimate purpose and meaning to life. "The LORD is my shepherd," writes the psalmist, "I shall not want" (Ps 23:1). But the Word's foundational commitment to an ultimate deity is itself a mistake according to many New Synthesis writers. Gary Zukav offers one explanation for the erroneous theology of monotheism when he posits "realms upon realms of intelligences" just beyond our immediate awareness," any one of which "we might think of as God."[69] Whereas these intelligences are often affirmed to be highly evolved spirit beings, none is presented by the New Synthesis as sovereign over the others, nor as humanity's creator. And the Other Spirituality never so much as hints that there exists somewhere a relationship-seeking redeemer God.

Second, with the prevalence of shamanism in the New Synthesis, private mystical, trance or hallucinogenic experience become important and authoritative sources of theology. This is true in spite of the fact that the shaman *as* shaman— whether UFO abductee, New Age teacher, occult medium or spiritual mystic— has no important connection to ordinary life lived in the external world. Every shaman, when functioning *as* shaman, enters through some esoteric method—drugs, incantation, fasting, self-inflicted pain, hypnosis, spirit possession—a solitary world of inner spiritual experience where the limitations of daily existence are suspended, and its problems irrelevant. On the basis of such a disconnected interior experience, spiritual knowledge is obtained that provides alleged answers to important moral and religious questions arising from daily life. It is important to contrast this approach to spiritual information with the life of Jesus Christ, lived authentically among ordinary people and under the limitations of daily existence in the villages of Palestine. We "have heard . . . have seen . . . and touched with our hands" the living Jesus, writes the apostle John of his and the other disciples' experience (1 Jn 1:3). The disregard for history shown by the New Synthesis becomes particularly pronounced and problematic in its embrace of shamanic insight—for how is the shaman's advice to be tested?

Third, among the most troubling aspects of modern shamanism is its tendency to preclude the possibility of evil intent on the part of the spirit guides. For Zukav it is a taken for granted fact that "there exists a realm that the religious language of the West would call the Angelic kingdom." In this realm are superevolved spirit beings "of numerous frequencies and qualities of consciousness, many of whom guide and interact with us upon the earth."[70] But according to Zukav, our spirit instructors "have evolved beyond" the possibility of doing evil. He writes, "The circumstances cannot be described in which [the inner teacher's] will might be bent in the wrong way, if there were such a way, or in a negative way."[71] This is a leap of faith if ever one has been taken. To submit one's judgment, indeed, one's life to a spiritual entity on the arbitrary assurance that it is incapable of evil seems perilous at best.

As with other components of the New Religious Synthesis, shamanism stands in sharp contrast to the Revealed Word tradition. Various shamanic practices were widespread in the ancient world, often associated with heinous rituals including human sacrifice. It is perhaps for good reason, then, that the biblical book of Deuteronomy expressed the following warning: "There shall not be found among you any one who burns his son or daughter as an offering, any one who practices divination, a soothsayer, or an augur, or a charmer, or a medium, or a wizard, or a necromancer. For whoever does these things is an abomination to the LORD" (Deut 18:10-12 RSV). New Testament sources express similar disdain for such activities, relegating them to the category of the demonic. Luke writes in the book of Acts that as he and Paul were on their way to the house of Lydia in the city of Thyatira, "we met a slave girl who had a spirit of divination and brought her owners a great deal of money by fortune-telling." Paul is reported to have said to the spirit, "'I order you in the name of Jesus Christ to come out of her.' And it came out that very hour" (Acts 16:16, 18).

Direct contact with spirits is viewed as a profound danger in the Revealed Word. Such is not the case in the New Religious Synthesis, where the practice is repeatedly commended, and almost never with cautions attached. This movement away from a humble approach in prayer to a personal and sovereign God and instead toward a shamanic elite interacting directly with the spirit world is a watershed event in Western spirituality. It marks a return to a repudiated spirituality that has, until recently, maintained a largely subterranean life. Enjoying again the daylight of popular acceptance, the practices of modern shamanism ought at the very least to be critically examined before becoming a fixed part of accepted religious practice.

MYSTICAL PLURALISM

That direct, mystical contact with the divine is the road to pluralism is an emerging consensus among advocates of the New Religious Synthesis. Correspondingly, the creedal pronouncements of the Revealed Word tradition are often seem as obstacles to the advent of an era of religious unity and hope. Theologians defending an authoritative revelation of God's nature must step down. The spirit person, the shaman, the mystic, the UFO abductee and even the drug experimenter are the pioneers of the soul's new way, explorers of the psyche's deeper reaches, heroes of faith pointing the way out of the old exclusionary doctrines and toward religious pluralism.

As he receives messages from "God" about the true nature of everything, Neale Donald Walsch is told, *"religion is your attempt to speak of the unspeakable."*[72] Thus, any and all conceptions of God are simply personal expressions of the unknowable truth that mystics encounter. "I am God, as you understand Him. I am Goddess as you comprehend Her. I am Conceiver and Creator of Everything as you know and experience. . . . [Y]our perception of reality is more limited than you thought, and the Truth is more *un*limited than you can imagine. I am giving you ever-so-small a glimpse of infinity—and infinite love."[73]

As we have already noted, for proponents of a new religious era, god is the undifferentiated consciousness present in all things, or, as Aldous Huxley and John Shelby Spong would have it, "the ground of being." This notion is not contradicted by Walsch's contact with "God," nor by Shirley MacLaine's conversations with a Higher Self, for these are simply highly evolved intelligences that make no claim to be a preexisting and creating divinity like Yahweh of the Revealed Word. Prescribed theology—theological doctrine of the type taught in the Revealed Word tradition—will never open the door into this realm of pure being, this sphere of light and ecstasy. A deeper, more subjective, more direct spiritual experience is needed to find the divine.

Deepak Chopra writes of the meditative effort to achieve a breakthrough to spiritual unity or ecstasy. "This process of shifting from activity to stillness," he writes, "is a simple yet very deep description of meditation." He adds, "We could modify the biblical injunction to 'Be still and know ecstasy.'" Of course, the biblical phrase is "Be still, and know that I am God" (Ps 46:10). Thus, Chopra makes the individual's experience of spiritual quietude a substitute for the Revealed Word's personal God. *"Expansion of consciousness is the road to ecstasy,"* writes Chopra.[74] And this experience of expanding consciousness is available in a variety of religious traditions, including the Christian when properly understood.

Christian apologist Ravi Zacharias has written, "The Christian faith is often castigated because the contemporary mind-set is infuriated by any claim to ideational elitism in a pluralistic society. How dare one idea be claimed as superior to another?"[75] It is true that Christianity's persistent claim to unique truthfulness offends modern sensibilities, outrages those seeking a rapprochement among the world's many religious systems. In fact, it is precisely Christianity's insistence that it alone is true among all of those systems that has driven the long public effort to unseat it and find a substitute, peace-making spirituality for the contemporary world.

But Christianity *requires* a unique claim to truth, and its internal logic runs dramatically and uncompromisingly at cross-purposes to religious pluralism. That logic states that God entered human history "in the fullness of time" and took on human flesh in the person of Jesus Christ. This event occurred but once and, when properly understood, is neither capable of duplication, nor does it have an equivalent. Christ's redemptive life and death must remain unique for Christianity to substantiate its foundational claims. And the same can be said of Jesus' resurrection—it must be unique if the logic of atonement is to be consistent. Why would God recognize another universal and ultimately sufficient sacrifice for human sin having recognized this one? Again, each of these claims—that Jesus Christ lived as God incarnate, that he died for human redemption, that he rose in conquest of death—is a sine qua non of Christian orthodoxy. Consequently, each makes the broad religious pluralism of the New Religious Synthesis impossible to reconcile with Christian orthodoxy. If Christians are to join the pluralistic parade, they must first jettison the old idea that Jesus is the unique manifestation of God in human form and reinvent their Messiah as one among many participants in the unifying mystic vision, as another highly evolved spiritual guide, a prophet among prophets or, in Marcus Borg's phrase, a spirit person.

The Other Spirituality presents itself as refurbishing the primordial human religious view, the first human spirituality. Mysticism is inherent to this ancient religious view, the core, it is argued, of all important subsequent religious experience and speculation. This notion clashes with the Revealed Word's account of early human spiritual experience. On the Revealed Word view, the very earliest encounter between humans and the supernatural was, indeed, pure and enriching. A sovereign God created human beings, called them good and entered a relationship with them. Humanity encountered the sovereign creator God and knew him intimately. That intimate relationship was, however, ruined through a disastrous fall into sin, a possibility that mystical experience cannot accommodate.

Many New Synthesis writers have suggested the pluralistic path for Christians if they are to enter the new millennium as good faith partners in the quest for a single, unifying spirituality. But again we encounter a problem, for Christians always have claimed that Christianity was just that—the single, true, universal and unifying spiritual view, the good news of God's act of saving people from every tongue, tribe and nation. The choice, then, between Christianity and the Other Spirituality is a stark one: Jesus Christ as the single divine redeemer of a lost human race or Jesus as one among many spirit people seeking to express the inexpressible.

FINAL CONSIDERATIONS: A NEW AND BETTER WAY?

At the center of the New Religious Synthesis is the striving human will seeking desperately to launch itself into minor godhood in an evolving cosmos through the mechanisms of directed spiritual evolution, spiritualized science and spirit contact. This Other Spirituality that now presents itself as the rightful replacement for the Revealed Word proclaims its spiritual liberation from the worldview that informs Christianity and its freedom from that worldview's personal and wholly other God. But this new way of self-salvation may be little more than the refurbishing of an ancient spiritual mistake.

The New Religious Synthesis promises to secure the soul's triumph over external restraints including time, space, evil, other people, conventional morality and especially traditional religion. But in the process it dispenses with a transcendent and personal deity, irrevocable forgiveness of sin, triumph over death, egalitarian spiritual community and the simple joy of accepting our unchangeable status as infinitely valuable but fallen creatures of a living and holy God. This "new way" in religion puts us on the path we are inclined to take when left to our own spiritual devices—to proclaim our own divinity, which, in spite of the idea's obvious absurdity when confronted with the undeniable facts of our individual and corporate limitations, will be proven presently once we learn enough secrets. Could this be the broad road leading to spiritual destruction spoken of by Jesus?

The New Synthesis stresses the exertion of the human will in the spiritual realm, the individual psyche throwing off the restraints of revelation and tradition, human reason crafting its own salvation out of the raw materials of psycho-spiritual technique, mysterious *gnosis* or subjective mystical experience. In response to such spiritual seduction, Jesus continues to urge, "Come unto me."

The combination of pantheism and its attendant nature worship, religious secrecy, spiritual elitism and hopes of scientifically assisted evolutionary progress toward a master-species has, at some historical junctures, had sinister consequences. According to Richard Noll, historian R. G. Collingwood "interprets the rise of fascism and National Socialism in the twentieth century as the direct result of the popularity of the neopaganism in the late 1800s that worshipped the power of the human will and that, in turn, arose to fill a spiritual vacuum created by this very eclipse of faith in orthodox Christianity."[76] Other observers of Western culture have warned against the advent of spiritual systems that jettison a sovereign God and elevate a divine man or race. According to A. N. Wilson, Thomas Carlyle held that "if [faith] was not directed towards the true God, it would be directed towards idols. Hence Carlyle's view—as we can now see, a fatal though perfectly accurate one—that the human race, having discarded belief in the unseen God of Israel, would always look towards *Ubermensch* or Superman as its God-substitute."[77] And the self-promoting candidates for this position have never been hard to find, nor have their followers been few.

The book of Genesis records that the first human temptation was to acquire a forbidden knowledge that would make them "like God." In the late sixteenth century the heretical teacher Giordano Bruno propounded a reworked system of Egyptian magic based on pantheism, demonic guidance and *gnosis*. As the first master of his own system, Bruno believed himself to be, in fact, divine. As Frances Yates writes, "Bruno has made the gnostic ascent . . . and so has become divine, with the Powers within him."[78] The advocates of a new way in religion have paid less attention to spiritual truth than they have to the grand project of inventing and promoting a self-aggrandizing substitute for an authentic religious faith, a faith, moreover, that made them accountable to a God who could not be bribed. M. Craig Barnes has written that "people who have a God do not need to become one themselves. They are too consumed watching the Lord's salvation unfold."[79] It may be time for us to relearn this simple but profound truth.

NOTES

Chapter One: Introduction: A Changing View of the Spiritual World

[1]Gary Zukav, October 2002, <www.zukav.com>.

[2]Gary Zukav, *The Seat of the Soul* (New York: Simon & Schuster, 1989), p. 67.

[3]Ibid., p. 71.

[4]Ibid., p. 83.

[5]Ibid., p. 102.

[6]Ibid., p. 92.

[7]Ibid., p. 97.

[8]Marija Gimbutas, *The Language of the Goddess: Unearthing the Hidden Symbols of Western Civilization* (San Francisco: Harper & Row, 1989), p. xiv.

[9]Marilyn Ferguson, *The Aquarian Conspiracy: Personal and Social Transformation in the 1980's* (Los Angeles: J. P. Tarcher, 1980), p. 25.

[10]Carl Jung, "The Difference Between Eastern and Western Thinking," in *The Portable Jung* (New York: Penguin, 1976), p. 476.

[11]Wayne Teasdale, *The Mystic Heart* (Novato, Calif.: New World Library, 1999), p. 4.

[12]Carl A. Raschke, *The Interruption of Eternity: Modern Gnosticism and the Origins of the New Religious Consciousness* (Chicago: Nelson-Hall, 1980).

[13]Quoted in Winifred Gallagher, *Working on God* (New York: Random House, 1999), p. xx.

[14]Michael D'Antonio, *Heaven on Earth: Dispatches from America's Spiritual Frontier* (New York: Crown , 1992), p. 13.

[15]Ibid., p. 17.

[16]Wade Clark Roof, *Spiritual Marketplace: Baby Boomers and the Remaking of American Religion* (Princeton, N.J.: Princeton University Press, 1999), pp. 37-38.

[17]Ibid., p. 38.

[18]Teasdale, *Mystic Heart*, p. 4.

[19]Ibid., pp. 4-5.

[20]Ibid., p. 5.

[21]Teresa Watanabe, "Spirituality Is One for the Books," *Los Angeles Times*, September 4, 1999, p. 1.

[22]Robert Wuthnow, *After Heaven: Spirituality in America Since the 1950s* (Berkeley: University of California Press, 1998), p. 14.

[23]Ibid., p. 13.

[24]Philip Jenkins, *Mystics and Messiahs: Cults and New Religions in American History* (Oxford: Oxford University Press, 2000), p. 10.

[25]Lisa Napoli, "When the Astrology Zone Aligns with the Internet," *The New York Times*, October 5, 1998, p. C11.

[26]Robert Wuthnow, *Rediscovering the Sacred* (Grand Rapids, Mich.: Eerdmans, 1992), p. 1.

[27]Karen Hoyt, ed., *The New Age Rage* (Old Tappan, N.J.: Revell, 1987), p. 11.

[28]D'Antonio, *Heaven on Earth*, pp. 12-13.

[29]Shirley MacLaine, *Going Within: A Guide for Inner Transformation* (New York: Bantam, 1989), and *Dancing in the Light* (New York: Bantam 1985).

[30]Ibid., p. 100.

[31]D'Antonio, *Heaven on Earth*, pp. 13.

[32]Carlos Castaneda, *The Teachings of Don Juan: A Yaqui Way of Knowledge* (Berkeley: University of California Press, 1969).

[33]Ibid., p. 7.

[34]Ferguson, *Aquarian Conspiracy*, p. 28.

[35]Carol P. Christ, *Rebirth of the Goddess: Finding Meaning in Feminist Spirituality* (New York: Addison Wesley, 1997), p. xiii. Other titles on goddess worship include Starhawk, *The Spiral Dance* (New York: Harper & Row, 1989); Elinor W. Gadon, *The Once and Future Goddess* (New York: HarperCollins, 1989); Zsuzsanna Emese Budapest, *The Holy Book of Women's Mysteries* (Oakland, Calif.: Susan B. Anthony Coven No. 1, 1986); Jean Shinoda Bolen, *Goddesses in Everywoman* (San Francisco: Harper & Row, 1984); Naomi Goldenberg, *Changing of the Gods: Feminism and the End of Traditional Religions* (Boston: Beacon, 1979).

[36]Carol P. Christ, "Why Women Need the Goddess: Phenomenological, Psychological and Political Reflections," in *Womanspring Rising: A Feminist Reader in Religion*, ed. Carol P. Christ and Judith Plaskow (San Francisco: Harper & Row, 1979), p. 277; quoted in Peter Jones, *The Gnostic Empire Strikes Back: An Old Heresy for The New Age* (Phillipsburg, Penn.: Presbyterian & Reformed, 1992), p. 55.

[37]Gimbutas, *Language of the Goddess.* p. xx.

[38]Ibid., p. xxi.

[39]Barbara Walker, *Restoring the Goddess* (Amherst, N.Y.: Prometheus, 2000).

[40]Akasha Gloria Hull, *Soul Talk: The New Spirituality of African American Women* (Rochester, Vt.: Inner Traditions, 2001), p. 1.

[41]Ibid., p. 2.

[42]Rich Poll, *Apologia Update*, winter 1999, p. 1.

[43]Deepti Hajela, Associated Press, June 4, 2000.

[44]See <www.bolt.com> link to Mystic.

[45]Phyllis Curott, *Book of Shadows: A Modern Woman's Journey into the Wisdom and the Magic of the Goddess* (New York: Broadway, 1998).

[46]Ibid., p. xii.

[47]Ibid.

[48]Ashleen O'Gaea, *The Family Wicca Book: The Craft for Parents and Children* (St. Paul, Minn.: Llewellyn, 1994), p. xi.

[49]Ibid., p. 6.

[50]David A. Cooper, *God Is a Verb: Kabbalah and the Practice of Mystical Judaism* (New York: Riverhead, 1997).

[51]Rodger Kamenetz, *The Jew in the Lotus: A Poet's Rediscovery of Jewish Identity in Buddhist India* (San Francisco: Harper SanFrancisco, 1994).

[52]John Heider, *The Tao of Leadership: Leadership Strategies for a New Age* (New York: Bantam, 1986).

[53]Ibid., p. 31.

[54]*O: The Oprah Magazine*, August 2001, p. 174.

[55]*Civilization*, December 1999, p. 61.

[56]*Transforming the Mind: Teachings on Generating Compassion* (London: Thorsuns, 2000); *The Art of Happiness: A Handbook for Living*, authored with Howard C. Cutler, M.D. (New York: Riverhead, 1998); *The Path to Tranquility: Daily Wisdom* (New York: Viking Arkana, 1999).

[57]Diki Tsering, *My Son: A Mother's Story*, ed. Khedroop Thondup (New York: Viking Arkana, 2000).

[58]See "Buddha Boom," *Civilization*, December 1999, pp. 57-71.

[59]Fritjof Capra, *The Tao of Physics* (Berkeley, Calif.: Shambala, 1975); *The Turning Point: Science, Society and the Rising Culture* (New York: Simon & Schuster, 1982).

[60]Fritjof Capra, *The Web of Life: A New Scientific Understanding of Living Systems* (New York: Anchor, 1996), p. 107.

[61]Ibid.

[62]Fred Alan Wolf, *The Dreaming Universe* (New York: Simon & Schuster, 1994), 344.

[63]Ibid., p. 343.

[64]Amit Goswami, *The Self-Aware Universe: How Consciousness Creates the Material World* (New York: Jeremy P. Tharcher, 1995), p. 11.

[65]Gary Zukav, *The Dancing Wu Li Masters: An Overview of the New Physics* (New York: William Morrow, 1979); Fred Alan Wolf, *The Spiritual Universe: How Quantum Physics Proves the Existence of the Soul* (New York: Simon & Schuster, 1996.

[66]Ferguson, *Aquarian Conspiracy*, p. 23.

[67]Jeremy Narby and Francis Huxley, eds., *Shamans Through Time: 500 Years on the Path to Knowledge* (New York: Jeremy Tarcher, 2001), pp. 301-5.

[68]Ibid., p. 302.

[69]Ibid., p. 303.

[70]Mark Epstein, *Going to Pieces Without Falling Apart* (New York: Broadway, 1998), p. xix.

[71]Ibid., p. i.

[72]Richard Noll, *The Jung Cult: Origins of a Charismatic Movement* (Princeton, N.J.: Princeton University Press, 1994).

[73]John E. Mack, *Abduction: Human Encounters with Aliens* (New York: Charles Scribner's Sons, 1995).

[74]Other books in this growing genre include *Summoned: Encounters with Alien Intelligence* by Dana Redfield and Linda Moulton Howe, *The Custodians: Beyond Abduction* by Delores Cannon, *Reaching for Reality: Seven Incredible True Stories of Alien Abduction* by Constance Clear and *The UFO Enigma: A New Review of the Physical Evidence* by Peter A. Sturrock.

[75]Helen Schucman, *A Course in Miracles and Manual for Teachers* (Tiburon, Calif.: Center for Inner Peace, 1975).

[76]Ibid., pp. 57, 63.

[77]Cadonna M. Peyton, "Schools Assist Students in Developing 'Sixth Sense,'" Associated Press, January 16, 2000.

[78]Ruth Walker, "Translating Belief in God into Health and Well-Being," *The Christian Science Monitor*, December 20, 2001, sec. 2, p. 13.

[79]James H. Austin, M.D., *Zen and the Brain* (Cambridge, Mass.: MIT Press, 1998), p. 695.

[80]Carl Jung, "The Spiritual Problem of Modern Man," in *Modern Man in Search of a Soul*, trans. W. S. Dell and Cary F. Baynes (New York: Harcourt Brace, 1933), p. 209.

Chapter Two: Antecedents of the New Religious Synthesis:
A Brief History of Alternative Spirituality in the West

[1]Leonard Levi, *Blasphemy: Verbal Offense Against the Sacred* (New York: Alfred A. Knopf, 1993), p. 55.

[2]Wayne Shumaker, *The Occult Sciences in the Renaissance: A Study in Intellectual Patterns* (Berke-ley: University of California Press, 1972), pp. 211, 209.

[3]Ibid., p. 201.

[4]See Gavin Ashenden, "The Influence of Hermeticism on Myth and Metaphysics in the Life and Works of Charles Williams" (Ph.D. diss., University of Sussex, 1998-1999).

[5]Shumaker, *Occult Sciences*, p. 233.

[6]Ibid., pp. 225, 214.

[7]Ibid., p. 215.

[8]Ibid., p. 220.

[9]Ibid., p. 228.

[10]Ibid., p. 229.

[11]Ibid., p. 230.

[12]Ibid., p. 235.

[13]Adolphe Franck, *The Kabbalah: The Religious Philosophy of the Hebrews* (1843; reprint, Secaucus, N.J.: Citadel Press, 1979), pp. 26-27.

[14]See ibid., chap. 3, "The Authenticity of the Zohar."

[15]Ibid., p. 16.

[16]Ibid., pp. 13-14.

[17]John C. Wilson, editor's introduction to Franck, *Kabbalah*, p. 8.

[18]Shlomo Giora Shoham, *Bridges to Nothingness: Gnosis, Kabala, Existentialism, and the Transcendental Predicament of Man* (London: Associated University Presses, 1994), p. 21.

[19]Franck, *Kabbalah*, p. 23.

[20]Shoham, *Bridges to Nothingness*, p.111.

[21]Ibid., pp. 110-11.

[22]Ibid., p. 112.

[23]Ibid., p. 97.

[24]Ibid., p. 103.

[25]Ibid., p. 72.

[26]Ibid., p. 73.

[27]Ibid., pp. 111-12.

[28]Hugh J. Kearney, *Science and Change: 1500-1700* (New York: McGraw-Hill, 1971), p. 24.

[29]Ibid., p. 100.

[30]Ibid., p. 48.

[31]Ibid., p. 39.

[32]Ibid., p. 37.

[33]Ibid., p. 100.

[34]Ibid., p. 39.

[35]Ibid., p. 110.

[36]Robert E. Sullivan, *John Toland and the Deist Controversy* (Cambridge, Mass.: Harvard University Press, 1982), p. 199.

[37]Carl A. Raschke, *The Interruption of Eternity: Modern Gnosticism and the Origins of the New Religious Consciousness* (Chicago: Nelson-Hall, 1980), p. 49.

[38]Sullivan, *John Toland*, p. 200.

[39]Kearney, *Science and Change*, p. 106.

[40]Franklin Baumer, *Religion and the Rise of Scepticism* (New York: Harcourt Brace & World, 1960), pp. 90-91.

[41]Kearney, *Science and Change*, p. 130.

[42]Ibid., p. 132.

[43]Roland Bainton, *The Reformation of the Sixteenth Century* (Boston: Beacon, 1952), p. 128.

[44]Bradford Verter, "Dark Star Rising: The Emergence of Modern Occultism, 1800-1950" (Ph.D. diss., Princeton University, 1998), p. 33.

[45]Shumaker, *Occult Sciences*, p. 205.

[46]Ibid.

[47]Ibid., p. 204.

[48]Ibid., p. 205.

[49]Quoted in R. W. Southern, *Western Society and the Church in the Middle Ages* (Baltimore: Penguin, 1970), p. 45.

[50]Ibid., p. 48.

[51]Bainton, *Reformation of the Sixteenth Century*, p. 125.

[52]Ibid., p. 124.

[53]George T. Buckley, *Atheism in the English Renaissance* (1932; reprint, New York: Russell & Russell, 1965), p. 17.

[54]Harold Hutcheson, *Lord Herbert of Cherbury's* De Religione Laici (New Haven, Conn.: Yale University Press, 1944), p. 60.

[55]On the nature of the ancient skeptical tradition, see Julia Annas and Jonathan Barnes, *The Modes of Scepticism* (Cambridge: Cambridge University Press, 1985). On more recent treatments of skepticism, see M. Jamie Ferreira, *Scepticism and Reasonable Doubt* (Oxford: Clarendon, 1986). See also P. F. Strawson, *Scepticism and Naturalism: Some Varieties* (New York: Columbia University Press, 1985).

[56]C. B. Schmitt, "The Rediscovery of Ancient Scepticism in Modern Times," in *The Skeptical Tradition* (Berkeley: University of California Press, 1983), pp. 225-51, esp. p. 228.

[57]Buckley, *Atheism in the English Renaissance*, p. 17.

[58]Mark U. Edwards Jr. *Printing, Propaganda, and Martin Luther* (Berkeley: University of California Press, 1994), p. 367.

[59]Buckley, *Atheism in the English Renaissance*, pp. 18-19.

[60]See James A. Herrick, *The Radical Rhetoric of the English Deists: The Discourse of Scepticism, 1680-1750* (Columbia: University of South Carolina Press, 1997).

[61]Benedict de Spinoza, *The Chief Works of Spinoza*, 2 vols. in 1, trans. R. H. M. Elwes (New York: Dover, 1951).

[62]Jonathan Israels, *The Dutch Republic: Its Rise, Greatness and Fall, 1477-1806* (Oxford: Clarendon, 1995), p. 1048.

[63]Spinoza, *Tractatus*, p. 8; quoted in Nigel M. de S. Cameron, *Biblical Higher Criticism and the Defense of Infallibilism in 19th Century Britain* (Lewiston, N.Y.: Edwin Mellon, 1987), p. 16.

[64]Spinoza, *Tractatus* 6.92; also quoted in Cameron, p. 14.

[65]Spinoza, *Tractatus*, chaps. 6-9.

[66]Edgar Krentz, *The History of Critical Method* (Philadelphia: Fortress, 1975), p. 14.

[67]Ibid.

[68]*The Works of Sir Thomas Browne* (London: n.p., 1857).

[69]Rosalie Colie, *Light and Enlightenment* (Cambridge: Cambridge University Press, 1957), p. 40.

[70]H. McLachlan, *Socinianism in Seventeenth Century England* (Oxford: Oxford University Press, 1951), pp. 325-27.

[71]J. C. D. Clark, *English Society: 1688-1832* (Cambridge: Cambridge University Press, 1985), p. 280.

[72]Krentz, *History of Critical Method*, p. 12.

[73]Ibid., p. 13.

[74]Ibid., p.5.

[75]Colin Brown, *Jesus in European Protestant Thought* (Durham, N.C.: Labyrinth, 1985), p. 281 n. 58.

[76]Krentz, *History of Critical Method*, p. 15. The other works included *Histoire critique du texte du Nouveau Testament* (1689), *Histoire critique des versions du Nouveau Testament* (1693) and *Histoire critique des principaux commentaires du Nouveau Testament* (1693).

[77]Krentz, *History of Critical Method*, p. 15.

[78]Ibid., p.16.

[79]Richard Popkin, *The History of Skepticism from Erasmus to Spinoza* (Berkeley: University of California Press, 1979), p. 4.

[80]Roscoe Pound, *The Development of Constitutional Guarantees of Liberty* (New Haven, Conn.: Yale University Press, 1957), p. 30.

[81]S. G. Hefelbower, *The Relation of John Locke to English Deism* (Chicago: University of Chicago Press, 1918), p. 3.

[82]See, for example, the anonymous *Reasons for Not Proceeding Against Mr. Whiston* (London, 1713), p. 15.

Chapter Three: The Rise of Biblical Criticism:
Allegory, Myth, Codes and the End of History

[1]Thomas Woolston, *Fourth Discourse on the Miracles of Our Saviour* (London: 1729), p. 33.

[2]R. M. Burns, *The Great Debate on Miracles* (Lewisberg, Penn.: Bucknell University Press), p. 10.

[3]Jonathan Swift, "Verses on the Death of Dr. Swift," in *The Poems of Jonathan Swift*, 2nd ed., ed. Harold Williams (Oxford: Clarendon, 1958), p. 564; also quoted in Burns, *Great Debate*, p. 10. Swift attacked Woolston in a note, writing that "Woolston was a Clergyman, but for want of Bread, hath in several Treatises, in the most blasphemous Manner, attempted to turn Our Saviour and his Miracles into Ridicule. He is much caressed by many great Courtiers, and by all the Infidels, and his Books read generally by the Court Ladies" (Williams, *Poems of Jonathan Swift*, p. 564).

[4]Peter Gay, *The Enlightenment: An Interpretation* (New York: Alfred Knopf, 1967), p. 375; Henning Graf Reventlow, *The Authority of the Bible, and the Rise of the Modern World* (Philadelphia: Fortress, 1985), p. 149; John Redwood, *Reason, Ridicule, and Religion* (Cambridge, Mass.: Harvard University Press, 1976), p. 149.

[5]Robert M. Grant and David Tracy, *A Short History of the Interpretation of the Bible*, 2nd ed. (Philadelphia: Fortress, 1984), p. 109.

[6]John Shelby Spong, *Rescuing the Bible from Fundamentalism* (San Francisco: HarperSanFrancisco, 1991), p. 21.

[7]Ibid.

[8]Ibid., p. 22.

[9]Ibid., p. 237.

[10]Ibid., p. 24.

[11]Anthony Collins, *A Discourse of Free Thinking* (London: n.p., 1713), p. 44.

[12]Ibid., p. 45.

[13]Henning Graf Reventlow, *The Authority of the Bible and the Rise of the Modern World* (Philadelphia: Fortress, 1985), p. 412.

[14]Thomas Woolston, *Six Discourses on the Miracles of Our Saviour* (London: n.p., 1727-1729), *First Discourse*, p. 4.

[15]Ibid., p. 34.

[16]Woolston, *Fourth Discourse*, p. 7.

[17]Ibid., p. 6.

[18]Ibid., p. 11.

[19]Ibid., p. 22.

[20]Ibid., p. 17.

[21]Ibid., p. 20.

[22]Simon Browne, *A Fit Rebuke to a Ludicrous Infidel in Some Remarks on Mr. Woolston's Fifth Discourse* (London: R. Ford, 1732), p. i.

[23]Bishop Edmund Gibson, *The Bishop of London's Pastoral Letter to the People of His Diocese* (London: Samuel Buckley, 1728), p. 33.

[24]See Colin Brown, *Jesus in European Protestant Thought* (Durham, N.C.: Labyrinth, 1985), chaps. 1 and 2.

[25]Ibid., pp. 51-52. Brown connects the Deists directly to a number of German Enlightenment theologians.

[26]Harold O. J. Brown, *Heresies* (Garden City, N.Y.: Doubleday, 1984), p. 404.

[27]Ibid.

[28]*New International Dictionary of New Testament Theology*, ed. Colin Brown (Exeter, U.K.: Paternoster, 1975-1978), p. 833; Brown, *Jesus in European Protestant Thought*, p. 2.

[29]Brown, *Jesus in European Protestant Thought*, p. 2.

[30]Gay, *The Enlightenment*, p. 381.

[31]C. Brown, *Jesus in European Protestant Thought*, p. 22; Gay, *The Enlightenment*, p. 332.

[32]Gay, *The Enlightenment*, p. 333.

[33]Eliot also translated Feuerbach's *Essence of Christianity* into English in 1854.

[34]Noel Annan, "Science, Religion, and the Critical Mind," in *The Victorian Age: Essays in Fiction and in Social and Literary Criticism*, ed. Robert Langbaum (Greenwich, Conn.: Fawcett Premier, 1967), pp. 69-74; quote p. 72.

[35]Ibid., pp. 71-72.

[36]J. W. Burrow, *The Crisis of Reason: European Thought, 1848-1914* (New Haven, Conn.: Yale University Press, 2000), p. 197.

[37]David Strauss, *Life of Jesus Critically Examined*, 2 vols., trans. Marian Evans (New York: Calvin Blanchard, 1856), 1:3.

[38]Ibid., 1:3-4.

[39]Ibid., 1:4.

[40]Ibid.

[41]Ibid., 1:33.

[42]Ibid., 1:43.

[43]Ibid., 1:47.

[44]Ibid.

[45]Ibid., 1:47-48.

[46]Ibid., 1:61.

[47]Ibid.

[48]Ibid., 1:63.

[49]Ibid., 2:892-93.

[50]Ibid., 2:895.

[51]Ibid., 2:896.

[52]Ibid., 2:898.

[53]Spong, *Rescuing the Bible*, p. 17.

[54]Ibid., p. 20.

[55]Ibid., pp. 16-17.

[56]Ibid., p. 24.

[57]Ibid., pp. 22-23, 21.

[58]Ibid., p. 37.

[59]Ibid., pp. 37-38.

[60]Ibid., pp. 98, 100.

[61]Ibid., p. 101.

[62]Ibid., p. 24.

[63]Ibid., p. 237.

[64]Ibid., p. 242.

[65]Ibid.

[66]Michael Drosnin, *The Bible Code* (New York: Simon & Schuster, 1997).

[67]Ibid., p. 20.

[68]Ibid.

[69]Ibid., p. 21.

[70]Ibid., p. 38.

[71]Ibid., p. 186.

[72]Ibid., p. 182.

[73]Ibid., p. 20.

[74]Ibid., p. 148.

[75]John Stott, *The Contemporary Christian* (Downers Grove, Ill.: InterVarsity Press, 1992), p. 15.

Chapter Four: The Ascent of Reason: Birth of a Deity

[1]Franklin Baumer, *Religion and the Rise of Scepticism* (New York: Harcourt Brace & World, 1960), p. 35.

2Ibid., p. 36.

3Carl G. Jung, "The Spiritual Problem of Modern Man," in *Modern Man in Search of a Soul,* trans. W. S. Dell and Cary F. Baynes (New York: Harcourt Brace, 1933), p. 209.

4Baumer, *Religion and Rise of Scepticism,* p. 74.

5Ibid.

6Quoted in ibid., p. 75. See Antoine Nicolas de Condorcet, *Sketch of a Historical Picture of the Progress of the Human Mind,* trans. June Barraclough (New York: Noonday, 1955).

7Peter Annet, *The Free Inquirer,* October 17, 1761 (reprinted London: R. Carlile, 1826), p. 3.

8Peter Annet, *Lectures Corrected and Revised* (London: J. Smith, n.d.), no. 11, p. 113.

9Annet, *Free Inquirer,* October 17, 1761, pp. 3-4.

10Ibid., p. 4.

11Annet, *Free Inquirer,* November 3, 1761, pp. 21-22.

12Peter Annet, *Deism Fairly Stated* (London: W. Webb, 1746), p. 9.

13Ibid., p. 10.

14Thomas Babington Macaulay, quoted in the introduction to Voltaire, *Zadig and Other Stories,* ed. Irving Babbitt (Boston: D. C. Heath, 1905), p. ix.

15Wayne Andrews, *Voltaire* (New York: New Directions, 1981), p. 9.

16Baumer, *Religion and Rise of Scepticism,* p. 47.

17Theodore Besterman, introduction to Voltaire, *Candide and Other Stories,* trans. Joan Spencer, ed. Henri Bénac (London: Oxford University Press, 1966), p. viii.

18Babbitt, introduction to Voltaire, *Zadig,* p. vi.

19Besterman, introduction to Voltaire, *Candide,* p. xi.

20Ibid., p. x.

21Ibid., p. 2.

22Ibid., pp. 7-8.

23Ibid., p. 20.

24Ibid.

25Ibid., p. 21.

26Ibid., p. 36.

27Ibid., pp. 39-40.

28Robert A. Wagoner, translator's foreword to *Voltaire,* by Gustave Lanson (New York: John Wiley & Sons, 1966), p. viii.

29Andrews, *Voltaire,* p. 2.

30William Covino, *Rhetoric and Magic* (Albany: State University of New York Press, 1997), p. 71.

31Ibid., p. 73.

32Ibid., p. 74.

33Thomas De Quincey, *Confessions of an English Opium-Eater and Other Writings,* ed. Grevel Lindop (Oxford: Oxford University Press, 1985), pp. 116-17; quoted in Covino, *Rhetoric and Magic,* p. 77.

[34]Covino, *Rhetoric and Magic*, pp. 77-78. Gregory Dart has written, "In his political writings, De Quincey frequently exhibited a violent fear and loathing of the urban mass" (*Times Literary Supplement*, June 1, 2001, p. 4).

[35]Quoted in Covino, *Rhetoric and Magic*, p. 79.

[36]Ibid.

[37]Thomas De Quincey, *Confessions of an English Opium Eater* and *Suspiria profundis* (Boston: Ticknor, Reed & Fields, 1850), p. 55.

[38]Ibid., p. 56.

[39]Ibid.

[40]Ibid., p. 62.

[41]Ibid., p. 57.

[42]Ibid., pp. 67-68.

[43]Ibid., p. 131.

[44]Ibid.

[45]Ibid., p. 132.

[46]Ibid., p. 133.

[47]Richard Kyle, *The Religious Fringe: A History of Alternative Religion in America* (Downers Grove, Ill.: InterVarsity Press, 1993), p. 49.

[48]Stephen Gottschalk, "Christian Science and Harmonialism," in *Encyclopedia of the American Religious Experience* (New York: Scribner, 1988), p. 903.

[49]Dennis Voskuil, *Mountains into Goldmines: Robert Schuller and the Gospel of Success* (Grand Rapids, Mich.: Eerdmans, 1983), p. 118.

[50]Ibid.

[51]Ibid.

[52]On Eddy and her relationship with Quimby and his ideas, see Gillian Gill, *Mary Baker Eddy* (Reading, Mass.: Perseus, 1998), pp. 119ff.

[53]Ibid., p. 119.

[54]From the Alliance's declaration of purpose; quoted in Voskuil, p. 120.

[55]Quoted in Voskuil, *Mountains into Goldmines*, p. 120.

[56]Quoted in ibid.

[57]Ibid., p. 122. Ralph Waldo Trine, *In Tune with the Infinite* (New York: Crowell, 1897).

[58]Quoted in Voskuil, *Mountains into Goldmines*, p. 122.

[59]Ibid., p. 123.

[60]Ibid.

[61]Ayn Rand, *Atlas Shrugged* (New York: Dutton, 1992), p. 1010.

[62]Ibid., p. 1011.

[63]Ibid., p. 1012.

[64]Ibid., p. 1011.

[65]Ibid., p. 1012.

[66]Ibid., p. 1013.

[67] Ibid.

[68] Ibid. For a discussion of how Rand's works are currently being used to provide moral justification for corporate greed, see Del Jones, "Scandals Lead Execs to *Atlas Shrugged*," *USA Today*, September 24, 2002, p. 1.

[69] Ibid.

[70] Ibid., p. 1015.

Chapter Five: Science and Shifting Paradigms: Salvation in a New Cosmos

[1] Edward S. Reed, *From Soul to Mind: The Emergence of Psychology from Erasmus Darwin to William James* (New Haven, Conn.: Yale University Press, 1997), p. 158.

[2] James Turner, *Without God, Without Creed* (Baltimore: Johns Hopkins University Press, 1985), p. 137.

[3] C. Maurice Davies, *Heterodox London: Phases of Free Thought in the Metropolis* (1874; reprint, New York: A. M. Kelley, 1969), 2:254.

[4] Ibid., pp. 256-57.

[5] Jacques Barzun, *From Dawn to Decadence* (New York: Harper Collins, 2000), p. 572.

[6] C. G. Jung, "The Spiritual Problem of Modern Man," in *Modern Man in Search of a Soul*, trans. W. S. Dell and Cary F. Baynes (New York: Harcourt Brace, 1933), p. 204.

[7] Philip Jenkins, *Mystics and Messiahs: Cults and New Religions in American History* (Oxford: Oxford University Press, 2000).

[8] Amit Goswami, *The Self-Aware Universe: How Consciousness Creates the Material World* (New York: Jeremy P. Tharcher, 1995), p. 60.

[9] Fritjof Capra, *The Tao of Physics: An Exploration of the Parallels Between Modern Physics and Eastern Mysticism* (1975; Boston: Shambala, 2000), p. 17.

[10] Thomas Paine, *The Age of Reason* (Secaucus, N.J.: Citadel, 1974), p. 60.

[11] Ibid., p. 70.

[12] Ibid.

[13] Ibid., p. 73.

[14] Ibid., p. 75.

[15] Hugh J. Kearney, *Science and Change: 1500-1700* (New York: McGraw-Hill, 1971), p. 127.

[16] Paine, *Age of Reason*, p. 79.

[17] Ibid., p. 80.

[18] Ibid., p. 80n.

[19] Ibid., p. 84.

[20] Ibid., p. 80.

[21] Ibid., p. 83.

[22] Ibid.

[23] Ibid., p. 82.

[24] Ibid., p. 84 and 84n.

[25] Ibid., p. 86.

[26]Ibid., p. 88.

[27]Ibid., p. 89.

[28]Paine was not the first to posit a number of inhabited worlds. This had been a mainstay of the magical view of science since at least the time of Bruno and had been explicitly argued in France by Fontenelle (1657-1757) in *Conversations About a Plurality of Worlds* (1685).

[29]Paine, *Age of Reason*, p. 90.

[30]Ibid., p. 91.

[31]Ibid., p. 92.

[32]Paine is likely engaged in the practice David Berman has called "theological lying," strategically implying his acceptance of theism while he advocates pantheism. See Berman's "Deism, Immortality, and the Art of Theological Lying," in *Deism, Masonry and the Enlightenment*, ed. J. A. Leo Lamay (Newark: University of Delaware Press, 1987), pp. 61-78.

[33]Paine, *Age of Reason*, p. 89.

[34]Paine's thinking may be rooted in what Hugh J. Kearney calls the "quasi-religious" Pythagorean belief that the universe is structured "in accordance with the laws of mathematics" (*Science and Change*, p. 137).

[35]Kearney, *Science and Change*, p. 215.

[36]Robert G. Ingersoll, *The Truth Seeker* (New York: n.p., 1890), p. 1.

[37]Ibid., p. 2.

[38]Robert G. Ingersoll, "The Mistakes of Moses," in *The Works of Robert G. Ingersoll*, vol. 1 (New York: Dresden Publishing, 1912), p. 98.

[39]Ingersoll, *Truth Seeker*, p. 2.

[40]Ingersoll, "Mistakes," p. 101.

[41]Ibid., p. 105.

[42]Ibid., p. 106.

[43]Ibid., p. 97.

[44]Ibid., p. 99.

[45]Ingersoll, *Truth Seeker*, p. 3.

[46]Robert G. Ingersoll, "The Foundations of Faith," in *The Works of Robert G. Ingersoll*, 12 vols., memorial ed. (New York: Dresden, 1912-1929), 4:290-91.

[47]The SETI project began in 1960 with Frank Drake's first experiment called Project Ozma. See Frank Drake, "Project Ozma," *Physics Today* 14 (1960): 40-46. For a more recent report on the effort to find intelligent life elsewhere in the universe, see P. Horowitz and C. Sagan, "Five Years of Project META: An All Sky Narrowband Radio Search for Extraterrestrial Signals," *Astrophysical Journal* 415 (1993): 218-35. Also of interest is Sagan's obscure early work on communication with alien intelligences, *The Cosmic Connection: An Extraterrestrial Perspective* (New York: Dell, 1973). See also Walter Sullivan's bestseller *We Are Not Alone* (New York: McGraw Hill, 1964).

[48]Carl Sagan, *The Demon-Haunted World: Science as a Candle in the Dark* (New York: Random House, 1995), p. 9.

[49]Ibid., p. 10.

[50]Ibid., p. 12.

[51]Ibid., p. 13.

[52]Ibid., p. 14.

[53]Ibid., p. 27.

[54]Ibid., p. 29.

[55]Ibid., p. 12.

[56]Ibid., p. 31.

[57]Ibid., p. 34.

[58]Ibid., p. 35.

[59]Ibid.

[60]Carl Sagan, *Contact: A Novel* (New York: Simon & Schuster, 1985), pp. 356-57.

[61]Ibid., p. 358.

[62]Ibid., p. 359.

[63]Ibid., p. 363.

[64]Ibid., p. 364.

[65]Ibid., pp. 366-67.

[66]Gordon Plummer, *From Atom to Kosmos: Journey Without End* (Wheaton, Ill.: Theosophical Publishing House, 1989).

[67]Gary Zukav, *The Dancing Wu Li Masters: An Overview of the New Physics* (New York: William Morrow, 1979), p. 331.

[68]Ibid.

[69]Marilyn Ferguson, *The Aquarian Conspiracy: Personal and Social Transformation in the 1980's* (Los Angeles: J. P. Tarcher, 1980), p. 146.

[70]Ibid., p. 148.

[71]Goswami, *Self-Aware Universe*, p. 11.

[72]Ibid.

[73]Fred Alan Wolf, *The Dreaming Universe* (New York: Simon & Schuster, 1994), pp. 343-44.

[74]Capra, *Tao of Physics*, p. 17.

[75]Ibid., p. 81.

[76]Fritjof Capra, *The Web of Life: A New Scientific Understanding of Living Systems* (New York: Anchor, 1996), 7.

[77]Capra, *Web of Life*, p. 295.

[78]Goswami, *Self-Aware Universe*, p. 60.

[79]Jeremy Narby and Francis Huxley, eds., *Shamans Through Time: 500 Years on the Path to Knowledge* (New York: Jeremy Tarcher, 2001), p. 305.

[80]Zukav, *Dancing Wu Li Masters*, p. 337.

Chapter Six: Evolution and Advancement: The Darwins' Spiritual Legacy

[1]Joseph Smith Jr., "King Follett Discourse" (1844) posted on Kingdom of Zion site

<www.kingdomofzion.org>. See also Joseph Smith, *Teachings of the Prophet Joseph Smith* (Salt Lake City: Deseret, 1976), pp. 342-61.

[2]Ibid.

[3]Ibid.

[4]Robert Ornstein, *The Evolution of Consciousness* (New York: Prentice Hall, 1991), p. 279.

[5]Ibid., p. 273.

[6]Robert Ornstein and Paul Ehrlich, *New World, New Mind* (Cambridge Mass.: Malor, 1989), p. 195.

[7]J. W. Burrow, *The Crisis of Reason: European Thought, 1848-1914* (New Haven, Conn.: Yale University Press, 2000), p. 43.

[8]For Rousseau's theory of education, see *Emile or On Education*, trans. Allan Bloom (New York: Basic Books, 1979).

[9]Erasmus Darwin, *Zoonomia*, part 1 (London: J. Johnson, 1794); 2nd ed. parts 1-3, 2 vols. (London: J. Johnson, 1796); 3rd ed., 4 vols. (London: J. Johnson, 1801).

[10]Erasmus Darwin, *The Essential Writings of Erasmus Darwin*, ed. Desmond King-Hele (London: McGibbon & Kee, 1968), p. 11. *The Temple of Nature; or the Origins of Society* (London: J. Johnson, 1803; 2nd ed. 1806-1807; 3rd ed. 1825). Interestingly, this poem was published in the Russian *Journal of the Ministry of National Education* in 1911, and this translation was reissued in book form in Moscow in 1956 and again in 1960.

[11]Edward S. Reed, *From Soul to Mind: The Emergence of Psychology from Erasmus Darwin to William James* (New Haven, Conn.: Yale University Press, 1997), p. 14.

[12]E. Darwin, *Essential Writings*, p. 97.

[13]Ibid.

[14]Reed, *Soul to Mind*, p. 39.

[15]E. Darwin, *Essential Writings*, p. 75.

[16]Ibid., p. 76.

[17]Ibid., p. 173.

[18]Reed, *Soul to Mind*, p. 41.

[19]Ibid., p. 42.

[20]Mary Shelley, *Frankenstein* (1831; reprint, New York: Dover, 1994), p. viii.

[21]E. Darwin, *Essential Writings*, p. 163.

[22]Ibid.

[23]Ibid., p. 165.

[24]A. N. Wilson, *God's Funeral* (New York: W. W. Norton, 1999), p. 162.

[25]John Passmore, *A Hundred Years of Philosophy* (1968; reprint, New York: Viking Penguin, 1978), p. 40.

[26]Wilson, *God's Funeral*, p. 162.

[27]Herbert Spencer, *First Principles* (1863; reprint, Westport, Conn.: Greenwood, 1976), p. 207.

[28]Wilson, *God's Funeral*, p. 158.

[29]Quoted in Adrian Desmond and James Moore, *Darwin: The Life of a Tormented Evolutionist* (New York: W. W. Norton, 1994), p. 315.

[30]Wilson, *God's Funeral*, p. 189.

[31]Frank Burch Brown, *The Evolution of Charles Darwin's Religious Views* (Macon, Ga.: Mercer University Press, 1986).

[32]Franklin Baumer, *Religion and the Rise of Scepticism* (New York: Harcourt Brace & World, 1960), pp. 147-48.

[33]Brown, *Evolution of Charles Darwin's*, pp. 29-30.

[34]Adrian Desmond and James Moore, *Darwin: The Life and Time of a Tormented Evolutionist* (New York: Norton, 1991), p. 293.

[35]Brown, *Evolution of Charles Darwin's*, pp. 29-30.

[36]"De-censoring Darwin's Religion," in *Classics of Free Thought*, ed. Paul Blanshard (Buffalo, N.Y.: Prometheus, 1977), p. 44.

[37]Ibid., p. 47.

[38]Ibid., p. 44.

[39]Ibid., p. 45.

[40]Reed, *Soul to Mind*, p. 169.

[41]John Angus Campbell, "Darwin, Thales, and the Milkmaid: Scientific Revolution and Argument from Common Beliefs and Common Sense," in *Perspectives on Argument*, ed. Robert Trapp and Janice Schuetz (Prospect Heights, Ill.: Waveland, 1990), pp. 207-20.

[42]Ibid., p. 209.

[43]Baumer, *Religion and Rise of Scepticism*, p. 148.

[44]Charles Darwin, *On the Origin of the Species* (1859; Cambridge, Mass.: Harvard University Press, 1964), pp. 201-2.

[45]Ibid., pp. 202-3.

[46]The same argument is advanced today by Stephen J. Gould in his many books. See, for example, *The Panda's Thumb*.

[47]Quoted in Campbell, "Darwin, Thales," p. 213.

[48]Ibid., p. 214.

[49]Baumer, *Religion and Rise of Scepticism*, p. 148.

[50]Robert Richards, *The Meaning of Evolution* (Chicago: University of Chicago Press, 1992), p. 86.

[51]Ibid., p. 87.

[52]Ibid., p. 89.

[53]Ibid., p. 90.

[54]Quoted in "De-Censoring Darwin's Religion," pp. 46-47.

[55]Reed, *Soul to Mind*, p. 173.

[56]Ibid., p. 173.

[57]Quoted in Baumer, *Religion and Rise of Scepticism*, p. 149. See George Bernard Shaw, *Back to Methuselah*.

[58]Quoted in Baumer, *Religion and Rise of Scepticism*, p. 149.

[59]Burrow, *Crisis of Reason*, pp. 99-100.

[60]August Forel, *The Social World of Ants*, trans. C. K. Ogden (New York: Albert & Charles Boni, 1930), 2:350; quoted in Richard Noll, *The Jung Cult: Origins of a Charismatic Movement* (Princeton, N.J.: Princeton University Press, 1994), p. 321n.

[61]Forel, *Social World of Ants*, 2:351; quoted in Noll, *Jung Cult*, p. 321n.

[62]"Transhumanism," in *Classics of Free Thought*, ed. Paul Blanshard (Buffalo, N.Y.: Prometheus, 1977), p. 80.

[63]Ibid.

[64]Julian Huxley, *Evolution: The Modern Synthesis* (1942; reprint, London: Allen & Unwin, 1974).

[65]Ibid., p. 556.

[66]Ibid., p. 561.

[67]Ibid., p. 563.

[68]Ibid., pp. 564-65.

[69]Ibid., pp. 572-73.

[70]Ibid., pp. 573-74.

[71]Ibid.

[72]Ibid., p. 575.

[73]Ibid.

[74]Ibid., p. 576.

[75]Ibid., p. 577.

[76]Ibid., p. 578.

[77]Ibid.

[78]Laurence Brown, Bernard C. Farr and R. Joseph Hoffmann, eds., *Modern Spiritualities* (Amherst, N.Y.: Prometheus, 1997), p. 209.

[79]Ibid., pp. 210-11.

[80]Ibid., p. 212.

[81]Ibid.

[82]Ibid.

[83]Pierre Teilhard de Chardin, *The Future of Man*, trans. Norman Denny (1959; New York: Harper & Row, 1964), p. 80.

[84]Brown, Farr and Hoffmann, *Modern Spiritualities*, p. 213.

[85]Teilhard de Chardin, *Future of Man*, p. 80.

[86]Ibid., p. 120.

[87]James H. Austin, *Zen and the Brain: Toward an Understanding of Meditation and Consciousness* (Boston: MIT Press, 1999).

[88]Ibid., p. 685.

[89]Ibid., p. 686.

[90]Ibid., pp. 686-87.

[91]Ibid., p. 687.

[92]Ibid., p. 688.

[93]Ibid., p. 689.

[94]Ibid., pp. 689-90.

[95]Ibid., p. 691.

[96]Ibid., p. 693.

[97]James Redfield, *The Celestine Prophecy* (New York: Time Warner Books, 1993), p. 98.

[98]Ibid., p. 99.

[99]Ibid., p. 100.

[100]Ibid., p. 120.

[101]Philip Jenkins, *Mystics and Messiahs: Cults and New Religions in American History* (Oxford: Oxford University Press, 2000), p. 73.

[102]Associates claimed that as a young man Hitler was taken with the principal character in Wagner's operatic adaptation of Bulwer-Lytton's *Rienzi*. The German leader acknowledged to Wagner's widow in 1939 that seeing a performance of the opera was the turning point in his life. See Nicholas Goodrick Clark, *The Occult Roots of Nazism: Secret Aryan Cults and Their Influence on Nazi Ideology* (New York: New York University Press, 1985), for a discussion of Bulwer-Lytton, the Victorian occult movement and Nazi ideology.

[103]George Edward Bulwer-Lytton, *The Coming Race* (Santa Barbara, Calif.: Woodbridge, 1989), p. 11.

[104]Ibid., p. 12.

[105]Ibid., pp. 14-15.

[106]Ibid., p. 25.

[107]Ibid.

[108]Bulwer-Lytton was not the first to write of the Aryans as a master race. In 1855, sixteen years prior to the publication of *The Coming Race*, Arthur de Gobineau had published his theory of Aryan racial superiority in *On the Inequality of the Races of Man*.

[109]See Chris Hodenfield, "The Sky Is Full of Questions: Science Fiction in Steven Spielberg's Suburbia," *Rolling Stone*, January 26, 1978, pp. 33-38.

[110]Herbert Spencer, *First Principles* (1863; reprint, Westport, Conn.: Greenwood, 1976), p. 207. On the spiritual impact of *Close Encounters* on another prominent Hollywood director, see *New York Times Magazine*, September 22, 2002, p. 59. Emily Nussbaum writes that the "existential revelation [of Joss Whedon, creator of *Buffy the Vampire Slayer*] arrived during an adolescent viewing of *Close Encounters of the Third Kind*." Whedon "became convinced that the pop genres he loved—sci-fi and horror movies among them—could be more than just entertainment. They could carry subversive ideas into the mainstream" (p. 58).

[111]Daniel Leonard Bernardi, *Star Trek and History: Race-ing Toward a White Future* (Rutgers, N.J.: Rutgers University Press, 1998), p. 56.

[112]Ibid., p. 126.

[113]Ibid., p. 119.

[114]Aldous Huxley, "Further Reflections on Progress," in *Huxley and God: Essays*, ed. Jacqueline Hazard Bridgeman (San Francisco: HarperSanFrancisco, 1992), p. 113.

[115]Marilyn Ferguson, *The Aquarian Conspiracy: Personal and Social Transformation in the 1980's* (Los Angeles: J. P. Tarcher, 1980), p. 159.

[116]Gary Zukav, *The Seat of the Soul* (New York: Simon & Schuster, 1989), p. 182.

[117]Wilson, *God's Funeral*, p. 165.

[118]Baumer, *Religion and Rise of Scepticism*, p. 147.

Chapter Seven: Pantheism in the Modern World: Nature or God

[1]Pierre Teilhard de Chardin, *The Heart of Matter*, trans. Rene Hague (New York: Harcourt Brace Jovanovich, 1978), p. 26.

[2]Ibid., p. 28.

[3]Ibid., p. 19.

[4]Ibid.

[5]Ibid., p. 29.

[6]Ibid., p. 30.

[7]Quoted in Fred Alan Wolf, *The Spiritual Universe* (New York: Simon & Schuster, 1996), p. 104.

[8]Richard Noll, *The Jung Cult: Origins of a Charismatic Movement* (Princeton, N.J.: Princeton University Press, 1994), p. 49.

[9]Ernst Haeckel, *The Riddle of the Universe at the Close of the Nineteenth Century*, trans. Joseph McCabe (New York: Harper & Brothers, 1900), p. 337.

[10]Wolf, *Spiritual Universe*, p. 95.

[11]Ibid., p. 86.

[12]Helen Schucman, *A Course in Miracles: Workbook for Students* (Tiburon, Calif.: Center for Inner Peace, 1975), p. 45.

[13]Hershel Parker, "Ralph Waldo Emerson," in *Norton Anthology of American Literature*, shorter ed. (New York: W. W. Norton, 1980), p. 265.

[14]Daniel C. Dennett, *Darwin's Dangerous Idea: Evolution and the Meanings of Life* (New York: Simon & Schuster, 1995), p. 185. See also Benedict de Spinoza, *Ethics*, in *The Chief Works of Benedict de Spinoza*, trans. R. H. M. Elwers, vol. 2 (New York: Dover, 1951); and Steven Nadler, *Spinoza: A Life* (Cambridge: Cambridge University Press, 1999), pp. 227-33.

[15]Robert E. Sullivan, *John Toland and the Deist Controversy* (Cambridge, Mass.: Harvard University Press, 1982), p. 196.

[16]Ibid., p. 44.

[17]Ibid., p. 175.

[18]Quoted in ibid., p. 182.

[19]Ibid., pp. 182, 183.

[20]John Toland, *Tetradymus* (1720), pp. 85; quoted in Sullivan, *John Toland*, p. 184.

[21]Quoted in Sullivan, *John Toland*, p. 185.

[22]John Toland, *Letters to Serena* (London: Bernard Lintot, 1704), p. 115.

[23]Sullivan, *John Toland*, p. 184.

[24]Ibid., p. 186.

[25]Robert D. Richardson, *Emerson: The Mind on Fire* (Berkeley: University of California Press, 1995), p. 21.

[26]Ibid., p. 23.

[27]Ibid., p. 24.

[28]Ibid., p. 198.

[29]Quoted in ibid., p. 198. See Sampson Reed, *Observations on the Growth of the Mind* (Boston: Cummings Hilliard, 1826).

[30]Guillaume Oegger, *The True Messiah*, trans. Elizabeth Peabody (1832; Boston: Elizabeth Peabody, 1842).

[31]Philip Jenkins, *Mystics and Messiahs: Cults and New Religions in American History* (Oxford: Oxford University Press, 2000), p. 71.

[32]Richardson, *Emerson*, p. 250.

[33]Ibid., p. 258.

[34]Parker, "Ralph Waldo Emerson," p. 266.

[35]Carl Bode, ed., introduction to *The Portable Emerson* (New York: Penguin, 1981), p. xxix.

[36]Ibid., p. xxxi.

[37]Parker, "Ralph Waldo Emerson," p. 263.

[38]Bode, *Portable Emerson*, p. xxx.

[39]Ibid., p. xxxi.

[40]Ibid., p. xxix.

[41]Richardson, *Emerson*, p. 153-54.

[42]Ralph Waldo Emerson, "Nature," in *Norton Anthology of American Literature*, shorter ed. (New York: W. W. Norton, 1980), p. 268.

[43]Ibid., p. 269.

[44]Bode, *Portable Emerson*, p. xxxiv.

[45]Ralph Waldo Emerson, "Divinity School Address," in *Norton Anthology of American Literature*, shorter ed. (New York: W. W. Norton, 1980), p. 287.

[46]Ibid., pp. 287-88.

[47]Ibid., p. 288.

[48]Ibid.

[49]Ibid., p. 289.

[50]Quoted in Bode, *Portable Emerson*, p. xix.

[51]Parker, "Ralph Waldo Emerson," pp. 264-65.

[52]Richardson, *Emerson*, p. 250.

[53]Noll, *Jung Cult*, pp. 43.

[54]Ibid., p. 47.

[55]Ibid., p. 49.

[56]Haeckel, *Riddle of the Universe*, p. 17.

[57]Ibid., p. 19.

[58]Ibid.

[59]Ibid., p. 20.

[60]Ibid., pp. 20-21.

[61]Ibid., pp. 148-49.

[62]Ibid., p. 109.

[63]Ibid., p. 138.

[64]Ibid.

[65]Ibid., p. 143.

[66]Ibid., p. 163.

[67]Ibid., p. 166.

[68]Ibid., p. 171.

[69]Ibid., p. 243.

[70]Ibid., p. 244.

[71]Ibid., p. 280.

[72]Ibid., p. 281.

[73]Ibid., p. 331.

[74]Ibid., pp. 336-37.

[75]Ibid., p. 345.

[76]Ibid., p. 347.

[77]Ibid., p. 353.

[78]Ibid., p. 356.

[79]Ibid., p. 357.

[80]Ibid., pp. 381-82.

[81]Ibid., p. 382.

[82]Noll, *Jung Cult*, p. 49.

[83]Ibid., p. 50.

[84]Ibid., p. 79.

[85]Henri Bergson, *The Two Sources of Morality and Religion* (1935; Notre Dame, Ind.: University of Notre Dame Press, 1977), p. 113.

[86]Ibid., pp. 209-10.

[87]Ibid., p. 210.

[88]George Bernard Shaw, *Man and Superman* (Baltimore, Md.: Penguin, 1955), p. 167.

[89]Ibid., p. 167.

[90]Ibid., p. 153.

[91]Ibid., p. 172.

[92]Ibid., p. 152.

[93]Ibid., p. 241.

[94]Ibid., p. 249.

[95]Ibid., pp. 251-52.

[96]Ibid., p. 252.

[97]Ibid., p. 253.

[98]Ibid., p. 256.

[99]Catherine L. Albanese, *America, Religions and Religion*, 2nd ed. (Belmont, Calif.: Wadsworth, 1992), p. 355.

[100]Danah Zohar and Ian Marshall, *The Quantum Society: Mind, Physics and a New Social Vision* (New York: William Morrow, 1994), p. 231.

[101]Ibid.

[102]Ibid., p. 232.

[103]Ibid., p. 233.

[104]Ibid., p. 235.

[105]Ibid., p. 236.

[106]Ibid., p. 237.

[107]Ibid., p. 238.

[108]Ibid.

[109]Ibid., p. 239.

[110]Ibid.

[111]Ibid., p. 240.

[112]Ibid.

[113]Ibid., pp. 240-41.

[114]Ibid., p. 241.

[115]Ibid., p. 242.

[116]Herman Hesse, *Siddhartha*, trans. Hilda Rosner (New York: New Directions, 1951), p. 117.

[117]Daniel C. Dennett, *Darwin's Dangerous Idea: Evolution and the Meanings of Life* (New York: Simon & Schuster, 1995), p. 520.

[118]Ibid., p. 502.

[119]Wolf, *Spiritual Universe*, p. 86.

[120]Ibid., p. 39.

[121]Ibid.

[122]Ibid., pp. 199-200.

Chapter Eight: The Rebirth of Gnosticism: The Secret Path to Self-Salvation

[1]Steven J. Hedges et al., "www.masssuicide.com," *U.S. News & World Report*, April 7, 1997, p. 28.

[2]Ibid., p. 30.

[3]This conventional view is challenged by scholars including Birger A. Pearson. See his

"The Problem of 'Jewish Gnostic' Literature," in *Nag Hammadi and Early Christianity*, ed. C. W. Hedrick and R. Hodgson (Peabody, Mass.: Hendrickson, 1986), pp. 15-35.

[4]See, for example, Michael Allen Williams, *Rethinking "Gnosticism": An Argument for Dismantling a Dubious Category* (Princeton, N.J.: Princeton University Press, 1996).

[5]Carl A. Raschke, *The Interruption of Eternity: Modern Gnosticism and the Origins of the New Religious Consciousness* (Chicago: Nelson-Hall, 1980), p. 20.

[6]Ibid.

[7]Yuri Stoyanov, *The Hidden Tradition in Europe* (London: Penguin/Arkana, 1994), p. 224.

[8]Hans Jonas, "Gnosticism," *The Encyclopedia of Philosophy*, vol. 3, ed. P. Edwards (New York: Macmillan, 1967), p. 336.

[9]Raschke, *Interruption of Eternity*, p. 24.

[10]Ibid.

[11]Jonas, "Gnosticism," p. 340.

[12]Jack Lindsay, *Origins of Astrology* (New York: Barnes & Noble, 1971), p. 121.

[13]Ibid., p. 120.

[14]Raschke, *Interruption of Eternity*, p. 70.

[15]Jacob Ilive, *The Oration Spoke at Trinity Hall in Aldersgate Street: On Monday, January 9, 1738* (London: J. Wilford, 1738), p. 7.

[16]Jacob Ilive, *The Layman's Vindication of the Christian Religion* (London: n.p., 1730), p. 4.

[17]Ibid., p. 7.

[18]Ilive, *The Oration Spoke at Joyner's Hall* (London: n.p., 1733).

[19]Ibid., pp. 22-23.

[20]Ibid., p. 25.

[21]Ibid., p. 59.

[22]Ibid.

[23]Ibid., p. 60.

[24]Pheme Perkins, *Gnosticism and the New Testament* (Minneapolis: Fortress, 1993), p. 40.

[25]Raschke, *Interruption of Eternity*, p. 73.

[26]Charles Gildon, "Letter to R. B.," in *The Oracles of Reason*, by Charles Blount (London: n.p., 1693), pp. 178-79; quoted in David Berman, "David Hume and the Suppression of Atheism," *Journal of the History of Philosophy* 21, no. 3 (1983): 375-87; quote p. 381.

[27]Charles Blount, *Anima mundi* (London or Amsterdam: n.p., 1678), pp. 63-64.

[28]William Derham, *Astro-Theology, or a Demonstration of the Being and Attributes of God from a Survey of the Heavens* (London: W. Innys, 1715).

[29]Ibid., p. 1.

[30]Ibid., p. 218.

[31]Ibid., p. 220.

[32]Ibid., p. xlix.

[33]Raschke, *Interruption of Eternity*, p. 41.

[34]Jacob Ilive, *A Dialogue Between a Doctor of the Church of England and Mr. Jacob Ilive* (London:

T. Cooper, 1733), p. 28.

[35]Ibid., p. 32.

[36]Ibid., p. 34.

[37]Jacob Ilive, *The Book of Jasher* (London: n.p., 1751), p. 3.

[38]Ibid., p. 3.

[39]Ibid., chap. 3, vv. 17 and following.

[40]Ibid., chap. 3, vv. 12 and following.

[41]For a standard biographical account of Smith, see Fawn Brodie, *No Man Knows My History* (New York: Alfred A. Knopf, 1967). For a more accurate understanding of Smith's spiritual orientation, see Harold Bloom, *The American Religion: The Emergence of the Post-Christian Nation* (New York: Simon & Schuster, 1992).

[42]Bloom, *American Religion*, p. 112.

[43]D. Michael Quinn, *Early Mormonism and the Magic World View* (Salt Lake City: Signature, 1998). See Smith's own account, in which he notes the date September 22: Joseph Smith, *History of the Church*, in *Pearl of Great Price* (Salt Lake City, Utah: Church of Jesus Christ of Latter Day Saints, 1981), p. 55.

[44]Quinn, *Early Mormonism*, pp. 136-77.

[45]Jan Shipps, "The Latter-Day Saints," in *Encyclopedia of American Religious Experience* (New York: Scribner, 1988), p. 652.

[46]Quinn, *Early Mormonism*, p. 70.

[47]Ibid., p. 136.

[48]Ibid., p. 98. On Smith's interest in the magical tradition see Lance S. Owens, "Joseph Smith and Kabbalah: The Occult Connection," *Dialogue: A Journal of Mormon Thought* 27, no. 3 (1994): 117-94. The essay received the Mormon History Association award in 1995.

[49]Ibid., p. 39.

[50]Ibid., p. 72-73. Stars figure prominently in Smith's theology. See, for example, *The Book of Abraham* 3:2-18, in Smith, *Pearl of Great Price*, p. 34.

[51]On the Smith family's involvement with folk-magic, see Quinn, *Early Mormonism*, chap. 4, "Magic Parchments and Occult Mentors," pp. 98-135.

[52]Quinn, *Early Mormonism*, p. 39.

[53]Harry L. Ropp, *Are the Mormon Scriptures Reliable?* (Downers Grove, Ill.: InterVarsity Press, 1987), pp. 39-40.

[54]Ibid., p. 38.

[55]George Arbaugh, author of *Revelation in Mormonism* (Chicago: University of Chicago Press, 1932), calls Rigdon the founder of Mormonism. See Ropp, *Are the Mormon Scriptures Reliable?* pp. 37-38. See also Joseph Smith, *Doctrine and Covenants* (Salt Lake City: Church of Jesus Christ of Latter Day Saints, 1981), sects. 35, 37, 40, for examples of Rigdon's prominence in early Mormonism.

[56]Ropp, *Are the Mormon Scriptures Reliable?* p. 38.

[57]For a detailed discussion of Smith's gnostic cosmology, see John L. Brooke, *The Refiner's*

Fire: The Making of Mormon Cosmology, 1644-1844 (Cambridge: Cambridge University Press, 1999).

[58]Bloom asks, "Is it not likely that Smith left other secret teachings that have been handed down only within the hierarchy?" (*American Religion*, p. 125). Access to Mormon temples remains restricted to Mormons in good standing with the Church.

[59]Bloom, *American Religion*, p. 111. Smith's famous statement is from his "King Follett Discourse," which is available online at <kingdomofzion.org>.

[60]Anthony Hoekema, *The Four Major Cults* (Grand Rapids, Mich.: Eerdmans, 1963), pp. 38-39.

[61]Bloom, *American Religion*, p. 114.

[62]See Quinn, *Early Mormonism*, pp. 70-83.

[63]Hoekema, *Four Major Cults*, p. 45.

[64]Ibid., p. 43.

[65]Joseph Campbell, ed., introduction to *The Portable Jung*, trans. R. F. C. Hull (New York: Penguin, 1976), p. vii.

[66]John P. Dourley, *The Illness We Are: A Jungian Critique of Christianity* (Toronto: Inner City Books, 1984), p. 72.

[67]Richard Noll, *The Jung Cult: Origins of a Charismatic Movement* (Princeton, N.J.: Princeton University Press, 1994), p. 6.

[68]Ibid., p. 23.

[69]Campbell, *Portable Jung*, p. viii.

[70]Noll, *Jung Cult*, p. 28.

[71]Dourley, *Illness We Are*, p. 99.

[72]Ibid., pp. 94, 95.

[73]Ibid., p. 74.

[74]Carl Jung, *The Collected Works of Carl Jung*, trans. R. F. C. Hull, ed. H. Read, M. Fordham, G. Adler, W. McGuire (Princeton, N.J.: Princeton University Press, 1953-1979), *Mysterium coniunctionis*, CW 14, par. 742; quoted in Dourley, *Illness We Are*, p. 98.

[75]Noll, *Jung Cult*, p. 21.

[76]Ibid., p. 18.

[77]Carl Jung, "The Difference Between Eastern and Western Thinking," part 1 of "Psychological Commentary on the Tibetan Book of the Great Liberation," from *Psychology and Religion: West and East* in *Collected Works*, vol. 2, pars. 759-87, in *The Portable Jung*, trans. R. F. C. Hull (New York: Penguin, 1976), p. 475.

[78]Dourley, *Illness We Are*, p. 78.

[79]Jung, "Eastern and Western Thinking," p. 475.

[80]Ibid., p. 476.

[81]Noll, *Jung Cult*, p. 6.

[82]Ibid.

[83]Ibid., p. 7.

[84]Ibid., p. 297. Noll quotes Edward Edinger, *The Creation of Consciousness: Jung's Myth for*

Modern Man (Toronto: Inner City Books, 1984), p. 90.

[85]Jean Houston, *A Passion for the Possible: A Guide to Realizing Your True Potential* (San Francisco: HarperSanFrancisco: 1997), p. 20.

[86]Ibid., p. 21.

[87]Ibid., p. 24.

[88]Ibid., p. 25.

[89]Ibid., p. 28.

[90]Ibid., p. 31. Similarly, Carl Jung entertained the possibility of "a quasi-spiritualist, quasi-biological idea . . . ancestor possession—that is, literally, spiritual possession by one's ancestors." Noll, *Jung Cult*, p. 23.

[91]Houston, *Passion for the Possible*, p. 32.

[92]Ibid.

[93]Ibid., p. 34.

[94]Ibid., p. 35.

[95]Ibid., p. 115.

[96]Ibid., p. 113.

[97]Ibid., pp. 116, 118.

[98]Ibid., p. 133.

[99]Ibid., p. 138.

[100]Ibid., p. 140.

[101]Ibid., p. 142.

[102]Ibid., p. 144.

[103]Ibid., p. 155.

[104]Ibid., p. 161.

[105]Ibid., p. 167.

[106]Ibid., p. 162.

[107]Catherine L. Albanese, *America, Religions and Religion*, 2nd ed. (Belmont, Calif.: Wadsworth, 1992), p. 357. Madame Blavatsky and her sources of spiritual information are discussed in my chapter nine.

[108]Ibid.

[109]Steve Kellmeyer, "The Gnostix," *Envoy* 4, no. 5 (2000): 34-39, quote p. 39.

[110]Ibid., p. 37.

[111]Carlos Castaneda, *The Teachings of Don Juan: A Yaqui Way of Knowledge* (Berkeley: University of California Press, 1969), p. 145.

[112]Raschke, *Interruption of Eternity*, p. 34.

[113]Theodor W. Adorno, "Theses Against Occultism," in *Minima Moralia: Reflexionen aus dem beschädigten Leben* (Berlin: Suhrkamp Verlag, 1951), pp. 238-41 (English translation *Minima Moralia: Reflections from Damaged Life*, trans. E. F. N. Jephcott (London: New Left, 1978).

[114]William Covino, *Rhetoric and Magic* (Albany: State University of New York Press, 1997), p. 90.

Chapter Nine: Modern Shamanism: Spirit Contact and Spiritual Progress

[1]Jeremy Narby and Francis Huxley, eds. *Shamans Through Time: 500 Years on the Path to Knowledge* (New York: Jeremy Tarcher, 2001), p. 1.

[2]Philip Jenkins, *Mystics and Messiahs: Cults and New Religions in American History* (Oxford: Oxford University Press, 2000), p. 170.

[3]Narby and Huxley, *Shamans Through Time*, p. 5.

[4]Ibid.

[5]Ibid., p. 6.

[6]Emanuel Swedenborg, *The Worlds in Space* (1758; reprint, London: The Swedenborg Society, 1998), p. 1.

[7]Ibid., p. 113.

[8]Ibid., p. 14.

[9]Ibid., p. 86.

[10]Ibid., p. 111.

[11]Ibid., p. 14.

[12]Ibid., p. 50.

[13]Ibid., p. 73.

[14]Ibid., p. 47.

[15]Ibid., p. 33.

[16]Ibid., p. 34.

[17]Ibid., p. 104.

[18]Again I am reminded here of the closing scenes of Steven Spielberg's *Close Encounters of the Third Kind*, in which the delicate features of advanced aliens are juxtaposed with shots of human beings exhibiting similar features. The suggestion is that some of us have already taken the next evolutionary step. Unfortunately, as our faces reveal, some of us have not.

[19]Swedenborg, *Worlds in Space*, p. 44.

[20]Ibid., p. 99.

[21]Ibid., p. 65.

[22]Ibid., p. 46.

[23]Ibid., p. 89.

[24]Ibid., p. 93.

[25]Bradford Verter, "Dark Star Rising: The Emergence of Modern Occultism, 1880-1950" (Ph.D. diss., Princeton University, 1998), p. 135n.

[26]Ibid., p.134.

[27]Ibid.

[28]Jenkins, *Mystics and Messiahs*, p. 73.

[29]Lawrence Sutin has recently published an extensive biography of Crowley: *Do What Thou Wilt: A Life of Aleister Crowley* (New York: St. Martin's Griffin, 2000).

[30]Ibid., pp. 2-3.

[31]Ibid., p. 4.

[32]Verter, "Dark Star Rising," p. 139.

[33]Ibid.

[34]See ibid., pp. 129-30n: "During the early and mid-nineteenth century, sensational yarns, ghost stories and Oriental tales were everywhere: newspapers, magazines, chapbooks, serial pamphlets, and books."

[35]Jenkins, *Mystics and Messiahs*, pp. 76-77.

[36]Carl Jung, "The Spiritual Problem of Modern Man," in *Modern Man in Search of a Soul*, trans. W. S. Dell and Cary F. Baynes (New York: Harcourt Brace, 1933), pp. 210-11.

[37]H. P. Blavatsky, *Isis Unveiled* (1877; reprint, Pasadena, Calif.: Theosophical University Press, 1998), 1:282.

[38]Judge Henry Steele Olcott, *The Sun*, September 26, 1892; quoted in Warren Sylvester Smith, *The London Heretics 1870-1914* (New York: Dodd Mead, 1968), p. 159.

[39]On Blavatsky see John Symnonds, *Madame Blavatsky, Medium and Magician* (London: n.p., 1959).

[40]Smith, *London Heretics*, p. 247.

[41]Ibid., 146.

[42]Mary K. Kneff, *Personal Memoirs of H. P. Blavatsky* (New York: n.p., 1937), p. 54; quoted in Smith, *London Heretics*, p. 147.

[43]Richard Noll, *The Jung Cult: Origins of a Charismatic Movement* (Princeton, N.J.: Princeton University Press, 1994), p. 65.

[44]Ibid.

[45]Ibid., p. 64.

[46]Jenkins, *Mystics and Messiahs*, p. 41.

[47]Blavatsky, *Isis Unveiled*, 1:93.

[48]Ibid., 1:94.

[49]Jenkins, *Mystics and Messiahs*, p. 84.

[50]Noll, *Jung Cult*, p. 83.

[51]Jenkins, *Mystics and Messiahs*, p. 96.

[52]Noll, *Jung Cult*, p. 83.

[53]Catherine L. Albanese, *America, Religions and Religion*, 2nd ed. (Belmont, Calif.: Wadsworth, 1992), p. 356.

[54]Blavatsky, *Isis Unveiled*, 1:296.

[55]Ibid.

[56]Adrian Desmond and James Moore, *Darwin: The Life of a Tormented Evolutionist* (New York: W. W. Norton, 1994), p. 538.

[57]Blavatsky, *Isis Unveiled*, 1:296, emphasis in original.

[58]Ibid.

[59]Jenkins, *Mystics and Messiahs*, p. 72.

[60]Blavatsky, *Isis Unveiled*, 1:296.

[61]See, for example, Jenkins's discussion of The Silver Shirts who followed self-styled as-

cended master William Dudley Pelley (1885-1965) in America of the 1930s and 1940s (*Mystics and Messiahs*, pp. 95-96). Many neopagan groups, e.g., Asatru organizations, teach a thinly veiled racialist philosophy.

[62]John E. Mack, *Abduction: Human Encounters with Aliens* (New York: Charles Scribner's Sons, 1994).

[63]Other books in the abduction genre include Dana Redfield, *Summoned: Encounters with Alien Intelligence*; Dolores Cannon, *The Custodians: Beyond Abduction* and Constance Clear, *Reaching for Reality: Seven Incredible True Stories of Alien Abduction*.

[64]Mack, *Abduction*, preface.

[65]Ibid., p. 3.

[66]Ibid., pp. 3-4.

[67]Ibid., p. 4.

[68]Ibid.

[69]Ibid., pp. 4-5.

[70]Ibid., pp. 6-7.

[71]Ibid., p. 8.

[72]Ibid.

[73]Ibid.

[74]Ibid., p. 9.

[75]Ibid., p. 32.

[76]Joseph Campbell, "Myths from West to East" in *The Universal Myths: Heroes, Gods, Tricksters and Others* (New York: Penguin, 1990), p. 59.

[77]Mack, *Abduction*, p. 18.

[78]Ibid., p. 17.

[79]Jenkins, *Mystics and Messiahs*, p. 172. See also Brad Gooch, " 'He's Only a Thought Away': Sleuthing *The Urantia Book*," in *Godtalk: Travels in Spiritual America* (New York: Alfred A. Knopf, 2002), pp. 3-62.

[80]Mack, *Abduction*, p. 32.

[81]Whitley Streiber, *Communion* (New York: Beech Tree, 1987); *Transformation: The Breakthrough* (New York: Beech Tree, 1988); *Confirmation: The Hard Evidence for Aliens Among Us* (New York: St. Martin's, 1998).

[82]Streiber, *Transformation*, p. 237.

[83]Paul Ferrini, *Love Without Conditions: Reflections of the Christ Mind* (South Dearfield, Mass.: Heartways, 1997).

[84]Ibid., p. 7.

[85]Ibid., p. 8.

[86]Ibid.

[87]Ibid.

[88]Ibid., p. 9.

[89]Ibid., p. 16.

[90]Ibid.

[91]Ibid., p. 18.

[92]Ibid.

[93]Ibid., p. 20.

[94]Gary Zukav, *The Seat of the Soul* (New York: Simon & Schuster, 1989), p. 180.

[95]Ibid., p. 181.

[96]Ibid.

[97]Ibid., p. 182.

[98]Neale Donald Walsch, *Conversations with God: An Uncommon Dialogue*, vol. 1 (New York: G. P. Putnam & Sons, 1995), p. 208.

[99]Narby and Huxley, *Shamans Through Time*, p. 305.

Chapter Ten: The Mystical Path to Pluralism: Discovering That All Is One in Religion

[1]Wayne Teasdale, *The Mystic Heart* (Novato, Calif.: New World Library, 1999), p. 72.

[2]Ibid., p. 75; emphasis in original.

[3]Ibid., p. 74.

[4]Ibid., p. 26.

[5]Ibid., p. 25.

[6]Ibid.

[7]Ibid., p. 45.

[8]Ibid., p. 46.

[9]Ibid., p. 47.

[10]Ibid., p. 48.

[11]Mircea Eliade, *A History of Religious Ideas*, vol. 1, trans. Willard Trask (Chicago: University of Chicago Press, 1978), p. xv; emphasis in original.

[12]Harold Hutcheson, *Lord Herbert of Cherbury's* De religioni laici (New Haven, Conn.: Yale University Press, 1944), p. 87.

[13]Franz Cumont, *Astrology and Religion Among the Greeks and Romans* (New York: Valor Publications, 1960), p. 3.

[14]Kenneth Scott Latourette, *A History of Christianity* (New York: Harper & Row, 1953; rev. 1975), 2:1123.

[15]Franklin L. Baumer, *Religion and the Rise of Scepticism* (New York: Harcourt Brace & World, 1960), p. 154.

[16]Rudolf Otto, *The Idea of the Holy*, trans. John W. Harvey (London: Oxford University Press, 1927), p. 52.

[17]Ibid., p. 6.

[18]Ibid., p. 17.

[19]Sigmund Freud, *The Future of an Illusion*, trans. W. D. Robson-Scott (London: Hogarth Press and the Institute of Psychoanalysis, 1928), p. 28.

[20]Ibid., pp. 33-34.

[21]John P. Dourley, *The Illness We Are: A Jungian Critique of Christianity* (Toronto: Inner City Books, 1984), p. 9.

[22]Peter Miller, "Jane Goodall," *National Geographic*, December 1995, p. 110.

[23]Eugene G. D'Aquili and Andrew B. Newberg, *The Mystical Mind: Probing the Biology of Religious Experience* (Philadelphia: Fortress, 1999).

[24]Roland Bainton, *The Reformation of the Sixteenth Century* (Boston: Beacon, 1952), p. 128.

[25]Ibid.

[26]Bradford Verter, "Dark Star Rising: The Emergence of Modern Occultism, 1800-1950" (Ph.D. diss., Princeton University, 1998), p. 30.

[27]Wayne Shumaker, *The Occult Sciences in the Renaissance: A Study in Intellectual Patterns* (Berke-ley: University of California Press, 1972), p. 205.

[28]Ibid.

[29]Charles Blount, *Anima mundi* (Amsterdam or London: n.p., 1678).

[30]Robert Hurlbutt, *Hume, Newton and the Design Argument* (Lincoln: University of Nebraska Press, 1965), p. 70.

[31]Ibid.

[32]Ibid.

[33]Blount, *Anima mundi*, preface.

[34]Ibid.

[35]*A Speech Delivered by an Indian Chief* (London: n.p., 1753), p. 4.

[36]Carl Jung, "The Modern Spiritual Problem," in *Modern Man in Search of a Soul*, trans. W. S. Dell and Cary F. Baynes (New York: Harcourt Brace, 1933), pp. 209-10.

[37]R. M. Bucke, *Cosmic Consciousness: A Study in the Evolution of the Human Mind* (1901; New York: Dutton, 1966), p. 17.

[38]Ibid.

[39]Ibid., p. 18.

[40]Ibid. See a similar discussion of mystical states in Andrew Newberg and Eugene D'Aquili, *Why God Won't Go Away* (New York: Ballantine, 2002), pp. 98-127.

[41]Bucke, *Cosmic Consciousness*, p. 18.

[42]Ibid., p. 22.

[43]Ibid., pp. 40-41.

[44]Ibid., p. 41.

[45]Ibid., p. 42.

[46]Ibid.

[47]Ibid., p. 52.

[48]Ibid.; emphasis in original.

[49]Ibid., p. 59.

[50]Ibid., p. 67.

[51]Ibid.

[52]Ibid., p. 69.

[53]Ibid., p. 71.

[54]Ibid., p. 96.

[55]Ibid., p. 99.

[56]Ibid., p. 72.

[57]Ibid.

[58]Ibid., p. 73.

[59]Ibid.

[60]Ibid.

[61]Ibid., p. 74.

[62]Ibid., p. 100.

[63]Huston Smith, introduction to *The Transcendent Unity of Religions*, by Frithjof Schuon (1957; Wheaton, Ill.: Theosophical Publishing House, 1984), pp. ix-xxvii.

[64]Ibid., p. xv.

[65]Ibid., p. xvi.

[66]Ibid., p. xxvi.

[67]Frithjof Schuon, *The Transcendent Unity of Religions* (1957; Wheaton, Ill.: Theosophical Publishing House, 1984), p. 47.

[68]Ibid., p. 14.

[69]Ibid., p. 38.

[70]Ibid., p. 21.

[71]Ibid.

[72]Ibid., p. 23.

[73]Ibid., p. 25.

[74]Ibid., p. 20.

[75]Ibid., p. 19.

[76]Ibid.

[77]Ibid., p. 26.

[78]Ibid., p. 27.

[79]Ibid., p. 33.

[80]Ibid., p. 81.

[81]Ibid., p. 125.

[82]Ibid., p. 125n.

[83]Ibid., p. 39.

[84]Ibid., p. 35.

[85]Joseph Campbell, *Transformations of Myth Through Time* (New York: Harper & Row, 1990), p. 93.

[86]Joseph Campbell, "Myths from West to East," in *The Universal Myths: Heroes, Gods, Tricksters and Others* (New York: Penguin, 1990), p. 43.

[87]Campbell, *Transformations of Myth*, p. 95.

[88]Ibid., p. 102.

[89]Ibid., pp. 104-5.

[90]Ibid., p. 106.

[91]Ibid.

[92]Ibid., p. 102.

[93]Ibid., p. 176.

[94]Campbell, "Myths from West to East," p. 45.

[95]Ibid., pp. 45-46.

[96]Huston Smith, *Cleansing the Doors of Perception* (New York: Tarcher/Putnam, 2000), pp. xvi-xvii.

[97]Ibid., p. 80.

[98]Campbell, *Transformations of Myth*, p. 94.

[99]Campbell, "Myths from West to East," p. 49.

[100]Ibid., p. 50.

[101]Marcus J. Borg, *Meeting Jesus Again for the First Time: The Historical Jesus and the Heart of Contemporary Faith* (San Francisco: HarperSanFrancisco: 1994), p. 29.

[102]Ibid., p. 14.

[103]Ibid., p. 15.

[104]Ibid., p. 17.

[105]Ibid., pp. 31-32.

[106]Ibid., p. 32.

[107]Ibid.

[108]Ibid., p. 33.

[109]Mack, *Abduction*, p. 9.

[110]Borg, *Meeting Jesus Again*, p. 34.

[111]Ibid., p. 36.

[112]Ibid., p. 37.

[113]Ibid.

[114]Ibid., p. 87.

[115]Ibid., p. 110.

[116]Ibid., p. 119.

[117]Ibid., p. 120.

[118]John G. Burke, "Hermetism as a Renaissance World View," in *The Darker Vision of the Renaissance*, ed. Robert S. Kinsman (Berkeley: University of California Press, 1974), p. 115.

[119]Peter Annet, *Judging for Ourselves* (London: n.p., 1747), p. 5.

[120]Teasdale, *Mystic Heart*, p. 26.

[121]Ibid.

[122]Ibid., p. 25.

[123]Gary Zukav, *The Seat of the Soul* (New York: Simon & Schuster, 1989), p. 182.

Chapter Eleven: Conclusion: A New Spirituality for a New Age

[1]John Stott, *The Contemporary Christian* (Downers Grove, Ill.: InterVarsity Press, 1992), p. 15.

[2]Shirley MacLaine, *Dancing in the Light* (New York: Bantam, 1985).

[3]Ibid., pp. 370-71.

[4]Ibid., pp. 372-73.

[5]Ibid., p. 113.

[6]Ibid., p. 112.

[7]Ibid., p. 375.

[8]John Shelby Spong, *Rescuing the Bible from Fundamentalism* (San Francisco: HarperSan-Francisco, 1991), p. 21.

[9]Joseph Campbell, *Transformations of Myth Through Time* (New York: Harper & Row, 1990), p. 106.

[10]Joseph Campbell, *The Hero with a Thousand Faces* (New York: MJF Books, 1949), p. 4.

[11]Brenda Brasher, *Give Me That Online Religion* (San Francisco: Jossey-Bass, 2001), p. 6.

[12]On the divine *Mens* and the Renaissance magical tradition, see Frances Yates's excellent study *Giordano Bruno and the Hermetic Tradition* (Chicago: University of Chicago Press, 1964).

[13]Gary Zukav, *The Seat of the Soul* (New York: Simon & Schuster, 1990), p. 185.

[14]Ibid., p. 67.

[15]Laurence Brown, Bernard C. Farr and R. Joseph Hoffmann, eds., *Modern Spiritualities* (Amherst, N.Y.: Prometheus, 1997), p. 224.

[16]Ibid., p. 226.

[17]Ibid.

[18]Ibid., p. 227.

[19]Joseph Banks Rhine, *New Frontiers of the Mind: The Story of the Duke Experiments* (New York: Farrar & Rinehart, 1937), pp. 3, 5.

[20]Ibid., p. 269.

[21]MacLaine, *Dancing in the Light*, p. 369.

[22]J. W. Burrow, *The Crisis of Reason: European Thought, 1848-1914* (New Haven, Conn.: Yale University Press, 2000), p. 198.

[23]Wayne Teasdale, *The Mystic Heart* (Novato, Calif.: New World Library, 1999), p. 72.

[24]Ibid., p. 74.

[25]Marilyn Ferguson, *The Aquarian Conspiracy: Personal and Social Transformation in the 1980's* (Los Angeles: J. P. Tarcher, 1980), p. 152.

[26]MacLaine, *Dancing in the Light*, p. 342.

[27]Ibid., pp. 341-42.

[28]David Gergen, "Trouble in Paradise," *U.S. News & World Report*, August 20, 2001, p. 80.

[29]Pierre Teilhard de Chardin, *The Heart of Matter*, trans. Rene Hague (New York: Harcourt Brace Jovanovich, 1978), p. 10.

[30]Pierre Teilhard de Chardin, *The Future of Man*, trans. Norman Denny (1959; reprint, New York: Harper & Row, 1964), pp. 190-91.

[31]George Bernard Shaw, "The Revolutionist's Handbook," in *Man and Superman* (Baltimore: Penguin, 1955), p. 251.

[32]Michael Cromarty, "A Conversation with Francis Fukuyama," in *Books and Culture*, July/August 2002, p. 9. Francis Fukuyama, *Our Posthuman Future: Consequences of the Biotechnology Revolution* (New York: Farrar, Straus & Giroux, 2002).

[33]Robert Ornstein, *The Evolution of Consciousness* (New York: Prentice Hall, 1991), p. 279.

[34]Ibid., p. 273.

[35]Robert Onstein and Paul Ehrlich, *New World, New Mind* (Cambridge Mass.: Malor, 1989), p. 195.

[36]Cromarty, "Conversation with Francis Fukuyama," p. 9.

[37]C. S. Lewis, *The Abolition of Man* (New York: Macmillan, 1947).

[38]Ibid., pp. 36, 37.

[39]Zukav, *Seat of the Soul*, p. 174.

[40]Ferguson, *Aquarian Conspiracy*, pp. 169-70.

[41]Burrow, *Crisis of Reason*, p. 215.

[42]Joseph Chilton Pearce, *The Crack in the Cosmic Egg: Challenging Constructs of Mind and Reality* (New York: Washington Square Press, 1971), p. 180.

[43]C. S. Lewis, *Mere Christianity* (New York: Macmillan, 1960), p. 185.

[44]Stuart Clark, *Thinking with Demons: The Idea of Witchcraft in Early Modern Europe* (Oxford: Clarendon, 1997), pp. 11-12.

[45]Neale Donald Walsch, *Conversations with God: An Uncommon Dialogue*, vol. 1 (New York: G. P. Putnam & Sons, 1995), p. 200; emphasis in original.

[46]Ferguson, *Aquarian Conspiracy*, p. 382.

[47]John Shelby Spong, lecture at Christ Community Church, Spring Lake, Mich., September 28, 2001.

[48]Dana Zohar and Ian Marshall, *The Quantum Self: Human Nature and Consciousness Defined by the New Physics* (New York: William Morrow, 1990), p. 226.

[49]Zukav, *Seat of the Soul*, pp. 71-72.

[50]MacLaine, *Dancing in the Light*, p. 360.

[51]Peter Jones, *The Gnostic Empire Strikes Back: An Old Heresy for the New Age* (Phillipsburg, N.J.: Presbyterian & Reformed, 1992), p. 59.

[52]Walsch, *Conversations with God*, pp. 201-2.

[53]Zukav, *Seat of the Soul*, p. 185.

[54]Ibid., p. 186.

[55]Walsch, *Conversations with God*, p. 126.

[56]Zukav, *Seat of the Soul*, p. 181.

[57]Ibid., p. 188.

[58]Phillip Pullman, *The Subtle Knife* (New York: William Knopf, 1997), p. 25.

[59]Dallas Willard, *The Spirit of the Disciplines: Understanding How God Changes Lives* (San Francisco: HarperSanFrancisco, 1991), p. 92.

[60]Cromarty, "Conversation with Francis Fukuyama," p. 9.

[61]Pearce, *Crack in the Cosmic Egg*, pp. 169, 168.

[62]Ibid., p. 166.

[63]Richard Noll, *The Jung Cult: Origins of a Charismatic Movement* (Princeton, N.J.: Princeton University Press, 1994), p. 39.

[64]William Covino, *Rhetoric and Magic* (Albany, N.Y.: State University of New York Press: 1997), p. 90.

[65]Noll, *Jung Cult*, p. 35.

[66]Walsch, *Conversations with God*, p. 1.

[67]Gerardo Reichel-Dolmatoff, "Shamans Are Intellectuals, Translators, and Shrewd Dealers," in *Shamans Through Time: 500 Years on the Path to Knowledge*, ed. Jeremy Narby and Francis Huxley (New York: Jeremy Tarcher, 2001), pp. 216-22, quote p. 216.

[68]Ibid., p. 222.

[69]Zukav, *Seat of the Soul*, p. 185.

[70]Ibid., p. 182.

[71]Ibid., p. 183.

[72]Walsch, *Conversations with God*, p. 195; emphasis in original.

[73]Ibid., pp. 197-98.

[74]Deepak Chopra, *The Path to Love: Renewing the Power of Spirit in Your Life* (New York: Harmony, 1997), p. 290; emphasis in original.

[75]Ravi Zacharias, *Can Man Live Without God?* (Dallas: Word, 1994), p. 121.

[76]Noll, *Jung Cult*, p. 38.

[77]A. N. Wilson, *God's Funeral* (New York: W. W. Norton, 1999), p. 59.

[78]Yates, *Giordano Bruno*, p. 239.

[79]M. Craig Barnes, *When God Interrupts: Finding New Life Through Unwanted Change* (Downers Grove, Ill.: InterVarsity Press, 1996), p. 158.

Index of Subjects